Copyright: 2023 by Gulliver Smith

Many characters and events depicted in this book are fictitious and any resemblance to real persons, alive or dead, is purely coincidental. Names of real people may also have been changed.

All Rights Reserved.

No part of this publication may be reproduced, stored in a retrieval system, or transmitted in any firm, or by any means, without the prior permission, in writing, of the author.

Mildly pretentious mission statement:

We try not to make plans. Decisions made on the spur of the moment, that's our travel philosophy. Finding the unexpected. New sights, experiencing different cultures and finding interesting people among total strangers. Setting off on a journey without a recognisable plan and just seeing where the road takes us. We're not tourists and we're most certainly not been-there-done-that box tickers, we're just travellers.
And, if you were wondering, no we don't take selfies as we already know what we look like.

Meet the Authors. Marigold has lived a full and interesting life and intends to carry on living in the same manner. Marigold isn't even her real name, but it suits her. She likes to travel, likes meeting people and talking to strangers. Most of all she likes coming across odd, interesting people and they do seem to find their way into her orbit on so many occasions.

Marigold used to spend her working days in dusty offices, working as a Legal Secretary for various Solicitors, Barristers and Judges. The decision, over thirty years ago, to abandon a regular income, job security and comfortable lifestyles was a mutual decision, a respectable married couple acting on impulse, not for the first time and certainly not the last, heading off to wander the world lacking a regular income, language skills and most of the attributes a sensible person would consider necessary.

Marigold's take on life may be considered unusual by some. She's one of a kind and nobody who's met her would ever want that to change.

Gulliver Smith used to be someone completely different – this current version is a massive step down. Gulliver was known by other names for many years. He was much younger then and considered to be rather clever, hirsute, handsome, good company, sensible and supremely fit. Of these virtues, very few remain. Since leaving home on becoming, technically, an adult he has never been a financial burden either to his parents or the State. With the benefit of hindsight he occasionally regrets these lost opportunities scorned.

As an author he initially wrote crime fiction with a hard edge, making use of a life which frequently brought him into contact with major drug dealers, hardened criminals, hard core addicts and many other residents of society's sordid underbelly.

During the course of an unconventional life, involving much movement around the globe, Gulliver Smith has shovelled coke into blast furnaces, taught English and History, been a work study engineer, restaurateur, civil servant, nightclub bouncer, antique dealer, owned a small French vineyard and also had another job that he's not allowed to talk about.

His debut novel stormed into the Amazon Top Ten Books Chart and further books followed to great acclaim. As with most other aspects of life Gulliver managed to constrain his astonishment behind a façade of justifiable expectation. To define Gulliver Smith in one word would be difficult. 'Wastrel' comes pretty close. He still writes, sporadically. Very occasionally his writing meets standards he finds acceptable.

Marigold on Tour

Marigold on Tour.

Fish and chips and a flu jab before we take our leave of England once more.

G Says...

I went for a flu jab the other day, in a branch of a well known Newquay chemists as they offered a walk-in jab facility, and the young man who came to administer said jab looked about fifteen. He asked my date of birth, checking against his paperwork, and I replied, 11 – 9 – 46.

'That's fine,' he said, 'would that be nineteen forty six?'

I thought he was having a bit of a joke, but he was dead serious.

Good grief, do I really look as if I was born in 1846? Well, as 2046 is well into the future being born in 1846 would mean he was asking questions of a 171 year old man. Did he really imagine I'm a hundred and seventy one years old? Did he ever even think before asking that question? If so, is he really qualified to stick a needle in my arm?

Anyway, he jabbed away and before leaving told me to 'sit in the waiting room for about five minutes in case you have a bad reaction and collapse.'

Where do they find these people?

While sitting for the mandatory five minutes - actually I left a minute early as an act of defiance - a woman sitting opposite said, 'you look brown, been away, have you?'

'Yes, just got back from a road trip to America.'

'Ew, what you wanna go there for? You're lucky to be alive, all them shootings and what not. What's wrong with England anyway?'

The questions were delivered in such a truculent fashion I wondered whether travelling had been made illegal or immoral during our absence, but my inquisitor appeared genuinely baffled by us seeking out foreign climes to visit.

We do appreciate our lifestyle wouldn't suit everybody. We're free spirits when it suits us, but can easily settle for quiet domesticity at times. Just, not all the time. We love experiencing different places, different cultures, meeting complete strangers whose life is so very different from our own and every trip is one less thing to be regretful about. We've talked about 'doing' a US road trip for several years and now we've done it. What's more, we've loved (almost) every aspect of our trip.

Some thoughts on travelling. I found a few quotes by people who expressed my thoughts far better than I could.

'Broad, wholesome, charitable views of men and things cannot be acquired by vegetating in one little corner of the earth all of one's lifetime.'

Mark Twain

'The world is a book, and those who do not travel read only one page.'

Saint Augustine

'Tourists don't know where they've been, travellers don't know where they're going.'

Paul Theroux.

'Never go on trips with anyone you do not love.'

Ernest Hemingway.

That Hemingway quotation is interesting. Helen Hayes, the 'First Lady of American Theatre,' held a very different point of view: *'when travelling with someone, take large doses of patience and tolerance with your morning coffee'.*

I really love travelling, but without Marigold to share the experience, it wouldn't be the same so I'm sticking with Hemingway.

'Wish I could do what you pair do, just swan off whenever you feel like it, seeing different places. I'd love to do that,' a friend said to us recently.

'Why don't you then?' Marigold, straight to the point.

A shrug of the shoulders, 'Oh, I will, one of these days.'

I'm not so sure that she will. Our friend is far more of a noun, an abstract noun at that, not a verb, a doing word. Marigold and I, we're verbs. We do things. Why harbour regrets for things you wish you'd done until your dying day? Why live your life in a conditional tense? 'If only' is a pretty awful mantra to live your life by.

Back home, we're still talking about our last Road Trip. So many diverse places: beaches, deserts, vast sprawling cities and towns that don't appear to have noticed it isn't the 19th century any more, we saw all this and more in just over five and a half weeks. Our favourite places, well, the Pacific coastline, Monument Valley and the Grand Canyon were highlights, but we also loved the quirky nature of Beatty and many other examples of small town America. Death Valley was somewhere we'd long wanted to see and met all expectations while Yellowstone and

Yosemite National Parks were perhaps best suited to immersion of a week or more to get full benefit from their sheer immensity.

Anywhere we didn't like? No, not really, but Los Angeles and Salt Lake City stood out as being big, noisy and crowded and we weren't sorry to leave either of them. San Francisco, which we expected to really like, had its moments, but has a real problem with homeless people and this wore us down after a few days.

The only place we'd not want to visit again was Las Vegas. We had a few laughs, met some lovely people, but its superficial glamour soon palled. That's just our opinion, obviously, and we can both understand how so many people love going there. Just, not us.

A few years ago now, we drove throughout New Zealand in a camper van. We've owned houses/apartments in France, Spain and Morocco and spent significant time in several other countries, but New Zealand was the one place we both said 'we could live here.' We don't say that very often. We could live, happily, in several of the places we've just visited. Malibu, perhaps? More sensibly, many of the coastal resorts along that California coastline have a good feel to them and even if we discount most of the arid desert regions as being less than perfect as a permanent home, a town like Moab has much to offer, but that 'New Zealand vibe' was hard to beat.

We're due to set off again any time soon. When we reach the stage of being able to say, 'we could leave tomorrow,' we'll go. We're not great 'packers,' but we're pretty good at travelling light. October in England means the air gets a bit nippy and realisation dawns that what passed for summer this year was definitely all we're going to get. Time to move on then. There's plenty of warm sunshine around, we just have to go and find it and that means heading south for the winter. Winters in Southern Spain, Portugal or North Africa are much like summers in England - a lot better than this year's offering actually - so why not keep ourselves warm and dry over the long winter months rather than huddling next to the fire coughing and sneezing? We've done both of them and we know which we prefer.

We were in St Ives the other day. Lovely place, St. Ives. A big sign said, 'try our delicious home baked biscuits.' We both said, 'with gravy' at the same time. No American breakfast menu is complete without 'biscuits with gravy.' What they call 'biscuits' are more like scones, but one serving of biscuits with gravy was more than enough for me.

We had fish and chips overlooking the harbour. St Ives is a working port with lots of fishing boats, yet they served us up pre-frozen fillets of fish. Why? Is the price difference between fresh and frozen so great? St Ives is busy, all year round, tourists clamour for fish and chips by the harbour and yet they serve up a product no different from what those hordes of tourists could buy back home. Seemed a missed opportunity to me.

We parked next to a miniature version of a VW camper, with a big VW badge on the front along with another saying Kernow Campers, so self evidently the product of a Cornish company. We've spent many a night in VW campers. They're great fun, very quirky, people's faces brighten up when they see one, but we're also only too well aware of the inevitable compromises they force on their owners. Now imagine one only about two thirds the size. Where I would put my feet when we went to bed wasn't exactly apparent. Even so, we both liked it. Liked the retro colour scheme too.

We wanted to visit the Tate in St Ives, but for the third time we've been here, it was closed, being prepared for a future exhibition. Grrr. By the time we get to set foot in the place it'll have been condemned as unsafe and recommended for demolition. Marigold decided she'd have a cup of tea instead. We found an almost empty café with décor aimed at the Pensioner's Day Out trade even though we try very hard not to fit into that particular stereotype. Earl Grey tea was served in delicate, almost translucent, bone china cups set on a lace table cloth. The room was a microcosm of Middle England with antecedents dating right back to the Raj when the British Empire was the envy of the world. In this room, those days may be long gone, but are certainly not forgotten. Facing Marigold a (presumably genuine) Sheraton cabinet contained leather bound books that didn't appear to have been opened since Disraeli was in Downing Street.

Our waitress, a vision in black and white, brought out Marigold's tea and swept away again, gliding as if on unseen casters.

The only other people in the cafe were a couple of locals, strong Cornish accents, with loud voices talking about Theresa May's cough. The man seemed to think she'd done it deliberately 'to gain sympathy,' but he 'wasn't buying it.' He said it was an 'egregious tactic dreamed up by Number Ten' and much more in the same didactic, and very intrusive, manner. I couldn't see the face of the person he was hectoring, but imagine it bore a long suffering expression.

'Interesting,' I said, quietly, to Marigold 'to hear the word egregious in conversation. Sort of goes with the surroundings.'

Egregious is one of those words that have completely changed meaning over the years. Its Latin root means flock, as in a flock of birds and its usage was based on 'standing out from the flock.' Originally, 'egregious' meant standing out from the flock in a good way; being superb or outstanding but now invariably is used to denote something really, really bad. Like Theresa May's carefully contrived and artificially induced coughing fit in the middle of a speech. Apparently.

A few days later we were in Looe. The weather wasn't brilliant, but it wasn't raining so we braved the narrow lanes of Cornwall to get there. Half way there and we wished we'd taken Ruby, our quirky Mini convertible, for this trip as she takes up so little room in these very narrow roads.

We wandered around Looe, visiting both sides of the fast flowing estuary. A sign saying, 'do not feed the locals; they're vicious' was slightly alarming until we saw the accompanying picture of a seagull. Every other shop sold pasties or ice cream. Not 'ordinary' pasties or ice cream, but 'award winning' pasties and ice cream. How many awards are there on offer? We didn't buy any, but when we came across Catch, a fish and chip shop on the quay, we decided to follow up on a recommendation from a couple of our gourmet friends. Oh, and it's an award winner too. This time, the award really means something as Catch were 'UK Best Newcomers' in the National Fish and Chip awards, which is the equivalent of a Michelin Star for fish and chip shops.

We had proper chips and line-caught fish from the Looe fishing fleet, straight off the boat. Delicious plump, pure white fish and tasting absolutely fresh. St Ives, take note.

One of our last days out in England for a while, as we'll be off on our travels again soon, but we found ourselves talking once again about that US Road Trip.

Thinking back, it's odd how our expectations of this last trip were perhaps different from, say, our extended journey through Eastern Europe a couple of years ago. The fact that we share (a version of) the same language, allied to the familiarity of American life gained from daily exposure through TV, all felt very safe and familiar when contrasted with instantaneous exposure to the vast cultural differences between Eastern and Western Europe. And yet, and yet...

America is reassuringly familiar in so many ways and yet so very different. With our long experience of living in different European countries as background, we're probably less 'British' than most visitors from the U.K. but we were constantly reminded we were spending time in a foreign land. We may share a common language with the US – and I'm not one of those people who regard the English language as 'ours' while other nations merely rent it – but the gulf in expression and perception between the two nations is enormous and at its most poignant in the small details.

While we were in the Napa Valley, we spent some time in an absolutely brilliant deli. We loved the wide range of fruit and veg, all organic too, but some of the other offerings brought home to us the differences between our respective cultures. Marigold did have to chastise me, not an unusual occurrence, for saying I liked the look of a Red Velvet cake. Well, it did look pretty scrummy, but I do realise that alarming shade of red does not remotely occur in nature and the cake must be absolutely stuffed with red dye to achieve that look. Organic dye, presumably.

We're okay with different foods when we're travelling. More than okay really as we've eaten and drunk some pretty alarming things over the years. Local colour, right? Even so, squirting cheese out from a can like shaving foam is not something I'd want to do regularly and why was almost every loaf of bread we saw on our trip packed with sugar? Bland, over sweet and tasteless, bread should taste like bread, shouldn't it, even if most of it is intended to surround a burger or to be slavered in peanut butter and runny jam?

Still in that deli: an aubergine is called an eggplant, a courgette is zucchini, that over-rated hybrid of lettuce and grass, rocket, is called aragula, a swede and/or turnip is a rutabaga and, I already knew this one, courtesy of Hannibal Lector, fava beans are nothing more exotic than the humble broad bean while haricot beans are called navy beans. We expected different names for our root vegetables in Ukraine, but in the Napa Valley?

Marigold asked one of the assistants – who told us he was from Hawaii and was about as big as a rhinoceros – 'what is this called over here?' pointing to a very large display of broccoli, and he replied, 'that's garden fertiliser, not food. You don't wanna be eating no green stuff, 'less you're a rabbit.' Maybe working in an organic delicatessen wasn't his ideal career choice.

What else is different? So many things to pick. Being told on checking in at hotels, 'You're on the second floor,' invariably made us frown, but of course this being America, in reality we were only required to haul our luggage up one flight of stairs, not two. Second floor means first floor and even more confusing they call the ground floor – that's street level, remember, on the 'ground, terra firma - the first floor. There's no logic to this.

One more: we were in Death Valley, no light pollution for twenty miles in every direction so the night skies were a feast of stars. I pointed out the distinctive Plough to Marigold only to find myself contradicted by a complete stranger standing nearby.

'Think you'll find that's the Big Dipper,' said Mister Star at Night Expert, wearing very tight shorts, knee length socks, heavy duty boots and a tee shirt that said 'Guns R Good' and a picture of a wolf with a machine gun.

After a period of amicable discussion – I wasn't going to argue with a man wearing that tee shirt - we both realised we were talking about the same constellation.

'My brain hurts,' Marigold said as we left.

Indeed.

Winter Avoidance Tip - Go to Spain.

Marigold Says..

We went to a closing down for the end of the summer party and belly dancing display which all sounded rather exciting. Luckily, we managed to find a table which had a 'reserved' sign on it, but it wasn't actually reserved for us! Fortunately, they didn't turn up.

It was on the beachfront and for me sitting right next to the sea eating and drinking something yummy seemed just about right. We were all hungry, but food had needed to be pre ordered yesterday, so crisps had to do, but I looked longingly at the curry and rice and feasted on the smell.

An exotic looking girl arrived with her hair piled on top, she was very pretty and slim. A bit later on she came out with a gold cloak, which she threw off and started to belly dance. Her hair was now loose and she looked splendid. She had a few props, and the finale was a candelabra on her head with lit candles. Luckily, she kept her head still as no one was following her around with a fire extinguisher, or a wet towel. We followed her outside.There was a rather large man jumping about next to me. Unfortunately, he jumped into me, knocked me over and instead of everyone being interested in the belly dancer, they were all looking at ME, and luckily my belly wasn't on view. Got up quick and said I was fine. Somehow, G got me into the car. We looked at the damage, cut knee and damaged toes, all already starting to bruise. Lesson to be learned. Stay away from drunk jumpy men on holiday.

Knee on the mend now with no lasting damage, other than to my dignity. Quite like having a black knee and foot. Quite stylish. Am sure people who saw me fall over thought I was drunk though.

G Says...

Browsing magazines in a hotel lobby, I came across this passage recently when we were travelling through France on our way to Spain : 'A paradigm is a gestalt constellation of beliefs, values and techniques shared by a community which creates preconceived assumptions.'

Leaving aside my (very considerable and entirely justified) irritation at the convoluted phrasing and a doomed to be unrequited urge to throw the remains of my drink over the writer of this pretentious twaddle, it served to remind me of a man we met on our travels, some years ago now, in Australia.

Jean-Pierre, or JP as he liked to be called, was a middle aged 'surfer dude' – his description, not mine – who somehow attached himself to us almost as soon as we reached Sydney. We'd decided we'd see more of Australia if we flew into different cities, stayed in hotels and hired cars to tour around than if we went down the camper van route. New Zealand, coming up next, would be explored in a van, but Australia is dauntingly big.

Sydney is not the capital of Australia, but acts as if it is. It's big, brash and exciting, but Marigold took against it from the very start so that was Sydney marked down for no more than a week's stay, at most! Not sure now what it was in particular, but Marigold doesn't take long making up her mind whether she likes a place or not and Sydney was doomed after the second day. Unknowingly, we arrived there in the middle of the Gay Pride festivities and our hotel was in Oxford Street, the epicentre of Sydney's gay scene. JP was wearing a wedding dress, a substantial beard and bright red Doc Martin boots when we met him in the hotel lift and he turned out to be staying in the room next to our own. It was quite late, our first night in the city, and we probably looked a little weary, but JP looked in imminent need of an undertaker! He assured us he was fine and, somehow, staggered into his room.

The next morning, at breakfast, JP arrived at our table, sat down and introduced himself. He told us he was 33, (he looked at least 45), had left his wife in Quebec five years ago – after telling her he was going away for a week or two - and had been travelling the world ever since. He had exchanged the wedding dress for a belly dancer costume, bright red, and the boots had now been replaced by flip flops. Only in Oxford Street, Sydney, does the appearance in a dining room of a large bearded man wearing a skimpy belly dancing costume pass almost unnoticed.

It proved impossible to have a conversation with JP without it denigrating into chaos due to his predilection for rambling off at inappropriate and seemingly random tangents. He used the word 'gestalt' frequently, each time saying it was a word without a direct equivalent in English, which is true. Gestalt is one of those words I'd occasionally written, but until then never heard spoken. It describes an organised entity that adds up to more than its constituent parts and I said something along these lines when JP badgered me for a description. A football team, for example, I said, playing as a collective unit will usually beat opponents with individual talents, even when the individuals concerned are better players.

JP threw a tantrum and proceeded to supply his own, almost identical, definition of the word. When he finished speaking Marigold said, 'isn't that the same?'

'Mine was better,' he said. 'We will go to Manley, on the ferry today. Don't bother going to Bondi Beach. Manley is better.'

An hour later, worn down by our new 'friend's persistence, we were on the ferry to Manley, still listening to JP spouting nonsense. In fairness, he was right about Manley. Much 'better' than Bondi Beach. He followed us around for three days. In the end, at Marigold's insistence. we moved hotels. The very next morning Marigold said, 'I miss JP.'

Our route to Spain, through France, has been both problematic and enjoyable. We were forced to divert from our planned route due to what a road sign termed 'a major security incident,' which added many hours to the journey and monumental traffic jams. As for the 'incident,' we saw nothing about it on the news that night or the next morning.

The enjoyment came from visiting an old friend. Old friend in every sense. When we first met Claude it was in his office in the centre of the village we'd just moved into. A French Mayor is an important person and he would be responsible for many decisions regarding the renovations we had planned for the house. Claude spoke no English, wore a shabby brown suit and wellington boots liberally spattered with evidence he was a farmer as well as the mayor and immediately made us feel welcome in 'his' village.

We were expected tonight and Claude, long since retired from Mayoral duties but not from farming, had made lavish preparations. The sun was setting over Mount Canigou, the sacred symbol of Catalonia, which dominates the village and serves to mark the border between France and Spain.

Dinner that night was one of those occasions that I'll remember forever. I lost count of the courses, the wine flowed endlessly and all had a spectacular time. Claude had invited several of his neighbours for the grand reunion with 'Les Anglais' and the festivities continued until the early hours. It had been eighteen years since we'd left the village – moving down to Spain for fresh vistas and the challenge of a ruined finca overlooking the Mediterranean to renovate – but the years of absence were washed away on a sea of conviviality.

The next day being Sunday, we watched the village hunters assemble for la chasse, essential equipment being a dog, a hat, a gun and enough ammunition to fight a war. Headgear varied from cowboy-style Stetsons to leather helmets with dangling earflaps, no two being the same.

This was even more the case with the astonishing variety of canine magnificence on display. We noted a few 'proper' hounds, a feisty and cantankerous Jack Russell Terrier, but also a pampered-looking poodle and many others *sans race* as the French call mongrels whose only common feature was their complete unsuitability as hunting animals. Complete bedlam reigned as the dogs barked, urinated and fornicated with impunity, their proud owners engrossed in hand-shaking, back-slapping, smoking and, inevitably, taking frequent pulls on the essential flasks and bottles. We'd managed to avoid participation by pleading tiredness after our long journey through France. As animal lovers, hunting holds no appeal, but having lived in the depths of the countryside, in England, France and elsewhere, we defend its continued existence stoutly.

A single thrush attracted a colossal fusillade of ragged gunfire, the noise was deafening, accompanied by clouds of smoke, all to no avail as the terrified creature winged its way to safety through the trees. Great excitement ensued with much boasting and hearty camaraderie. The inability to hit the target appeared immaterial and would set the tone for the rest of the day.

When we met up with them again at lunchtime, taken precisely at noon, a single rabbit was the only evidence of success. Many of the dogs had failed to return with their owners, their excited yelps being heard in the distance as they chased shadows and fought imaginary enemies.

Lunch had been anticipated and was to be confirmed as the highlight of the day. A good hunt obviously called for a special picnic. Any true Frenchman adores le *picnic*. The French version bears no relation to the cucumber sandwich and thermos flask variety so familiar to the British. A French picnic is a true feast with each person trying to outdo their friends in the variety and scope of provisions.

Prior to 1789, hunting in France, as in England, was reserved for the nobility. The owners of grand Chateaux arranged their lands around the pleasures of la chasse. Most had pigeonniers or dovecotes, providing homes for thousands of pigeons, all destined for eventual extermination in the great hunts, and, eventually, for the immense kitchens of the chateau. In the aftermath of the French Revolution, la chasse became a classless sport, albeit with the proviso that only the edible are at serious risk. This seems to cover most species, as far as I can see, but unlike fox hunting back in England, here at least most of the resultant bag goes in the pot.

Game has been scarce around here in recent years, unsurprisingly, but wild boar are becoming a menace once more and there remain enough reasons to justify the excitement as hunting season arrives in the autumn. Claude, our host and the most prominent viticulteur in the area is president of the hunt and very proud of the combined skills of his troops. Last season they shot several wild boar, two deer and half a dozen foxes. I made the mistake, cursed once again by my ingrained British politeness, of admiring the stuffed and mounted fox which took pride of place in his lounge. Apparently, I was a little too fulsome in my admiration, as he promised me a similar trophy next time I'm passing through. The stuffing and mounting will amount to a mere 250 euros, trés résonable, non? I'm sure it's the bargain of the century, but now had the problem of explaining why I must decline this kind offer. Where will we find room to mount a stuffed fox? Not that I want the remains of the unfortunate creature anywhere near me. Oh well, a hard lesson learned. In future, I'll reserve my praise and admiration for his wine; I'll gladly take any amount of that.

Hunting in this area is only 'allowed' on Tuesdays and Sundays, seemingly honoured more in the breach than the observance and most serious hunters belong to clubs and associations who have areas reserved for them. In exchange for payment of a club subscription the chances of finding game are vastly increased. The clubs finance the rearing of pheasant and similar game birds which are 'farmed', reared from young chicks in the same way as the gamekeepers of an English, or Scottish, estate rear young birds for the hunt. There are several of these large netted farms nearby. The unfortunate creatures, virtually tame and with no fear of humans, fly trustingly towards the massed ranks of hunters and their eventual doom. Oh well, not my idea of an ideal way to spend an October morning, but in this company I keep my opinions to myself.

We'd brought our own contribution to the fare – including a few items sourced from Marks and Spencer so not exactly food from the surrounding area - and ate delicious food, washed down with wine from bottles that bear no labels, all made from local grapes, and were reminded once again of the pleasures of living in France. Even though I'm far less fluent in the language than I used to be, this proved no barrier. We ate, drank, roared with laughter in most convivial company and were transported back almost twenty years to the last time we'd shared a meal with these delightful people. It may be a cliché, but it really did feel like yesterday.

On our second evening in Spain we went to the 'last evening of the summer season' at a local beach bar. The resident singer was Clive Sarsted, (his better known brother Peter died recently), a swing band and... a belly dancer. She didn't even remotely resemble JP, fortunately for her and the audience.

We saw a young girl, tattooed and wearing Moroccan clothing, on our way in and both said, 'she looks interesting.' Her boyfriend/partner/ manager/whatever was even more interesting, like a young Errol Flynn. The swing band were a hardworking group of fine musicians, Clive Sarsted gave us 'where do you go to, my lovely' and much more while the young Moroccan girl we'd noted earlier swivelled her hips furiously, gyrating and whirling with great abandon despite the meagre floor space available, while balancing an array of objects on her head including a curved sword and a lit candelabra. A very odd way to earn a living, we decided.

When she moved outside to dance with flaming torches, a man who'd perhaps had a few too many beers managed to trip up Marigold and she was black and blue the next day. Turns out belly dancing with naked flames is a lot safer than being a spectator.

The swing band were brilliant, as befitting a group of gypsy musicians from Granada. We've been lucky enough to have enjoyed off the cuff concerts in the caves set into the hills opposite the Alhambra Palace and marvelled at the prowess of the players. Forget any notion of itinerant vagabonds; these are a proud people with a long and distinguished lineage and that heritage is a valued aspect of life in Granada.

The previous evening had been spent in a sea front bar eating a three course meal accompanied by a group of strolling players performing a theatrical extravaganza and regarding this well attended event, with absolute certainty I can say I enjoyed the performance enormously, for all the wrong reasons.

We've also been to an afternoon session featuring a group of ukulele players who were rather good and not at all what we were expecting. More rock 'n roll than George Formby, that's for sure.

The 'Catalan Problem.'

Marigold Says...

We do like the café life in Spain, and I start most days with a strong coffee and then perhaps twice a week I have a large fresh orange. Don't have any more orange juice as don't want to look like Donald Trump.

Thank you everybody for enquiring about my recent fall, well only one person actually. I do not need medical attention, and it looks much worse than it is, I am pleased to say.

G has sorted out the odd assortment of clobber he brought with him and chucked out into the communal bin a couple of very old moth eaten jumpers. Then, when we were out yesterday, we saw the local tramp wearing one and also G's old tee shirt which I had used to clean the car windows. He did look quite fetching, except for his own trousers which were tied up with string and were splattered with many stains. We have seen him over several years and apparently he is looked after by local cafes and allowed to shower at one. Not a bad life and the weather is good. Would like to know his story, but risky as he's a bit whiffy.

Went to Cabo De Gato, which is only about an hour away. The low sun played havoc with the windscreen view, but we managed. Sometimes you wish for cloud. The run in is fab and one of our favourite places. Met some friends on their way to Morocco in a van. We ordered some tapas and took in the view of the sea. We tried some Spanish wine the cafe people were promoting. Bottles with fantastic labels. That gets me every time, not the wine quality. I always choose by the label. Producers take note.

Went to one of my favourite shops which sells lovely knickknacks. It was closed for Xmas! Bit early I thought.

Anyway, my dosh is safe for another day.

Went back to our friends' camper van and had cake and coffee, then set off back with the sun behaving itself. Five minutes later I was asleep and very content.

G Says...

Yesterday, we treated ourselves to a run out into the National Park, one of Marigold's favourite places. The sun was beating down, clear blue skies overhead and a sparkling sea. Perfect place to spend a November day. We walked up to look at the view of the sea from an abandoned gold mine. Many years ago, gold mining was big business here, but no longer.

There's no real 'industry' left in this desert region now, apart from tourism and a few dedicated farmers of aloe vera, one of the few plants that will survive in these arid conditions. Hotels are of the 'off the beaten track' variety and focus on walking, trecking and getting back to nature. The (very few) roads are blissfully deserted, beaches are hard to find and even harder to get to, but well worth the effort and we've loved each of our trips through this virtually untouched region of Spain.

When we stopped for tapas and a cool drink the view out to sea was stunning and a middle aged couple were swimming. I remarked on the man wearing a white cap, but when he came ashore it soon became clear the cap was his only item of clothing. His female companion continued to splash around in the sea and was still there when we left.

A young woman wearing Ugg boots, a very short skirt and a Barcelona football shirt was serving behind the bar. She spoke perfect English and told us she had just taken delivery of a new batch of wine, so far only available in this tapas bar.

'Are you Spanish?' Marigold asked as her English was so good.

'No, I am Catalan,' she replied, 'I was born in Barcelona, but now I live here, in Spain. Please, come and see my wine.' She took us to the back of the tapas bar and showed us some of the wine she was introducing to the area. They were from small unknown boutique vineyards and all featured labels she had designed herself. She has worked in England, hence the impeccable command of the language, in France and the USA, but has now decided to give up work to pursue her passion for wine. 'I earn very little, but I am happy,' she said. We heartily approved and approved of her wine even more.

Marigold wanted to look in a shop window that never fails to interest her. It's packed with ethnic jewellery and on the three occasions we've been here in the past the shop has been closed. As it was today.

We had been warned. Marigold had mentioned she was going to look at the shop around the corner and the girl in the tapas bar said, 'It's never open. The owner has a frisky new boyfriend and she only opens up the shop when he gets tired' and laughed.

The Catalonia 'problem' dominates the news here. Just about everyone we talk to has an opinion and almost all in this area regard the leaders of the Freedom for Catalonia movement as enemies of the state. This young woman held very firm opposing views and we could relate to her passion. Many years ago now, we moved into a house we had bought in the South of France close to the Mediterranean border between France and Spain.

A neighbour came across to say hello. She sold flowers on market stalls and the front of her house was covered in them. We explained we spoke next to no Spanish and only fairly basic French and she said, 'but you are not in France or Spain now. This is Catalonia and I am Catalan.'

Broadly speaking, many people living in the area between Perpignan, in France, and Barcelona, in Spain, consider themselves Catalonians, the Catalan language is widely used and despite the privations of General Franco's brutal regime there's a clear desire for Catalonia to be an independent nation once again amongst so many. Others disagree, equally vehemently, but the Catalan 'problem' seems unlikely to be resolved any time soon.

Catalonia was first recognised as a wholly autonomous region in the 8th century and, despite the best efforts of our flower selling former neighbour, the Roussillon area is now resolutely part of France, but, across the border, Barcelona and Gironès remain hotbeds of revolution. Money, as much as an urge for autonomy, has prompted the recent strife. Catalonia is a prosperous area, far richer than most of the rest of Spain, and people are fed up of the Madrid government taking far more in taxes from the region than is ever returned in public services. Echoes of the pro Brexit lobby here.

The Catalan dialect, whether based on French or Spanish, is very, very different. Our friends from that time have three children in school and their children are taught Catalan as a 'first language' with French and Spanish as 'foreign' languages.

This national obsession with all things Catalan reaches a peak at the summer solstice when thousands descend on Prades for the Festa de Sant Joan (Catalan Spelling). Thousands of people climb the mountain and remain there overnight, congregating around an enormous bonfire and watching the dozens of similar fires burning brightly on every hilltop for miles around.

Many years ago, we made our one and only ascent of Canigou for the Festa. We climbed past two ancient monasteries, recently restored after being damaged by an earthquake well over five hundred years ago, yet still accessible only by hiking up a brutally steep path. From the summit the lights of Barcelona were clearly visible and the feasting and drinking went on all night long.

It's a long slog up the mountain, but not really hazardous and even quite young children can make the ascent. Could we do it today and if we did would we notice the difference between now and almost twenty years ago? That's no and yes, respectively.

None of us are what we once were, but that doesn't mean we have to accept it without question. Age creeps upon us all. It's inevitable. We'll fight it though. Keep on 'not acting our age' as we've managed to do for most of our lives. Very, very occasionally we still ask our battered bodies and damaged knees to do things they don't really want to do in the certain knowledge that the cardigan and slippers years cannot be deferred for ever. I hope it will be long time before that fateful day dawns. Meanwhile, we're still travelling. Meeting new friends and keeping up with old ones. Keeping our wandering life going. Doing what we love to do. Having adventures, large and small, and trying hard to savour every minute of every day. Just don't ask us to climb many mountains. It's our sore knees, you see? The spirit may be willing, but the knees know best. Marigold's recent fall has left a massive bruise. If she turns up on your television screen one day soon you'll know that recent enquiry to Embarrassing Bodies has been accepted.

Writing this in a café, the flat screen TV on the wall is still dominated by protest marches in Barcelona. The recent referendum produced an overwhelming vote in favour of cessation from Spain and the heavy handed approach from Madrid and the Monarchy has only worsened the situation. As a woman cashier in a Motorway Services who gave me my change when we filled up with petrol in Figueres said, 'Madrid cannot put all of us in prison.'

Enough politics. The latest ten-day forecast is for unbroken sunshine, temperatures more akin to summer than November and that's exactly how we like it. Last night was warm and around midnight we went out to stand on the balcony overlooking a moonlit sea. The faint susurration of waves breaching the shore was the only sound we could hear.

'Not bad here, is it,' Marigold said. No, indeed.

Revisiting old haunts, thirty years later.

G Says...

Our visit to a café for the Wi-fi and coffee routine was a fair bit later than usual so it was eleven o'clock before we were ready to venture forth. Outside the café, the sunshine was glorious, as it has been throughout the whole of the past month. Blue sky and warm sunshine, in November. It's why we come here after all.

'Shall we go off for a run,' I asked. Meaning, a 'run' in the car, for those who don't know us personally. Marigold has never regarded distance running as a viable option, an opinion I have come to share over time.

We set off with a fixed plan in mind: turning right at the motorway entrance and stopping when we felt like stopping. Not much of a plan, but hey ho.

Heading towards Murcia, we bypassed several likely stopping points, chatting away, enjoying the scenery on a virtually empty road until we passed a sign saying 'Torrevieja' and were instantly (figuratively, not literally) transported back in time almost thirty years.

Before we sold up and shipped out to live abroad, we were like most other people, taking 'normal' holidays, in the U.K. or abroad. One such holiday was to a newish Resort, in Spain, Torrevieja.

Friends told us of a couple who rented out their villa in Spain and we got in touch. We only ever met Sid and Nancy, in person, once. If you were expecting Sid Vicious and Nancy Spungen, think again. (Just looked up how to spell Spungen and saw she died in 1978 - 39 years ago. Feel very old now).

Sid (that's 'our' Sidney, not Mister Vicious) was a teacher and Nancy a 'proud housewife,'in her words. Sidney taught woodwork, but gave it a somewhat grander title, which I have now forgotten, and Nancy's every utterance was in praise of her remarkable husband. Every woman's dream, assuming you were a woman without a feminist cell in your body, who had willingly signed on for a life of indentured servitude and hadn't had an original thought since birth. She chain smoked, sucking furiously at her cigarette every three or four seconds. Vast intakes of nicotine had deprived her blood of oxygen over a prolonged period and surrounded her mouth with the characteristic finely drawn lines of a serious addict. Marigold and Nancy were never likely to become friends.

Sidney was tall, skeletal and intense with dark rimmed eyes receding into their sockets like two dried up waterholes and hectored us at the same volume he presumably deemed appropriate to quell a class of unruly schoolboys. He was unlikely to become my best mate either.

'One hears you're interested in renting out our Spanish casa,' Sid said as we arrived at 'Chez Nous.' Yes, really!

We agreed we were indeed interested, viewed the only photographs they had available, just three of them, each showing only a fuzzy view of what may or may not have been a house. Not a villa after all, but a 'town house,' in other words a terraced house. It was very cheap, Marigold and I both fancied the idea of driving across Europe to get there and an agreement was reached.

'The little lady will pop directions and a few pointers in the post,' Sid announced and we somehow managed to get twenty yards away from their front door before collapsing in hysterics.

Directions arrived in the post, as promised. Three sheets of them, in vast detail, denoting every turn of the road to what was still termed 'the villa' and every line of all three pages spellbinding otiose.

We'd said, on several occasions, we were going to drive there, by car, but the directions were mostly concerned with leaving Alicante airport, locating a car hire firm and where to find a nearby shop that sold 'English provisions.'

Also included was a separate sheet of paper telling us how to work a flush toilet and remember to add water before switching on the electric kettle. A final, underlined, paragraph said, 'please leave the villa in the same state you found it.'

When we eventually turned up at the 'villa' some weeks later, we spent the first two hours cleaning it and putting away the solidified remains of partly opened packets of food left in various places. The two bedrooms each contained twin beds with sagging springs and mattresses which looked as if they'd been scavenged from a skip. We went out and bought a pair of blow up mattresses, some sheets and pillows and slept on the floor for a fortnight. As with so much in life, memories of disasters endure long after those of better times have faded and we still laugh about our time in Stalag Sid and Nancy.

We remembered Torrevieja as being slightly seedy, surrounded by building sites, prone to graffiti attack, packed out with Brits and and with a huge open air hippy market, selling tat to tourists, every evening by the port. In short, a place we have never wanted to return to.

Until today.

The hippy market was still there, not as seedy as it used to be but still fairly lacking in charm. The old town, the original part, has narrow streets and is still very 'Spanish.' The remainder of the town is entirely based around tourists. The weather was lovely, we enjoyed strolling around, there were people swimming in the sea and it was all very pleasant.

So pleasant, we decided we'd have lunch at one of the many sea front restaurants. We picked the only one that didn't have a waiter outside beckoning customers inside – we don't like pushy waiters – and decided to have fish and chips as a trio of ladies, and a single harassed looking man, with Birmingham accents who were just leaving said 'the fish and chips was bostin', the highest praise a Brummy can offer. Over the centuries, this area of Spain has been home to Celts, Greeks, Romans, Iberians and Muslims, all of whom have left their mark on the gastronomy of the region. Despite this, thanks to the recommendations of our fellow citizens, we ordered fish and chips! One of the women, slightly the worse for drink, clung to my arm and said, 'you're like me, you look like you fancy a bit of F and C.'

It took me a few moments to realise she meant fish and chips and not some form of fetish native to Birmingham.

We ordered and eventually a young lad brought our meal to the table. It looked okay, maybe not 'bostin,' but okay.

Oh dear.

The batter was soggy, the fish itself was grey in colour and had a texture more like a fish cake than a fillet of any known fish. A hundred yards from here, fishermen were unloading their catch so there could be no excuse for serving up what was on our plates. There were peas, garden peas too, in a beaker at the side. When Marigold tipped the peas onto her plate half a cup of water came out with them.

We did wonder about the palates of the three ladies from Birmingham, with some concern!

Complaining wasn't easy. The young waiter didn't speak any English and seemingly very little command of Spanish either. He did say 'sorry' at one point. We are not 'complainers,' in general, but this was inedible.

Marigold was magnificent.

She decided, unilaterally, that I would be best placed in reserve while she went off to remonstrate with the chef. She was away for quite a while, but came back like a victorious Roman Emperor. No charge, even for the drinks we'd already drunk and a fulsome apology. We left, still peckish, but with the scent of victory in our nostrils.

There are still a lot of Brits, both visiting and resident here, but there are no more empty building sites. For many years, Torrevieja was a magnet for Brits. Property was cheap and the sun shone almost every day. A no-brainer, then. Over-expansion led to crashing property prices and many sorry tales to satisfy the 'Brits ripped off in Spain' diet of English tabloids.

When we were here last, we drove through Torrevieja and kept on going for a while past half finished, or abandoned, building projects until we reached Sid and Nancy's place. Today, it took us ages, the traffic was relentless, new apartment blocks lined the road and one shop or restaurant in three catered to an English clientele.

Cabo Roig was a brand new development thirty years ago. Today, it looked pretty impressive. We found Sid and Nancy's old house almost straight away. It's now inside a gated complex, very secure, and the communal grounds are superb. Mature trees and shrubs, none of which we remembered, and it all looked very smart. We'd happily rent a house here. Preferably one with beds fit for purpose.

There used to be a winding narrow track down to a small marina and we walked along it every day. This is now a paved walkway, the beach was packed and the marina is about five times bigger.

It was now obvious we wouldn't get back before dark, but we still took a couple of detours. The first being a beach, far from tourist traffic with only a dozen of the motor home brigade in residence - they always seem to find the best beaches. Glorious sandy beach, a good beach bar too. We were still hungry so tuna and salad baguettes went down very well.

Our other brief stop was to seek out the salt pans and flamingos of the Mar Menor, the largest sea water lagoon in Europe. The Mar Menor is separated from the Mediterranean by the 24 kilometre long La Manga del Mar Menor (The Strip). The average depth of the Mar Menor is four metres and at its maximum it is still only seven metres which means that the seabed slopes very gradually and you have to wade out a very long way before the water reaches a depth where swimming becomes necessary.

The water in the lagoon is incredibly salty, so like the Dead Sea, it's very safe for swimming as it is almost impossible to sink.

We found a few flamingoes, but not many today and mostly young ones. Where flamingoes are concerned, you are what you eat. Flamingo chicks are born grey, and do not become pink until they reach maturity at the age of five. For the first five years of their lives the pink pigmentation is gradually acquired by means of the carotenoids in their diet, which includes large quantities of brine shrimps.

The shrimps themselves do not create the pigment: this comes from the bacteria and microscopic algae which live in the saline plankton which are consumed by shrimps and flamingoes. The tiny organisms need the pigment to protect them from the high salinity, low oxygen levels and strong sunshine in the water of the salt flats.

We learnt all about saline shrimps on our recent visit to Antelope Island, near Salt Lake City. The Mar Menor is also a Salt Lake and we went to look at the huge mounds of salt painstakingly gathered from the lagoons. The pumps used to be powered by windmills, but nowadays the process is all electric. The windmills are still here though.

We're planning a longer trip soon, maybe next week, but as with all our 'plans,' no details are available yet. This next trip is at Marigold's instigation, based on some article she read in a newspaper, but she's a bit vague on detail, so far. Should be interesting.

Amongst Millionaires.

Marigold Says...

Yes, it's been mentioned G seems to do all the writing work, so today you're getting me. Just, don't expect this to be a regular occurrence!

Benahavís is one of those places you're unlikely to go to unless you know it's there. We first came here about twenty years ago, but only because we got lost! We have been back a few times since then and we wanted to see if it had changed since last time. It has.

There's a new very posh Country Club right at the top of the village so we drove up to take a look at it. Not that Country Clubs are where we normally find ourselves. A sign said Hills Café was up the road so I said to G 'that sounds like an English Café.'

How wrong I was.

Hills Café is really a restaurant, not a café, and is part of the Benahavis Hills Country Club. We drove up a very steep hill, behind a Fiat 500, and on one of the very tight bends the Fiat stopped, stalled and started to roll back down the hill towards us. G didn't panic, but I did. Quite a lot. It stopped about an inch away and the driver told his passenger to get out and walk, obviously because she was so heavy.

Charming!

She wasn't exactly slim, but it was very hot and the road was very, very steep so after the car in front started up again and crawled off up the hill in first gear G asked the woman if she wanted a lift up the hill. She jumped into our car in less than half a second.

The Fiat driver was parked in the only parking space at the top of the hill so our passenger got out while we drove up an even steeper road to where she said there was more parking. Lovely views over the new estate down to the sea.

We walked down to Hills Café and a sign on the door said please use lower entrance. I suggested G should go back and bring the car down as he wouldn't be very keen on walking all the way up again from the lower entrance. He didn't even thank me for my thoughtfulness, just went plodding up the hill back to the car while I waited in the shade.

G picked me up and we found a parking space near the main entrance. A sign said 'Hills Café is a secret and magical spot run by Michelin star chef Jean Francois Job. The menu features a variety of delightful fusion meals.' Secret and magical sounded good.

Inside the very swish entrance there were brochures of houses for sale. I found one I liked for only two million euros, but G said the pool was a bit on the small side and he much preferred the larger one for four and a half million. There are 38 villas - 'a collection of luxury rustic contemporary villas uniquely located at the Pinnacle of the historic town of Benahavis, overlooking spectacular views of the Mediterranean Coastline,' as it said in the brochure. We didn't bother the receptionist about making an offer as she was very busy sending text messages on her phone. Her thumbs were normal sized, but as she was tapping away so fast I expected them to be worn down to about half an inch.

We went upstairs, gave the gym and Wellness Centre a miss, for now, and were met by Jean Francois himself who was really nice. He told us about his Indonesian themed 'specials,' which all sounded pretty grim, and said they also did speciality sandwiches, the cheapest of which were twelve euros. For cheese and tomato. Not very special. We said we'd think about it. There was only one customer, a woman eating a doughnut and feeding it to her little dog. Not sure if it was a Michelin star standard doughnut. The dog didn't appear to be bothered either way.

As we were going out we met the woman who we had given a lift up the hill again and she took us by the arm and pushed us back inside. Jean Francois looked much happier to see us this time, in the company of someone who was obviously well known here. He kissed her on both cheeks, very enthusiastically, then me. G went to hide behind a palm tree.

Our new friend, Gina, was originally from Canada, but now lived in Marbella and her boyfriend was thinking of buying one of the villas. I wanted to ask, like Mrs Merton, what attracted her to the obviously very rich man in the little Fiat who had abandoned her on the hill, but somehow I stopped myself.

Gina told us lots of things about Benahavís and also quite a lot about herself, but mostly about herself. We suspect she is a bit of a good time girl, as the locals probably say about her in Spanish.

'Benahavís', Gina said, is 'the wealthiest town per inhabitant in the whole of Spain, which means there are all sorts of subsidies here that just don't exist anywhere else.' This is what attracted her rich boyfriend who runs an import/export business. G said 'drug dealer then,' but only after we had left.

There are nine golf courses around here, Gina said, and almost all of them are 'full up' and not taking in new members. She told us how much membership cost for a year, which I forget now, but it was a lot and her boyfriend has joined two of them. Wonder why her boyfriend only has a Fiat 500 that can't climb hills?

We had a cool drink next to the pool as a thanks for the lift up the hill present from Gina, and then we went outside. G was glad now he didn't have to walk all the way up the road to get the car.

We went into town and parked in a space after only driving around for five hours, well it seemed like five hours. It's all narrow winding streets and little squares, all very pretty with dozens of restaurants and lots of artists. The best known is a man we met once, not that I suppose he remembers. David Marshall, who must be about 75 by now, but still works as a sculptor, mostly in metal. He was a welder, from Scotland, but found out he had artistic talent and now sells all over the world. We found his gallery, La Aldea, straight away, part of what seems to be the oldest part of the town, but is one of the more recent. David Marshall had all this area built to look 'old.' We had a cold drink at the Bodega which looks hundreds of years old, but the painted barrels outside are actually older than the building itself. It's all very well done and very clever. Most of the town, Benahavís, is 'recent' after it was 'discovered' in the 1960s and became fashionable with the Marbella set.

While in the bodega we saw an article about a visit by the BBC Holiday programme which said Benahavis was 'as close to Paradise as you can get'. Not sure I'd go that far, although it is lovely, but who are we to argue with Judith Chalmers? Thinking back, she looked like Donald Trump does now, but even more orange.

It appeared to be a typical Andalucian village, but it's much more like Portmeirion in North Wales which was the setting for 'The Prisoner' back in the 1960's, as most of the buildings, which look ancient, were built in the 20th century and it only got a reputation for fine dining at the end of the 1970s.

We drove back down to the coast and realised the hotel we only booked this morning hadn't given us very good directions. We found the address of the road it was in, set the Sat Nav and drove on listening to the sat nav woman being bossy. When she said, 'you have reached your destination' we were a bit surprised as we were outside a sewage works.

G decided to ignore her, turned round, and we eventually found the hotel, an old finca done up in Moorish style. It was lovely, very Moorish, not many mod cons, but had a lovely garden, two parrots in a cage and the girl on reception was lovely as well.

I said 'is there a Café near here?' And she said 'No.'

Then she said there was a bistro on the beach, but it might not be open. We walked to the beach, found the bistro and had tuna and avocado panini each on a terrace overlooking the sea. Lovely.

On our way back we saw our waiter pinching lemons off a tree in someone's garden. He said, 'nobody here now,' and we all laughed. He had about twenty in a bag.

The breakfast at the finca next morning was weird. Cold meats and cheese, yes ok. So far. Followed by bread and marmalade, still ok. Asked for butter but it never came. Followed by muesli and yoghurt, followed by two (over ripe) pears with a piece of choc and 6 walnuts. Bits of odd 'stuff' really, all brought out at different times so never knew what to expect next.

Of course we ate it all, even the nuts. Felt a bit sick and went to lay down again for half an hour. Oh and the tea was like hot water with loads of milk in it, but no taste of tea. G had coffee which he said tasted like turps. (This too clever by half IPad changed 'tasted like turps' to 'tasted liked turds,' so good job I noticed. It was bad, but not that bad!)

Off to Tarifa today then a wander up the coast towards Jerez. Hope G writes the next blog as I am exhausted. He hasn't even checked my spelling and punctuation. Not that it needs checking, but just in case! He's a writer, I'm a good time girl, like Gina. Still not found a millionaire though, but our car is better than his and it even goes up hills. If G ever stopped the car and told me to walk up the hill I would explode. Don't think he will.

Old Favourites and the glorious beaches of the Costa de la Luz, the Coast of Light.

G Says...

On the road to Tarifa we find time for a quick coffee in a bar with a good view of Gibraltar. The coffee isn't wonderful (Marigold likened it to tepid gravy), but the views are quite some compensation.

The Rock of Gibraltar, in ancient times, was one of the two pillars of Hercules and the Romans called it Mons Calpe, the other pillar being Mons Abyla on the Moroccan coast. Both are clearly visible today. Yesterday evening, in our finca style hotel, I ended up talking to a Frenchman who obviously wished to practise his English. He spoke English about as well as I speak French so with some switching around we were able to communicate. He went off and fetched a second wine glass so I could share the bottle by his side. I expected sophistication, he was French after all, but the wine was very far removed from sophistication. The last time I had wine as rough as this was in Algeria. He seemed to like it though, even praising its tannin levels.

He taught history at the Sorbonne for thirty years, he said, and did indeed appear very knowledgeable on the history of this area. He told me the twin pillars marked the end of the known world, which I already knew, but added a personal opinion that this myth had been propagated by two other ancient seafaring civilisations, namely Greeks and Phoenicians, as a means of dissuading future ventures into the vast expanse of the Atlantic Ocean which they had already explored and visited. Interesting idea.

Marigold had long since taken herself off to our room at about the same time the former history teacher stopped 'chatting' and began 'lecturing.' Shame as she missed out on the wine! Given a free choice Marigold would choose Vimto over wine anyway.

'Marigold, you missed a treat,' I said as I got back to our room. 'As you know, the strip of land joining Gibraltar to the mainland is called an isthmus, but historian call it a tombolo, from the Latin word tumulus which means a mound?'

Marigold didn't appear too impressed with this for some reason.

'Over an hour talking about Latin rubbish. He was awful and I bet his wine was awful too.'

'Yes,' I admitted, 'he was and it was.'

We stop at the viewpoint next to a tiny and rather dingy café overlooking the Straits of Gibraltar. We've stopped here many times and at certain times of the year the place is packed with 'twitchers,' (bird watchers), drawn by the sight of thousands of birds migrating across the narrow stretch of water separating Europe and Africa. Good views across the Straits of Gibraltar today, a calm sea and not as much wind as usual, but no flocks of birds. Plenty of bikers here, as there always are.

There was a three masted tall ship far out to sea, like a galleon, which reminded us we must visit Cape Trafalgar later today. Unusual, us having a plan, but as it turned out the rest of our day's travels were as amorphous as ever, although we did get to see Cape Trafalgar!

Our first stop, as ever in Tarifa, was the cemetery. Yes, an odd choice maybe, but this is a very special place. Apart from a few conventional graves, one hosting a couple of imitators of Greyfriars Bobby – two black cats whereas Greyfriars Bobby was a Skye Terrier - there is a sort of horizontal locker system in place, stacked five or six 'boxes' high and extending along numerous rows.

It's Sunday morning so mourners were out in force. Virtually every last resting place is festooned with flowers, the whole area is immaculate and there's a palpable air of respect for others in the air.

On our last visit here we saw many 'graves' bearing the legend 'unknown African,' each accorded exactly the same respect and care as the other 'residents.' Today, we saw only references to 'Immigrante de Marruecos.' Adding to the pathos, many of these victims washed ashore after unsuccessful attempts to cross illegally from Morocco to Spain bear the same date of death. Equally sad was the sign on the grave of an identified victim of drowning, that a mourner directed our attention towards - 'Hope Ibriam, Nigeria.' Hope died in 2005, the poignant irony of that name must surely strike everyone who sees it here.

I was fascinated by the concomitant accoutrements to the grave of Professor Wolfgang W Wurster; one dead flower and two empty wine bottles. A not exactly cryptic suggestion the late Professor was a bit of a lush, perhaps?

The graffiti on the end walls of houses just up the road from the cemetery have been repainted as we noticed last time we visited they were getting a bit shabby. The residents of this small estate, by no means a prosperous area, are very proud of their art work and rightly so.

Down by the port we saw the creamy wake of one of the hydrofoil ferries racing across to Tangiers. We've been on one of these many times, and also used the larger, slower, ferry from Algeciras to Ceuta. Incidentally, as we passed Gibraltar we saw the long queues for vehicles entering and leaving. Spanish officialdom takes a dim view of Gibraltar remaining British and often makes life difficult for those entering or leaving the entry point between the Rock and mainland Spain. It invariably strikes me as somewhat irrational when we're travelling to Morocco from Algeciras as we arrive in North Africa at the Spanish enclave of Ceuta, a tiny area of Morocco that remains Spanish territory. At least Gibraltar is in the same continent. Different, in what way?

We love beach bars and Wet café, just off the N340 road, is a special favourite, but today we went for a long walk on Tarifa's virtually deserted beach and had a smoothie at Café Aqua right on the beach. The smoothies weren't very good, but it's such a laid back place we didn't mind. Much.

There's a slack rope, ie not a tightrope, between two trees for those who like showing off. I felt adventurous and was about to try it when a group of young kite surfers arrived, most sporting beards and tattoos, so I sat down again, fearing ridicule. One of the young girls, no beard but many tattoos, hopped onto the rope and instantly fell off again. She tried again, same result. I almost wished I hadn't abandoned my plan as I couldn't have been any worse, but the moment had passed.

One of the girls said, 'they shouldn't let fat people go on beaches, not without a shirt on anyway. It's gross.' Her friend agreed. I stood up to look at who had offended them, hoping it wasn't me, and saw a middle aged couple walking along minding their own business. Yes, they were on the plump side, but even so. I hope those girls realise, the couple in question probably were just as skinny as them in their youth.

All along the beach here are camper vans, large and small, expensive and falling apart, there's every type. We saw several from very far afield: Estonia, Moldova, Lithuania, Finland, but very few Brits. Distance travelled appears to have no correlation to quality of vehicle, there was one with a Belarus number plate which we wondered how it even got the hundred yards from the road to the beach in one piece. We never stayed here in our van owning days, but one of our favourite places is just up the coast.

As we were leaving the beach we detoured to admire a separate group of vehicles, the wildest of wild campers living year round in old vans and converted buses. We occasionally come across old friends in groups like this, but didn't know anyone here today.

A sign in one van warned potential intruders, 'beware, Staffies on guard,' in several languages. I met the Staffies, apart from the likely prospect of being licked to death I found them very far from dangerous.

A couple having a (very well organised) picnic in the woods waved at us and invited us over for a drink, but we have, unusually and somewhat irrationally, booked a hotel for tonight and it is many hours away from here so we had to move on.

Our next stop was Bolonia, another place we return to often. There's a great beach here, with many camper vans 'wild camping.' We've been here many times and it's a delightful place. The main draw for visitors is the ruined Roman city in a perfect location, right next to the beach.

Entry costs 1.5 euros, it was only one euro last time we came, but if you can prove you are entitled to call yourself 'European' by showing an EU passport, it's free. After Brexit, this visit will cost us three euros!

Maybe not as nobody asked to see our passports. As we went through the unguarded entrance we saw the attendant having a ciggie break in the sunshine. She waved to us to carry on. We obviously looked sufficiently 'European.'

It's all gone a bit more upmarket since our last visit, hence the 50% entry fee rise, with a humongous museum complex, but the main attraction remains the ruined forum and other remnants of Ancient Rome. This was once a prized asset of the Roman Empire. Then, it was known as Baelo Claudia and its importance came from the fishing industry, much as this area does today. Baelo Claudia supplied the popular Roman delicacy Garuda, a sort of fish paste, to the whole Roman Empire. It was thriving at the time of Emperor Claudius who was so impressed with the produce he gave the town his name.

By the second century AD the town was in decline and was nearly destroyed by an earthquake. By the sixth century AD, Baelo Claudia was abandoned.

In its heyday as a fishing centre, the fish-salting factory - located in the lowest part of the town, right on the beach - allowed the prized Garuda to be preserved and sent throughout the Empire. The salting vats have been excavated and the stone columns of the forum and basilica are remarkably well preserved. The weather was great and we enjoyed wandering around for an hour or so.

The beach itself was stunning in the sunshine. There are many sand dunes, one of which is now a National Monument. Many people climb to the top of the biggest one, as we have in the past, but not today!

Marigold decided those struggling up the slope were just show offs and declined to be associated with them. Very wise.

Moving on, we diverted again to the coast to Zahara de los Atunas. This is at heart a fishing village, but is rapidly approaching 'resort' status and is now, apparently, probably one of the Costa de la Luz's most upmarket areas where house prices have soared in recent times.

There's a good beach, of course, as there is everywhere else along the 'coast of light,' which remains unspoilt, and empty, but the town itself has definitely gone upmarket since our last visit. Designer shops and gourmet restaurants – we hardly recognised the place.

At the side the of the road we see numerous reddish coloured Retinto cows, many with calves alongside. Very often we've seen them on the beach at Bolonia and they're the ultimate free range grazers, wandering at will between beaches and forests. They survive, apparently happily enough, on hay and acorns from the woods throughout the summer. In Cádiz province the 'winter 'problem isn't really a problem for livestock, but the summer heat and drought is where the herds are at risk. They're placid creatures, even the bulls seem friendly, despite those scary looking horns, and the meat is highly prized – very lean and low in saturated fats – with a big festival every year in Zahara to celebrate the breed.

A few miles along the coast road and we're in Barbate. Known throughout Europe as the epicentre of tuna fishing it may be, but not to us, as whenever we see the sign for Barbate we say in unison, 'Kenneth Noye.' This has been a hectic day, so our observations on fugitives from justice, tuna fishing and Trafalgar will have to wait a little longer.

Tuna fishing, beachfront restaurants, fugitives from justice and sea battles. Oh, and naturists too.

G Says...

I spent an hour or so, (it felt a lot longer at the time), recently in the company of a French historian, so please allow me some leeway if this post contains more 'history' than would normally be the case. Marigold could have written something far more interesting and engaging, but she didn't so you'll have to manage with me. In mitigation, one of our regular followers wrote in praise of the factual content, interspersed with nonsense, and told us he had learned a great deal. Yes, really!

Barbate is a fairly scruffy town, in fairness – not surprisingly, I suppose, as the local newspaper declares it to be Andalucia's most deprived town and unemployment here is at record levels - but there's a good beach and a well cared for promenade and as we arrive on Sunday afternoon the beachfront restaurants are packed, almost entirely with extended Spanish families.

The centre for traditional tuna fishing, a holiday home for a notorious dictator and the setting for the arrest of a notable fugitive; that's Barbate.

It used to be known as Barbate de Franco as Spain's former ruler liked the place so much he spent much of his free time here. Not something to boast about these days, perhaps, but in harsh economic times it's surprising how some people yearn for the 'old days when Franco ensured Spain's prosperity' which is the gist of a remark made to us yesterday by a young waiter in Estopona. In any rational context, that's the opinion of one far too young to remember the Franco years, but since when has actual life experience been any barrier to absolute certainly of conviction? In an era where 'fake news' is swiftly acknowledged and regurgitated with seemingly irrefutable assurance, one person's random opinion can soon reach out to a wider audience. No wonder that Donald Trump is showing signs of paranoia.

Tuna fishing has been important to Barbate ever since the Phoenicians arrived here over three thousand years ago and even today the system they pioneered back then remains in use. Thousands of giant blue-fin tuna pass through the narrow passage between the Atlantic and the Mediterranean on their annual migration in spring and once again in the reverse direction in winter.

The ancient method of catching them is known as the *almadraba* method in which a series of long nets are anchored to the sea bed fairly close to the shore. Tuna, on their way to spawn in the Mediterranean, are then trapped in the nets. Once the huge fish are captured in the final chamber, fishermen in boats pull the net into a tightening circle. The men raise the net, gaff the tuna and haul them on board. It's dangerous work as those fishermen have to wrestle those huge fish, weighing as much as three hundred kilograms, that's approaching 50 stone, onto their small boats, but the resale value of their catch is enormous. There's an insatiable demand for tuna in the Far East and the majority of the catch is shipped, frozen in situ, to upmarket sushi bars and restaurants in Tokyo.

Due to indiscriminate overfishing, the Atlantic bluefin tuna, confusingly known as in Spanish as *atún rojo*, (red tuna), is in danger of extinction. The local fishing industry in Barbate and the surrounding region claim, this was again taken from the local newspaper, that *almadraba* fishing is sustainable and the decline in numbers is entirely due to offshore fleets of so called 'factory ships.' It is estimated that only about 0.01 percent of the tuna that migrate through the Straits are captured in the coastal *almadraba* which would certainly suggest the traditional method is no threat to the continued existence of the blue fin tuna. In contrast to the factory ships, the traditional nets allow smaller fish, and dolphins, to escape and only fish weighing over 70 kilograms are captured. 70 kilograms is over 11 stones in weight so no tiddlers are involved. These are mature fish who have made the journey to spawn many times and have thereby already added to their numbers.

We managed to find an available parking space and a free table for lunch, both involved great ingenuity, and sat people watching while we waited to be served. I recently learned a new Spanish word, *abuelos*, meaning a grandparent, as a couple of our friends have recently gained grandparent status, and there were very many *abuelos* here today, busily engaged in the vital task of doting on new arrivals. One baby was so tiny it must have only been a few days old, but it's never too early to enjoy a family meal in the sunshine on the seafront.

A little further along the promenade is a very famous gourmet restaurant specialising in tuna, naturally, and it was on the terrace of *Al* Campero one sunny day in August 1998 that Kenneth Noye was finally arrested.

Kenneth Noye had been on the run for two years after becoming the main suspect for the murder of Stephen Cameron in a road rage incident while on licence from prison in 1996. He'd been convicted in 1986 of handling stolen goods from the Brink's-Mat robbery and was serving eight years in prison of a 14 year sentence.

Noye had been among those involved in laundering a huge quantity of stolen gold bullion taken during the Brink's-Mat robbery by six armed men in 1983. While he was being investigated for his involvement in the crime, Noye stabbed and killed a police detective involved in police surveillance in the grounds of his home and, although cleared of murder on the grounds of self-defence, was found guilty of handling some of the stolen gold and conspiracy to evade VAT.

Britain's most wanted man had also been 'spotted' in Spain, Tenerife, Lanzarote, Gran Canaria, France, Morocco, Turkey and Russia and police visited 13 countries in the course of their investigation.

The police account says they were tipped off about Noye by a holidaymaker who recognised him. Noye was put under surveillance and detectives tracked his wife and son when they visited him. Spanish police officers cooperated with their British counterparts and a glass from which the man had been drinking was taken to obtain the fingerprints that identified him beyond doubt. Stephen Cameron's fiancé, the key witness to the killing, was flown to Spain, she discreetly identified the suspect in the restaurant and after her return to the U.K, Kenneth Noye was finally arrested and returned to England for trial.

19 years ago, yet we still can't see the name 'Barbate' without saying, 'Kenneth Noye.' Yes, I know, but it will pass, in time.

Barbate looked very peaceful today and even the man whom Marigold suspected of being a wanted fugitive as he kept looking around and repeatedly glancing at his watch turned out to be only a long suffering dad waiting for his teenage daughters to arrive. Very disappointing.

Lunch was great, not as fancy as it may have been at *El Campero*, but we loved the lively beachfront scene and the unceasing chatter of our fellow diners. Marigold enjoyed her (very) large glass of tinto de verano - literally 'red wine of summer' being a mix of red wine and lemonade - so much, she ordered another one! Our waiter wagged his finger and suggested she would be in urgent need of a siesta very soon. How right he was.

One of the waiters dropped a tray of drinks and the whole place erupted in gales of laughter at the poor man's misfortune with the table of diners who had ordered the drinks leading the way. Odd, isn't it, how we all invariably find such mishaps amusing? I banged my head on the open rear door of the car on setting out today and thought Marigold would have to go and have a lie down as she was laughing so much. 'I've got jelly legs,' she gasped, as if that was my fault for deliberately smacking myself on the head with a car door.

We were heading for Jerez and had already decided to bypass Cádiz as we've been there several times over the last couple of years. This left some time over for another trip to the coast.

Cape Trafalgar is essentially a beach, naturist in parts, an impressive lighthouse and not much else, but it was off these shores that the definitive sea battle of all British history was fought.

We walked the entire length of the beach, up to the lighthouse, no naturists today, and beyond where we found a dozen or so windsurfers and one intrepid kite surfer way out to sea, soaring up high and as we watched, admiring his skill, misjudged a landing and vanished beneath the waves. We were just about getting concerned when his head popped up. No damage, other than loss of dignity. No wetsuit either and the Atlantic water would have been pretty nippy that far from shore.

Returning in the direction of the lighthouse, we saw two items of interest we'd missed on the outward journey: a plaque commemorating the sea battle and, rather less impressive, three naked sun worshippers, two males, one very much so, the other not as much, and a woman who we may have mistaken for a large boulder when we walked past previously. They were sprawled, arms akimbo, supine, ie on their backs. If they'd been 'prone,' lying face down it may have been less arresting a sight. On second thoughts, maybe not.

'Is it a rule that only people who look like that can go on nudist beaches?' Marigold wondered. It's a fair point as we've been on many a naturist beach and invariably come away reflecting on how much better the vast majority of human bodies look when clothed. Today, it wasn't even a close call as this particular trio just made the place look untidy. We weren't tempted to join them. Don't expect naturist photographs; that wouldn't be seemly. Trust me, it wouldn't be much appreciated either in this case.

Trafalgar holds such significance for the English that I had to check the victory wasn't merely a jingoistic over-exaggeration. Nelson's stellar reputation as a certified hero of the nation certainly seems justified.

The battle itself took place in 1805, (I knew that, having paid attention in school history lessons. My ability to remember random dates never ceases to bemuse and occasionally even irritate Marigold), and Napoleon was allied with Spain in planning an invasion of England. He needed to assert his supremacy on the seas and the English fleet, commanded by Admiral Horacio Nelson and the combined Franco/Spanish fleet under the command of General Villeneuve had been pursuing each other around the Atlantic, the West Indies and the Mediterranean for a couple of years, before finally coming together for what became known as the Battle of Trafalgar.

Villeneuve formed a battle line three miles long with his forty ships. The rival fleets sailed onward and Nelson hoisted a flag signal "England expects every man to do his duty" as he gave the orders that unleashed a series of unexpected and quite revolutionary manoeuvres, throughly confounding the opposing fleet.

During the battle, a French sniper fatally wounded Nelson and the great man uttered his famous dying words, 'Thank God I have done my duty.' Yes, he also is rumoured to have said, 'kiss me, Hardy,' to the captain of the Victory as he lay dying, but the 'done my duty' words were destined to be his last.

Stirring stuff!

Of the forty French and Spanish ships, only ten survived and over 4,500 men died in the battle.

The English had far fewer casualties, but lost their best and much beloved admiral, Admiral Nelson. Napoleon was to remain a threat to England for a further ten years, but if Waterloo marked an end to hostilities, Trafalgar had been the point of no return as far as an invasion of England was concerned.

Nelson's body was brought ashore and placed in a brandy vat to preserve it during the long journey back to England. The English sailors who were not buried at sea, but who later died of their wounds, were buried in the Trafalgar Cemetery in Gibraltar. We've been to Gibraltar several times – not one of our 'favourites' in fairness, (is it possible to be too British?), but never been to the Trafalgar Cemetery. Better put it on our 'to do' list, if only we had one!

Jerez is famous for sherry and Andalusian horses.

Marigold Says…

Two days in Jerez. Before we set off, someone said to me, 'you must go and see the horses.' Jerez is best known for sherry, but also for the very fancy named Royal Andalusian School of Equestrian Art and I got a bit of a bee in my bonnet about it because the woman who told me to go said it was the best thing she'd ever seen.

I had wanted to go to the horse show today, when we arrived, but they apparently don't do it today. Sulking now. Never mind, i have been talking to some Americans. Talked rather posh so they might think I am Royal. They never mentioned Harry and his fiancé once.

G just 'negotiated' a deal with the hotel, so we are staying over in Jerez and going to the horse show tomorrow.

It's December, the hotel is very big, very lavish and most of the staff are standing around doing nothing so they were happy to do a deal. Our system is to find the right person, offer to help them out by sleeping in one of their many empty rooms, but paying very little as even a little is much better than an empty room earning the hotel nothing. Oh, and we'd like breakfast as well.

I should add that when I say 'we' haggle, I mean G haggles and I stand about ten yards away looking as if he's nothing to do with me. I'm the same when we go to Morocco where G barters, not me, as I'd just say 'okay' to the first price they mention.

We promise to keep quiet about paying quite a lot less for our room than everybody else, or there would be a riot, and the girl on the desk even gave us sweets. So, that's two nights in a plush hotel for a lot less than everyone else paid for one night. Our system only works properly in the winter months though, but we can't have everything.

There's a piano bar with a man playing to an empty room so we sit and listen for a bit, but then as soon as he sees he now has an audience he thinks he's Liberace and starts flouncing around, so we don't stay long.

Today we walked for miles all around Jerez. We passed a convent called Convento de Capuchinos – ancient order of coffee drinkers, perhaps – and later on found a church with a sign outside. G said it said something like, 'closed due to foot and mouth epidemic,' but a man told me it said the church was closed as it was being decorated. I assumed he meant for Christmas, but he was working there and said 'come in.' So we did.

His workmen were all supposed to be painting the walls, but they were sitting in one of the pews smoking. He started shouting at them, but they took no notice and he went away grumbling. The men all laughed after he left. It's a gorgeous church, even though it's called something like St Gertrude the Unworthy or something very like that and may be even nicer when they finish painting the walls. May be a year or so yet at this rate.

I was supposed to bring a map from the hotel, but I forgot, and we couldn't get a signal on the phone so we were soon lost. Never mind, it was a nice place to walk as long as we walked in the sunny side of the street. In the shade it was perishing. We sang 'on the sunny side of the street' as we walked along, but had to stop when we got a stern look from a policeman. He was smoking a cigarette so it was a bit much to give us a dirty look just for being cheerful.

We came across two statues, busts really, one of Cervantes, fair enough, but the other was Shakespeare, not so obvious. They both bore me rigid, but I have been told, many times by many people, that is my fault.

We followed a sign that said Cathedral as we thought there would be lots of cafes around there, but found some enormous buildings instead which turned out to be sherry bodegas. We went inside the one that supplies Harvey's, it's massive, and wandered around the shop part for a bit. G knocked a cupboard with his elbow as he walked past and one of the display bottles wobbled but he caught it in time. The girl on the desk looked a bit alarmed. When we saw the name, the Imperial Reserve, and the price, three hundred and ninety euros, we gulped and scurried off before we knocked into anything else.

We walked past a bar, a really dingy bar, but there was a man on a motorbike outside and on the back was a grinding wheel and when he ran the engine the wheel whizzed round and he was just finishing off sharpening knives for the man in the bar. I wished we had a knife for him to sharpen.

We did a tour of Fundador, a really massive place with thousands and thousands of barrels. Walked around with a very friendly girl, practising her English, and didn't have to pay, but no free samples. Never realised so much sherry was drunk, but they export all around the world and their biggest market is South America, the girl said. Then we went to Tio Pepe, even better as they gave us tastings, but we had to pay a few euros to go inside the warehouses and look at lots more barrels. Outside, the walls were stained very dark. We have seen this before, in Cognac, as a percentage of the alcohol evaporates into the air and over a hundred years or so stains the walls. In Cognac they call this 'the angels' share,' which I always thought was a nice idea.

We found the Cathedral, more walking, and ended up at the bottom of a really steep flight of steps. We both looked at each other, but decided we had better go up them as we could perhaps see where we were better from the top. After about 500 steps, may have been less but felt like 500 we were in a big square with a huge Christmas tree, about a hundred little school kids all eating packed lunches, a brass band and, best of all some cafes.

We plonked ourselves down and a waiter, dressed like a punk with spiky orange hair, took our order and talked us into having a Spanish omelette, between us, as he said it was delicious. It was.

We sat basking in the sunshine, wondering why all the little kids were so well behaved. We reckon their teacher must've been a real dragon but when she stood up and clapped her hands they all went and stood in neat lines and the teacher was tiny, not much bigger than them, and looked very sweet. She took a group photo and then asked our waiter to take another with her in it as well and she was pulling faces and all the kids were laughing.

All of a sudden the sun went behind a big building and everyone put on an extra coat. All except us as we were wearing all we had brought with us. We had no idea how to find our hotel again and I told G I had a blister. He didn't look convinced by this sudden blister, but we went and found a taxi. The driver drove down cobbled streets that looked as if they were too narrow for cars, but he did it anyway, and came out on the big roundabout near our hotel, only about a mile away at the most. We must have walked three or four times further than that.

'I preferred the scenic route', G said, but I was too busy scurrying into the warm hotel to reply.

'Your blister seems better now,' G said and I only just stopped myself from saying, 'what blister?'

Oops!

Fab breakfast this morning and a big 'Hola' from the girls on the desk who are our best mates now we are 'regulars,' well, this is our second day here. The most chatty one speaks English with an American accent as she has a boyfriend from Texas and came over to us last night when we were reading our Kindles in one of the lounge areas and said, 'would you like a gin and tonic? They were doing a photo shoot yesterday and she wheeled over a trolley with lots of bottles of gin on it.

'Not sure whether they are coming back for this or not,' she said, pouring us both a big measure and another for herself. She fetched tonic, ice and lemon from the bar and sat chatting with us for over an hour until her boyfriend turned up and she went home. She wheeled the trolley of gin away too before she left. Just as well as when I got in the lift I noticed I had a very red face.

Today we went to the dancing horse performance. We looked on the map and it was only five minutes walk away. Good job as we might have ordered a taxi to take us just up the road and it might have been the same one as yesterday which would have been embarrassing.

There was only one woman in front of us at the ticket office, but about fifty others standing around. Trouble was, she was the one buying tickets for everybody and it took ages.

The main building was like a mini chateau with lovely gardens all round it and there were lots of stables and a big open air exercise ring. The performance was to be in a building that looked like a covered bullring, very old, and when we went upstairs there were seats all round a floor area of raked sand. There was a Royal Box, empty, and a VIP section in front of it. There were only three VIPs and they didn't look very famous at all and one of the women was eating crisps. Call yourself a VIP?

The woman in charge of our stairway told us where to sit, in a very bossy manner.

It was due to start at noon and I said to G, 'bet it's late starting. This is Spain.' At half past twelve, half an hour late, they played some very loud music to wake everyone up and then there was a message over the loudspeakers in three different languages which took ages. It was 'forbidden' to talk, to take photographs or to leave your seats during the performance and the bossy woman glared at everybody as the message ended as if daring us to do anything 'forbidden.' One little boy tried to take a photo as the horses came out and she wagged her finger at him and glared so much I thought he might start crying. I think I would have done.

The horses looked fabulous, were obviously well cared for and the riders, all middle aged men and very serious, rode around the ring while the horses did clever things. After that there were a pair of horses pulling a carriage with two men and another set of four horses pulling another carriage. They whizzed around, missing each other by inches as they passed and it was all very clever and impressive.

But.

I looked at G and he didn't look very impressed. 'You don't like it, do you,' I said and he shook his head.'

'Neither do I,' I said.

It was very clever, but we weren't happy to see the horses being asked to do so many unnatural things like walking backwards on their hind legs and every time the rider flicked them with a whip they jumped in the air kicking their legs out. Everybody clapped and seemed to enjoy it so it seemed to be just us that was unhappy.

We don't like the idea of having performing animals like elephants in a circus either and this seemed to be very similar. When there was an intermission, we decided we'd go somewhere else.

'My bad,' I said when we got outside. Just like our gin swigging friend last night would have said as it had been my idea, but G just said, 'this is lovely though' and we walked around the gardens, looked at the horses in the stables and almost got run over by the men driving the four horse carriage who came up behind us and we never noticed.

We are hitting the tapas bars, for lunch not for drinks as G has to drive later when we leave for Seville. Last time we went to Seville they told us to drive our car into what we thought was going to be an underground car park but turned out to be a very narrow box, only just bigger than the car. When the door behind us closed, they sent our car up to the roof in a rickety old lift and we had to drive out and park on the roof. Hopefully we will be staying somewhere more modern this time.

A Return to Glorious Seville.

Marigold Says...

Our hotel was the best yet, but really cheap as it was nearly empty. Our room faced the back of a football stadium, bet it's noisy on match days, but there were lots of comfy seating areas and the staff were lovely. So many of them too. I suppose they're rushed off their feet when the hotel is full, but there's hardly anyone else apart from us in a huge modern hotel.

This is our fourth visit to Seville and we know parking is impossible in the old part so the girl at the desk rang for a taxi for us. The car was a hybrid, G said – I never noticed – and most of the way we drove on electric power so it was very quiet. The driver went through lights on red, cut across traffic lanes and made me wish I'd stayed in bed, but we got there in one piece.

It's a Bank Holiday so the city centre was packed with lots of queues.

Went round the cathedral in Seville. We had to queue to get in of course, but played the old pensioners' card again and only paid 4 euros. G laughed when the woman asked him to prove he was a pensioner and didn't even bother to ask me. How rude. I don't look a day over twenty five.

There were several different pricing categories with big reductions for pensioners, students and the disabled so we limped up to the booth hoping to get a double reduction. No luck. I went through the wrong gate as I was too busy looking at a weird woman who was eating an ice cream even though it was cold and ended up back in the queue. G came and rescued me and the woman taking the tickets gave me a funny look. She might have been considering giving me a refund as I was obviously in a completely different category.

Luckily, there were no dancing horses inside.

Afterwards, we walked round the Jewish barrio and had a few tapas, no pork on offer of course. There was some street entertainment, which made it rather jolly. The best were a group of girls and an older woman who went around playing guitars and singing. They were really good. When G went to take a photo the girl on the end went 'ooh, a photo, I had better smile, in case that man fancies me,' or something like that. Honestly, teenage girls are the same the world over.

I had 2 'speciality' sherries in different bars, both were recommendations of the barman and both tasted vile, but felt I ought to investigate its popularity. Will never have another until I reach 100.

Over to G now.

G Says...

It's good to be back in Seville once more. Such a fascinating city. Seville was founded as the Roman City called Hispalis and is steeped in history. We find it's best explored in spring, autumn or winter. We came here once in summer. Temperatures hit 100 degrees and stay there for weeks on end. They call this area the frying pan of Spain; even the Spanish complain about the heat in Seville. We also learned, to be polite you have to say it properly. It's not Seville, which is how we misguided Brits say it, but Sevilla, pronounced – Sev – ee – a – with each syllable enthusiastically extended.

Our hotel was almost empty, but when we went down to sit in one of the lounges a man came over and sat down right next to Marigold. He was very thin and completely bald. After seeing that bust of Shakespeare in Jerez, I thought immediately how much his head resembled the skull of Yorick, the former court jester exhumed by the gravedigger in Shakespeare's Hamlet. Holding the skull, Hamlet's ensuing soliloquy is a meditation on the fragility of life. That's the famous soliloquy that begins, 'Alas, poor Yorick.'

When the speech continues with 'I knew him, Horatio, a fellow of infinite jest, of most excellent fancy,' well, that's where the likeness ended. This man was surely a quip free zone, can't imagine he has ever cracked a joke and certainly never been amused by one. Even his mother, on the day of his birth, must have thought, 'he looks a miserable little devil.'

Naturally, Marigold started talking to him!

I couldn't hear what they were talking about, but when he finished his drink he got up and walked away without another word.

'He wasn't much fun,' Marigold said.

'Really?' I replied, trying to look surprised.

We got a taxi, accompanied by a mad taxi driver, to the Cathedral area. Seville (pronounced Sev-ee-a, remember) was madly busy with holiday crowds so we had to queue. It was pretty nippy out and the locals had their furs on. A strong smell of mothballs permeated the air. We've never been inside the Cathedral before, so why pick a day with long queues outside? No answer came to mind. Maybe we thought huddling together with a herd would be warmer?

First impressions: this place is big. As in massive.

A hand out leaflet on entry – couldn't find one in English so made do with the French version – tells us that after its completion in the early part of the 16th century, (the precise date wasn't given and I didn't get around to looking it up) the Cathedral took the title 'biggest in the world' from Hagia Sofía, which had held this claim for well over a thousand years. Hagia Sofía, once a mosque, but now a museum, is certainly spectacular and the Blue Mosque also in Istanbul is even more so. We passed through Turkey a few years ago and visited both of them.

When people complain about traffic in city centres I think back to the time I drove through Istanbul and the several times I have driven through the centre of Marrakech – trust me, European cities may be busy, but at least there are rules! Marrakech and Istanbul, no rules or rational driving conventions are present there.

Reading on, the leaflet said this was the third largest church in the world, which makes one wonder on the precise definition of 'church,' and also the largest Gothic church in the world. We were in Milan a few years back and I distinctly remember an identical claim made by Milan Cathedral. It also gave the 'correct' name: the Cathedral of Saint Mary of the See. Yes, that's See not Sea, now that would be confusing, but the shorter version, Seville Cathedral, certainly rolls off the tongue better.

Like many of the post-reconquest churches in Spain, the cathedral was built on the site of a former Almohad mosque; the newly reinstated Catholic Church making a point by demolishing the places of worship used by former rulers. Announcing the intention to build with the phrase, 'we shall build a church of such a kind that those who see it built will think we were mad,' certainly conveys a fair degree of chutzpah, particularly so as the local worthies who instigated the project were unlikely to survive until its completion. The canons of Seville committed to a subsistence existence to make sure the project was funded, which is pretty laudable. Work started in 1402 and a mere 104 years later it was complete! In fairness, just over 100 years is pretty swift as far as cathedral building goes, as the citizens of Barcelona can testify. It was designated a World Heritage Site by UNESCO in 1987.

Seville Cathedral was built on the same large, rectangular base-plan of the mosque it replaced, but the Christian architects added the extra dimension of height. The result is an astonishingly large building that breaks several size records. Measured by area, Seville Cathedral is the third largest in Europe after only after St Paul's in London and St Peter's

Basilica in Rome, but when measured by volume, it surpasses them both.

We didn't realise at the time, but were told later by a fellow visitor, whom Marigold christened Senor Know-all, that we'd entered by what had been the original Moorish entrance court, the Patio de los Naranjos, and the only other remains part of the original mosque was the Giraldo, now a bell tower but originally a minaret. It's possible to climb up to the bell tower for a view of the city. We decided this could wait until another visit, when the weather would be warmer. It was decidedly nippy inside the cathedral, must have been freezing at the top of the bell tower.

As is the norm, many famous historical figures are buried in cathedrals. Christopher Columbus has a vastly ornate tomb and his son is also buried here. It was at this point we met Senor Know-all who told us he knew 'for a fact' that the remains in the tomb were not of Columbus and DNA testing was under way to prove this. It may even be true. He was very insistent and got quite worked up about his 'for a fact' conspiracy theory. There's the head of John the Baptist here as well, but surely not even the most devout would accept this as an authentic relic.

The centre-piece of the altar is huge, ornate and seriously over the top, in our humble opinion. Intricate carvings, more gold than Fort Knox, it's the largest and most expensively decorated altarpiece in the world, according to Senor You Know Who!

It was a little warmer when we left the Cathedral and we walked back through the Jewish Quarter, the Barrio de Santa Cruz, a labyrinth of narrow pedestrian streets, all intertwined and with unexpected entrances into picturesque squares. We had a drink, a tapa or two and wandered around for an hour or so discovering hidden gems. Order a drink, get a free tapa. It's a good system, especially for the many 'bar hoppers' we came across during our own bar hopping.

The barrio was originally a means of walling off the city's many Jewish residents from the rest of Seville, but after the Christian Reconquest in 1248 they mingled freely once more.

History teaches us these situations never endure for long and so it was here in 1391 when the entire Jewish community was violently persecuted and their synagogues were converted to churches. Thousands of Jewish lives were lost. Today, it's an area filled with sunshine, orange blossom and good humour. Even a statue of Don Juan.

Marigold decided we'd walked these cobbled streets for far enough and we looked on Google Maps to see if there was a shorter route back. It said the walking distance from the tapas bar we were in to the Cathedral was 1.6 miles, but we must have walked at least twice that given how winding the alleys were. It estimated 26 minutes for the journey, again it took us over three times that but we are nosy, stop often and need refreshments, frequently. It also said the same journey, ie from 'here to there,' would take 44 minutes by car. Seville city centre traffic is evidently no worse today than normal.

Back in the wide open spaces, we toured the tapas bars, just 'window shopping,' so to speak, this time. Lunchtime crowds, harassed waiters and the deafening babble of the Spanish enjoying themselves. Spanish bars are about as far removed from the awed hush of the Cathedral as it's possible to imagine. There were musicians, jugglers, mime artists everywhere, not seeking donations but putting on an entertainment for the Bank Holiday crowds. Enormous fun. A group of girl singers, with a responsible adult in tow, were delightful.

We took a taxi back to the hotel, footsore but happy, and were even happier when the return journey turned out to be far more sedate than that piloted by the would be racing driver we'd endured in the outward trip.

This is a delightful city, especially away from the searing heat of high summer. It's a great mixture of ancient and modern buildings, palm tree lined promenades, a river to stroll alongside, olde worlde street lamps and the rattle of horse drawn carriages. We love it and we'll be back again one day.

We had intended to return to the Roman Ruins of Italica, just outside the city itself, but that will have to wait until next time. It's a Roman Amphitheatre, said to be the first evidence of Roman occupation in the whole of Spain. We loved our last visit a few years ago as we were the only people in the arena and could recreate gladiatorial battles while unobserved. Yes, it probably was embarrassing, but it never seems so when there's nobody around to play the critic. From memory, it's about half the size of Rome's Colosseum, but we had to share the Colosseum with a few hundred others so Italica was much more fun. It was free too, for EU citizens, so there's another future cost to take into account after Brexit. We may have to pay a euro each next time we go there. It's a consideration!

We didn't visit the bullring either. Bull's heads are a common sight in the tapas bars and matadors are heroes around here. Seville has one of the biggest arenas in Spain, the Real Maestranza has seating for 14,000 spectators. Built in 1761, the bullring has an oval shape, which is unique among Spanish bullrings. We're no fans of bullfighting, but the historic buildings are always impressive and it's part and parcel of Spanish life and has been for hundreds of years.

So much more we could have done. In past visits we've visited a recreation of Pontus Pilate's house in Jerusalem, the fabulous Royal Palace (queues all around the block today) and the intriguing Barrio de Triana across the River, home to a thriving pottery industry and the centre of the gypsy community. We didn't even catch a flamenco show! These omissions, together with much else besides, are reason enough to come back again. Can't be bad.

A historical Site to Rival anything in the World.

Marigold Says...

Just arrived at a vile hotel in Cordoba. A real flea pit. The air con is set on ice cold and I can't turn it off. Never mind we shall be stoic and go down and moan a bit, except the girl on the desk has big tattoos and so we will be pathetic, and hope she doesn't turn violent. This was the only hotel in Cordoba, which is heaving at the moment, with any rooms left. Just one room, as it turned out. Last minute decision to come here, so we were due a bit of a comedown after getting such great deals in hotels so far. Will venture out in a bit amongst the hordes. Hope we don't get bitten by bed bugs tonight, but may be too cold for them.

Traffic hasn't been too bad except for when we were leaving Seville. I only screeched a bit.

G had to wait outside the hotel to park the car, which took ages as the only free parking space was filled with a woman breastfeeding a baby so he had to wait until she finished and was ready to go on her way.

I asked the tattooed girl if she could sort out the air con. She came up with me in the tiny lift and we had to take it in turns to breathe. She wasn't as tall as G but was much, much wider so we were both glad when it got to the third floor.

She tried to work the air-con, nothing happened, so she said, 'control needs batteries' and tried to take the old ones out. She didn't want to risk breaking her false nails so she banged the remote control on the wall to loosen the batteries and broke it in half. She glared at me as if it was my fault and stomped off to get a new remote. The new one worked, but the machine still pumped out freezing cold air.

'Solo frio,' she said. Only cold air .

I decided we should turn it off then as the night was supposed to be very cold. It had been such a lovely day and people were still sitting outside, but with a clear sky and being high up above sea level here, everyone said tonight will be cold,

When G got back from parking the car, very fed up, he said the reception girl had something for me. We went down, much more room in the lift with only G and me in it, but still very tight space, and found a coffee and drink waiting. The girl had asked G on his way in what I would like to drink to make up for the faffing about with the air con. He said 'Tia Maria' and there was a huge measure of it and a coffee waiting by an armchair. Very nice.

G showed me the garden area, which was a bomb site, and the overflow parking area which was even worse. We both laughed.

'What's the room like?' G asked as he'd only been as far as the door so far.

'Awful,' I said and we laughed again. Must be all that Tia Maria. As things turned out, it wasn't too bad. The beds were on the firm side, but no more so than lying on the road outside would have been, and the shower cubicle was a dead ringer for the one in Psycho. I insisted on a dramatic recreation. G rolled his eyes at first, but then played the knife wielding killer so realistically my screams were genuine.

The people staying here are very friendly, the hotel is packed, and we took part in a sort of pub quiz in the dining area. We didn't understand most of the questions, being obviously all in Spanish, so were never likely to win, but everybody else had been to a wedding and were pretty drunk so we didn't come last. It was funny and we even slept well. Until five o'clock anyway when the people next door had a storming row. We saw them briefly last night and he looked just like Art Garfunkel and his wife/partner was about two feet shorter than him. It was her making all the noise though and she sounded very fierce,

When we went downstairs, G went out to get something from the car. He came back and said the car windows were frozen up as the temperature was minus three. I went off and ordered a pot of tea and some toast. Not going out there until it warms up.

Everybody from last night was already there and we realised the idea of toast was a good one as they used the local fat, doughy, bread rolls so you got huge chunky pieces of toast. Art Garfunkel turned up and had breakfast on his own. No black eye though.

After breakfast, we checked out, put the luggage in the car and only then realised we were blocked in by several other cars, two of them looked abandoned and were completely blocking the exit. The man from the hotel came out, in just a tight tee shirt and jeans to look at all the chaos, shrugged his shoulders and rushed back inside.

We decided to flag down a taxi, which is what we did, and sort out the getting out problem later. G will tell you all about Cordoba, but I just remembered something about a café we went into. It was packed with customers and the people running it were both very old. They made the coffee and drinks and three other men and a woman took food out to customers. They kept getting the orders wrong, taking food to the wrong tables and it was chaotic. Obviously, we loved it.

We only had a cup of coffee each, but when we offered one of the waiters some money he looked terrified and backed away saying no, no, no. We realised the 'staff' were not allowed to handle any money and we had to wait for the old granny to shuffle out from the kitchen part to take our money. After ten minutes, we hadn't had any change, from our 20 euros note, so we went up to the counter. The old woman gave us a very suspicious look as if we were trying to rob her and then gave us the right change. I don't think they were coping very well with those Bank Holiday crowds. As we left an American man started shouting as the waiter took yet another wrong order to their table. They had been there when we arrived and were still waiting for their order. I started laughing and G pushed me outside quickly as me finding it all very funny didn't seem to improve the American man's temper.

G Says...

The Mezquita of Cordoba is one of the world's most impressive buildings. We've been here before so we know what to expect, but even so, there's a buzz in the air as the taxi drops us off. Just as well we have been here before as we were dropped off right next to a vast herd of people waiting outside a building with some very big doors. Not the mosque/cathedral though, no fooling us, these people were waiting for an official tour.

There's a long queue of people trying to buy entry tickets, it's very cold in the orange tree lined courtyard and we're not equipped for Arctic conditions so we go and find a man in uniform fiddling around with a wall mounted ticket machine under a sign saying Out of Order.

The sign has evidently deterred everyone else, but that was a very, very long queue. After a couple of minutes, the man started to screw back the faceplate.

'Is it working now?' asked Marigold.

The man shrugged and said what we took to mean, 'no idea, but if you want to risk 10 euros, give it a try.'

We put a note in and tickets came churning out. Four of them. We only needed two, so the man frowns and says he will need to do some more repairs. He asked for the spare tickets, which we had intending giving to whoever in the queue looked most cold, but never mind, we had our precious tickets to enter the Mesquita.

Each year approximately 1.5 million tourists come here and surely none of them could fail to marvel at what's inside the gates. It's a fully functioning Cathedral now, but the Cathedral was built inside the former grand mosque of Cordoba, not only the largest mosque in the world, but the largest temple in the world, as well. It's huge, jaw-droppingly huge. There are 856 supporting red and white columns – no, I didn't count them – made of marble, granite or jasper and the mosque tails away into the distance in every direction between the twin arches supported by these ornate columns.

A minaret, the highest ever seen at that time, was added by Caliph Abd Al-Rahman the Third and became the inspiration for minarets in Seville and Marrakesh, both of which we've had the privilege of visiting. The minaret is now the bell tower of the 'new' Cathedral.

The original mosque was built to symbolise the sophistication of the Islamic culture that had conquered Spain and much of the rest of Europe in the 8th century. Given its size and sheer magnificence, no wonder the building took over 200 years to complete after work began in 785 AD with succeeding generations adding new additions. Its pattern was based on the basilica model, following on from mosques built in Damascus and the al-Aqsar mosque in the centre of Jerusalem.Underneath the foundations, archaeologists uncovered sections of the Basilica of San Vicente, a much earlier building presumed to have been erected by Visigoths and also containing fragments dating back to the Ancient Greeks.

Cordoba became the capital of Spain at the time of the Moorish Conquest, it was easily the largest and most cultured city in the known world and remained so until the Christian re-conquest many hundreds of years later.

After Cordoba was recaptured by King Ferdinand III in 1236 and the Moors were driven out, the mosque began to be used as a Christian church.

In the centre of the mosque, beneath the dome, Bishop Alonso Manrique began the building of a Renaissance cathedral in 1523 and work on the project continued until the beginning of the 17th century. When a further addition, a Renaissance nave, was added, encroaching still further into the original mosque, even King Carlos I, who had commissioned the most recent work, deplored this as 'desecration' and condemned the Church for 'having undone something that was unique in the world.'

The row rumbles on as although Mass has been conducted here every single day since Christianity was restored as the dominant religion of Spain in the 13th century, but worship by Muslims in the mosque is forbidden.

As recently as 2006, the diocese of Córdoba paid 30 euros to register ownership of what it calls the cathedral-mosque, or sometimes they refer to just as the cathedral. The universally approved name is the mosque-cathedral of Córdoba. The local council in Cordoba stood their ground, denying the right of the Diocese, representing the Catholic Church in Rome, to claim legal ownership of the mosque-cathedral, declaring that "religious consecration is not the way to acquire property."

The council's report says the building does not belong to the Catholic Church nor to any other organisation or individual as the site has been classified as a UNESCO world heritage site "of exceptional universal value" and therefore cannot be owned by anyone.

In 2014 the Mezquita bell-tower reopened for the public. This means we could have taken the opportunity to clamber up a few hundred uneven stone stairs, walk around the bell tower in the frigid air of a December morning and take in the views. We watched a group come back down. They didn't just look cold. Think far beyond cold. They looked close to death. We decided the bell tower could wait for a warmer day.

I really liked a winding mechanism, part of the bell tower, removed and replaced from above after a supporting beam broke causing one of the bells to become dangerous, mainly for its Heath Robinson construction. The bell, and the offending beam, are also on show.

On our second circuit, we took more time to fully explore the architectural differences between the Renaissance Cathedral and the Moorish mosque. Ornate splendour contrasted with almost rustic simplicity, on the surface, but even the most simple original arch was extensively carved. A Byzantine mosaic we discovered, covered with inscriptions of praise and holy passages, would have been very easy to miss, but was compellingly impressive.

Of course, the 'bling' elements of a Catholic Treasury, common to most large cathedrals, were to be found here too. One magnificent item, which a helpful security guard, not Spanish at all, but from South Africa, (he introduced himself as a "Seth Iffrican") told me was called a 'monstrance' (hope that's the correct spelling) and had been manufactured by a German goldsmith Heinrich von Arfe in about 1510, was particularly impressive.

The Treasury and the ostentation of the altar in the Catholic area stood out starkly against the spartan simplicity of the mosque, but this particular mosque was significant in its own way. There's none of the majestic extravagance that defines the Blue Mosque of Istanbul, for instance, which had so bewitched Marigold and myself, but the sheer scale of this place with its seemingly endless lines of arches and columns, had a unique majesty all of its own.

The same security guard told me this is the only known mosque that does not face Mecca, but instead turns its face towards Damascus in Syria. He added this was an assertion of the dynasty that began the construction of the mosque, the remnants of the Umayyad dynasty, in the face of the rise of the Abbasid faction from Baghdad.

He wrote it down for me when when I looked perplexed so if there are any errors here, blame the security guard's handwriting and not my lamentable failure to check his assertions.

Outside again, the sun was shining and it was warm enough now for shirtsleeves. Not that the Spanish people readily abandon their winter clothing at the first glimpse of the sun. We Brits may imagine this was a warm day, but the locals remained huddled down in their fur coats and boots, shivering.

After passing an interesting twenty minutes or so having a warming drink in a café Marigold selected, from a vast choice available, which was full of customers shouting at the waiters and vice versa, we walked across the Roman Bridge in the, by now, warm sunshine.

The bridge was built over the Guadalquivir river on the command of the Roman emperor Augustus in 918 AD, although it's safe to say that most of that original bridge has been repaired and restored over the past thousand years or so. Today's bridge is based on 16 ancient Roman foundation sections with the river flowing freely between the arches. The Roman Road, the Via Augusta, linking Rome with the coastal port of Cádiz, passed through Cordoba and the bridge was constructed to allow both traders and armies to travel freely throughout this far flung section of the Empire.

In the middle of the bridge we found a statue of San Rafael, the patron saint of Cordoba, dated 1651. Nearly new, then, by Cordoba standards! On the return journey, we passed through the Triumphal Arch, mostly known locally as the Roman Bridge Gate, which leads up into the city.

For any Game of Thrones fans out there, the ancient Roman Bridge of Cordoba was reclassified as the Long Bridge of Volantis in the TV series.

We got a taxi back to the hotel, found the car park exit was now clear and set off for Granada. Or that's what we'd intended. As were were about to set off, I decided to surprise Marigold and go somewhere very different. Would she like it? She's not fond of surprises. I'll let you know.

Living in a Cave doesn't have to be Primitive.

Marigold Says...

On setting off from Cordoba, we were originally intending to go to Granada, another place we've been to several times, but after seeing the weather forecast on the tv news – warm sunny day, freezing overnight on high ground - we had a rethink. Granada is close to the ski resorts of the Sierras Nevada and G reckoned Granada at about 5,000 feet above sea level definitely qualified as 'high ground.'

G disappeared with his iPad while I chatted to the lady running the coffee machine about politics and high finance. No, not really, she wanted to know why English people came to Cordoba when they could go to Marbella instead. I asked her if she'd ever been to Marbella and she said no. It was a bit of a strange conversation really as her English was even worse than my Spanish so we just waved our arms about and smiled a lot.

G came back, said 'all sorted' and off we went. He wouldn't tell me where we were going, even after I had taken about fifty guesses. Usually, this irritates him so much he ends up telling me, but not today.

We whizzed past Granada where every other car we saw had skis on the roof and the snow covered Sierra Nevada mountains looked gorgeous in the sunshine. When I saw the sign for Guadix, I got excited and said, 'caves.'

We've been to Guadix before, even stayed here, in a hotel, and have seen the cave houses, but never stayed in one. Well, we would be staying in one today.

The directions G had been given were terrible but we found it in the end. The lady who met us, who I called Linda as I misheard her name and she was too polite to correct me, was lovely and spoke good English. She took us to 'our' cave and showed us round. She looked after ten caves in all and was a cave expert. She told me she was fifty years old and had been born in a cave, had lived in cave houses most of her life and her mother still lived in the same cave house where she had been born.

Our cave house was lovely, with a living area and a little kitchen, not that we had anything to cook in it, a separate bathroom and a really cozy bedroom, all the rooms with whitewashed rough ceilings but Linda's own cave house had been very different. There was no electricity or heating, no water and no bathroom so they had to collect water from the river, a long way away. Hard times. She said it had been very exciting when her father dug out an extra room for a bathroom when Linda was thirteen.

Linda said over half the people in Guadix still live in cave houses, but that people from all over Europe have been buying them up lately so some people have moved out. There are 'thousands' of gypsies living in caves, Linda was from a gypsy family, and she said her people will never sell their homes to foreigners. 'Where else would we go?' She said. We'd driven through Guadix on the way here and the sign post leading to here was called 'Barrio Trogladyte.'

G tells me we're actually in Benalúa, just outside Guadix, and to be honest there's not much going on around here. It's a desert area, very dry with lots of humps and hollows and it's here, in this land that nobody else wants, that most of the cave houses are found.

Linda, I still don't know her real name, took us into a restaurant nearby that had only opened a few days ago and introduced us to the owner, a big, not very friendly woman, and said we should walk down to eat here tonight as it would be 'an experience'.

G wasn't that keen, but we were quite hungry and I didn't fancy banana sandwiches so we booked in for eight o'clock. Six o'clock would have been better for me, but Spanish people eat late and eight o'clock is still very early for them.

We got to the restaurant and were the only people in there apart from two young girls and a lad, aged about 18, who were sitting at a table with about twenty empty beer bottles on it. The music was deafening and we asked our waitress if she could turn it down. She went off and turned it down, only a bit, and the lad on the beer table started shouting at her to turn it back up again, but she ignored him.

'Go here, by the fire,' the waitress said. 'It's very cold in here.'

It wasn't, actually, but we sat down next to a roaring metal stove, a really big one that burns pellets. They're very expensive things, but even sitting right next to it we couldn't even feel any heat.

The girl slid over again in her patent leather shoes with slippy leather soles, about as bad a choice as is possible for waitressing, but they looked nice which is important when you're seventeen. She said she was the only one there who could speak English, but she didn't speak it very well. There wasn't a printed menu, but she told us what we could have, I hardly understood a word. G asked her, in Spanish, to repeat what the choices were but we still didn't understand her replies.

'How bad can it be?' G said and we ordered a starter and a main course. He ordered pate and I ordered a 'special' salad as starters, but we had no idea what the main courses were. 'Lamb something' was about as far as we got with one and 'no idea' for the other..

My salad was okay, just a salad, not very special, with a slice of very hard goat's cheese perched on top. G's pate looked interesting, but was pretty vile. It turned out to be black pudding, but looking like a slice of cake. Pigs' blood cake. Vile. He still ate it though.

Main courses were lamb chops for me, with a fancy name, and G got a big pile of chips smothered in a weird sauce with chunks of meat on top. We couldn't decide what the meat was. I said pork and G said donkey. We both left at least half, very unusual for us. Oh, we had a free glass of local white wine too. It was called mencal and comes from the bodega up the road somewhere or other, the waitress said, which was called Pago de Almaraes. We both agreed not to bother visiting the bodega.

Sorry to go on and on about food, but it was one of the worst meals we've ever eaten. Loved the cave, hated the restaurant. Linda was right about it being an experience. Not in a good way. We walked back, grumbling, and passed some locals going the other way, to the restaurant. I wanted to shout, 'Go back home and have beans on toast. You'll be glad you did.'

Obviously, I didn't.

Everybody talks about the main thing about living in a cave is that it's cool in summer and warm in winter. Very energy saving and 'worthy.' Bet those people buying them up are all Guardian readers. It was cool inside when we arrived here, pretty warm outside at that time, and when I got up in the morning I looked out of the window and saw frost on the car windscreen.

'It's cold out, but really toasty in here, in our very kind to the environment cave,' I shouted to G, just before I walked past a radiator I'd not even noticed last night and it was very hot. Central heating. In a cave. How decadent. What about the environment?

Saw Linda on leaving. She asked about our meal. We both said "fabulous, thanks". Pathetic!

Guadix is fascinating, but G will tell you about all the history stuff.

G Says...

Interesting stay in a cave house. It took a bit of finding. In fairness the directions I had been emailed were a bit vague. Cave dwellings are fairly random as regards having actual addresses and the 'map' that accompanied the directions resembled a Venn diagram crossover. We got there, eventually, after discarding the instructions and relying on local knowledge. The man I chose to ask would not have been my first choice, but this wasn't exactly Regent Street so there weren't many to choose from. He had a spectacularly large nose, very thick glasses and was wearing a coat tied at the waist with hairy string. He didn't speak English and I didn't understand his spoken Spanish – I suspect it wasn't even Spanish – but he knew where to find cave houses well enough. There are thousands around here, but I showed him a photo of the cave house in question, looking like every other cave house I've ever seen, on my iPad and he nodded, waving his arms about and 'speaking in tongues,' at high volume the whole time.

No idea what he actually said, but 'keep straight on for a bit and stop at the top of the hill' was the gist of what I perceived his gestures to mean. Of course, after driving on for a bit and stopping at the top of the hill, we found the very place we were to spend the night.

The lady who greeted us was very slim, very dark and exotic. Marigold is pretty exotic herself, so they hit it off immediately. My only contribution was to mend the printer in the office. Paper jam, if you're interested.

The cave house itself was one of many around here, each with a while chimney poking up from the earth on the hillside above. On entry it didn't appear much different from a conventional house, after dark in particular, and much more comfortable than our hotel in Cordoba. I'd expected it to be dark inside, but there was a big window at the front and a glazed door so it wasn't at all gloomy. It all felt very peaceful, admiring the rough hewn walls and ceilings and simply watching the languid progress of dust motes reflected in the sunlight outside. Very hushed, very peaceful, a place for relaxation, for contemplation.

This peaceful interlude didn't survive the arrival of Marigold and her insistence there was a wolf on the hillside. We went outside again where a scruffy dog was busily engaged in digging a hole in the sandy soil accompanied by excited yelps. In fairness, he did, very slightly, resemble a wolf, but we felt able to take a walk around the area without fear of being savaged.

We were persuaded to go to a restaurant last night and can safely say I've enjoyed root canal work at the dentists more.

Our waitress, first job and it showed, was lovely though. I'm still worrying about her slippery and completely inappropriate shoes and whether she ended up in A and E last night. Just hope, when she eventually slipped over, as she must surely have done, she wasn't carrying a great load of food out from the kitchen.

On second thoughts, it would have been better for us if she'd dropped all our food and we'd gone home for banana sandwiches instead. Not the finest example of Andalusian cuisine, but perhaps standards are not very high in Guadix. Food to be endured, not enjoyed. Pity we're British, so we don't complain. Not at the time, anyway. Marigold will probably still be grumbling away about last night in a fortnight's time.

The name Guadix stems from the Arabic 'Guadh-Haix', which means 'River of Life.' A famous French explorer once said, 'Guadix is a city that should not be described; it must be seen.' That's true of many places, but I'm not going to argue with a revered French traveller. Guadix is one of the most oldest cities in Spain with a rich history behind it.

Evidence exists of prehistoric settlements as both Neanderthal and Palaeolithic remains have been found.

Guadix certainly dates way back to pre Roman times when the early Phoenicians settled here, naming it Acci, but it gained much of its importance with the arrival of the Romans as it formed a staging post on the Roman Road, the Via Augusta. Julius Caesar instigated the mining of silver from the nearby hills in 45 Ad, renamed it Julia Gemella Acci, and Guadix became important for the minting of silver coins.

Guadix was taken over by the Moors who ruled Andalucía from the 8th to the 15th Centuries. They built the Alcazaba, the magnificent Moorish fortress that still overlooks the city in the 11th Century. As with the Roman occupation, Guadix was an important trade town, as it was midway between the great Moorish stronghold of Granada, with its magnificent Alhambra Palace, and the coast.

Over the course of two thousand or so years, Guadix has suffered more of the vicissitudes of history than most places, but it still survives.

It was the Moors, or perhaps more accurately the decline of the Moors after the Christian Reconquest, who were responsible for so many of the population adopting cave dwellings as their permanent homes and it is this prevalence of cave houses that drew us, along with so many others, to this ancient city on a plain overshadowed by the majestic Sierras Nevada.

The Moorish citizens of Guadix founded an important silk industry, on a par with that of the more celebrated Granada, but after the reconquest of Spain, those remaining who still espoused the Moorish ways and beliefs were expelled by the newly arrived Christians and many from Granada arrived in Guadix as refugees.

Their only option was to retreat into the surrounding hills and live in existing caves, or create new ones. The rock in this area is favourable for excavations as it is soft and pliable, but hardens after exposure to the sun. One great advantage of a cave house is the year-round constant temperature, a comfortable 20 degrees centigrade, and whether in the grip of winter or even more beneficially in the savage heat of a Spanish summer, when it's 40 degrees outside, the benefits are obvious.

There are over four thousand cave dwellings in this area, the biggest inhabited cave settlement in Europe. Half the population of Guadix are Troglodytes. This area is like a lunar landscape, unsuitable for farming or for anything else I could imagine, which surely explains why the original cave dwellers, and many of the present residents, were those with low incomes or victims of persecution.

I looked up some details, reluctant to rely entirely on Linda's facts and figures, only to find everything she said was correct. Sorry, Linda, for doubting you. Guadix may have 4,000 habitable caves, but we've seen cave houses before, in the Loire Valley, near Saumur, and also visited several of those vast underground wine 'cathedrals' where hundreds of thousands of bottles are stored at a reliably constant temperature. All this pales into insignificance against the reality of China where thirty million people make their homes in caves dug into the hillsides. 30 million may be only a tiny fraction of the population of China, but even so, that's a lot of cave houses.

This area, said the knowledgeable Linda, is famous for 'star gazing' with very little distraction from ambient light and on this clear, almost frigid, evening the stars were out in force. We've lived in truly remote areas, several times, and this place doesn't begin to compare with the views of the heavens we've seen in the past, even so, a starry sky is always an impressive sight.

I remember, one star filled evening a few years back now, discussing with an old friend the celestial bodies overhead - my friend's term, not mine. This was when we were living in an old finca where there were no street lights anywhere to be seen and he reminded me that what we were seeing was not the light emitted by stars but only the light emitted by stars several thousand years ago. Such is the incomprehensible vastness of space, even starlight travelling at the speed of light only represents what had once occurred, not the here and now. Yes, we'd probably enjoyed a glass or two, or more, of wine before debating such philosophical matters, but every time I see the full majesty of a star filled sky I am drawn back to that evening.

Sensibly, we studiously avoided last night's restaurant as we set off and stopped instead for breakfast at a service station an hour later. One of those where lorry drivers arrive at set times as the bar was crammed with brimming coffee cups indicating a rush was due. We ordered quickly, just in time as it turned out as about fifty or so men arrived in the next five minutes. By the time they left, twenty minutes later, the floor was knee deep in paper napkins and we could hear ourselves think once more.

We love workmen's bars in Spain for their bustle and good humoured banter – notwithstanding the fact we actually understand very little – but they are seriously loud! In France, there's little more than a hum of conversation, but Spanish bar-goers carry on conversations across a crowded room in a raucous bellow.

Seated at our table with a delightful view of the car park and three cats exploring the overflowing rubbish bins, Marigold drew my attention to a couple of men at the next table. They were evidently English, middle aged, portly and possibly en route to a fancy dress party. Unkind, I know, and I'm rarely mistaken for a male fashion model myself, but this pair were dressed in the style of Bertie Wooster.

When the last of the truckers departed and we were able to hear their conversation, we realised they were on a golfing break where ludicrous outfits are not only tolerated but encouraged. One of them, in a booming, orotund voice redolent of the Shires, explaining his reaction to the Brexit referendum, announced he had been 'throughly discombobulated by the whole affair' at one point which gives a fair picture of the nature of our fellow Brits. We finished our coffee and left hurriedly before they attempted to talk to us. Marigold used the word 'discombobulated' in every spoken sentence in the next half hour, regardless of context or any perception of whether it was appropriate while I tried to concentrate on the road ahead.

Later on, we passed through an arid, uninhabited area of desert. One like many others in this sun baked and isolated region, but there's something different to be found here. Hollywood used to film 'cowboy' films, Westerns, in the wild states of the Old West in the USA. Whether for financial reasons or because the Italian backers for what became known as Spaghetti Westerns didn't fancy travelling outside Europe, I'm not sure, but film sets were built and filming began in this area and still continues even now.

The 'Western' town, Fort Bravo was expressly built for the shooting of 'The Good, the Bad and the Ugly' and now is a sort of theme park with all the Western settings: a saloon, a jail, shops, a bank and stables. There's a Mexican film set too, fully fitted out as a Mexican Town.

Fort Bravo is one of three similar opportunities for the tourist to experience the Wild West. Entry costs 19.70 euros per person. Did we dally here for an hour or so to watch the recreation of a shootout at the bank or marvel at cowboys riding into town brandishing six-shooters? No, we did not. We didn't even hang around long enough to meet Clint Eastwood.

We did stop, however, at a 'Roadhouse' modelled on the diners lining Route 66, a little further on absolutely crammed with 'authentic' fixtures and fittings and as a token sop to minimalism only a couple of ancient, rusty, classic American cars on the forecourt.

We drove part of the 'real' Route 66 a couple of months ago. This place doesn't really compare, but I'm sure they've tried their best. After all, imitation is the sincerest form of flattery as the well known saying goes.

'If a thing's worth doing,' Marigold said, just before we both joined in completing the well known phrase, not with the conventional 'It's worth doing well,' but with "our version," – 'if a thing's worth doing, it's worth over doing.'

The full "imitation is the sincerest firm of flattery" quotation, as said by Oscar Wilde, however, is: 'imitation is the sincerest form of flattery that mediocrity can pay to greatness.' That's a bit of a downer, then, for these people who fondly imagine they're recreating a revered image of a traditional roadhouse. As with the 'Old West' a few miles back down the road, the original is the best and anything else merely artifice.

Almost Christmas and we've missed out on the office parties, the last minute dash to buy presents, the tree and decorations and just about everything else, not to mention the Arctic blasts hitting the UK. Same as last year, then. Not sure where we'll be on Christmas Day yet. That decision can wait a while longer. After all, there's best part of a week to go yet. Hope Marigold likes the DVD box set of Love Island I've bought her.*

*No, of course I haven't.

Christmas Day in Spain isn't the Main Event. We Were 'Spanish' this Christmas Day. Not Entirely By Choice.

G Says...

Christmas Day morning. The Royal Family will be getting ready to attend church. This year there'll be a new focus of attention – Meghan – to add to the perennial question about whether Prince Philip will finally accept he is 96 and accept a lift in a car rather than walking in on a freezing late December morning. Obviously, as I saw on tv later, Phil declined the offer of a ride in a warm car. He's no wimp! Being 96 years old is no reason to go soft. I think it was Luis Bunuel who said 'age is something that doesn't matter. Unless you're a cheese.' Oh, and Meghan performed a curtsy. Not just any old curtsy, oh no, but the best curtsy in the history of the world, according to most commentators. *O tempora! O mores!* Oh, the times, oh, the customs as Cicero said when describing the various nonsensical obsessions afflicting Ancient Rome.

Elsewhere, families will be gathering for the annual orgy of presents, eating far too much rich food, then complaining about the repeats on television and building up to the traditional family row that can last until Christmas Eve, next year.

Obviously, we do none of these things. If I want an argument, there's only Marigold here, so that's out. Why pick a fight I can't win? Not that I'd ever do such a thing. We don't have a Christmas tree, no decorations either and the rented apartment we've just moved into for a change of scene has a brand new oven and induction hob but no saucepans that will work with an induction hob and no container even remotely suitable for roasting a turkey. We decide to give Christmas a miss, at least for today. Here in Spain, Christmas Day itself is not the main event. Not even close for most Spanish families. Christmas Eve, yes, the Festival of the Three Kings, very much so, but Christmas Day, not such a big deal, so we reasoned we'd be in good company.

Thinking back, we had a similar 'Christmas Day Avoidance' episode last year, but at least then we had the excuse of being kidnapped by complete strangers in camper vans and forced to spend an entire afternoon and evening eating and drinking with outrageously convivial Irish families we'd never met before that day. I was secretly hoping to do the same again this year.

We set off in the car with Marigold looking gorgeous and wearing her brand new earrings and necklace. (No, not just earrings and necklace, obviously. My life isn't that perfect!). Mainly empty roads and a lovely sunny day with blue skies. I'm not one of those people who pine for a white Christmas.

We decided it was such a lovely day, a beach walk was in order and one of the best beaches in Europe was, relatively, close by. Monsul Beach is pretty isolated and scarcely anyone visits it. Certainly not in the depths of winter. If you can call a day like today 'winter.' Its pristine shoreline and sense of isolation persuaded Steven Spielberg to use Monsul as one of the settings for Indiana Jones and the Last Crusade.

We only found it during our motor home days when we got directions from an elderly Irish couple who have been wintering there for several years. San José has a good beach and a few cafes, restaurants and shops, but it appears to be the end of the line. The best beaches are along a pretty rough track, but not too bad today, about three miles after leaving 'civilisation' in San Jose. There's an occasional shuttle bus in the summer, but obviously that's not running now. The bonus is not having to pay for parking when we get there as that's restricted to high summer as well. We got as far in the car as we deemed reasonable and walked the rest of the way. Beyond Monsul are a couple of other even more isolated beaches, but getting to Monsul was enough trekking for one day.

We weren't really expecting the beach to be packed and it wasn't. Apart from us there were only two other people in sight. A few weeks ago, many miles from here, we met and briefly chatted to a German couple living, full time, in a magnificent, albeit scruffy, van conversion. What were the odds on meeting them again, on Christmas Day? Yet, here they were, parked up overlooking one of the best beaches in Spain.

Until we arrived today, they had been the beach's only occupants - a blessed state we remembered well from our own van-based travels – and we were quick to reassure them we weren't intending to stay here for long! They're off to North Africa in the New Year and going first to Algeria this trip as they've 'done' Morocco many times. The van is well suited to desert travel so they can wander at will. We were just a tiny bit jealous, especially of their van, its huge tyres that would have thought the rough access track leading to here was a motorway and the 'back to basics' living quarters.

If I'm giving the impression of 'chatting' to these people I apologise. We lacked any sort of common language as they spoke very little English and my command of the German language extends only as far as being able to say good morning and thank you! In fairness, I could sing the whole of Silent Night in its original German form, (*Stille Nacht, Heilige Nacht, etc*) and the German sections of the Elvis Presley hit, Wooden Heart, but I'm not sure how viable that would be in normal conversation.

We walked along the beach, had a quick paddle in the sea, quickly decided against going swimming and climbed the (not very big) sand dune instead and then decided we'd carry on down the coast to see what took our fancy.

We looked in to see if the street market we'd visited last Christmas Day at El Alquin was up and running – it wasn't – so we drove right along the coast road until we reached Almeria. We've been here several times and the traffic is pretty stressful, but not on Christmas Day! There were three big ships in port, none of the shipping lines were familiar to us, and the only one we thought of as being a 'cruise ship' catered for passengers travelling to Ghana. We've never been there and weren't tempted to buy a ticket today either. As a ferry port, Almeria is best known for its passenger routes to Morocco and Algeria, but it's important for freight as well and there were three bulk carriers far out to sea but heading into port as we arrived.

Christmas Day, in Spain, may not be the 'main event' of the holiday season, but even so the pavement cafes were packed with families enjoying the sunshine. 29 degrees, so pretty exceptional, even for Spain, in late December. Spanish families get together on Christmas Eve for a big party, but the festivities really get going on January 6th with the Festival of the Three Kings and that's when many Spanish children get their presents.

We were chatting to a couple of dog walkers, originally from Australia, the other day and they'd invited us to join them for a Christmas Day supper. I'd been busy dog stroking and talking to the woman so didn't say much to the man as he was obviously far keener on monopolising Marigold. I heard her say, 'that would have been lovely, but...' at one stage.

He did tell me one interesting 'fact' – he was a man who knew a lot of 'facts' – when I asked him whereabouts in Australia he came from.

'In the bush, nowhere you'd possibly have heard of,' he replied before continuing, 'do you know the plural of a platypus?'

I'd actually seen a duck billed platypus, in Australia, but had not given much thought to what a few of them would be called.

'Platypussies,' Marigold said without much conviction.

'Platypi,' I offered.

He shook his head, pityingly, at our ignorance.

'Platypode, there's your answer, and a baby platypus is called a puggle.' (Annoyingly, I looked up these dubious 'facts' later and was irritated beyond measure to find they were correct.)

'He must be the boring man I've ever met,' Marigold said after we left them to their dog walk. Even their dogs looked as if they'd rather be with somebody else. Anybody else. 'Can't imagine spending an evening with them. Told me all about Spanish customs and Christmas traditions, even after I told him we'd lived in Spain for ten years longer than he had so we knew all that stuff. He's so pedantic.' Marigold hates pedants because they tend to interrupt the flow of conversation. Too much 'accuracy' harms the flow.

I was very relieved. I had hardly spoken to the man, but even so a brief acquaintance was more than enough. Marigold said he took issue with almost everything she said and told her they had only asked us round as he thought we would be lonely on our own. Ha!

I told her a suitably pedantic joke to lighten the mood.

Q. How many pedants does it take to change a lightbulb?

A. Well, strictly speaking, what you're referring to is replacing a lightbulb…

Marigold didn't laugh.

We spent well over an hour in Almeria, taking advantage of the traffic free roads. The thousand year old Alcazaba dominates the city. It's the largest fortress ever constructed by the Moorish invaders and originally housed several mosques and palaces inside the citadel housed within its triple walled palaces and mosques. When it was built in the 10th Century, Almeria was the main commercial port in the Caliphate of Cordoba, with more than 10,000 textile mills inside its medina. We walked up to it a few years ago, but it was a steep climb and we're much more sensible these days.

We didn't go inside the Cathedral either. It's much more of a fortress than most others of its ilk due to the frequent raids on the city from Berber pirates after the Christian reconquest and its thick walls and forbidding appearance are not exactly welcoming.

Bypassing most of Roquetas de Mar, we reached Aguadulce, one of the few places along this coastline we've never visited and it was so charming we parked the car and went to look for our 'substitute' Christmas lunch. Aguadulce means 'sweet water' and the name supposedly comes from the natural springs that filter down through the rocky hills that tower over the beach. In the sea itself, there are more natural springs of fresh water that bubble up through the sand.

The beach is about a mile and a half long and was virtually empty, but the promenade which runs along the entire length was very busy with Spanish people dressed in their Christmas finery. It was warm, bordering on hot actually, but I seemed to be the only one there wearing shirtsleeves. Most of our fellow strollers were dressed as if for an expedition to the Arctic.

All along the promenade there are wonderful views of the Bay of Almeria and at the near end a rather smart marina which was getting very busy with the lunch trade. Oysters were being eaten in vast quantities, sparkling wine was flowing, but it was all a bit 'dressy' in those places and everyone inside looked very serious so we chose more prosaic fare in an 'outside' restaurant run by a very jolly woman who greeted everyone like old friends.

We had a big (huge) salad, and I ordered the 'local to the area special': ajo colorao which was a stew with potatoes, red bell peppers, eggs, sausages, cod, garlic and drizzled with olive oil and was one of the best things I've ever eaten. Marigold chose rape a la barraca - monkfish served with leek and mushrooms and the jolly woman said 'English' to us as she brought out a big bowl of chips and crunchy bread as well. We were absolutely stuffed by the time we finished and wished we'd ignored the jolly woman's insistence we try her home made sponge cake veined with dates and served with thick and very tart Turkish yoghurt. It was delicious, but would have been best enjoyed in its own right, not as an adjunct to such a big meal.

After lunch as we wandered rather more sedately the mile or so back to where we'd parked the car we saw two naked Santas arrive in a car. As it turned out, they were two young lads, not naked at all, just wearing very brief shorts and Santa hats, who set off at a fair old pace running along the promenade. We stopped for a bit of people watching at a bar where the waiter invited us to take a seat and have a free drink. Not a con either, everybody who passed by was offered a drink 'for Christmas.' We weren't pestered to order food, just a kind gesture and a very nice one too.

A man in bulky overalls who had been assiduously sweeping the street and the promenade – on Christmas Day – sat down too and had a welcome drink. He seemed to be a local 'character' who everybody knew, but his accent was so strong we couldn't understand him. Another free drink 'customer' explained he was telling everybody that he was getting double pay for working on Christmas Day, but that with so many people about he had to do three times as much work.

As we left the two Santas reappeared. It was still pretty hot and they had run about three miles in full sun so were well and truly lathered. Practically deliquescent.

We got back as the sun was setting. Still lacking saucepans that worked, no turkey, no sprouts, not even a family row, but we didn't feel shortchanged. Not at all. At the very least we were very happy not to be setting off for supper with pedantic Australian dog walkers for an evening of detailed instruction on collective terms for random Australian wildlife.

Spanish New Year.

G Says...

Youth is when you're allowed to stay up late on New Year's Eve. Middle age is when you're forced to. That's a quote from someone else, obviously, as we've been frolicking through to the end of 2017, even if we didn't party until dawn like we once did.

Okay, it wasn't every year!

A new year brings its own problems, the chief one for me is remembering to write 2018, not 2017, when filling in the date on official forms. I usually get it right by mid-February. Marigold can still be observed pondering, pen in hand, as late as next August. As we lack any form of structure or routine in our lives – by design – we very often wonder what day it is, so getting the year right is a minor matter.

Marigold has made the same 'new year's resolution' for many years now – to be kind and helpful. Annoyingly for those of us who lack perfection, she is both kind and helpful anyway. Many years ago now, I made a New Year's resolution to never make New Year's resolutions. Unsurprisingly, it's been the only resolution I've ever kept!

Alfred Tennyson wrote:

'Ring out the old, ring in the new,

Ring, happy bells, across the snow:

The year is going, let him go;

Ring out the false, ring in the true.'

That's not bad, is it? It even rhymes.

P. J. O'Rourke's contribution was rather more prosaic. He observed:

'The proper behaviour all through the holiday season is to be drunk. The drunkenness culminates on New Years' Eve, when you get so drunk you kiss the person you're married to.'

We observed many disciples of Mister O'Rourke in Nerja where we spent New Year's Eve. Not remotely unpleasant, but most certainly 'well oiled' in honour of the occasion.

We spent a couple of New Year's Eves amongst the throngs around the Balcon de Europa in Nerja back in the day when we lived in the area full time and it was good to be back. When it comes round to New Year's Eve 'festivities', we've 'done' Trafalgar Square, we've 'done' Edinburgh, we've even 'done' Sydney Harbour and the Balcon is just as manic, jolly and memorable as any, just on a smaller scale.

We arrived early, hoping to beat the crowds – a vain hope – and decided we'd go for a drink just off the main square first. We even got a seat. On the next table were three English matrons, all decked out in their best sparkly outfits. 'Didn't realise the cruise ships stopped off here,' Marigold murmured. Even the stone deaf, and I'm not quite there yet, would have overheard every word they said.

Here's a sample.

'What did Joe get you for Christmas?'

'A sparkly toilet seat.'

'Oh, God.'

'I know. It's not even a nice one. Told him there's no way I'm parking my bum on that. He looked disappointed.'

At least half of the people in the bar understood spoken English well enough to laugh out loud.

One more, on the subject of 'what are the best and worse ways to die' – yes, it was an odd subject for New Year's Eve - 'The worst way to die has got to be in a house fire. If I smelled smoke and knew the house was on fire, I'd commit suicide.'

'How would you do it, though, commit suicide?'

'No idea, but I'd definitely do it.'

We finished our drinks and left them to it. At this point I realised I had left my phone in the hotel room, so no photos would be forthcoming.

The local Town Hall had pulled out all the stops and there were free goodie bags on offer containing Champagne and grapes. They even offered silly hats. Before you all book in for next year, it's Spanish Cava, not 'real' Champagne and it's only a small bottle. The idea is to eat a grape and take a sip of champagne with each chime of midnight and if you manage it, then it is supposed to bring you luck for the coming year. We'd both tried and failed miserably in the past but this time I came armed with a secret weapon, my own seedless grapes.

There's a live band there performing their medley of hits. Pretty dreadful in my view and largely ignored by the crowd despite the noise. Spanish people don't mind noise; they just shout even louder. There's also a man on a small stage shouting something or other, very loudly, but again being largely ignored. Hey, it's his one night of the year in the spotlight and he's milking every moment. As the band decide they may as well stop playing and start drinking, the Nerva Council Glee Club President sees his moment. Marigold says he's speaking in tongues while I decide he's a Tourette's sufferer. No idea who is right but every vein on his forehead is standing out by now and he's still only warming up.

As the excitement of the man on the dais reached fever pitch, the bell in the Iglesia El Salvador struck the first peel of the midnight dozen. I popped in a grape, took a swig of Cava and was pretty confident of success. As the fifth peel rang out, I realised my seedless grapes were at least half as big again as the seeded variety and took grape chomping to a whole new level. By the seventh ring I was swallowing grapes whole and by the tenth ring I was a spluttering wreck, admitting defeat. Marigold, even after chewing down a thousand pips failed as well. It's not as easy as it sounds.

The grape swallowing tradition goes back at least 100 years or so, presumably when there was a vast surplus in the grape harvest and many regions of Spain now observe the tradition. There's much kissing going on. Tonight I seem to be far more attractive to complete strangers than I'd imagined and Marigold is practically submerged by a scrum of well wishers. There's even more alcohol to be drunk as the New Year begins and the firework show, reflected in the sea for added effect, is magnificent.

Our Christmas may have been low key, but New Year certainly made up for it. As we're in Spain, the main event, the Festival of the Three Kings, is still to come. How will they all cope? We love the pageantry of Spain and the way they involve the entire family, babes in arms to grannies in wheelchairs, in every aspect of the holiday season. We've often talked about the different ways in which Christmas and New Year differs from England and, indeed from the many Christmases we spent in France where in the days leading up to Christmas we received many visitors. Even though our first French house was so remote we never saw a bin man in all the years we were there, they still called to say 'bonjour,' as it's Christmas tip time.

Then there's the postman who, in December, called at the door to hand deliver a calendar. Always tatty with washed out photos of kittens in a basket. He's a lovely man, always gives a toot on his horn as he puts our post in the box, but even so, the calendar he's come to sell us isn't the best value aspect of Christmas. We get another calendar, one year it was the same as that from the postman, from the firemen. Les Pompiers, the French fire service, are the ultimate first responders if there's a house fire, a road accident or just about any emergency. The ambulance, the police, they're all on the way where necessary, but the firemen are always first on the scene. When we moved to the Pyrenees, we realised they do mountain rescue too. Another pricey calendar, another wine bottle opened, a ten minute chat and away they go for another year. When we left France, we missed it. Possibly the only ritual of Christmas we do miss. We don't decorate a tree as we wander around so much, don't get cards for the same reason and we don't miss any of that either. Especially those greetings cards given out by work colleagues which require another in response.

Despite us having talked repeatedly about going to a Verdiales Festival this year, usually on December 28th which is also the day of Santos Inocentes, holy innocents, we forgot all about it. Shame as we've been before and loved it. Oh well, maybe next year.

December 28th is a religious holiday in all Spanish speaking countries. It's also the day for practical jokes similar to those on April Fool's Day in Britain. Santos Inocentes originates from the killing of children by King Herod around the time of the birth of Jesus, hence the name Holy Innocents as they were both young and innocent. Although it stems from a religious festival on the Catholic calendar, nowadays as with so much surrounding the Christmas period the religious meaning has almost been forgotten and it is far more widely known as a day of pranks and practical jokes.

We regard every day as April Fool's Day, so we don't pay December 28th any particular attention, but have enjoyed several Festivals de Verdiales. The best are in the Malaga area, just along the road from where we're staying, but we forgot, plain and simple.

The best of the festivals used to be on La Venta de Tunel just outside Malaga where bands of musicians compete to prove they can outlast the opposition in longevity and sheer volume. It's all a bit mad, but gloriously so. I've heard since it didn't take place there this year anyway, but there would have been plenty more to choose from.

Verdiales is a form of flamenco that originated in the Los Verdiales olive-growing region and the name comes from a specific type of olive grown in the area around Malaga. We used to have fifty or so Verdiales olive trees on our land which we allowed our neighbour to harvest in return for enough olive oil to last us all year. An olive harvest can be fairly lucrative, but our trees were mostly at the bottom of a very steep hillside and we much preferred to let our neighbour harvest the olives as it's a job best left to the experts. Not to mention being absolutely backbreaking. Not that that was a factor of course!

Verdiales music is lively, very lively, and intended for dancing. It's, apparently, one of the earliest forms of fandango, one of my favourite Spanish words, possibly dating back to the time of Bohemian Rhapsody. The players wear a variety of odd costumes and in some ways it's like very, very spirited Morris Dancing, but much better! We've seen and heard a different variation of Verdiales in several areas of Morocco and presumably like so much else in Andalucia the fandango originated there.

A Spanish friend, who we last saw well past midnight last night when he was rather the worse for wear, has just turned up and told me my failure to down a dozen grapes at midnight doesn't necessarily mean 2018 will be wretched. I get credited with a month of good fortune for every grape so I'll be okay until the end of October. Good news.

I apologised to my friend for my ignorance and he replied, 'El burro sabe mas que tu' which translates, roughly, as 'A donkey knows more than you.' I shall have to reassess the status of my 'friends,' it appears!

This same 'friend' tells me, 'me gusta pedo,' the most literal translation of which would be, 'I like to fart,' but, fortunately, I know quite a few examples of colloquial Spanish vulgarity and understand he means to say he likes to get drunk. To fart or to be plastered, the meaning is in the context.

Should you ever wish to announce at a dinner party, for instance, in Spain, that 'I have just passed wind,' simply say, 'me acabo de tirar un pedo.'

There, hope that will be helpful to you next time you're dining with the Spanish Ambassador. No need to thank me.

A couple of days later we called in at one of our favourite places, the charming, unspoilt and virtually tourist free fishing village, Isleta del Moro, which sounds as if it should be an island, but isn't. It's virtually surrounded by the sea, however and there are always fishermen mending their nets on the beach, as there were today. They don't even look hung over - the fishermen, not the nets. As the only other sober people in Spain we still feel virtuous. There's a decent beach here, a great big rock, a few small whitewashed houses, a very good fish restaurant in the harbour and not much else. Which is why we like it.

We walked along the (not very long) Playa de los Escullos with the two rocks of the Isleta at the far end. It was from this spot that Philip II and his armada sailed off to fight the Turks in the 16th century. Scarcely credible, looking at this tiny beach next to a small fishing village today.

Last time we were here there were a few people selling art and jewellery, of the ethnic style favoured by Marigold, and one girl is here again with ear rings galore on offer. She remembers Marigold, as most people do, and they are soon chatting away. A man walks past with a rubber bucket absolutely crammed with fish, straight from the sea, and goes into the back door of the restaurant, ready to be served for lunch. Can't get any fresher than that.

An Abandoned Hotel, a town that resembles Workington, but with better beaches and the Beach of the Dead.

Marigold Says...

First effort of 2018 for me and it will be brief. Probably should have said 'pathetically brief,' not just 'brief,' but anyway... life's too short to type as Shakespeare once said. Well, he may have done.

We're back in Mojacar the Beautiful after some pretty exhausting New Year celebrations and we're very happy to be here in one of our favourite places in Spain. It hardly ever rains here, the sun shines almost every day, even in winter, there's lots to do and the people here are nice too.

I said to G the other day, 'let's go off for the day, but not too far.' We ended up driving no more than about ten miles and had a brilliant day. We drove out of Mojacar up the hill leading to Carboneras. Every time we pass this way we look at the Macenas golf course and think what a shame it is as everything is brown, hardly a blade of grass anywhere.

We played golf there a few years ago when it was still 'green.' More accurately, G played golf and I drove the electric buggy, very fast and G said very dangerously at times. Well, how was I to know there was a steep hill just round the corner? We flew down it at what seemed like 100 mph, but probably wasn't. I remember I had a very sore throat from screeching and G said he wouldn't have been so worried if I hadn't closed my eyes and taken both hands of the wheel.

I'm a very good golf caddy. I don't actually carry any clubs or know anything about golf, but I do clap wildly at good shots and pretend not to notice the bad ones. Sometimes we have a putting competition on the practise greens and the rule is that I can have another go if I do a bad putt and we only stop playing when I win three holes. Or when it starts to get dark!

We drove past the tapas bar at the top of the first hill as it was full of cyclists and there were no free seats. Cyclists love going up the hill from Mojacar, over the top and down to Carboneras and then going straight back again. Very exhausting and rather sweaty, especially when wearing Lycra. The cyclists today were quite fat, especially for Lycra shorts and tops, and very sweaty so we carried on going.

G stopped at the top to take some photos of the winding road going down the hill and the sea looked fantastic, very blue and no waves at all. There were two people on motorbikes in the lay-by, looked like a boy and a girl, snogging. Not easy when leaning over, sitting on their bikes and wearing crash helmets, but it didn't seem to bother them. The 'girl' took her helmet off and she was about 60 with a huge nose. I was quite glad the 'boy' kept his helmet on. Two cyclists puffed past us, looking very red and very hot. One of them had a woolly Santa hat on his head which he took off as he passed me and bowed which made us laugh.

I also waved to a man driving a camper van going the other way, just because I liked the camper. We saw it parked up the next day, but it was empty. Perhaps he was in hiding from mad English women who wave madly at him as he's trying to go round a very sharp bend at the top of a mountain.

At the bottom of the hill is a big hotel complex which was never finished. I could tell you all about it, but would have to look up stuff so have told G to do it instead. I meant 'asked,' not 'told' in case you think I'm a bossy woman.

We went through Carboneras which is an odd place. It has lovely beaches, a good promenade and the sea is very clear, but there's lots of industrial buildings here as well. We went to one of the best beaches in Spain, which took a bit of getting to but was worth it. Nobody else was there even though it was a gorgeous day.

G Says...

January, in Spain, is one of our favourite months. There are no crowds, you can park the car anywhere, the beaches are empty, the sun usually shines all day and we can walk along a sea shore gazing at a cerulean sea and golden sands under a bright blue cloudless sky. Perfection!

On a day just like this, we set off over the mountain top towards Carboneras, the starting point for the Cabo de Gata National Park. Carboneras translates as 'coal bunkers' in English, coal mining and charcoal burning are no longer the main industries, but even so, with a name like that, expectations for a visitor are never going to be sky high. Even so, we're here and determined to find something of interest.

Even before we reach Carboneras, there's one of the saddest sights, or sites, in Spain: the abandoned hotel complex perched right above the beach, known as El Algarrobico.

Twenty years or so ago, a developer, Azata del Sol, submitted plans for a 21 storey, 411 roomed four-star hotel, to be followed by an 18-hole golf course and 1,500 houses/apartments. The Carboneras council and residents would benefit greatly from the development, many jobs were on the way and the addition of so many taxes into the Town Hall coffers was eagerly anticipated.

In 2003, the local Junta granted a licence to start building work, but problems soon arose. Environmental activists argued that the site was (just about) within the Cabo de Gata Natural Park, one of Europe's largest marine and territory nature reserves, and within two years the Spanish government overruled the local council, claiming the hotel development had broken Coastal Law, which forbids building within 330 feet of the sea and ordered its immediate demolition.

The hotel construction was almost complete by now, but a judge cancelled the building licence amidst numerous claims of bribery, corruption and falsification of planning permission documents.

Very Spanish, this great divide between the Government in Madrid and the local council, and the row rumbled on through the courts with no sign of resolution, but the real drama was yet to come.

In 2007, Greenpeace activists took direct action, scaling the building and daubing the slogan, 'Illegal Hotel' in huge letters across the freshly painted façade. Those Greenpeace activists kept the pressure on, occupying part of the empty hotel until a fresh court judgement ruled the project legal and that work should continue.

'This monstrosity is the symbol of the destruction of our coasts,' a Greenpeace spokesman said, but locally, everyone on the local council was unhappy. 'The council continues to believe that the best option for this hotel after such a huge investment is that it is completed and opened to provide wealth and jobs for the town,' Salvador Hernandez, the mayor of Carbonera said.

The hotel remains empty, a daubed slogan on the side now reads, 'Hotel, Si' and the legal wrangles veer between allowing the project to be completed or be demolished. I was talking to a couple of locals in a bar recently. One said the hotel being demolished would deprive the town of hundreds of potential jobs. The other suggested the jobless of Carboneras could always apply for work at the demolition firm. I suspect the hotel, which is a bit of an eyesore in its present condition, will still be here in another ten years.

We parked up in the town and made our way to a café on the almost deserted promenade. The sea was gleaming and even the Island of San Andres looked attractive. It's no idyllic desert island, just a small lump of volcanic rock just offshore. Even so, it's a bit special, this barren, uninhabited hump in the water as it supports any amount of fish, crabs and seabirds. The fish feed on the lush and splendidly named Poseidonia Oceanica, (also referenced by the rather more prosaic name of Neptune Grass,) which is a type of lush weed only found in certain areas of the Mediterranean and it is the presence of this weed that helps keep the water so crystal clear. We snorkel dived here a few years back, and we're the only people on the beach today, but weren't tempted to go skinny dipping in January no matter how pleasant the sunshine.

As we drive on along the road bordering the sea, it gets more 'industrial.' Not exactly a backdrop to the the set of Peaky Blinders, but even so the port area stands out starkly from the strictly conserved (random hotel developments notwithstanding,) and seemingly untouched inland nature reserve of the Cabo de Gato.

The background to the port is tall chimney stacks, a relentless procession of lorries going to and from the harbour, a particularly unattractive (coal burning) power station with its accompanying noxious eructations and the scarred remnants of what were once dense forests and coal deposits on the surrounding hills.

There's an impressive desalination plant here as well, one of the largest in the world and any method of obtaining water in such an arid region is welcome. Producing fresh water from seawater will have great benefits. I just about understand the basic theory – stripping out the salt content of sea water by means of reverse osmosis – but anyone seeking any more detail has come to the wrong place! I read a leaflet about the plant where it says output is 120,000 cubic metres of fresh water every day. That's impressive. Much will be of lower quality and intended for irrigation, but thousands of litres of fresh drinking water, recovered directly from the sea, is being sent all around this parched region every day. Water is a precious commodity in this area, but even so there are limits on what agriculture will pay for it so the plant is currently operating welll below its capacity as the farmers consider the costs are too high. I read recently that water will become as vital in this century as oil was to the last, but supply and demand, as ever, sets prices and desalination remains an expensive option, for now.

I've read about a 'hidden' beach near here, usually accessed by boat, and today we're determined to find it. It turns out to be scarcely hidden at all, there's even a signpost for 'Playa de los Muertos.'

Beach of the Dead? Pretty grim name, but when we eventually find our way to the viewpoint overlooking the beach it's a real treat. The French word trouvaille sums it up best. An unexpected and almost overwhelming delight, like one of those Caribbean beaches the holiday industry use to persuade their stressed out potential customers of their pressing need to seek out a little piece of paradise. It's been voted 'best beach in Spain' for three consecutive years, a pretty impressive claim. It's a beach, no facilities, no shade, nothing but sand and the clear water of a gently lapping sea.

One way of ensuring a 'perfect' beach is to have its only viable access, unless you want to try the sea kayak method from Carboneras, be extremely difficult. The track is steep and rutted, certainly no place for flip-flops, and we're wary of twisting an ankle, or worse, as we edge our way down. I'm wearing shorts and sandals today and reject Marigold's suggestion of changing into the pair of shoes in the car boot.

At one point, having helped Marigold across a particularly difficult section, I manage to stub the same big toe that had required the removal of an ingrown toe nail. It's significantly more painful without a protective toenail, as I point out to Marigold who is remarkably unsympathetic with an unsaid 'I told you to put shoes on' expression in evidence. She even fails to comment on my remembering being told the medical term for a big toe is a hallux, even though I was given that information during the amputation procedure, a time not best suited to memory retention! Perhaps she's doubting my claim of this being a 'pretty easy track down to the beach.' In fairness, it's not easy at all.

Once we arrived though, it's worth every careful step. The name comes from the vast numbers of shipwrecked pirates who supposedly washed up here, but we're relieved to find a deserted stretch of sand and dramatic pyroclastic rock formations without a single drowned pirate to be seen. It's a nudist beach too, but we aren't tempted to remove our liberty bodices. What's the point if there's nobody else here to marvel at our magnificent bodies?

We walk along the beach, clamber over rocks, paddle in the clear water, admire the graceful progress of a brightly speckled fish and, as we finally prepare to clamber back up the track to where our car is baking in the sun, we see a pair of dolphins swooping and gambolling their way along the coast. The perfect end to any day. Of course, we still have to climb up this goat track to the top of a mountain.

La Manga. Some People love it. Not everybody though. Especially in January.

Marigold Says...

We went to La Manga to meet some friends who are staying there and when we got there it was closed! Try coming here in August and there are crowds everywhere, but we went past so many empty apartment blocks and hotels I started to sing 'This place is getting like a ghost town' until G threatened to put me out and leave me at the side of the road unless I stopped singing. I switched to 'any old iron' instead which is even more annoying.

We found our friends, it wasn't hard as there were hardly any people about. They were talking to the most miserable people in the world who were parked up on a beach in camper vans. We usually like camper van people, but this lot were awful. Can't even blame the Brits either who are normally the most miserable campers of all as there were no GB badges to be seen.

Eddie, our friend, (a retired musician, orchestral version, not heavy metal) said, 'we thought these people might know you as you've done so much travelling in camper vans.' G told him we don't hang around with people who are miserable. One of the women was really staring at me and I said to G she was making me feel very uncomfortable. He pointed at the little girl playing in the sand right behind me and said 'I think she's looking there, not at you' and of course she was.

Our friends took us to look at a bridge and we had to pretend to be fascinated. It's a really, really steep humped back bridge at the far end the 'strip' that a developer wanted to be just like Venice, but it's not exactly the Bridge of Sighs in Venice.

La Manga is a weird place as it is on a very narrow strip of land between the Mediterranean on one side and an enormous lagoon, a bit like Lake Como but nowhere near as pretty, on the other. If you stand in the middle of the road you can see both 'seas' as they are only about twenty yards apart in places. I stood in the middle of the road for ages as there was no sign of any traffic.

I saw a shop that looked open so I shouted, 'stop,' which was rather dramatic. I went in to ask if they knew any restaurants that were likely to be open. Everything on sale was from Poland or Romania, which was interesting and a bit of a surprise. I found several things we'd eaten when we were in Eastern Europe and shouted for G to come and look. He was very patient and even took a few photos while I posed with things off the shelves. Our friends already think we're a bit odd so they weren't surprised.

We found somewhere to eat, eventually. I found a really nice place with a huge terrace that was open, but when I asked the man if he was serving food he looked a bit worried and said no, but he had three different flavours of crisps. We'd already been to a lovely restaurant where our friends had eaten before, it was in the shape of a boat, but of course it was closed.

We found a bar/cafe eventually where they were actually serving food. On the terrace, a group of about thirty people were munching away at a huge buffet style banquet. As we passed I said 'what's the celebration?'

One of the group turned to me with a very sad face and said, 'I just buried my brother.'

Oops!

The people running the bar were English, from Devon, and had been in business there for ten years. We were dreading the offer of an all day full English breakfast, but the food was very nice. Just as well as I was at risk of entering a 'grumbly' state.

Recently found out we were very law abiding over Christmas. Oliver Cromwell passed laws forbidding gluttony on Christmas Day - no Christmas pud, no mince pies – and those laws were never abolished. Mind you, we do make up for it in the rest of the year.

I also read recently that King Richard II really knew how to celebrate Christmas. Apparently, his Christmas Day guests in 1377 had to make do with 28 oxen and 300 sheep as a main course washed down with many gallons of wine. Trifle wasn't mentioned. No wonder Oliver Cromwell felt so strongly that the 'real meaning of Christmas' was getting put to the back of the queue.

There was a dog hanging around looking hopefully at everyone and obviously hoping for scraps. The woman who owned the bar said he belonged to the people next door but he came to her bar straight after he'd had his breakfast and stayed all day. His name was Rocco and the bar woman said Rocco was the patron saint of dogs.

That sounded very unlikely so I looked it up later. I thought St Francis would be the 'dog's saint' as he is the patron saint of animals, but it was true. Saint Rocco, or Saint Roch as he is called in some countries is the patron saint of dogs! So there. If you want to pray for a lost or poorly dog though, pray to Saint Anthony. A lot more involved than I had imagined.

A group of four middle aged people came and sat at the table behind us and one of the men pushed his chair right back so I had hardly any room. Of course I didn't say anything, but it got even worse as he kept burping really loudly. I wanted to shout 'Settlers' or 'Tums' really loudly back at him.

We wandered around a fair bit after saying goodbye to our friends, visiting beaches. This is the Costa Cálida, the warm coast, and we saw several people swimming in the sea. Not New Year's Day Fancy Dress swimming either, but 'proper' swimming. I had a paddle at a lovely beach called Calblanque and the water was quite warm. G waded in a bit further and said it was 'just about' warm enough to swim, but only just. He didn't go in any further though. Said he was just being sensible as we didn't have a towel with us. I think his Prince William haircut is the real reason. Didn't want to get his head wet.

Calblanque is a lovely place. Very peaceful and very popular with nudists, but only one there today, a very fat man who looked like Winston Churchill. Did anyone ever imagine Churchill would look attractive without his clothes on? I don't think so. We seem to go on rather a lot of nudist beaches considering I am the very last person to ever want to run around naked, but nudists like quiet beaches in out of the way spots and so do we. There was a sign up telling people to 'respect' the sea turtles, but we didn't see any. Perhaps the naked Winston Churchill had frightened them off.

We went to some other places, but G will have to tell you the names as I was sitting in the passenger seat and it's the driver's job to remember the names of places. Unless I'm driving.

G Says…

Not every day is perfect. Some days are, let's face it, crap. We had one of those days on Monday. We went to La Manga to meet up with some old friends. We've been to La Manga before and we thought then it was both 'interesting' and 'awful.' On this visit, we just thought it was awful.

Spain is the least densely populated country in Europe, with plenty of wild and wonderful open spaces, deserted beaches, craggy peaks and areas that resemble a lunar landscape and we love them all. Then there are places built around tourism such as Benidorm. Add La Manga to that list.

The interesting part is in its situation: a narrow strip of land, about 14 miles long but very, very narrow in places, so narrow you could stand in the middle of the road and throw a pebble into the water on either side.

Marigold tried to demonstrate this at one point, but her throwing skills appear to have deserted her!

This tiny ribbon of land separates the Mediterranean Sea from the Mar Menor, a saltwater lagoon which is the largest in Europe, over 100 square miles of it. There are natural channels that keep the two 'seas' in contact with each other; these so-called 'golas' allow water to pass from the Mediterranean into the lagoon.

This strip of land known as la Manga (the sleeve) encloses the Mar Menor (small sea) which is vast, but fairly shallow so the water is warm all year round. I swam here one summer and it was like swimming in a bath tub. The water is incredibly salty, very rich in minerals and, as I confirmed today, warm enough for swimming. I walked 'across the road' and dipped a toe into the Mediterranean for contrast. Not 'cold' as such, but nowhere near the temperature at which swimming becomes a pleasure not an ordeal.

It was very hot, record high temperatures for January in Murcia Province, but we were driving along empty roads and the beaches were deserted. We saw more people in Ghost Towns in the Arizona desert.

Until the 1960s this strip of land was uninhabited. Not any more. The only road is now hemmed in on both sides by towering hotels and apartment blocks, each as featureless and hideous as the next. In the summer, the place is packed, the hotels are full, the road is one long traffic jam and the traffic fumes are a nightmare. I speak from experience as the last time we were here was in mid summer and we both agreed it was somewhere we should avoid in the summer months.

January is even worse.

The sun shone, glinting and sparkling on the deep, blue Mediterranean on one side and the placid waters of the vast lagoon on the other, but there was nobody there to enjoy the sunshine. Any resort, out of season, can be a pretty grim place, and we've been to a fair few of those, but never felt so depressed as we did in La Manga.

In mitigation, the fact that it didn't even exist as a town until the mid 60s means that La Manga inevitably lacks old buildings or quaint winding streets to give it what we tend to call 'character,' but I'm only giving a personal view as many visitors return here year after year and love it.

Even the camper van community, parked up in what looked an idyllic spot overlooking the Mediterranean were miserable. One van had a sign saying 'Noli Me Tangere,' which we took to mean keep away from me and my property, but the scowl on the face of the van owner made the sign redundant.

There were good parts too. We saw another sign, on a café that was closed like almost everywhere else, that said 'How beautiful it is to do nothing, and then rest afterwards' which appealed to me. The 'special' – on days they were open - was something I couldn't decipher containing 'humus,' which is that dark organic matter that forms in the soil when plant and animal matter decays. Presumably, they meant hummus. If not, I was glad they weren't open.

When we finally found somewhere that sold food, the people on the next table sat really close. That was bad enough, but the one sitting right next to Marigold kept making certain noises which the rest of us found amusing. We couldn't decide on the correct term: belching or burping? I decided his frequent interruptions were 'eructations,' which is what one of the teachers at my school used to say when one of the class 'lapsed.' I remember the word very well, as a frequent offender.

It was lovely to see our friends and we had some real laughs in their company. Nobody admired my new haircut though, even though I was somewhat more hirsute last time we met up. I like it as it's not exactly difficult to manage and I use far less shampoo. One slight annoyance is finger combing my hair when I get up in the morning, even now it's no longer there. It must be a similar effect to that form of neuropathic pain often called   phantom limb syndrome when an arm or a leg has been removed because of illness or injury, but the brain still receives pain messages from the missing limb. On a far less serious level, obviously.

Our friends are all keen golfers so La Manga, or the area around La Manga, is sheer Heaven for them. Playing golf in the sunshine, on perfectly manicured courses, no waterproof clothing, no drizzle of rain down the back of your neck, well, you get the picture. We talked of the old days, as old friends do, and congratulated ourselves on still being alive, as all of our old friends seem to do with great regularity lately as news breaks of one of our rather more famous contemporaries popping their clogs! Those shining examples of good diet, healthy living and treating one's body with respect: Keith Richards and Iggy Pop are still alive and kicking. Very much so. As is Shane MacGowan who turned 60 on Christmas Day.

Is this fair?

I first saw the Pogues, then still called Pogue Mahone (the Irish for 'kiss my arse,') perform live many years ago, before they were 'famous' and thought even then their lead singer's life expectancy would be reckoned in months, not years! Shane MacGowan reaching the age of 60 must be a misprint, surely? Good on yer, Shane.

Before leaving La Manga we'd been to Veneziola, at the far end of the Strip, which had been originally developed to rival Venice with a network of canals and some pretty beaches around a housing development. Venice? Not even close.

The best part of Veneziola is El Puente de la Risa, a small, very steep, humpbacked bridge where we saw more people than we'd seen all day, driving back and forth over the bridge and getting out at the midpoint to take photos. Great fun. For five year olds!

We drove over, looked around, drove back like grumpy non-tourists. One of our number walked back up to the mid point and took a photo then jogged down again and on his return was rubbing his (recently replaced) knee joints ruefully. Serves you right, we all said with unbearable smugness.

El Puente de la Risa has only recently been reopened to the public following a repair and renovation project which cost 90,000 euros. Seems a lot of money for what was already a working bridge.

There's another, better, little bridge on La Manga, a rather more modern one, like a mini Tower Bridge in London as it splits in the middle to allow tall masted boats to pass from the Mediterranean to the lagoon and back again. It opens every two hours, but we managed to see it open on the way back. A sign says maintenance of the bridge, El Estacio, costs 116,651.62 euros a year. Bridge repair and maintenance seems a good trade to be in around here.

I like signs, when they're interesting. We saw another one on Las Palmeras, the biggest beach on the Mar Menor that warns of draconian punishments, a minimum of 300 euros, for dog owners who fail to 'pick up.' On the other hand, another sign right next to it says the beach is 'dog friendly.'

Even the rather posh La Manga Club was disappointing this time. Very security conscious, which is fair enough, but made it all feel very remote and off putting which is surely out of kilter for a resort. We pressed on, back to just the two of us by now, and headed for beaches to cheer us up. We like beaches, for looking at and walking on, but never as places for lying on all day in full sun.

Today we enjoyed Isla Plana, a small village in the eastern half of the Gulf of Mazarrón with a lovely uncrowded beach, La Azohia and

Mazarrón itself where we've been many times before. Not quite enough to banish the disappointment of yesterday, but a decent effort.

Jaen. Far from Pretty.
I haven't been everywhere, but it's on my list.' Susan Sontag.

G Says...

We've ended up in Jaen today. Not planned, nothing unusual there, but we were on the way to Toledo (planned) when we turned left instead of right and ended up in Jaen. We've passed by this place many times, admired the wonderful castle and Parador perched on the hill, but never actually been to Jaen. Until now.

This 'system' of taking random turns in the road brings to mind that famous Robert Frost quote: 'I shall be telling this with a sigh somewhere ages and ages hence: Two roads diverged in a wood, and I – I took the one less traveled by, and that has made all the difference,' but I prefer the quote attributed to baseball legend Yogi Berra, 'If you come to a fork in the road, take it.'

Yogi Berra also gave the world such spoken gems as 'It ain't over till it's over' and 'It's like déjà vu all over again' in post game interviews – a wise man, indeed.

It's a (rare) dull, overcast morning as we set off and as we very soon find ourselves driving through the heart of Europe's only desert there's not much to look at. The 'western inspired' theme parks of Texas Hollywood and Fort Bravo look even more desolate today than usual, which is really saying something! There's a lone 'cowboy' on a horse, trying, and failing, to look like Lee Van Cleef and even he appears not to be bothered about looking the part today. We wave as we go by as we're perhaps the only car he's seen for quite some time and he makes an effort to doff his Stetson which falls off and blows away. Will be a long day in the saddle today.

When we finally reach the high ground just outside Guadix the clever temperature thingie on the dashboard tells us it's two degrees outside. We decided against getting out to check if this was an accurate figure.

Long before we reach Jaen it gets warmer and the landscape begins to resemble a pointillist painting by Georges Seurat or Paul Signac as on both sides of the road and seemingly stretching to infinity are serried ranks of identical dark green blobs. Infantry battalions of olive trees in battle array, each tree set a precise distance from its neighbour; it's a remarkable sight.

Almost half of all the world's olive oil comes from Spain, most of it from Jaen province and Spain produces vastly more olive oil than the rest of Europe combined. Much of the supposedly 'Italian' olive oil originates in

Spain as the canny Italians import olive oil, rebrand it and resell it as Italian produce, at a healthy premium. I remember reading there are over 220 million olive trees in Jaen province. Is that all? Looks a lot more than that to me, but I'm not tempted to count them.

Jaen isn't a pretty city. Far from it and the traffic is a bit of a pain here as well. We find a hotel on the outskirts, lovely hotel too after haggling the night's stay down to Premier Class level, reasoning we can pop into town easily enough from this hotel on the outskirts. Well, not all that easily as it turns out.

We eventually find an underground car park, hidden away down a narrow alley in the middle of Jaen, but the almost new car we follow down the ramp demolishes the entry ticket machine. A man comes out, waves his arms about and tells us to go ahead and park while he sorts the mess out. We creep past the car in front, which is barely dented even though the ticket machine is a write off, and park in an unreserved free space. As I get out of the car, the irate man from outside rushes back in and shouts 'not there.' I move the car up one space, despite it appearing exactly the same as its predecessor, and he nods approvingly. Perhaps J17 is his lucky number and he resents anyone else having it.

We walk up the hill, over the very rough uneven pavement interspersed with equally treacherous cobblestones, bound for the cathedral, and are blowing a bit when we get to the top. The cathedral is, of course, closed. I ask a woman eating a sandwich, sitting on the pavement, outside the door if she knows why it is closed. She shrugs and says, 'they open when they feel like it. It was open only five minutes ago when I came here. They told me to go away and closed the doors. 'Very strange.

I take a photo of the cathedral façade. It's magnificent, one of the very best examples of Renaissance architecture I've ever seen. Inside, behind those massive locked doors, is an important relic, the veil of Veronica (Santo Rostro) which appears to bear an image of Jesus' face after Saint Veronica used her veil to wipe the head of Jesús as he carried the cross to Calvary. As with the Turin Shroud, the authenticity of this relic is in doubt, but it doesn't seem likely we will get the chance to see it today.

We pass a man, he's also seated on the pavement and he calls out, in English, 'please help me.' Assuming he is a street beggar we are about to walk on when he calls out again. We turn back and see he is holding a broken walking stick and has a huge bandage on his leg. I help him to his feet and a man runs out from a shop holding an ornate walking stick and says, 'please take this. Return it when you can.' The poor man has an injured leg, his walking stick snapped and he couldn't get up again. Even after these Good Samaritan deeds, the cathedral remained closed. The man who brought over the walking stick said, piously, 'God hears our prayers, inside or outside a church,' so that's us told.

We decide to go to lunch and perhaps try again later. We find a café with tables outside and order a drink. Drinks come with a free tapa here, but what we get is deep fried bread crumbs containing tiny pieces of fish. It is really disgusting, but when the waiter sees we have only eaten a tiny bit he brings us another, Barbate tuna and red peppers, which is delicious.

We pop into a dark and dingy tapas bar, just for a look around, and discover it's a delightfully 'authentic' bar, full of weird characters, most of them smoking roll up style cigarettes. Those new-fangled laws prohibiting public smoking don't yet appear to have reached this area of Jaen. A swarthy man with huge brass earrings makes room on a bench and invites Marigold to sit down, which she does. Nobody offers to move up for me!

I order coffee for me, tinto verano for Marigold, and the barman pours me a glass of dark, almost black, liquid from a brown bottle bearing no label to drink while I wait for the coffee to arrive. I take a sip. It's the strongest sherry I've ever tasted. It's pretty grim, but after the third sip I start to enjoy the taste. By the time my coffee comes, I have finished the whole glass. Marigold is 'talking' to the group on her table by now. Nobody seems to be speaking the same language, but they're all laughing. This is not unusual as Marigold manages to hold conversations wherever we find ourselves.

After lunch, we decide to visit the the Baños Arabes, one of the best examples of Moorish hammams in Spain. The ones in Jaen are over a thousand years old and the extensive information leaflet says they are 'probably' the largest in Europe. The horseshoe arches and brickwork ceilings with star-shaped windows letting in the light are delightful. The baths are in the basement of the Palacio de Villardompardo which was built on top of them in the 16th century. We start our visit in the hallway, a big room with a brick vaulted ceiling with 18 star shaped skylights, move into the warm room and finally into the hot room which is about 50 feet across, alongside the boilers and also covered by stars, allowing sunlight to stream in. The baths were used on a daily basis by Moslems, but also later on by both Christians and Jews. Women were even allowed in, but of course only at certain times and never when any men were around!

We didn't actually bathe. We have been to hammams in Morocco and in Granada, as fully participating bathers, but decided we were already clean enough today.

The palace above the hammam was built by Fernando Torres de Portugal, the viceroy of Peru, and Count of Villardompardo, so a pretty well connected chap! It's as impressive a Renaissance palace as the Count himself and contains A Museum of Popular Arts and Customs and the Naïf International Art Museum, neither of which we could be bothered to walk around as we'd decided to brave the Jaen road system once more and drive up the hill of Santa Catalina to the Parador.

The Parador de Jaén sits alongside a 13th-century Arabic fortress and mimics its architecture to perfection. The main public rooms have high ceilings and vast fireplaces, it's all very impressive. We had coffee in the café, sitting alongside three police officers in uniform. They stopped talking when we sat down, but when they realised we were English, carried on telling what we assumed to be their favourite dirty jokes. They certainly laughed a lot. I nudged Marigold and said, 'laugh with them next time' which she did and they all stopped laughing and looked a bit sheepish. Marigold wagged her finger at them and then burst out laughing so they knew she hadn't actually understood the joke.

The policemen have a dozen empty bottles of beer on their table, but perhaps they're off duty. Hope so. I read in one of those lists that proliferate at the start of any New Year that amongst beer drinking nations, per capita, Britain comes 28th. Czech Republic tops the list. Never particularly noticed this myself on our travels there, but then again beer is very cheap in the Czech Republic. They're 'only' 9th for alcohol consumption in general though, but Eastern European countries still fill 9 out of the top 10 in that list. The odd one out, ie not in Eastern European, is Andorra in 7th place. Not many of 'em, but they certainly like their grog. Britain? An unremarkable 25th. We seem to meet a fair few British 'good imbibers' on our travels. Must get thirstier when they leave the U.K. One of our best friends lives for part of the year in Andorra, part in Spain, so we're wondering if Spain will now replace Andorra in the top ten as she certainly does her best to keep the figures up.

Back in our hotel, we're sitting in overstuffed armchairs in a room just off Reception reading a book and Kindle respectively when a middle aged couple come barging in, talking at the top of their voices and generally causing havoc. They're English, of course. The woman has one of those

voices whose natural habitat is endless kvetching, whining, complaining*
and finding fault with everything. The man says nothing at all.

*Yes, tautology, with bells on, but one simply cannot overstate the
irritation of this woman's voice and attitude.

Worse is to come as they strut into 'our' sitting area, banging luggage
about and creating havoc. The whining woman evidently sees Marigold is
reading a book with an English title and decides this gives her the right to
come over and talk to us.

'Come over here, Jim,' she says to her companion, 'but don't you dare sit
down in that low chair.'

She turns to Marigold and says, 'he's got terrible trouble with his
rhomboids,' which, predictably sets Marigold off in a fit of rather
unseemly giggles. The woman glares at her.

'It's no laughing matter,' she says, sniffily, and goes away again. I know a
bit about rhomboids: there's a rhomboid major   and a rhomboid minor
and they are two of the big muscles on the back that link the scapula and
the spinal column. I once had 'rhomboid trouble' myself and know how
painful they are when overstretched, but my attempt to send a
sympathetic glance at poor Jim is interpreted by his wife as a
demonstration of male solidarity. She sniffs again, loudly, and drags the
wretched Jim out of the room.

'Good riddance,' says Marigold and we return to our novels in peace.
Just as well Jim's problem was 'only' a bad back. I dread to think how I
would have coped with a hysterical Marigold if flatulence had been his
problem.

Fabulous Toledo.

Marigold Says...

Toledo is an ancient and remarkable city and we can scarcely believe this is our first ever visit. It won't be our last.

Set off early, well, early for me, then stopped at bottom of road for coffee and toast which wakes me up and gets me ready for anything.

Journey along motorway going past the many hills and villages, lovely. Police stopped all traffic on motorway, lots of policemen, big dogs, all wearing full body armour, (no, not the dogs), and police cars parked across the road so we had to go around the narrow gaps between the cars very slowly. The police stopped every car, a man with a machine gun looked inside and in the boot. They let us go and didn't even mention how untidy our boot was. Phew!

G said, 'could you possibly look more guilty?' I know, I go bright red and would be a hopeless smuggler. Every time I go through security at an airport they pull me to one side, make me empty my bag and put that bleeping stick all over me. They look very disappointed when I am just an innocent tourist. They never stop G, which is annoying.

Getting into Toledo with sat nav telling us to 'take the eighth exit on the next roundabout' and things like that was a bit of a nightmare as we got tooted at a few times for late decisions due to both of us arguing with sat nav, but not with each other, about where to go. Sometimes Hillary (sat nav) doesn't know as much as she pretends to and is very bossy. She sounds just like Hillary Clinton and I imagine her standing up in the sky above our car, wearing a pastel coloured trouser suit, pointing at people she pretends are waving to her and grinning. Just do your job, Hillary, and get us into Toledo before it gets dark.

The old part of the city, as we're driving in, was wonderful, we glanced at the huge gates and high walls surrounding the city, so our appetite was whetted.

Hotel is very modern and our room has a huge bed, and we get to it in a glass lift. We arrived at the desk with our usual luggage, three carrier bags and a bag of munchies. The man on the desk said 'is it for just one night?' I think he was expecting someone with Louis Vuitton suitcases. Wish we could travel a bit more tidily, but will never happen. Our room has a fantastic view of the city so we're very happy. The hotel has five stars and the outside is lovely, all Roman columns and a huge wooden entrance door, but we had to walk a long way to our room, far enough for us to wonder if we were still in the hotel or had taken a wrong turn and were now in the next postcode.

Most of the rooms we were passing must have been empty as there was only one other car in the big car park. G said this was the hotel getting their own back for us haggling them down on price. By the time we found our room, number 6,865 – no, not really, but it seemed like it – I was wishing we'd paid full price and wondering how I'd ever find my way back to Reception again. Not asking Hillary as she'd probably direct me to Peru.

Self off for Toledo by taxi as the very helpful man on the Reception desk said, 'only a mad person would try to park a car in Toledo' and rang for a taxi. Only a few euros. Stunning place, all the first shops we saw were selling swords and armoury. For 160 euros I could have bought a brilliant sword. Would be handy if they're still looking for extras for Game of Thrones.

Found the War museum, which the man in the hotel had recommended, which was in a huge, ancient building and even better it was free to over 60s. G was thrilled that the girl on the desk asked us to prove we were genuinely ancient by showing our passports, but she was only about 17 so everybody will have seemed old to her and she probably asks everybody.

Toledo is most famous for swords and we found lots of info about them and some of those on show were covered in jewels and diamonds. A bit over the top, but apparently that's what you get given for a pressie if you are rich. Then there was the armour, modelled for everybody, from big fat blokes, down to children, and the horses wore it as well. Must have all sounded very clanky.

Outside, in the courtyard, there was a tank and an army helicopter guarded by a very tough looking soldier with a shaved head and a fat girl soldier who looked as if she normally guarded doughnuts, not very well.

The main building is huge and a bit like IKEA as you have to follow arrows to find your way around and if you decide you want to leave now the only exit is about three miles away from wherever you are at the time.

Loads of shops in the town were selling hams hanging from ceilings. We found one where you could taste, but it was a bad decision, as the 'ham carver' wouldn't shut up talking, instead of carving, and we just wanted to go. Fortunately another couple came in, so we scarpered, without having to buy any ham. To be truthful, judging by the miserable scraps he was giving out as samples, it was a bit salty and chewy.

Stopped for a drink at a lovely little bar just off the main square and had free tapas. Don't know what was in them but quite delicious.

When we got outside again I said 'we should have ordered a proper meal' and G said 'just pick somewhere you fancy then.' I spotted a restaurant with a big awning outside and those tall heaters going full blast. G didn't look very impressed, said it would be full of people smoking and looked like a place for ripping off tourists. I said that it was my choice and we went in.

We sat next to one of the heaters and looked at the menu which was written in German. I rummaged around and found one in Spanish which was a lot better as the words were a lot shorter. G went off to look at a book shop and left me to order for us.

There were a lot of people smoking, but I tried to concentrate on the menu and hope I was the only one who'd notice when G got back. The couple at the next table had their backs to me, but looked very interesting. The man was really, really fat and wearing a fur collared parka and his mother kept passing her plate over so he could help himself. He'd already eaten a pizza and by the looks of the cardboard container it came in it was one of those that serves ten people. The mother was not as fat as her son (impossible) and had long grey hair with a flower broach in it. She had a walking frame next to her and every time the waiter came past he had to climb over it.

When they left I had two shocks – the 'mother' was only about 35 so must have been his wife and the walking frame was for the man as he was too fat to walk on his own.

I'd been too busy watching the couple to concentrate when ordering food and when G came back and asked what we were going to eat I said 'the speciality sandwiches and two glasses of Tinto Verano' and he seemed happy enough with that. When the waiter came he brought two really big jugs of Tinto Verano. I said we hadn't ordered these and he said, 'we only serve Tinto Verano in one litre jugs and you ordered two.'

Gulp!

Persuaded the waiter to take one of the jugs away. He came back with 'sandwiches' which were supposed to contain smoked salmon. There were a couple of thin strips of smoked salmon, a lot of green slimy stuff and lots of mayonnaise. We ate them, of course, supped the litre of weak red wine mixed with flat lemonade and were both very unimpressed. I'm not going to say what the bill came too, but G's suspicions of it being a tourist rip off weren't far off the mark.

We walked through the narrow little streets and found the cathedral, but even though we were prepared to pay the admission charge there was nobody on duty to take our money and they were only letting people with pre - booked tickets inside. We could have booked a guided tour, starting in 40 minutes and only in Spanish, for 18 euros each. We didn't bother!

We walked round the back and found a door that was open. This allowed us inside, but only just. The main area was behind iron railings but we could get some idea of how magnificent a building this is. It was first founded in the 6th century, turned into a Mosque after the Moorish invasion and then turned back into a Cathedral when the Moors were driven out. They knocked down the existing mosque and rebuilt it as it is today in 1227.

Inside the whole building is supported by massive stone pillars, 88 of them, and there are over 750 stained glass windows. I know all this because I found a leaflet on the way in.

A man wagged his fingers at us and said, 'no photos,' even though there were lots of people taking photos on the other side of the railings, the part you pay to go in. G said it was 'elitist' and took two photos, very quickly. There are pictures by El Greco and Goya on display, apparently, but we were unable to confirm this. 'Seen one Goya, seen 'em all,' I said. G said he was impressed by my philosophical attitude to unavoidable cultural deprivation.

It was starting to get cold and dark by now, so we hailed a taxi and set back. The driver went back by a different route, driving very fast over cobbled streets, and we were back at the hotel in no time, extremely shaken and stirred. All we had to do then was find our room again. Should have brought a ball of twine!

Next morning at breakfast a great number of Chinese teenage girls arrived with masks on. There must have been pollution in the hotel which we didn't know about. Wondered if they would take them off to eat and drink. Should we put a napkin over our noses to go in the lift?

Chinese people are great tourists these days. They do like to take a photograph or two, don't they? One of the girls ran past us, squealing, to take a photo of Toledo through the window. What's the rush, I thought, Toledo has been standing here for a thousand years or so, it's not going anywhere. It started to snow as we finished breakfast and this sent the teenage hordes into a frenzy. Lots more photos, absolute bedlam.

I've missed out loads, there's so much to see here, and we didn't get to see the historic Jewish Quarter at all. Will save that for our next visit. One of my favourite places in Spain. We will return.

Las Alpujarras. Medieval North Africa without crossing water.

G Says...

Las Alpujarras is a region like no other in Spain. We've visited Berber villages in the High Atlas Mountains, but there's no need to make the long trek through Morocco to see exactly the same villages, recreated south of Granada, in Southern Spain.

We love it here, but all our previous visits have been in the summer months where the high mountains and perched white villages are a relief from the baking heat. It's February now, there's snow on the hills and we're not sure what to expect.

This region was the last refuge in Spain of the Moors of the El Andalus kingdom. Long after Boabdil, Granada's final sultan, was thrown out of Granada in 1492, bands of rebels were still waging a guerrilla war from the isolation of their mountain strongholds in the Alpujarras. It was to be another eighty years before the Moorish presence in Spain could truly be said to have been extinguished.

This Moorish influence is most evident in the place names, the traditional North African artisan crafts that thrive here and the plethora of flat-roofed, Moroccan-style houses that typify the numerous villages that define the region. The High Atlas, or the Alpujarras, I'd be hard pressed to tell the difference, from a distance. Up close, the difference is evident: this region may still have medieval architecture, but the roads are good, there's a bus service and even a pretty decent Wi-fi signal. You don't get any of that in the High Atlas.

The publication in 1999 of Driving over Lemons, an account of rural simplistic living on an isolated farm near Orgiva had a significant effect. Much as Peter Mayle introduced Provence, particularly the Luberon region, to a wide readership, prompting an instant surge in house ownership and bringing much tourism to the area, so it was with the Alpujarras.

A personal view: South from Granada: Seven Years in an Andalusian Village, an autobiographical book by Gerald Brenan, first published in 1957, is a far better read. Its subject matter is life in these villages during the 1930s and much of Brennan's writing still resonates with us as we drive around here today.

A good few years back, we spent a few weeks in Calpe. This was in the pre Internet era and pre Sky tv, so the evenings were long. We took ourselves off to the local cinema, long since closed to nobody's great surprise, to see an English language film, Carrington. We remember the evening vividly for the half time 'interval' where the projector stopped, jerkily, in mid frame and the entire audience trooped off to the foyer for free coffee, a slice of cake and a stiff brandy, all included in the ticket price. You don't get that at your local Odeon.

'Carrington' is Dora Carrington, a talented artist and the film details her relationship with Lytton Strachey, the author of Eminent Victorians, one of my favourite 'serious' books. Strachey was a founder of the Bloomsbury Set and one of its peripheral figures was Gerald Brennan. We loved the film and the next two books I read were Eminent Victorians and South from Granada.

We start on familiar ground, two large villages or small towns, the biggest and most affected by tourism in the region, Lanjarón and Órgiva.

Lanjarón is the first village on the road into the Alpujarras from Granada. We cross the Tablate Bridge which marks the official start of Los Alpujarras. This bridge was the site of a fierce battle between Moors and Christians in 1569, seventy-seven years after the last of the Moors were supposed to have been sent back to North Africa in full retreat. There's a ruined castle here as a reminder of times gone by, dating back to the eighth century when the splendidly named Yusuf the First served as Sultan of Al Andalus.

Lanjarón is best known for its spring water, there's a big bottling plant as you enter the town, and Lanjarón water is one of the best known brands in Spain. A sign indicates a spa featuring 'Chalybeate Baths' which I associate with Tunbridge Wells. I look it up later and confirm the natural springs at Tunbridge Wells, sorry, I really meant to say, Royal Tunbridge Wells, contains Chalybeate water and they were first promoted by Dudley, the Third Baron North who claimed the spa waters could cure, 'the colic, the melancholy, and the vapours; it made the lean fat, the fat lean; it killed flat worms in the belly, loosened the clammy humours of the body, and dried the over-moist brain.'

Pretty impressive claims as in reality Chalybeate water is basically nothing more than plain old water enriched with iron deposits. We don't notice anyone skipping a round shouting 'I'm cured of those flat worms in my belly,' but tourists and spas, seven natural springs in the town, are a heady mix and there are more hotels here than anywhere else we'll visit on this trip.

Obviously, we're not staying here. Tonight we shall be spending a night in rustic style somewhere very different. As yet I haven't found the 'actual village' on any map, so let's hope we find the place before dark.

One of our 'friends' emailed us recently, pointing out how 'bourgeois' we had become with our patronage of five star hotels. One night in a five star hotel and we've lost our street cred forever! Never mind that we only paid a two star price at the aforesaid accommodation, the damage is done.

In Voltaire's satire Candide – another of those 'did this for A Levels so unlikely to ever go near it again' works of literature – responding to perceived jealousies, our hero declares 'Il faut cultiver notre jardin,' which roughly translates as 'Look after your own garden.'

Don't worry about us, mind your own business, as we'd love to say, but Voltaire's wisdom is written in French, so much less likely to offend.

As confirmed hodophiles, the act of travelling being far more relevant to overall enjoyment than where we choose to lay our heads at night, we're going very, very rustic tonight. As far removed as can be from five star. Bourgeois? Not likely. How very dare you?

The issue may be thought complicated by tomorrow being Valentines Day. Some may question the wisdom of choosing a resting place very far removed from any semblance of 'luxury' for one's beloved to awaken in on Valentines morn, but Marigold is no ordinary woman!

Lanjarón is very clean and surprisingly busy (it's a Tuesday morning in February after all) but we're not 'tourists' so we give the gift shops a miss and move onwards to Órgiva, the largest village and very much the region's 'capital.'

Órgiva has a thriving 'hippie' population and a brilliant Thursday market, but today it's far less frenetic than we've seen in the past. We've got friends here, but a quick dash around their usual haunts fails to find any trace of them. They're van dwellers so may have moved on. Maybe next time.

We stop and look around at the Molinos de Benizalte, a 15th century Arabian oil mill which is always fascinating and then take ourselves off to one of our favourite places in Spain, Café Baraka, just above a car park in Órgiva.

We first discovered Café Baraka – 'baraka' means 'blessing' - almost twenty years ago and are relieved it is not merely still here but thriving. Step inside and it's just like being in Fez or Marrakesh. Most of today's customers are wearing dreadlocks, have multiple piercings and wear baggy clothes, this is Órgiva, after all, a 'hippie' stronghold, yet all are busily engrossed in their laptops.

Café Bareka is owned by a Sufi Moslem, there are copies of both the Bible and the Koran on the bookshelves, and this is just one of the many ways in which this place encapsulates the diverse nature of Órgiva. The town's population is a little under 6,000, but includes 68 resident different nationalities, as well as a sizeable Buddhist community and a sprawling and long established 'Rainbow' collective just outside the town called Beneficio of which more anon.

We order breakfast from the vast choice available and Marigold takes an age studying the list of thirty-six different varieties of tea before deciding on café con leche! No alcohol here, but if you're vegetarian/vegan you're in paradise. They do serve meat though, halal meat where requested, almost everything on the menu is 'organic' and there's not a microwave oven in sight! .

A man with a mass of curly hair and a very dark long beard sits behind us. He's very black, very big and very exotic looking in flowing robes and a bright headband. He also has a broad Irish accent. No, it doesn't pay to judge by appearances. He tells me to order baba ghanoush as it's 'superb here.' We last ate baba ghanoush, basically mashed baked aubergine with garlic, spices and lemon juice, in very different surroundings in Bristol and were massively disappointed. His meal arrives and does look enticing, but not sufficiently so to convince us.

Three girls, older teens, who we'd passed on the way up from the car park, sitting cross legged on the stone steps comparing their piercings, come inside and take an age deciding where to sit. Choosy over which padded sofa or bench to sit on, yet seemingly happy enough to sit on the floor outside. They're wearing billowing tie-dye dresses, thick socks and heavy, lace-up boots and I imagine they think of themselves as rebels against convention. Marigold catches my eye and we share a conspiratorial grin. Marigold dressed exactly like that in the 1960s, back when my hair was longer even than that of the dreadlocked hippie in the corner seat. Been there, done that.

The teenage 'rebels' order toast and jam, speak English with Home Counties convent school accents and gaze adoringly at a couple of (male) Danish backpackers who turn up along with their bikes, a hairy dog and all their worldly goods. Everybody moves up to let them in and the waiter brings over a bowl of water for the dog. No wonder we like coming here.

We go for a walk around Órgiva in the sunshine, much warmer here than it will be later in the mountains, and have to cross over the road pretty smartly when a Guardia Civil van screeches up alongside two scruffy young men, several officers climb out and push the men up against the wall. It looks pretty drastic, but is over almost as soon as it starts. The men show some documentation, turn out their pockets and are soon released. It's break time at a nearby school and the released men get a round of applause.

A man with a lived-in face, one of the old school hippies, tells us his name is Kurt and that there has been trouble for a few months now between the local police and anyone suspected of being a member of the long established Beneficio commune. The man said he had lived in the commune for fifteen years, the members believed in 'peace and love' and wished only to live their lives in harmony with nature. We've been to the community, twice, in the past and never saw anything even remotely threatening. About 250 people live there full time, more in the summer months, on land gifted by a benefactor in the 1970s as a self governing centre for 'peace and harmony.'

Last time we were in Órgiva I got the impression the townspeople were becoming less tolerant of their near neighbours which Kurt confirmed. Things escalated a few months ago after an American tourist claimed to have been sexually assaulted by a member of the commune. Kurt said the allegation was 'a load of bull' but police raided the camp, arrested about twenty people and brought over a hundred charges against the community members.

'Including me,' Kurt added. We intended to refrain from asking for details, but he told us anyway.

'Owning an illegal vehicle,' Kurt said. 'The van I arrived in 15 years ago. It's not taxed, not insured, so they charged me with a couple of traffic offences. Never been off the land, never driven it on a road since I came here, it's where I sleep at night and that's all. Still charged me though.'

I'm enough of a cynic to know there's more than one view of any situation, but this did sound fairly trivial.

'Were most of the charges like that?' I asked.

Kurt frowned. His chosen lifestyle presupposes a certain bias against him by authoritarian figures, but he's obviously trying to be fair.

'They did arrest some guy they accused of strangling a woman, his wife I think, in France, but he'd not been here long so I don't really know him.

Mostly it was about our vans or growing a few cannabis plants. For our own use, not to sell.'

As we were leaving, Kurt called after us, 'they never found my little garden though' and laughed.

Later on we picked up some more detail on the raid. The man accused of murder was aged 23 and still had his wife's phone in his possession which was how the police traced him. A woman waiting for the tourist office to open told us most of the other charges had been dismissed and the only ones left were related to diverting water supplies or the digging of illegal wells. She added there had been uproar in the town over what they regarded as overzealous police action. Dozens of police vans invaded the site, along with a helicopter and the scene we had just witnessed was all too common. She dismissed the allegations of the American tourist as 'fanciful' and had never heard of any arrests connected with this complaint.

Beneficio is a fascinating place and when we've been before we've always been welcomed. It reminds us of a hippie community on the outskirts of Copenhagen we spent a few days in, but Beneficio is much more 'authentic' in my view and certainly more attuned to the lofty ideals of its founders. Last time we were there, Marigold said, 'if we'd found this place when it first started up, we'd still be here.' As ever, she's probably right.

It helps to take something along as a present for the community. Last time I offloaded fifty or so spare books. It's entirely self sufficient. There are no mains services, but a modicum of civilisation exists as there's very considerable use made of solar power and wind turbines for power. We don't want to risk another raid so we decide against a visit today, time is getting away from us and I still haven't the faintest idea how to get to where we're spending the night.

Beneficio isn't the only 'hippie' hang out in Orgiva; there's another campground, a rather less well known place called El Morrion which we've visited only once, but it's quite charming with numerous dogs and young, happy children running around. Not so many rules as Beneficio, much more laid back and far less emphasis on spiritual enlightenment.

We've spent some time knocking about in La Mancha recently where Miguel de Cervantes Saavedra, always referred to as simply 'Cervantes' set his classic novel, Don Quixote. Widely regarded as the first modern novel, Don Quixote has been translated into more languages than any other book except the Bible. Cervantes died way back in 1616, but he's the Shakespeare of the Spanish language and we saw effigies of the writer and his best known characters, Don Quixote and Sancho Panza everywhere we went in Orgiva.

Okay, this is Spain's most famous literary figure, but why is there such a massive bust of Cervantes in Orgiva? I waited, camera phone in hand, for ages, waiting for a lady in funeral black to walk alongside the bust in order to give an accurate idea of its size. She walked so slowly Marigold wondered whether the old lady was a statue herself.

Back in 1967 the local librarian, Agustin Martin Zaragoza, started to encourage people and institutions to send him copies of the book, Don Quixote. Today the collection, housed in the library and available to anybody who wants to read them, contains books translated into 82 different languages, far more than anywhere else. They're still looking for more as Don Quixote has been translated into 140 languages and dialects. The 'next best' collection in Madrid, where Cervantes is actually buried, only contains translations of 59 languages.

Anyone can see the collection, we just asked at the reception desk, and there are over 150 editions of the novel on display along with many other books, papers and essays together with numerous biographies of Cervantes. There's artwork and sculptures in here as well. It made me want to read the book again. Marigold's reserving judgement, for now. Wonder if there'll be a library devoted to Driving over Lemons in a few hundred years time? I rather doubt it.

The book's full title in Spanish is 'El ingenioso hidalgo don Quijote de la Mancha' – Not exactly catchy, is it? I noted two copies that had been signed by members of the Real Madrid and Barcelona football teams and another copy signed by King Juan Carlos I during an official visit to Órgiva in 1994 – although that copy had already been donated by him to the Orgiva library from his own collection. Nobody asked us to sign anything. We drove along the road overlooking the El Morrion camp on our way out. There are numerous vans parked up all along the valley, a couple of communal 'big tents' and a fair few buildings that appear 'almost' permanent.

Hippy communes behind us we decide we must put aside lofty ideals of peace and harmony and, selfishly, go off to find our place to spend the night. I've already reassured Marigold that even though a yurt was available in the same area I had booked a one bedroom house. The house took some finding, it's along a narrow and precipitous track, and is just about as remote as is possible to find. We see a very smart house coming into view, but of course that's not it and we have much more of this narrow track with an unfenced sheer drop on one side to go yet.

We've climbed up through the mountains by now, it's late afternoon and bitterly cold. The shade temperature shows as two degrees, but when we get out it reminds us of a day we spent at Europe's most northerly point, Denmark's North Cape when even the reindeer were shivering.

The woman who meets us there is lovely, there are four cats, a ridiculously silly dog, hammocks and a tiny one roomed house with a bed, a 'kitchenette' and a small bathroom. When we're on our own, I look at Marigold and we both start laughing. 'I love it,' she says.

We both agree the yurt would have been a very bad idea as the house has thick stone walls, a solid flat roof and it's still freezing! The friendly dog, a bearded collie with matted fur and a lolling tongue, turns up, rolls around in the dust and tries to climb up onto my lap. He's a real character and takes us off for a walk.

We eat our meagre rations, yet more lamentably bad planning on our part, augmented by a packet of crackers and a pot of jam the house owner had given us. Our adopted friend polishes off half the crackers. His table manners reflect his general appearance,

'You must be the scruffiest dog in Spain,' Marigold says and he wags his tail in agreement. I point out the nearby hammock, reminding Marigold it will be Saint Valentines Day tomorrow, and suggest a means of starting off that special day tomorrow morning. The suggestion, however, does not meet with any great enthusiasm. I am secretly quite relieved. The spirit may be willing…

Day two in the Alpujarras.

G Says...

We're up bright and early, partly due to worrying about frostbite in this chilly little house and decide jumping into a car with not only a heater but heated seats will be a good idea. The scruffy dog leaps out from the bushes as I get to where I parked the car, determined not to let us leave without saying a lengthy goodbye. He brings me a filthy and much chewed stick which is almost as unwholesome as himself and I throw it for him for a while. He's a gorgeous dog and a real character. We will miss him and I tell him so. I glance at the rear view mirror as we leave and he is sitting on the car park looking absolutely bereft. I'm so relieved we've only stayed for one night; any longer and I'd have smuggled him into the back seat.

Marigold decides today she would like to choose our route solely on which place name takes her fancy, so that's what we do. It's not sensible, it's not particularly practical, but we do it anyway, so be aware if you ever wished to recreate today's odyssey, there are easier ways of getting from place to place.

Even so, 'a good traveller has no fixed plans and is not intent on merely arriving,' as Lao Tzu once said. He also gave the world 'a journey of a thousand miles begins with a single step,' and several other quotes that have become part of everyday language. Not bad for someone who died in 531 AD, so there's hope yet for Marigold's undoubted wisdom to be recognised, eventually.

Random directions are one of the chief joys of travel and today throws up some unexpected gems.

We set off up the very steep track, very relieved not to meet anyone coming the other way, and head for Atalbeitar, the nearest village. It turns out not be car friendly as there's no access road and only donkey tracks leading into and throughout the village. We don't see any donkeys, but don't see any people there either.

We brave the morning chill and wander around a bit. There are no shops, no bars and seemingly no inhabitants but a couple of smoking chimneys suggest they are inside keeping warm, sensible folk.

Altabeitar is the smallest of the seven villages which make up the ancient Moorish district of La Tahá in the high Alpujarras. Taha is the Moorish word for obedience and this whole region used to divided into separate groups or 'Tahas,' but this group of seven is the only one to retain the name.

Mostly untouched by tourism, life in this isolated area life goes on much as it always has, in an unhurried and peaceful manner.

We find out the village stands at 1,150 metres above sea level, hence the early morning chill, and, supposedly, has 31 permanent residents. There are more than 31 houses, so even if they have one each there won't be a housing shortage and the church looks as if it could contain the population three times over.

We go on to see whether the nearby village, Pitres, is any livelier. Well, it's bigger, quite a lot bigger, but still not exactly lively. There's an artisan chocolate company – Chocolates Sierra Nevada - here so we're quite excited, but not for long as it's closed. As is everywhere else, apart from a tiny shop, a terraced cottage with one room turned into a 'shop' which contains absolutely nothing we want to buy. They do have such oddities as carrot jam and artichoke jam for sale though.

'Who buys this stuff?' I wonder.

Marigold shrugs her shoulders. The man standing in the doorway, presumably the owner, walks over and points at a display of firelighters which he's taken the trouble to arrange in a pyramid shape. We smile in appreciation and finally find a small bag of biscuits to buy so his feelings won't be hurt. Oh, the pressures of being a foreigner in another land, ever mindful we are representing our nation in the eyes of others.

Hint, that last sentence may contain sarcasm. Even though it's true as well. Let's call it a slight exaggeration then.

The biscuits were dreadful, of course. Soggy, probably went out of date in the last century and almost entirely tasteless. Yes, of course I ate them. Marigold is far too fussy sometimes. She mutters something that sounds like 'war boy,' a reference to the one time I mentioned spending my early years in the days when rationing was in force. Times were hard then, I said, only having one potato a week to eat and wearing my grandad's old clogs. Not to mention still wearing a gas mask every day to make sure it didn't go to waste. It all falls on deaf ears.

There's a small cage with a few chickens in next to one of the houses, that shop in someone's front room and that's about it for Pitres. The chickens do their best, but even their efforts to please can't sustain us for long. There are bars here, two discos, several hostels and a hotel, but they're all closed. Bet this place is a riot in summer. They may even get

111

the chance to buy chocolate. Spring onion jam too. Yes, really. I have photos to prove it.

Pitres is somewhat a figure of fun locally as a politician once asked the residents what amenities they would like him to obtain on their behalf if he was elected. The villagers conferred and came up with the idea that Pitres could become a port so the men would have more work. The politician didn't hesitate before agreeing to bring the sea up the mountain to Pitres and thus set up a port. There's a boat and a big anchor to greet visitors to the village so at least they're now able to laugh at their own expense. The request for the village to be made into a port has another legacy: a fiesta where sardines are 'planted' in a dry riverbed and solemnly watered to make them grow. Side splitting stuff, I imagine for those lucky enough to be there at the time. Perhaps not...

We drive next to three of the nearest villages: Capileira, Bubion and Pampaneira, perched on the slopes of snow covered Mulhacen, the highest point in mainland Spain.

We start at the highest point, Capileira, and work our way down. Capileira is not the highest village we'll reach today, it's only the second highest in the region, but we notice the immediate drop in temperature. When we left the coast a couple of days ago the car showed 18 degrees as the outside shade temperature; up here it's showing as 2 degrees and the 'warning, frost alert' symbol lights up even more brightly on the dashboard. Even so, it's sunny, there's blue sky above and we wander around looking and feeling like (inadequately equipped) Polar explorers for at least twenty minutes, admiring hand woven rugs we don't need, artisan style rustic pottery that's ludicrously expensive and of course hams.

The Alpujarras are famous for hams, hung outside in the frigid mountain air to dry naturally and add flavour. Alpujarras hams are highly prized, the Spanish love them, and we were offered samples wherever we went today. Far more samples than normal, this generosity must be prompted by the scarcity of tourists in the winter months.

Marigold declines all the offers; I accept – it's a 'Marmite' situation. Or, as Marigold says, quite often, I'm just greedy.

We love the haphazard nature of these mountain villages, narrow streets twisting and turning, whitewashed stone walls and simple pots of flowers everywhere – more geraniums here than at Kew Gardens. There's a uniformity about the roofs, even a 'new build' house has a flat roof, but there aren't many new houses, this place looks much the same as it did a few hundred years ago. Flat stones are laid over chestnut wood beams and the gaps are packed with clay and grey sand. As they do in the Moroccan mountains, these roofs appear to be a misguided design choice, but they endure throughout even the harshest climate. On top are tall chimney stacks, often several of them on the same roof and they offer a touch of individuality.

These houses were built with the living quarters above a ground floor level where the animals were housed, pigs, goats, chickens, perhaps a mule. That's still the case in the High Atlas, but here we glimpsed only the odd motorbike or washing machine, not a pig to be seen. Such is progress.

Later on we're driving merrily along, admiring the tenacity and optimism of farmers who cultivate vines to make wine at such high altitudes when we see one such farmer hard at work. He's following a pair of horses, ploughing the land between rows of vines. This isn't an immaculate Bordeaux vineyard, it's a scruffy, stony field, on a steep slope many hundreds of feet above sea level and surely these ancient vines will struggle to produce enough grapes to justify his labour. We decide the low yield from these venerable stumps will produce either very bad wine or something very special. The oenophile in me hopes it's the latter.

There are four official languages in Spain (Castilian, Catalan, Basque and Galician), plus several regional dialects such as Andalusian and Valencian. In England, natives of Liverpool, Gateshead and London speak the same language, but in full flow their accents make perfect understanding difficult for many of their fellow citizens. Spain is a big country and a Catalan or Basque speaker would be almost unintelligible to a Spanish person in Madrid. When we bought our first finca our closest neighbour came over for a 'chat.' We spoke and understood a little Spanish, but couldn't understand a word he said. A few days later a Spanish friend came to visit us. He's a university lecturer in Barcelona, a throughly cultured and erudite man, like all our friends, (!!!) but his 'Spanish' proved sadly inadequate when he tried to speak with our neighbour.

'Andalusian is not Spanish,' he said, 'you have much work to do here before you can carry on a conversation.'

And so it proved.

We were reminded of that day as we tried to speak with the man following along behind his horses. Even the tried and trusted truncations of the 'me Tarzan, you Jane' variety proved useless. Whatever variation of Spanish he was speaking was far beyond our comprehension.

Persevering, I learnt that the two horses were 'amigos' and had been together as a pair for fifteen years and that his father had 'retired' from ploughing only two years ago. At the age of 88! He pointed out his father, several fields away, snipping away at the vines on a steep hillside. Presumably, this pruning work being the 'light duties' he now performed after all those years of ploughing.

'I don't even think I could get up to where he is working,' Marigold said.

'Me neither.'

We waved goodbye after asking if we could take a photo of him and his horses. He was happy to do so and we left with our respect for these Stakhanovite sons of the soil raised even higher in our estimation.

A few miles further on we saw two very old men shaking olive trees and collecting their bounty in a net. No fancy machinery, just a couple of octogenarians doing what they've done all their lives. Will the next generation be performing back breaking labour into old age as subsistence farmers as their fathers did and their fathers before them? We already feel we know the answer to that question. This may be the end of a way of life that's survived over many hundreds of years. We're sad to see the old ways die off, but opportunities in education and travel have revealed other ways of earning a living. I wonder aloud whether I'd ever contemplate spending my extreme old age scrabbling around on a steep hillside with just a pair of secateurs for company. Marigold doesn't say anything, but gives me one of her 'looks.'

There are cork trees, chestnut trees, olive and almond trees and a riotous display of blossom lining the roads and always, always, the views of the surrounding hills are magnificent.

On the road to Bubión we watch a pair of eagles swooping and soaring, their keen eyes no doubt watching the valley floor far below. As we're so high, they're practically at our eye level. I try, without success, to capture them on film, but they're so fast and change direction so unpredictably I give up. Later, I see they've both appeared in shot in another photo I took of the hillside views opposite and I hadn't even noticed them at the time. As we prepare to drive on another pair of eagles appear, much higher in the sky. Not a good day to be a rabbit in this valley.

We've seen many walkers setting off for a day in the hills, festooned in many layers of clothes and sturdy boots. Most of the visitors we've seen are here for the walking, but it's an area renowned for bird watching too and we see a pair seemingly equipped for a trip to Antarctica getting very excited about a pair of hoopoes, of which we've seen dozens on this trip, completely oblivious to the four eagles soaring overhead.

Yet more exciting stuff going on in the Alpujarras.

G Says...

Bubion is only about a mile from Capileira and it's the village we're most familiar with in this area as we had stayed there for a couple of nights about ten years ago. Needless to say, we can't find the house we stayed in even though so much else is familiar. A few walkers are setting off in little groups, wearing odd knitted hats, big clumpy boots and (perceived) expressions of superiority. They've all got sticks and weatherbeaten faces too. I've nothing against walking, we certainly do plenty of it, but there's a certain 'type' of walker where being in a group appears to give off vibes of superiority, especially towards those who are sitting in a car.

'Look at us' I suspect they are thinking, 'see how fit we are, how smug and comfortable in our presumption of longevity.'

Marigold points out the three at the back, two men with very red faces and a woman who looks as if she'd rather be sitting by the fire, eating biscuits yet are probably the most expensively equipped of the whole group. They are puffing a fair bit and they've only walked a few hundred yards and are still on a firm, even surface. That's another thing that annoys me: the competitive nature of the 'leaders,' making a point to the less accomplished members at the rear. As with cyclists where one, almost always the man, rides half a mile in front of his female partner, particularly on the hills, what's the point? If I walk or cycle with Marigold, we stay together, we talk, we share the experience. Why can't this 'group' stay together as a group? They've already fragmented and they've only been walking for ten minutes, at most. Walking 'group,' do me a favour.

'You're ranting, again,' Marigold says as I grumble away. Yes, I know I am, but I have no problem with 'walkers' at all; wonderful exercise in the open air in the company of others, but I really do wish it didn't so often denigrate into a competitive display of showing off.

A social group, walking together as a united group, in the countryside, sharing the experience, I'd happily join that group. As would Marigold, although if there were too many hills she'd resent getting out of breath as it may mean talking would become difficult.

We don't go down as far as the church (not because it's too far to walk, but because I'm still hoping to stay in touch with the eagles) but move on instead, not very far, to another pretty village, neighbouring Pampaneira.

Pampaneira has hams, of course it does, but is also renowned for its chocolate.

It's only a small village with narrow streets, but amongst these narrow alleys is Abuela Ili (Grandma Ili) which specialises in artisan chocolate. We bustle along, still very much aware of how 'nippy' it is out of the sun, only to find Grandma's shop is closed. Cue much weeping, wailing and gnashing of teeth.

We console ourselves, well not really, by visiting the Fuente de San Antonio, (Saint Anthony's Fountain), known locally as Chumpaneira, very popular amongst 'unattached' young men. The closest I can get to a translation of the inscription it bears is 'it has such a magnitude that, a bachelor who drinks with the intention of marrying does not fail, because he has a girlfriend at once. You'll see!'

Marigold points out a couple of local men sitting on a wall nearby. They're tucking into a stercoraceous concoction with evident relish, presumably a shared breakfast on a paper plate placed between them. Like their meal the pair are quite spectacularly unattractive in appearance and their chances of finding a girlfriend are surely pretty remote, Marigold suggests.

She wonders if she should take a glass of water from the fountain over to them as it may improve their prospects. On second thoughts, she decides such an approach could be misconstrued and leaves them to their bachelor state. Even worse, they may ask her to share their meal.

We know what to expect when we get to Trevélez: hams and cold air. Trevélez is 1,476 metres – that's just over 4,840 feet - above sea level, making it the highest permanent settlement in Spain, but this altitude makes it a pretty nippy place. The last time we were here was in summer and it was certainly not a teeshirt day on that occasion either.

Hams are the first thing we see on entering the village, a fancy sort of delicatessen with numerous hanging hams. If the mountain air of the Alpujarras is ideal for drying hams, then Trevélez is ham drying perfection. The village is divided into three barrios: bajo, medio and alto. The lower section, Barrio Bajo, is the most tourist friendly of the three with handicraft shops, bars and restaurants. We wander up to a restaurant with an inviting lunchtime menu, but inside is bedlam – the young lad behind the bar seems happy enough to have his rap music blaring out at distortion level, but nobody else is there to share the experience - while the plastic seats outside in the cold are hardly inviting.

There's a ham museum, complete with a giant ham outside, further up the hill, but it's closed. Of course it is. Back down in the square, we meet up with a couple of walkers, Brits, who are topping up their water bottles from one of the fountains.

'The water is freezing,' the man says to us, sipping from his bottle. He's drinking what is almost certainly melted snow off the mountain, but still seems surprised. They tell us they got up at dawn and have walked all the way up from the valley. Impressive, but given the man is a) in his 60s, b) at least three stones overweight and c) has both knees heavily strapped perhaps a little foolhardy as well. His wife, Muriel, is small, very thin and looks as if a strong gust of wind would blow her over.

Marigold rolls her eyes as this brief chat seems likely to develop into a lengthy exchange. The man seems intent on bloviating away, talking at us rather than to us, purely because we share a common language.

They may be perfectly nice people, but seem intent on rabbiting away for hours and I'm well aware Marigold would far rather be indoors out of the cold with food and drink in front of her.

The man, I've either forgotten his name or deliberately blotted it from my memory, and Muriel stop talking for a moment while he tries to open a very narrow door on the assumption it is the entrance to a public toilet. Which it isn't.

I point out to him that it doesn't have a handle with which to open it, just a decorative knob. I don't say, 'you'd never get your belly through that door anyway,' but I want to. He's getting a bit cross, banging on the door and getting very red in the face. I notice he has eyes of different colours and whisper 'heterochromia' to Marigold at the exact same instant she whispers 'David Bowie' to me.

'I see your David Bowie and raise you Benedict Cumberbatch,' I hiss, relishing Marigold's annoyance at not being able to think of another with this condition.

Hours later Marigold shouts out 'Kiefer Sutherland' and I look at her doubtfully, but if course when I check her 'facts' the next day, she is right. Kiefer Sutherland does indeed possess eyes of different colours.

By now Beryl has got her husband under control. 'We've decided to walk to the summit of Mount Mulhacen,' she announces, waving a bony talon up at the snow capped mountain high above the village. 'Where does one find a map of the best routes?'

There is indeed a walk to the summit, starting from this village, and we know people who have done it. But, the round trip is a two day expedition not just a hike, it's only to be recommended in ideal walking conditions, basically meaning in the summer months when the snow has melted, and the people we know who have done this climb all look a lot fitter than this pair of crocks. Who would carry that man back down the mountain if he twists an ankle? Certainly not Muriel.

'There's a tourist office over there with all the info,' Marigold says, brightly, and they toddle off. He's already limping and this is a paved village square, not a mountain.

I look quizzically at Marigold. 'Well, there might be a tourist office over there,' she says. 'Why don't we go and find a café?

So we do.

It's not easy to find food here that doesn't feature ham. I choose habas con jamón, which is basically broad beans and ham and Marigold picks an item off the menu about which neither of us have a clue as to what it is (she does this quite often) and when it arrives we still have no idea what's in it. Apart from chunks of ham, obviously. It tastes good though and we munch our way through another couple of dishes happily enough. The local speciality, Plato Alpujarreno containing potatoes, peppers, egg and black pudding with very thinly sliced ham is delicious, and I'm not normally all that fond of black pudding.

This is rustic food, peasant food, of a kind these villagers have been eating for generations, but it hits the spot. We've enjoyed our few days up in the mountains very much. Would we consider coming back here again in February?

Of course not.

'Change of scenery?' I say.

'Will it be warmer?'

'Much.'

Marigold throws her top layer onto the back seat and gets into the car.

'Drive,' she says.

Valentines Day should involve warmth, in all respects, so we're back on the coast soon enough and the difference in temperature is staggering. One or two degrees in the mountains, here it's a tee shirt and shorts day. Not that I have shorts with me, but we remove layers as far as decency permits - must think of others - and we set off with a specific place in mind.

Roquetas del Mar is by the sea – there's a bit of a clue in the name – but it's mostly shops, plastic greenhouses and fruit and veg packing depots as far as the eye can see. We press on as there's a wonderful beach area here for those with enough perseverance to find it. We've been before, so we know it's here, but there's a lot of Roquetas del Mar to get through on the way.

We're late for lunch, Valentines Day or not, but meal times in Spain are a movable feast, literally, and everywhere along the promenade is open. There's one beachfront restaurant advertising a Valentines Day lunch for 'only' 37.50 euros. It's empty and judging by the waiters' bored expressions has been empty all day.

We jump into the only spare seats at the place next door which is packed.

We've been here before and the waiter recognises us, always nice, and serves up a couple of tapas even before we order a drink which is even nicer.

We munch away and decide to stick with tapas. 1.50 euros each and big portions. We order another four (no, not four each) and share a lovely meal in the sunshine looking out at a blue sea and a cloudless sky.

Perfect Valentines Day lunch? Well, we think so, but we're in a minority on this terrace. Every other group of diners here is having a 'domestic.' The Germans next to us – three couples - are all dressed up and have ordered huge amounts of food and several bottles of wine between them. They're at each others' throats – I blame the wine – with the respective couples only stopping their arguments to temporarily join forces in an attack on their 'friends.'

Of course, we're loving it. Our waiter comes to our table, winks at us and says 'everybody happy here?' We laugh with him and he dashes off as further along the terrace a chair is over-turned and a fresh commotion breaks out.

'Aren't we a boring pair?' Marigold whispers. No need to whisper really, it's bedlam here. Even the 'lookie-lookie men are turning back and avoiding the area.

It all settles down, eventually. The Germans next to us start singing, badly but very loudly, arm in arm, their differences now apparently forgotten and we decide we need to leave. Riotous alcohol fuelled argument is fine as a spectator sport, but alcohol fuelled singing is quite a different matter.

'Time to go, Zebedee,' says Marigold.

Film locations, a Beatle, Picasso, exotic architecture and Game of Thrones. Busy Day!

G Says...

I read recently there are 17 kilometres of coastline in Carboneras, and as we drove down the hill towards the town with the long abandoned hotel on the left we reached the first of many beaches, that of Playa Los Algarrobicos. Latterly, this has become merely the foreground to 'that' hotel, or more accurately, putative hotel, that has blighted the landscape since the denial and then withdrawal of planning permission left a building site as its legacy.

Before the ill fated project even began, this beach was seen by millions throughout the world as it was one of the settings for the film Lawrence of Arabia.

One of the most spectacular scenes in the film was an attack on the city of Aqaba which was reconstructed on Algarrobico beach as it would have looked back in 1917. This was quite a task, involved the building of over 300 buildings and employed more than 200 local people over a period of three months. Four huge cannon were installed and they also built a Turkish military camp with more than 70 tents. Best of all, most of the residents of Carboneras were engaged as 'extras' and able to boast of being part of a major Hollywood blockbuster.

Unsurprisingly, nothing remains of 'Aquaba,' but if the film producers wanted to build their set in this spot today, they'd first have to demolish and remove any trace of the abandoned 'hotel' which now dominates the end of the beach. Maybe they should have kept the cannons in situ.

There's a statue of a robed 'Lawrence' in the town which we've admired on previous visits, but today our attention turned to an equally legendary figure of more recent vintage as we came across a mural commemorating the association of John Lennon with Carboneras. In fairness, the association is on the minimalist/tenuous spectrum as the former Beatle's stay in the area was scarcely extensive, but, come on, this is John Lennon we're talking about and Spain's largest Beatles-themed mural is right here, in Carboneras.

Lennon had described himself as being 'at a loose end' after the Beatles decided their touring days were over in 1966. The final break up of the band was four years in the future, but John Lennon was then only in his mid twenties and perhaps viewing an uncertain future out of the public eye, so he took himself off to Almeria for seven weeks to make a film, How I Won the War. The Director was Dick Lester who had directed the Beatles' films and offered John the part of Private Gripweed, a fairly minor character who serves as Batman – no, not 'that' Batman – to an officer played by the film's main star, Michael Crawford.

During his stay in the region, John Lennon wrote 'Strawberry Fields Forever,' and gave a rare interview to the press, seated on a beach in Carboneras. Strawberry Fields has stood the test of time, but Carboneras has made a big effort to ensure the visit of a Beatle hasn't been forgotten either. The 50th anniversary of that visit was wildly celebrated in Carboneras, as was the 50th anniversary of the filming of Lawrence of Arabia, and the mural itself is pretty impressive. I read that magazine interview, however, and John Lennon wasn't exactly thrilled to be in Carboneras. The location was intended to mimic North Africa, but the great man himself was far from enthralled by a desert landscape and the relentless heat. This was in September too, so just as well they weren't filming a month or two earlier!

There's a John Lennon statue in Almeria which we saw recently. There were a constant stream of people waiting their turn to take a photo next to John Lennon. The Beatles broke up 48 years ago and it's almost 40 years since John Lennon was killed, so the majority of those surrounding his statue weren't even born when Lennon was killed. A poignant moment for me too. I saw the Beatles play 'live' many times even before Love me Do hit the record stores in 1962 and John Lennon was even then the heart and soul of the group.

As for Strawberry Fields, the song was inspired by a Gothic-style mansion in Liverpool which had been converted to a Salvation Army children's' home. It's long gone now, but those bright red gates remain a place of pilgrimage for Beatles fans.

John Lennon apparently used to play as a child in the grounds of Strawberry Fields, but I only remember it for the annual party the Home put on for the children of Liverpool in Calderstones Park. I'm sure John Lennon would have attended these too, but I'm less sure whether me and my friends 'gatecrashed' the event as I'm sure we didn't get invitations. Maybe John Lennon was a gatecrasher as well.

A short distance away, approaching the port area of the town, is another remarkable mural which serves as homage to Pablo Picasso. We sat on one of the benches, studying each individual section of an extensive mural and could have stayed much longer, but we had much more to do today.

I do like high quality 'street art,' as distinct from 'graffiti,' but architecture has been a 'fascination' of mine - less than a passion but more than just an interest - for many years and I especially like boldness and originality of design. When we lived in France, a few years back, We came across a house, by chance, and I've never forgotten it. 'Position, position, position' is the oft repeated mantra of estate agents and that house was sited next to the lighthouse on Cap D'Antibes, arguably the most desirable area of the entire French Riviera.

Perfection of location brings its own pressures and the house that Claude Parent built to the exact specifications of his fellow architect, friend and mentor André Bloc as Bloc's summer home back in 1966 was unique. It has produced many imitators, but when we saw this house for the first time in 1971 it took my breath away, and still does. Built to make the most of one of the world's most enviable vistas it was an architectural triumph.

I never expected to find another Claude Parent/André Bloc house almost on our doorstep, but their experiment in shape and form, a melange of architecture and sculpture, sits on a hillside in Carboneras. Again, it was built as a holiday retreat for André Bloc and was termed 'The Labyrinth' for its bizarre layout. In fairness, I'd rather live in the house at Cap D'Antibes as the 'Labyrinth' is more of a sculpture than a house, but art doesn't have to conform to perceptions of normality. The man who founded Architecture Today while still a young rebel was never going to build 'just' a house, was he?

We carried on, through the industrial areas and to the top of the hill overlooking Carboneras with one destination in mind. Our second visit to the Beach of the Dead in a couple of weeks and we chose the perfect day for it. We even found an easier way down. It turns out there are two paths, one we already knew about from the viewpoint overlooking the beach and the other, much easier, route from the car park which we parked right next to on this occasion.

Last time we risked life, limb and stubbed toes, but today's newly discovered route was significantly easier. Not 'easy,' but not the 'never doing that again, ever' trek through a lunar landscape we'd previously experienced. We scrabbled down, complaints being just a necessary part of the routine, no toes were stubbed, scarcely any blood was shed, (only mine, not Marigold's, so insignificant) and eventually reached sea level.

The only delay was when one of Marigold's ear rings, one of a favourite pair, fell off into a bushy group of yellow flowers. I scrabbled around, squatting uncomfortably on a stony pathway, for what seemed like hours before they were found and returned to their anxious owner. Is Superglue a viable solution to prevent ear rings becoming detached?

The couple we'd glimpsed from far above were now nowhere to be seen. Did they drown, bury themselves in the sand? Who knows? We were in sole possession of this magnificent beach, the sun was shining, the blue sea sparkled and we'd entered a world of silence interrupted only by the soft whisper of tiny waves lapping the shore.

Marigold turned and waved to the group of tiny people on the viewpoint far above. One may have even waved back, but I imagine most were simply seething with jealousy. We were down here, experiencing this glorious setting and they were mere observers. Yes, maybe I shouldn't allocate my own inadequate personality to others, but that's easier said than done.

We followed the footsteps of the only people who'd crossed this stretch of sand today. They grew less and less defined until they faded away completely.

'Spooky,' I said.

Marigold looked out to sea. 'No sharks,' she said.

'Well, not now, but...'

We gave up on the vanishing footsteps and walked from one end of the beach, a glorious half mile or so, to the other with one foot in the sea and the other on dry land. This activity has both mystical and healing powers.

No, it doesn't.

It's hard to imagine a beach anywhere where the water is so clear and so blue. It's pretty steeply sloping so in a heavy sea with strong breakers bathing may be hazardous, but today the surface is flat calm and we're only paddling anyway.

As we were climbing back up the track which appeared to have steepened in the last hour, we caught a glimpse of the missing couple, almost but not quite hidden amongst some scrubby bushes and very obviously involved in matters with a distinct possibility of becoming rather more unbecoming. We averted our eyes and moved swiftly, well as swiftly as possible, onwards and upwards. 'Wise to wait until they were almost at the top of the hill,' I said, puffing with exertion.

A couple, no longer in the first flush of youth, albeit younger than us, were about to set off down the path. English, obviously, but dressed as if for Ascot not a beach located down a dusty and uneven track and bedecked with the appurtenances of an overland to India expedition. They were perhaps best described as the secretary of the WI and a Methodist lay preacher respectively.

'Is it worth it?' The woman asked Marigold.

'Oh, yes, well worth it. The beach is lovely, but you need to keep your eyes open on the way down as there's lots to see.'

Off they went, taking a route that would take them within a couple of yards of the amorous couple. We were tempted to hang around, but didn't.

'Should have warned them,' Marigold said.

'Yes, we should.'

We drove off instead, heading for Torre de Mesa Roldan, a fortress originally intended as an artillery watchtower perched high up on Mesa Roldan, actually an extinct volcano. The fortress was built in 1766 and hasn't been well cared for at all. There's a lighthouse up here too, but it's to the fort we are headed. It's one of those buildings where the planners were on a different page to the builders as although it was built to house a couple of large cannon on the roof, it proved massively not fit for purpose. The location, a pretty significant aspect of the design, meant the planned cannon were far too far away to be able to fire on any sea attack, which was the sole reason for building the fort.

Useless planning then and even though it was pressed into use as a lighthouse even that secondary facility was superseded when a replacement lighthouse, in a far better position, was constructed.

It's been abandoned for a while and it shows, but even great lumps of crumbling stone in remote locations have their uses and it's for this reason we've come here today. Immediately, we look at each other, nodding in recognition as this abandoned fort was used as a filming location for Game of Thrones. We've been to a fair few of these locations by now, the last one being the ancient Roman bridge in Cordoba regenerated as the Long Bridge of Volantis, and recognise this site on a hill above Carboneras as the fortification in Meereen where Daenerys (Khaleesi) arrives with her army of Unsullied soldiers.

There's just us here today, no sign of Daenerys, not even Grey Worm, but we can still imagine their presence. Next, we're keeping up the theme of film locations and heading just a few miles up the coast, but that will have to wait until the next posting.

If you want a hint, try Sexy Beast. That's a film title, not a description of Marigold or myself. Oh, hang on though…

Sexy Beast in Agua Amarga and onwards to Cabo de Gata.

G Says...

Marigold asked me to tell you she'll be back writing again very soon after her somewhat prolonged absence. By absence, I mean in her capacity as scribe as in every other way her presence enlightens and gives purpose to our various excursions.

Today, we're not travelling far from our base in terms of distance, but in every other respect we're bound for a different world. We're visiting the Cabo de Gata National Park once again. One of our favourite places for a day trip, as distinct from visits farther afield.

Agua Amarga means bitter water in Spanish, not the most attractive name for such a little gem. Why a gem? Well, Agua Amarga is a small fishing village, there's just a few rows of simple white-washed houses hugging the shore and not much else, right on the edge of Cabo de Gata nature reserve. There's a delightful, sandy beach, about half a mile or so, end to end, sheltered by cliffs and today the sun is glistening on the almost transparent waters of a turquoise sea.

In our recent US Road Trip we spent a few weeks meandering down the Pacific coastline between San Francisco and San Diego. Close to Los Angeles we were advised to take a detour to view a little known surfing beach at a point where Agua Amarga Canyon meets the sea. The California version is pretty much just scrubland, part of a significant nature reserve and I remember it very well, not just because the name was familiar but also because of the plethora of signs triumphantly announcing the saving of the endangered Californian gnatcatcher from extinction. We never saw a single one!

Agua Amarga, the Spanish version, has been described as one of the last hidden paradises in Europe and that's born out on this day in early March as we're the only people walking on the beach, none of the (very) few shops or restaurants are open and the only signs of life we see are around the dozen or so motor homes parked on a scruffy piece of land at the edge of the village.

We came to Agua Amarga today, not for beach bars or a vibrant café scene, but to look at a house. No chance of anything vibrant here, even in summer this quiet backwater is no rival to Marbella and is all the better for it. The house we seek was the setting for one of the best British films of its era, Sexy Beast. Not at all suitable for those of a delicate nature it starred Ray Winstone, Ben Kingsley and Ian McShane.

I read an article about Ray Winstone where he waxes lyrical about this simple fishing village. 'It's the genuine article, it restored my faith in Spain,' he said, having no idea such an unspoilt spot still existed on the Spanish coast. We've come across many unspoilt seaside places on our travels, but this is certainly idyllic on such a lovely day.

Palm House has sea views which made it ideal as a filming location. There's an apartment under the main house which the owners rent out to holiday makers and it's safe to assume the Sexy Beast history is quite an inducement. We can't get inside or wander around, obviously, but we recreate the sea views the film audience saw with a little ingenuity and a fair bit of scrambling.

The film dates back to the year 2000 and Ray Winstone played a former safe-cracker now living in retirement on what is portrayed as being the 'costa del crime.' Ben Kingsley's character tries to recruit him for a final 'job' and it is his performance as a manic sociopath that dominates the film and earned him an Academy Award nomination for Best Supporting Actor. This isn't anything like his portrayal of Gandhi. There's a scene in which he speaks to camera, while facing a mirror, all shaven headed malevolence, and Kingsley said he forgot his lines when he saw his own rage - contorted face staring back at him!

No chance of finding a restaurant open around here, so we move down the coast to one of our favourite places: Las Negras, deep inside the gloriously unspoilt nature reserve of Cabo de Gata. We've explored great cities and marvelled at their scope and diversity, but it's in the wild places we find our greatest pleasure. High mountain ranges, snowy peaks and crystal clear lakes, forests and deserted shores, we love them and continually seek them out, but best of all, by far, are desert landscapes. We've traveled through the ever changing sand dunes of the vast Sahara, explored the weird rock formations of Nevada and Utah and been delighted by the absolute silence, the sheer tranquility and sense of majesty that every step, every turn of the wheel brings in a desert.

Cabo de Gata 'ain't the Sahara, but its climate is practically unique in Europe; as arid as North Africa due to minimal annual rainfall and more sunshine than just about anywhere on this side of the Mediterranean. We come here often and are never disappointed. Yes, there are areas on the outskirts where the plastic greenhouses providing fruit and vegetables our culture demands to be available all year round hold sway, but almost all the rest is a virtual wilderness. There are some fine beaches on the coast, their purity sustained by difficulty of access or simply by being well off the tourism trail, but Las Negras doesn't have a great beach. What it does have is a superb setting where we drop down from the surrounding hills towards a beautiful little bay where the water lapping gently at the shore is often the only sound you hear.

We park up and walk down to the beach front only to find our favourite eating spot on the beach is closed for renovations. Not to worry, we go next door and get the last table on the terrace.

The beach here is mostly pebbles, but it's still a great place to sit down with a cool drink, look out to sea and find peace. The clear blue sea sparkles, the cliffs over to the left are strikingly attractive in this clear light and the sun brings warmth and comfort, even as the rest of Europe freezes in the icy grip of yet another cold spell. There are a few fishing boats drawn up on the shore, a couple of men mending nets and the boats waiting to take the 'day tripper' hippies back to Cala San Pedro Beach, a small cove, almost completely isolated and reached only by boat, unless you fancy an exceedingly strenuous hike across the headland over very rough terrain. We've never tried the overland route, but were invited to go there by boat once and we loved it. There's a fresh water supply from a steam, a few ramshackle 'houses' and not much else.

The small colony who live there year round pop across to Las Negras for supplies or, as was the case today, to obtain a dozen or so wooden pallets to extend one of their shacks. The tiny boat set off with one lad balanced precariously on top of the stacked pallets after arranging to return to collect the two dreadlocked men and their scruffy dog who we seem to meet almost every time we come here. Their cheery response suggests they were not particularly keen on boarding the already overloaded boat anyway.

As we sip our drinks a fat man in a very tightly stretched wet suit comes ashore, carrying a spear gun in one hand and two, maybe three it's hard to tell, octopuses in the other. The water here is crystal clear and is a divers' paradise, perfect for spear fishing.

Marigold takes issue with 'octopuses,' championing 'octopi,' but I'm sticking to my guns, for now. Resisting any rash accusations of being an awkward doryphore, I decide that a little research is in order. It's clear Marigold isn't wrong, heaven forbid, as octopi is certainly in common usage, but the word octopus is derived from Greek not Latin and hence the plural version should surely be 'octopodes.' Which both looks and sounds ridiculous.

As for 'octopi,' however, the word grates, with me. The plural of hippopotamus, in my view, is hippopotamuses. Even my annoying and significantly more pedantic predictive text 'assistant' bears the word no malice, yet it dislikes hippopotami. Language is variable, isn't it? We, mostly, say 'termini,' not terminuses,' and yet say 'syllabuses,' not 'syllabi.'

Marigold just said I should write 'he was carrying an octopus and he also had another one or two of them as well.' Such a sensible woman, or more likely she has had enough of my nonsense for one morning .

We're sitting, watching the boats, admiring the peaceful waterfront, when we hear a regrettably familiar voice boom out behind us and both of us enter panic mode.

'Edgar,' Marigold says, and Edgar it is indeed.

We travel a lot. Visit places, countries, we've never been before, where we know not a soul and most of the time it's great. We're happy enough in our own company, a self contained unit, tried and trusted, but our life style inevitably brings us into contact with total strangers. This interaction can be invigorating, enlightening and very occasionally leave in its wake memories that last for years. We can both vividly remember strangers we met for a few brief hours many years ago who remain with us in spirit. Comparisons are made, fleeting moments recalled, oddities fondly called to mind. Meeting other people is surely one of the greatest joys of travel.

Life has to be balanced and I'm still barely recovering from our exposure to a group we met by chance about a week ago. I asked Marigold if she could summarise them in a few words. She just needed the one.

'Prats,' she said.

We met Edgar in the lobby of the Parador Hotel in Mojacar as we were meeting friends who were passing through. Paradors are pretty swish, usually, but we've stayed at a few in our time and so can confirm they'll let anyone in! The appalling Edgar was a hotel guest, but we were merely waiting for our friends to get changed into their glad rags, as they put it. No idea why as they were only going out with us.

Throughly 'English', resolutely and unmistakably middle class, tall, stout and overbearing, he sauntered over, the heels of his sturdy brogues clopping on the tiled floor and introduced himself in orotund tones that must have been audible at the far side of the car park.

'Edgar,' he boomed, shaking my hand vigorously and favouring Marigold with a rictus smile while raising the brim of a non existent hat. 'On our own, are we?'

Well, no, we're sitting next to each other on a sofa, reading books and minding our own business, but of course we don't say any of that. I half stand, shake his hand and try desperately to prevent a feeling of dread from showing on my face. Marigold looks stricken, but fortunately by now Edgar seems to have forgotten she exists.

I'm half expecting Marigold to come out with the Glenn Close speech from Basic Instinct; the 'I'm not going to be ignored' outburst, but she seems happy enough to find Edgar's attention fixed solely on me.

He hitches up his trousers, hideously red corduroy and high waisted, to preserve their immaculate creases and sits down, heavily, next to me. We've commandeered a leather sofa, technically a three seater but vastly more comfortable for just the two of us. Edgar's arrival – he's very broad in the beam – removes all aspects of comfort at a stroke.

Edgar didn't seem to regard conversation as being any substitute for a monologue. Marigold returned to her book, now obviously happy enough to be ignored, while our new acquaintance lectured me in a ceaseless torrent of magniloquent speech, every word boomed out at full volume.

Finally, he stopped talking, in mid sentence, leapt to his feet and rushed out. Marigold burst out laughing.

'What did you say?' She asked, 'whatever it was, it worked.'

'Nothing. I never even got a word in,' I reply and we settle back with our books.

'Goodbye Edgar,' Marigold says. Peace is restored.

Five minutes later the doors open and in walked Edgar, this time at the head of a phalanx of people just as awful as himself. Two other men, one of them wearing identical red trousers to those adorning Edgar's lower half, and two women who look like sisters. I want to say ugly sisters, but that'd be facile as although it's fair comment, it's unfair. No one can help what they look like, but this pair are talking, very loudly with much arm waving and the subject of their conversation is their perception of Spain, Spanish people, Spanish food and, especially, the Spanish check-in staff at the front desk. It's not remotely complimentary. In fact, it's a philippic denunciation of just about everything related to the country in which we and they are guests.

We remember the courteous manner of both the girls on the reception desk, the attention they paid us, their smiles of welcome and their ability to speak English, not fluently but well enough to put our own command of their language to shame . We're also aware they can hear every word these two harpies are saying.

'Surely they should all have to learn to speak English properly to work in a hotel,' one of the women is saying, loudly, 'I mean, how many people speak Spanish compared to all the countries that speak English?'

Marigold nudges me as she can see how tempted I am to get involved. I keep quiet, for once, and, quietly look something up on the free Wi-fi this excellent hotel provides, for free, even to transient visitors like us.

'Approximately 470 million people in the world speak Spanish as their first or native language', I whisper to Marigold.

'Quite a few, then.'

'Only about 360 million people speak English as their first language while Chinese is the language with most native speakers.'

We find comfort in this vindication of what we'd already surmised, but this air of satisfaction brings scant respite.

Hector joins in, his braying voice probably audible up in the Old Town two miles away and we share a resigned glance, put away our books and leave, swiftly.

I leave a message at the desk for our friends to meet us at a local café and say 'sorry' to the receptionist, nodding my head at the noisy quintet in the lobby. She grins, says a word in Spanish I don't recognise (maybe it means 'prats') and giggles. They must meet a fair number of people like Edgar in their line of work. Shamefully, I imagine a fair few few of the worst offenders will be Brits.

We thought we'd seen and heard the last of Edgar, yet here he is, spoiling our peaceful interlude. Once more, we gathered our belongings, girded our loins and vamoosed.

We hadn't ordered a meal, just had drinks, in any case as there's smoke coming out from the kitchen and the staff are harassed, so when we get back on home turf we're starving. We go to a beach restaurant specialising in fish and Marigold's initial order of Sea Bream has to be changed to another fish, the name of which escapes both of us.

The fish arrives, only one side (half) of a fish actually, accompanied by four asparagus (asparagi? oh, behave) and that's it. We get a chunk of bread between us too, but when the bill arrives we find there is an added charge for this 'extra' as well. I had ordered pork loin, invariably excellent in Spain, and it was tasteless and anaemic. The bill is deflating, the food disappointing and we grumble about it for the rest of the day. Shame as we'd had a great time until then.

We drive past the motor homes parked nearby, five less than when we left this morning, and say hello in passing their apartment to the long term rental couple from Halifax who are recently retired and enjoying their first ever trip abroad. They're always on their terrace, don't have a car and obviously have no intention of moving from their apartment apart from shopping trips for food.

'Been off out again, 'ave yer?' the man says in ripe Yorkshire tones, his skin by now having moved on from lobster pink to a rich vermilion.

'Yes, had a lovely day.'

He shakes his head. 'Wouldn't do us at all, that gadding about.' His wife nods in agreement.

I could offer up a favourite quotation from Rumi, the 13th-century Persian Sunni Muslim poet and Sufi mystic who is in any case probably not that well known in Halifax - 'You were born with wings, why prefer to crawl through life?'

But I don't. Each to his own. They enjoy basking on the terrace, we like to explore. Fair enough. Takes all sorts, as they definitely do say in Halifax.

An infestation of motorhomes.

G Says...

Not been out and about much lately. Marigold fans rejoice, she's in fine fettle, but, sadly (for me at least) the same cannot be said for your ailing correspondent. On the mend now, so Marigold has cancelled the trip to Exit in Switzerland she'd kindly arranged on my behalf. She's absolutely right, of course, she's just not cut out to be Florence Nightingale.

One (dubious) advantage of being marooned locally has been we didn't miss the greatest controversy since Brexit – the invasion of the sea view snatchers!

There have been an unusually high number of motorhomes spotted along the shore where we're based recently. Hard to miss them, over sixty at one stage and that's just along the sea front. 'An infestation' one woman said in the middle of a rant about her perception of these winter visitors as being vile despoilers of the landscape, occupiers of prime positions directly on the sea front, rampant polluters of the environment and harbingers of the end of civilisation. If you imagine that last concern is an over exaggeration, just wait until they drop the word 'pikey' into the mix and see the difference in attitudes and perceptions.

I should at this point declare an interest as they say in Parliament. We were members of the transient motor home community for many years and the experience afforded us much joy.

I'm differentiating between transient and fixed motor home residents; the former wander at will (like us) and the latter park up on a site and remain there for months on end (not like us). Both have their adherents, but as the vast camping grounds around Benidorm, for example, are filled to capacity year round, almost exclusively with 'long stay' residents it appears the 'wanderers' are in the minority.

Three weeks ago that minority status looked unlikely around here after an influx of fresh seasonal visitors. They've gone now, all bar a few stragglers, and all those spurious claims of impending Armageddon have proved groundless. They arrive, park up to enjoy exactly what drew the permanent or long term residents to this area and then move on. 'Moving on' being the entire ethos of the motor home community, its *raison d'etre.*

Even so, the recent 'infestation' has been unusual. All crammed together along the sea front with scarcely room to walk between neighbouring vans, all gleaming white with all mod cons included vans each costing a minimum of £50,000 and several having cost a great deal more than any of the front line neighbouring apartments sharing their view.

As former motor homers, we don't 'get' this. Gathering together in a 'clump' appears to me to impinge on one's personal sense of space and liberty; thereby nullifying at a stroke the reason we enjoyed the life so much. This isn't a rally, not even a convivial group of fellow nationals, there are motor homes there from Britain, France, Holland, Germany and many other countries. Don't expect an answer, I don't have one.

They all left, within twenty four hours, leaving only the usual sprinkle of seasonal visitors who routinely arrive, stay a day or so and move on. 'Our' type of motor - homer.

One of the 'remainers,' – not a Brexit reference – was an artist from Holland living in a garishly painted van with his easels and artists' paraphernalia strapped to the back. One of those eccentric travellers who brighten our day, he also had a tiny dog on a lead that bore more of a resemblance to a gerbil than a dog. No need for a muzzle anyway. He told me he had moved from the edge of a 'clump,' (my word not his as I can't translate the Dutch word he used) as a fresh arrival had brought their number to thirteen. It seems triskaidekaphobia* is rampant in Holland.

*No, I don't often, or ever actually, speak this word in conversation, but I like it as a word and write it when the occasion arises.

The woman who coined the 'infestation' description had first attracted our attention by talking about a funeral she'd recently attended. Such fun! It's odd, isn't it, how many people enjoy a funeral. In fairness, it's the wake not the actual internment they recall with such fondness, but even so. An example of this person's twisted logic could be inferred from her saying, 'I always make an effort to go to people's funerals, otherwise they won't come to yours, will they?' Well, no they won't. Being dead renders one pretty damn antisocial.

The remark isn't original, I've heard it before, but there's no shortage of folk who make the use of bizarre logic a foundation of their lives.

We were out and about in the Cabo de Gata National Park recently and found many examples of 'our' sort of motor-homer. No gleaming white behemoths, no fancy airs and graces, just a place to sit, wash (ideally), do basic cookery and sleep while retaining the ability to move on the next day with a bare minimum of fuss.

We've recently visited the US and our former vans, or anything like them, were nowhere to be seen. In the US of A, bigger is undeniably better and some of the Recreational Vehicles, RVs as they're ubiquitously called, were very big indeed. Many Americans retire, sell up and take to the road in an RV, criss crossing that vast continent as the mood takes them. Good for them! Must be better than sitting vegetating in a lay-zee-boy armchair in front of the television until it's time to rustle up the next meal. Not that the RV fraternity miss out on TV or, indeed, their habitually gargantuan meals. We were invited inside a couple of RVs and the flat screen televisions were bolted to the walls by massive carriage bolts while the 'snacks' we were offered would have fed a family of four for a week.

We toured New Zealand by camper van, a vehicle far too puny to rate even being called a motor home and loved every minute. We're not envious folk, but the converted buses, usually but not always of the single deck variety, really took our breath away. There seem to be thousands of them in New Zealand and Australia and we love them. Both countries are 'motor home friendly,' but this isn't the case elsewhere. France welcomes motor homes, providing hundreds of *'aires'* where you can stay overnight, either free or for a nominal fee. The British, however, are deeply suspicious of campers in vans outside their prescribed habitat of official campsites, fearing they will be robbed, attacked or forced to buy lucky heather at the first sight of a van in the locality. Spain we'd always found to be reasonably tolerant, but evidently there is a 'tipping point.'

In the Cabo de Gata there are many hidden coves the tourists hardly ever seem to find. Pristine beaches, sand dunes, sparkling clear water and all hidden away. Hidden from everyone but the motor home brigade. The big tyres help as there's no real 'road' to the best places, but as we know very well, 'van dwellers' are happy to share their finds with others.

The un-named beach we walked along a couple of weeks ago was a case in point. A Dutch couple I had swapped paperback books with a few years back told us about this place. On our first visit we found five motorhomes, no cars, and only three people on the beach. This last visit it was busier. Seven motorhomes, each of the 'cobbled together van conversion' variety, still no cars, other than ours, and a gloriously empty beach. Three Brits, three French and a solo traveller from Lithuania riding around in what looked like a former World War Two vintage ambulance.

We chatted to a French woman, in her mid twenties, who left France three years ago with two children, a husband and a dog and they have been wandering ever since. She plays guitar and sings, her husband is a skilled diesel mechanic and also makes exquisite jewellery – an unlikely combination, but if he's as good a mechanic as he is a silversmith, he'll be sure to find plenty of work on their travels.

Their van is an old lorry with hand cut openings for door and windows; one of the most 'basic' conversions I've ever seen, but it has been to 28 countries, so far. Their children ran around, happy, content and healthy and it would be hard to find a family more content with life. They have so little, but sunshine and freedom are a heady mix.

The delightful French woman struck an exotic pose for a photograph alongside our van, calling out 'sell to Paris Match Magazine.' As I took the photo, another of the 'temporary residents', a Brit from Scunthorpe, called out, 'Eh up, we have a visiting paparazzo' which intrigued me, the singular (and therefore correct) form of the more usual plural version, paparazzi, being heard so rarely in recent times. Evidently, folk hailing from Scunthorpe are sticklers for correct grammar.

In fairness, the word paparazzi has been so widely used it has been unofficially adopted as a plurale tantum.

A plurale tantum being a noun used only in its plural form such as scissors, jeans, trousers is common enough, but I did over hear a shop assistant in a rather smart clothes shop in Lewes once say to a customer, that's a very smart trouser, sir,' thus defeating the whole point at issue as he was surely not intending to sell only one leg of a pair of trousers!

Later that same day we were in Los Negros and came across a bizarre mixture of vehicles on waste ground just behind a deserted beach. I'm at a loss to describe such a confused mixture of styles – a Gallimaufry perhaps - but all serving the same purpose: a means of containing the absolute essentials of life, and virtually nothing else, in one small space and then giving it the priceless freedom of mobility. No big flat screen televisions here.

Every day we take 24,000 breaths and waste most of them in useless pursuits. We all do it. Some choose to live life to the full, in absolute simplicity. These van dwellers don't have anything the Western World regards as desirable. Yet they appear happy and they certainly look healthy living an outdoor life. Food for thought.

Yes, I know I do get occasional flashbacks to my lapsed hippie past.

I'm not a Buddhist or a Hindu, but can appreciate the spirituality of this quotation from Guru Arden.

'After many lives as insects and worms and many more lives as elephants, fish and deer, after many lives as snakes or birds, and then as trees for lives unnumbered; after countless ages you are graced with a human life.'

What he leaves unsaid must surely be 'don't waste it.'

Untitled*

***No idea why.**

Marigold Says...

Seem to have been packing the car for ages ready for the off. Moving on. Again. I said to G I know that space is limited but this is ridiculous, vans are much better than cars. He replies in a rather sarcastic manner that we could always send everything ahead in a shipping container and seemed to find this very funny. Anyway, have got round it by sneaking things in when he is not looking. Got a bit worried when he said he was going to empty it and re-pack. Luckily, that never happened.

The journey to Peniscola was brill. Hotel, which included breakfast and evening meal was a bargain. The (included) evening meal was a fab buffet and I got so excited I ran in. There was no need to really as we were the first in at 8 o'clock. The Spanish don't eat till 10. Filled our faces nicely and didn't over indulge.

Journey to Begur was a different matter, rain, rain, rain. We went through a toll booth and I dropped the change and got peeped at by the man behind. Very stressed by this point so went to sleep to recover.

The sat nav didn't recognise any hotels in Begur, so we blundered round and passed the same tramp three times, in fact he waved at us. Then the hotel we wanted was there suddenly in front of us. I ran down in the rain and a cleaner let me in and shouted "Mercedes, No Inglese." I said we haven't got a Mercedes, but she was just telling me her name and saying she didn't speak English. I told her my name, in Spanish and said I spoke a little Spanish. She told me, again, she didn't speak English which was a bit much as I thought I had been speaking Spanish. G turned up from parking the car and Mercedes understood every word he said. Very annoying!

Hotel just lovely, very old with stone walls and domed ceilings and a lovely bedroom. Shame we can't explore the town as it's still raining hard, but hopefully tomorrow I can spend the change I had dropped.

No evening meal, so banana sandwiches with squashed bread. Good job we like this as an emergency feast.

G Says...

I know this is a short piece, but it's raining outside, we're prevented from doing what we want to do and we're both a bit grumpy.

We were sitting on a rather nice bench, looking out across the sea towards the majestic castle at Peniscola when a woman walking an elderly collie dog appeared. They've both wrapped up as if in readiness for the next Ice Age.

'She'll be English,' I say, gloomily, 'what's the betting she wants to sit here?'

'And talk,' contributed Marigold. Thirty seconds later, we're both proved right. It's not a very big bench and there are several others in sight, but it's 'our' bench she chooses to rest upon.

Our bench sharer starts by asking us, in woeful Spanish, if we've seen a woman wearing a red hat go by. We haven't and I, foolishly, say so, in English.

'Ooh, more Brits, that's good. So many here now, used to be all French, but that wretched Game of Thingies brought a lot more Brits here.' Game of Thrones is, indeed, filmed here, the castle being an important setting for the narrative. Peniscola becomes the city of Meeren, for the purposes of television at least, and I imagine the people living in the five hundred or so houses that surround the castle will have strong opinions, for or against, the excitement and disruption that a major film crew brings. I imagine the many hotels will be happy though.

'We're just here for the day,' Marigold says and the woman and her dog adopt the same sad expression at this news.

'Are you comfy, Brucie?'

The woman sitting next to us had abandoned conversation for a bout of fussing over her dog's outerwear as the sad looking collie was wearing the canine version of a Christmas jumper, a sort of onesie with four leg holes which no self respecting dog would want to wear, even if it was a present.

'I'm Joyce and this little chap is Brucie,' the woman said. 'I named him after Bruce Forsyth because his nose is so long and pointed.'

I somehow refrained from pointing out the late Mister Forsyth was best remembered for having a long, pointed chin, not a nose with the same attributes. Brucie, the collie, didn't seem to mind what his name was.

'Me and my dog both suffer from the same complaint,' she said. 'Have a guess. Go on.'

I didn't say 'distemper,' but I wanted to. As our new friend's attention was focussed on the dog, Marigold whispered 'I was going to say a wet nose but that's healthy, isn't it?'

'For dogs, it is,' I whispered back, 'maybe not so desirable in humans.'

We guessed arthritis, cataracts and another one I've forgotten, all to no avail.

'Brontophobia,' she announced, with some pride. We looked blankly back at her.

'Some people call it astrapophobia.'

Deep in the dark and dusty corners of my brain a faint spark ignited. 'Is that the same as astraphobia, the fear of thunder and lightning?'

The woman's annoyance was evident. Obviously she wanted to prolong this game of twenty questions a little longer.

'Yes,' she reluctantly admitted, ' we're both in therapy.'

Marigold nudged me, quite hard, in the ribs.

'Really?'

'Yes, only I have the normal type and Brucie has the doggy kind.'

'A canine therapist?'

'Yes and he charges me more for Brucie than my therapist charges for me.'

'Is it working?' Asked Marigold, her face the embodiment of serious concern, even though the faint tremor of suppressed laughter was certainly evident to me.

Joyce looked at her askance. 'We won't know until we get a thunderstorm, will we?'

'Oh.'

'I've dreaded them all my life and now I'm waiting for one to happen. Funny, isn't it?' We agreed it was indeed funny and she toddled off with Brucie trotting alongside.

Peñíscola gets its name from the Romans who named it Pene Iscola – almost an island – as it is connected to the shore by only a tiny sliver of land.

The castle that sits atop the 'almost an island' was built on the orders of the Knights Templar in 1294 and until Game of Thrones came calling is best remembered for being the Papal seat of Pope Benedict X111 for twelve years. In 1411, Cardinal Luna had succeeded the first Pope of Avignon, Clement the Seventh and claimed the Papacy. Eager to restore some order to the succession, Rome denied his claim and, no doubt, more than a little miffed by this, the claimant and many cardinals arrived in Peñíscola making the castle the third papal seat in history after Rome and Avignon, thus prolonging what we now call the Western Schism that divided the Roman Catholic Church for many years.

Born Pedro Martinez de Luna the new Pope was mainly known by his family name and the main road through the town is called Papa de Luna. El Papa Luna made the town famous, or for a period infamous and the Luna name is found wherever you turn, together with his family crest, a crescent moon.

We stayed the night in neighbouring Benicarlo, mostly famous for growing artichokes. Both towns share a splendid beach but today is not a day for beaches. We set out for a walk, twice, in bright sunshine only to be driven back indoors by sudden squalls.

We had been planning on staying for a few days in Begur, just over the border from France, as the Costa Brava is delightful and Begur is a great base for touring the area. The glorious bays of Sa Tuna and Aqua Blava, the sheer luxury of Empuriabrava, all will be denied to us. We used to come to this area for 'days out' back when we lived just across the border in France and we stayed a few times in a glorious waterfront villa in Empuriabrava where there are over fifteen miles of navigable waterways which make it the largest residential marina in Europe. It's very posh, very luxurious and a reminder of times gone by when we had rich friends! Sadly, that particular friend sold up, moved to Florida and died within a week of his arrival.

Once again, forward planning is revealed to be a flawed concept as the weather is vile. We're not used to this, we wail, and it's true, we've not seen rain of any significance for many months. Well, it's here now and Begur is not only storm lashed but shrouded in thick mist. Our hotel is superb though and we rest our grumpy bodies in armchairs, reading our Kindles and looking in vain for a ray of sunshine. Oh well, there's always tomorrow.

Life's too short for Titles.

Marigold Says...

It's me today, how lucky are you? Our lovely hotel in Begur made up for yesterday's vile weather. Liberated some gorgeous brown crunchy bread from the breakfast bar which will be ok later with a banana for G and two yoghurts. There was a machine that you cook your eggs in. Thought he could have one and hack it about as he's, temporarily we hope, stuck with a restricted diet and one of the many things he can't eat for a bit is egg yolk, but egg white is okay.

Plopped egg in said machine, but I plopped it in from a bit too great a height, not keen on getting close to boiling water part, and it sent white of egg stringing in the water, so walked away from that one. 5 minutes later there was a kerfuffle as they were all trying to sort it out and carry the container of boiling water away. I sat there looking eggless but innocent. I have got a real phobia about machinery. I shouted yesterday as we stopped at the tolls, "oh my god there is nowhere to tell you what to do, or where to put the money in". Then the woman opened the hatch and said "bonjour," waiting for the dosh. I am not meant for the open road.

Into France now, en route to England.

G said if the weather was okay this morning we should go to the Puy de Dome, the volcanic peaks that are a feature of the countryside up the hill from Clermont-Ferrand. We went past the Michelin factory which is huge and very 'industrial.' Bet the workers need a good wash when they get home after working there all day.

There's a visitors' centre as well where I suppose they just show you around the clean parts and talk about tyres. It didn't seem to me to be be a 'must see' place at all so now we still don't know everything there is to know about tyres. I have enough trouble with the things when G stops at a garage to check tyre pressures. He does all the fiddly bits, grubbing around taking the dust caps off, which he always moans about as they are always right at the bottom of the wheel. I say, 'don't blame me, you're the driver.' When we set off for this trip we went to a different one where the pumping up is done at the pressure gauge so I had to press a button until it said 33, or 333, something like that while G was holding the hose end next to the tyre.

I'd been pressing the button for ages until G shouted, 'what are you doing, it's nearly flat.' I hadn't realised one of the buttons took air out instead of putting it in. We sorted it out eventually though and G's mood improved after I gave him a wet wipe to clean the black marks off his hands. Aren't wet wipes wonderful?

We got to the Puy place at last. G said it was historic. I said it looked like a slag heap. He then said I am not cultured and I said whoopy doo. There wasn't even a coffee shop. G said, 'there is, but it's up on the top.'

He was just reading from a notice that said something like, 'going to the Puy de Dome and not climbing to the top is like going to Athens and not going to the Parthenon.' Well, we went to the Parthenon and I can still remember all the hundreds of steps we had to climb up so perhaps that wasn't the best incentive.

While we were looking up at the Puy, three young walkers came down the path from the top. They were wearing clumpy hiking boots, about five sweaters each and woolly hats, but were blowing on their hands and were blue with cold. G said, 'must be a bit cold up there,' bit obvious really, and said the car temperature thingie was showing as only three degrees. That's at the bottom of the Puy! I said it must be minus fifty up there and he agreed it may be best to stay in the car. We took a photo and that will have to do. The notice said the track to the top is steep in places and takes an 'experienced walker' about an hour and a half. I'd better not do it then as it will be dark before I get to the top. It also said the volcano was formed in an eruption about ten thousand years ago so I told G we'd better move on sharpish as it was probably due to erupt again by now.

The sun was shiny on the Michelin factory but it still didn't look pretty. We stopped at a motorway services at lunch time and went into the cafe part which was packed with hungry French people, all very agitated as it was ten past twelve and their lunch was overdue! The couple at the next table were having a 'domestic,' but in between the arguments they said 'Merci' when one of them passed the salt or topped up the other's wine glasses. Very polite.

We end the day in Chartres. I always know when Chartres is getting close as the land around is very flat so we see the huge cathedral looking as if it is suspended in air and we don't even see the city around it until we get much closer. We've been inside before – lots and lots of stained glass windows – but we just get close enough to have a good look at it this time from the outside. It was built in the twelfth century, but by the look of it, the builders who added new bits over the years mustn't have thought much of the builders who did the previous job as the two big spires are so mis-matched. One is much bigger than the other, one is very plain, the other is very fancy, maybe they just didn't notice at the time or were afraid if they upset the builder he'd walk off the job!

We're in a cheap chain hotel tonight, a B and B one if you want to know everything, but it is brand new and very nice with a fancy lift and even armchairs in the lobby for those customers who sulk if there isn't anywhere to sit in comfort and read a book. Yes, they do exist and one of them is sitting next to me as I write this! A couple with a screaming baby have just come in. I ask G if he'll go and ask the girl on reception to tell them the hotel is full, but he seems reluctant. When we booked in, in G's very best French, he did it so well the girl must have thought he was either French or completely multi lingual as she started telling him a very long tale in very, very rapid French. G said afterwards he was always three sentences behind and never caught up.

Off to bed now. The bedroom has a mural on the back wall of an open window looking out to the cathedral just down the road. Very realistic.

England tomorrow, going through the Tunnel, and hoping it won't be raining when we get there.

G Says…

One of the highlights of the year for Hastings residents is Pirates Day. Hastings proudly holds the record for most people dressed as pirates in one place, as verified by the Guinness Book of World Records. So what, I hear you say. Trust me, it's pretty damn important in Hastings. Despite attending several Pirates Day events, neither Marigold nor myself ever took the trouble to don piratical attire, so can claim no credit whatsoever, but many thousands do take the trouble and it's a remarkable sight.

We're in Penzance today, of Pirates of Penzance fame, and are keeping our former association with Hastings very much to ourselves. Penzance and Hastings are deadly rivals and the world record has alternated between the two towns for several years.

We park alongside the harbour and sit in the car for a while watching a man struggling to launch a boat on a fast receding tide. The boat is half on water, half on mud and the mud is winning hands down. He wisely gives up, eventually, and clambers ashore leaving muddy footprints all across the car park.

Penzance is one of those towns with a rich variety of shops, confined almost exclusively to just a couple of roads. We walk up the hill, just steep enough to make the building housing Lloyds Bank at the top look even more imposing. There's a statue of one of the town's most famous citizens, Sir Humphrey Davy, in front of the bank.

Humphrey Davy was born in 1778 in Penzance, was apprenticed to a surgeon and aged 19 went to Bristol to study science. In 1800, the Italian scientist Alessandro Volta had introduced the first battery. Davy used this for what we now call electrolysis and was able to isolate a series of substances for the first time - potassium and sodium in 1807 and calcium, strontium, barium and magnesium the following year. Pretty impressive stuff.

In 1815, he received a letter from some Newcastle miners which told of the dangers they faced from methane gas. The gas often filled the mines, and could be sparked off by the candles they had in their helmets to light their work. The resulting fires and explosions caused many deaths. Davy separated the flame from the gas, and his 'Davy' lamp later became widely used.

His assistant, Michael Faraday, went on to establish an even more prestigious reputation than Davy, but Penzance is quite rightly proud of its most famous son.

I have a particular interest in Sir Humphrey Davy, dating back to being a twelve year old boy at school. My best friend's first name was David, shortened to Dave. When chemistry lessons threw up the name of one of Britain's foremost scientists, 'Dave' became 'Davy,' then 'Humphrey' and finally 'Stumpy.' Another friend's given name, Gordon, morphed into Gorgonzola, onwards to 'Cheesy' to which 'Richard' was eventually added. In fact, Richard was not the actual end of the process, being merely the respectable form of his universally used nickname, but that's as far as I'm prepared to go on the subject without using the word 'Dick.'

We wandered around town, met someone we'd not seen for many years and had no idea they now lived in Cornwall and enjoyed an hour's browsing and window shopping. Returning to our car, the harbour by now a sea of mud and stranded boats tilted alarmingly at their moorings, we can't decide whether to turn left to look at the (relatively) newly restored Lido or turn right to St Michael's Mount. In the end, we do both.

We're too early to swim in the Jubilee Pool – it doesn't reopen for the season for a few weeks – but the café is open and we get some idea of its setting and the Art Deco architecture. The original Jubilee Lido, Penzance's 'concrete beach,' dating back to 1935, the 'Jubilee' name commemorating King George V's silver jubilee, was devastated by the massive winter storms of 2014, when freak waves breached the walls, twisted railings, and demolished the changing rooms and terraces. Locals fought many a battle to ensure the lido's survival and their reward is the restoration of what is one of only a handful of saltwater tidal pools left in Europe. It's fully restored now and looks magnificent. We just wish it was open for business.

We've been to St Michael's Mount many times and are well aware of the parking difficulties in the narrow roads close to the causeway approaches. As I dared to pause for a moment, off the road, to consider the limited options for parking, an officious panjandrum wearing a spectacularly ill fitting uniform dashed across and told me I had to 'move along.'

We moved along. The tide is out so access to the Mount would be a pleasant stroll, but we took umbrage at the attitude of the local 'jobsworth' and decided to keep on 'moving along.' St Michael's Mount is a smaller version of Mont St Michel in Normandy, one of our favourite places, and was given to the Norman Abbey of Mont St Michel by Edward the Confessor after the Norman Conquest. I read recently that the Mount featured in the 1979 film Dracula as the exterior of Castle Dracula.

There's well over a thousand years of history there, yet my first thought as we approached had been its connection to the St Aubyn family. The Mount was sold in 1659 to Colonel John St Aubyn whose descendants, the Lords St Levan, retain an ancestral home on St Michael's Mount.

One of my favourite writers, based on writing ability rather than actual content, is Edward St Aubyn whose almost completely autobiographical series of five novels form the basis of the Patrick Melrose television series with Benedict Cumberbatch in the title role. I've just finished reading the books again and they are not an easy read. St Aubyn was repeatedly abused by his father as a child, devoted much of his adult life to the consumption of heroin and cocaine and the novels are both harrowing and brilliant in equal measure. I said to Marigold when I heard about the forthcoming television series, 'I've no idea how they'll film that story, or if it will retain an audience beyond the first episode.' The main character has no obvious redeeming features, his hedonistic lifestyle is utterly repellent, yet credit the author with the courage to expose his weaknesses and bizarre actions to public scrutiny and, above all, the man is a consummately brilliant writer. As a television series though...

We watched the first episode the other night. Cumberbatch makes a fine job of his role, but television cannot possibly convey the full nature of the novels. It's a universal truism that films/television fail to do justice to the original book. I can only think of the first two Godfather films as examples of the written word being adequately represented on screen.

Edward St Aubyn was born in 1960 into a family that has been prominent in Cornwall since the Norman conquest. His cousin is Lord St Levan, whose ancestral home has been St Michael's Mount for hundreds of years, and he is godfather to Earl Spencer's son, Louis. Even for the famously 'posh' Benedict Cumberbatch, the role requires him to play the part of someone with far greater claims to upper class status than himself!

I'm writing this in a café – as I often do - and it's one of the least suited environments to the creative muse that I've ever experienced. Whoever decided the caterwauling that's blaring from the wall hung speakers is conducive to a relaxed atmosphere needs to seek urgent medical attention. I suppose it's jazz, but as background music it's appalling. I think it was the late George Melly who said 'bad' jazz sounded like a fire in a pet shop. Nail on head, George.

Breaking Wind is Nothing Like Breaking Bad.

G Says...

One of our most loyal followers took me to task after a recent offering: the centrepiece of her complaint being, 'this one's a travelogue with scarcely any light relief.'

In mitigation, Shakespeare's genius shines through only 90% of his work – he had his off days - and I'm light years away from being a second Bard of Avon.

You want more than just an account of our travels? Okay, let's get right down to basics then with a brief meander around the most basic of all subjects: flatulence.

We're in a café just outside St Mawes on the morning of the Royal wedding, watching a procession of well-off women ordering cakes and pastries for their 'watch the wedding on tv parties.'

'Let me see,' one says, 'I think I need 8 muffins, 6 cupcakes, plus my usual order. Let me check.' She whips out her phone and starts a lengthy conversation with her, obviously very picky guests back at the house, while the queue behind her gets more and more agitated.

Rude? Inconsiderate? Undoubtedly. Even worse, she breaks wind, loudly, twice, while relaying messages from her phone to the long suffering girl behind the counter.

'Do excuse me,' she says to the girl, 'tummy's a bit off this morning.'

Never mind apologising to the girl standing three feet in front of her, it's the poor devils standing right behind her who rate an apology. When she leaves, the whole place collapses in hysterics. Farting is funny, isn't it? Especially when the one responsible is dressed up to the nines and has just driven off in a Porsche.

When someone sneezes the phrase 'bless you' soon follows.

Oddly, there's no commonly known polite word or phrase, the equivalent of 'bless you' when someone else breaks wind. Farting is presumably considered too impolite to deserve a salutation. How unfair. Sneezing and breaking wind are both involuntary acts common to every person who's ever lived so why stigmatise one aspect of human physiology and not another?

When the great French writer Honoré de Balzac was starting out as a writer he told a friend he wanted to be sufficiently famous to be able to fart in public with impunity. Having seen photographs of Monsieur Balzac I don't imagine even his strongest admirers would have ever included the word callipygian when describing his hindquarters so credit must be paid to the ambitious nature of the activity he aspired to upon achieving fame.

The unfortunate link between what most people regard as an antisocial act and the surname of the current US President is hardly conducive to the association of statesmanlike gravitas and 'the Donald,' but as it's only the Brits who find the word 'trump' childishly amusing his large band of admirers will, presumably, not dwindle away any time soon.

In our recent trip to America I had a conversation with a fellow hotel guest, a man from Texas, about the different meanings between words in our supposedly common language. The Texan was intrigued to learn the word 'trump' has connections with flatulence in England. He raised an ample buttock cheek off the chair, broke wind quite remarkably loudly and said, 'get out and walk, Donald.'

I didn't claim he was a particularly sophisticated conversationalist.

In ancient Rome, the Emperor Claudius, fearing that holding farts in was bad for the health, passed a law stating that it was acceptable to break wind at banquets and apparently set a very fine example.

Inuit people in Canada consider farting after a meal to be an expression of thanks and appreciation to the cook while an Indian tribe in South America, the Yanomami, fart as a means of greeting one another. Different cultures, eh? Wouldn't go down too well in Tunbridge Wells.

Scientific research establishes the average person farts 14 times a day and that most farts take place at night while sleeping. Imagine slogging away to earn your Masters Degree and choosing to devote your working life to the scientific study of nocturnal emissions.

The doom and gloom merchants forecasting global warming and an imminent end to civilisation decided long ago that the internal combustion engine is the greatest threat to our continued existence. Every time we return to England we realise there are a lot of cars on the road. No more than in France or Spain, I'm sure, but those countries are several times larger so we hardly ever come across a traffic clogged motorway.

Evil cars, pumping out carbon monoxide and destroying the ozone layer. The recent volcanic eruption In Hawaii added more carbon dioxide to the atmosphere than the emissions of every car that has ever rolled off a production line which should give pause for thought.

Natural phenomena aside, nobody ever seems to mention cows, a far greater threat to the environment, and there are, apparently, 1.5 billion cows in the world compared to 1 billion cars.

Cows - along with many other ruminants such as sheep, goats, giraffes and deer - produce methane gas when digesting their food. Methane produced by cows is more damaging to the environment than the carbon dioxide produced by cars. Over twenty-three times worse! Leave cars alone and get rid of cows if we really want to preserve the life of our planet. Even though there is more carbon dioxide in the atmosphere, methane traps more heat from the sun, meaning it contributes far more to greenhouse gases and global warming.

Not that cows are the greatest 'offenders' when it comes to breaking wind, but there are a great many of them. The most prolific farters in the world are termites. Bonus point to anyone saying, 'I knew that.' Next in line are camels, then zebras, sheep, then cows, elephants, dogs (I can vouch for labradors!) and way down the list, humans.

No idea what Google will make of my recent search history, or how they will apply this knowledge, after I spent over an hour researching farting!

One more thing, as Steve Jobs used to say, while I'm on this somewhat unsavoury subject: flatulence has featured in the works of many great men. Geoffrey Chaucer, no less, offered this in The Miller's Tale, part of The Canterbury Tales.

'This Nicholas anon leet fle a fart

As greet as it had been a thonder-dent'

I 'did' Geoffrey Chaucer as part of my A level syllabus and can still remember the expression on the face of the wretched boy struggling to keep a straight face while reading this passage aloud to a classroom full of ribald teenagers.

'Fart for freedom, fart for liberty, and fart proudly.' Worthy sentiments indeed, offered up by Benjamin Franklin, one of the founding fathers of the United States.

James Joyce, who deserves to have the recognition of his full name - James Augustine Aloysius Joyce – was surely one of the most influential and important authors of the 20th century. He is best known for Ulysses, Dubliners, A Portrait of the Artist as a Young Man and Finnegan's Wake. I've read them all. Great literature they may be, yet I derived far more enjoyment from letters he wrote to the splendidly named Nora Barnacle who later became his wife.

The letters are a comparatively recent discovery and are graphically explicit love letters. His twin obsessions appear to be sex, not unusual in a love letter, and farting, somewhat more unusual. Here's an example: 'I think I would know Nora's fart anywhere. I think I could pick hers out in a roomful of farting women. It is a rather girlish noise not like the wet windy fart which I imagine fat wives have.'

Beats Finnegan's Wake any day!

Okay, back to our travels now.

We'd visited the café with the flatulent customer - not likely to be confused with Jeffrey Archer's wife whom a High Court Judge called 'fragrant' at Archer's trial for perjury – after coming across the actual bakery that supplied it on a small industrial estate between Truro and St Austell. The tiny bakery supplies many of the upmarket hotels and restaurants in Cornwall and also trains each new entrant onto Jamie Oliver's 15 scheme on the art of bread and pastry making. The café is hugely successful with its local clientele, mainly wealthy visitors with (expensive) second homes on the gorgeous Roseland Peninsula.

On the road to St Mawes, we called at Pendower Beach. The road beyond the top car park was closed due to coastal erosion, so we walked down the hill and strolled along the beach. The sun went in behind clouds as we reached the furthest point making the long slog back up the hill even more of an ordeal. Just before we reached the car park we were overtaken by a very stout, red faced man being dragged along by a pair of Irish wolfhounds. 'You need to get yourselves two of these,' he panted. The trek up the hill may have been both quicker and easier with the benefit of canine assistance, but judging by his florid complexion he may have been suited to a more gentle ascent. Not that we were exactly pallid of face when we wearily climbed into our car.

St Mawes looked as lovely as ever and the sun had come out again. We drove along the sea front and stopped to admire the view from St Mawes Castle on the headland. The castle dates from 1539, in the reign of Henry The Eighth. In the early stages of his 'wives' saga, Henry's attempts to persuade Pope Paul III to annul the long-standing marriage to his wife, Catherine of Aragon and remarry failed and he took the drastic step of breaking away from Roman Catholicism and founding his own church, the Church of England. As head of the church he could now divorce Catherine and take another wife.

The solution to Henry's problem threw up many more in its stead. Catherine was the aunt of Charles V, the Holy Roman Emperor, and he took the annulment as a personal insult. This resulted in France and the Empire declaring an alliance against Henry in 1538, and the Pope encouraging the two countries to attack England.

When invasion of England appeared certain, Henry issued instructions for the "defence of the realm in time of invasion" and the construction of forts along the English coastline.

The stretch of water known as Carrick Roads at the mouth of the River Fal was an important anchorage serving shipping arriving from the Atlantic and the Mediterranean. Pendennis and St Mawes Castle were positioned on each side of Carrick Roads and able to provide overlapping fire across the water.

St Mawes Castle is the best-preserved of Henry VIII's coastal artillery fortresses and the most elaborately decorated bearing carved Latin inscriptions in praise of Kings Henry VIII and his son Edward VI. The cannon facing out across the narrow strip of sea between the castle and Pendennis Castle set on the opposite hill above Falmouth are still there, even though they were never used.

Marigold collected her new glasses, always a time of great excitement (!) and to 'try them out' we went to the cinema in Wadebridge. The Regal resembles a small town cinema from a bygone era, which it is of course, but what it lacks in facilities it makes up for in charm. Very 'Cornish' and that's a compliment.

We also met a man named Paul, originally from Yorkshire, who proved to be excellent company. Paul is tattooed, all over, from head to foot and everywhere in between. Yes, everywhere, although we had to take his word for that claim! Not that we doubted it. He's been on television many times, usually when being questioned about the plight of the homeless.

'Are you homeless?' Marigold asked.

'No, but they obviously think I look as if I am.'

Fabulous.

Into Zummerset, cider apples, Wells, Glastonbury, Wookey Hole and Murmerations.

Marigold Says...

We've been in Wells for a couple of days, which is lovely. We've been to Bristol and Bath many times, but never Wells, and we both think it's the nicest of the three. I love its oldness. Don't know if that is a word, but it was very, very old. It's not very big, of course, so easy to walk around the centre, but because it has a cathedral it's a city, the smallest city in England, I think. We were in Truro the other day, also a city, but that's only the size of a small town as well, but if there's a cathedral there you can be called a city. Very confusing.

First off we we started off at the interestingly named Wookey Hole, which of course we sniggered at. Well, I did. Changing it to Wonkey Hole made me titter the most. We didn't do the caves, but the surrounding houses were just lovely.

Had a walk about and decided which one we would have if we had two million to spare. We settled on a mill house with loads of stuff growing up the walls, and it had a thatched roof, ducks and 3 geese. I would have to factor in a gardener and a full time person to protect me from the geese. All in all a stupid idea then. That's saved us two million quid. Liked the public toilets in the car park with signs saying witches and wizards very much welcomed but didn't need to visit either of them.

We had a latte at the local café and a bacon butty. The latte had more froth than coffee and we both ended up with a white moustache. Mine looked quite attractive, I was sorry to wipe it off.

We got back to the car park after our walk and there was a Morgan sports car parked next to us, the same Morgan that we parked next to at a motorway services about 150 miles away. Small world, unless he's a stalker. I mentioned this to G and got the impression he thought it a bit unlikely. You never know. Will be checking for the rest of the day to see if I am being followed.

We went to find a cemetery, still nobody following us, which a woman walking her dog had told me about. She said 'you'll never find it, dear, it's very well hidden.' We both said, how hard can it be to find a cemetery, but she was right, it was very, very well hidden. In the end we asked another lady dog walker, very posh lady indeed, and she told us where to go. (Just realised, that sounds as if she told us to clear off, but she was very nice and gave brilliant directions)

We drove into a housing estate and, eventually, found a very narrow gap between two houses which led to the cemetery. Of course, it was closed and a notice said it only opened on a Sunday mornings in the summer. Another dog walker, they like dogs here and like chatting too, showed us the best places to peep into the cemetery and told us all about it. The cemetery was the burial ground for the Somerset and Bath Pauper Lunatic Asylum, later known as the Wells Mental Hospital, and later still, the Mendip Hospital. There are nearly 3,000 former patients and a few staff buried here and the last ones were buried in 1963, so quite recent.

Our dog walker friend told us the grass is only mown once a year to encourage birds, and wild flowers. There's a wildlife pond too. Most of the people buried here were very poor and classified as 'lunatics' so there are very few gravestones, just numbered metal markers. Very sad. The cemetery isn't sad at all, it's really lovely and peaceful and there are some wooden sculptures in the grounds which we weren't able to see. Will have to come back again another time on a Sunday morning.

Next stop was Glastonbury. We didn't wear the 'uniform' - either Jesus Sandals or wellingtons – and it was very hot. There were quite a few people wearing those funny trousers with a very low crotch or crutch which look as if they have filled their pants! The shops were full of fairies, crystals and vegan food. We were not tempted by any of their offerings. The street musicians were brilliant, and it was great fun.

I was chatting to a couple wheeling a little dog in a shopping trolley and I never even noticed the man was wearing a skirt until they had gone and G told me. He was very nice so I suppose he thought a skirt would be a good idea on a hot day. Saw him again a bit later and the skirt was a kilt, so that's okay. The dog in the shopping trolley looked very fed up, think he wanted to get out and run around a bit.

We drove to Street as well, just for a quick visit. It used to be just a small village, but is now larger than its next door neighbour, Glastonbury. Again, it's very old, Roman times, and its name comes from a road used to transport stone from a quarry to build Glastonbury Abbey.

Clarks Shoes, was founded in Street and still has its headquarters here. When a few empty factory buildings were converted into the Clarks Village retail park Street took off and today thousands of people visit the 'outlet village'. Not our sort of thing at all so we carried on and found our hotel in Wells instead where the bar offers over 100 different varieties of gin. Not that I sampled all of them.

We had intended to be staying at Wookey Hole, which I suggested as I liked the name, but we ended up at a hotel in the middle of the 'city' of Wells which was great as we could walk around Wells and not bother about parking.

I read a leaflet about the Vicars Close when we got up the next day and told G we should go there. He said, 'okay, that's easy enough, it's just over there.' I took notes so I could pretend to be knowledgeable when I wrote about it. We walked across the green facing the cathedral, just across the road from our hotel. and a man in long robes, a vicar/priest/ whatever, nearly knocked us over. He dashed into the Deans' House so we decided he was running because he was late for morning coffee and the Dean gets cross if people are late.

Vicars Close is fabulous. Like a scene from Dickens, but much, much older. Vicars Close is the oldest purely residential street with its original buildings surviving intact in Europe. John Julius Norwich called it 'that rarest of survivals, a planned street of the mid-14th century.' The street has appeared in Harry Potter films, so it gets even more visitors now.

On 30 December 1348, Bishop Ralph of Shrewsbury presented '44 dwellings newly built for the use of vicars, and quarters with appurtenances built and to be built.' He made it quite clear in his original deed that each house in the quadrangle was designed to accommodate one vicar, but some of the houses were joined up to make a bigger house following the Reformation when vicars were allowed to marry, so there are now only 27 separate houses, occupying the original double sided street.

That's the end of what I found out in the hotel leaflet so don't expect any more facts and figures from now on. If G was writing this he would have told you what 'appurtenances' are. I haven't a clue, but that's all the 'research' you're getting.

We chatted to a man who was repairing windows, one of two men who carry out repairs to all the houses. He told us the work was very involved as all the houses are Grade 1 Listed and only the original materials can be used when doing repairs. He said the people who lived in the street still included all twelve men forming the Vicars Choral, plus the organists and vergers. The Vicars Choral have sung at Wells Cathedral since the 12th century and are recognised as a world-class choir.

'You should do guided tours,' I said.

'No thanks, can't stand all the visitors we get here,' he replied, 'can't even leave the front door open when I'm working in case someone wanders in so I have to put up with working in clouds of dust.'

Unsurprisingly, and despite my many hints, we didn't get to look around the empty house he was working on! G was talking to him about different types of plaster so I wandered off and looked for the other workman thinking he might be a bit more obliging but couldn't find him.

There were lots of young children, only about four or five years old , being taken to school by their parents or nannies. They looked lovely in their uniforms, all the girls were skipping and all the boys had their hair sticking up at the back. One of the nannies was skipping too. It's obviously a very rich area, but almost everybody smiled and said hello. I told G, 'I could live here,' and we walked up one side of the road and back again on the other side, picking out which house we would choose. I would love all the tourists going past looking madly jealous, and I would say "just another property we own."

We both picked out the same house, but G said he didn't think they'd let him join the Vicars Choir. I hope not. He thinks he can sing, but unless he's being Elvis, he can't. He does Elvis quite well though. We didn't go inside the cathedral because it was such a sunny day, so we walked back into the centre.

Wells has been in existence since Roman times, because there are three natural springs here, fresh water wells. A man in a shop tried to sell me a hobby horse. That doesn't happen every day. Perhaps he thought I was seven years old. He did have very thick glasses and I aren't very tall.

Wells is named after the three wells, what a surprise, and there is a fountain in the market square, but I'm not sure that's one of the three wells. There's also a plaque marking Mary Rand's World record long jump – she was born in Wells - and there's a brass strip on the pavement marking out the distance. It looked a very long way to me. If I did my best ever long jump, repeated six times, I'd still only be halfway there! She was the first British woman to win an Olympic gold medal and also held the world record in the Triple Jump. No wonder they gave her the Freedom of the City.

We spent the whole morning in Wells, but some gourmet friends had recommended a pub in 'the Levels' and we decided we'd try and find it and perhaps have lunch. One of our very best decisions! It's only about ten minutes or so from Wells and on the way we stopped and looked around an architectural salvage yard which was brilliant. Like a huge junk yard with some things you never even imagined to find for sale. If we had bought the big house in Wookey Hole we would come here for 'stuff' to go in it. Obviously, we didn't, so we didn't buy anything.

The pub in Lower Godney is called the Sheppey Inn and has been there for hundreds of years. It's not exactly inviting from the outside, pretty scruffy actually, but inside it's lovely. The owner is named Liz and she told us all about the pub. She and her partner, Mark, used to own the Wookey Hole Inn and won very many awards there, but took over the Sheppey eight years ago when it was very run down. Liz collects glass, Mark collects toys and the pub is packed with knick–knacks, big pictures and wonderfully eccentric furniture. We loved it.

They have lots and lots of different beers and ciders and also brew kombucha, which we used to do when we lived in France. It's very trendy now and Liz gave us a sample of their experiments with different flavours. The menu was very inviting so we ate lunch in the garden, next to a stream, with cows looking at us from the opposite bank. They dig out peat from all around here, people do, not cows, as they have for hundreds of years, and it's a very peaceful scene.

Our waiter told us that every year between November and February, starlings flock together and their displays are so spectacular that hundreds of people turn up to stand and watch them. 'A murmuration,' G said and the waiter laughed. 'I didn't want to say the word,' he said, 'because people think I've made it up.' Yes, it is the correct word for those amazing shapes made by many thousands of starlings in flight.

We've seen them in Spain and it's a fabulous sight, but if you want to see them in England, the area around the Sheppey Inn is the place to go.

Meandering around Cornwall.

G Says...

We decided if Prince Charles could find time to visit the Royal Cornwall Show, we should as well. Mind you, we had to pay to get in and I suspect the heir to the throne didn't. The Wadebridge show ground is massive, the queues equally so and the car parks on fields around the show ground were packed. We're tough so we persevered, parked our car at the far end of a field and trudged back the equivalent of three postcodes to the entrance where an officious man wearing a bowler hat told us we would have to wait twenty minutes until the ticket office reopened. At that point it began to rain.

Heavily.

We did what any red blooded English people would do in these circumstances.

We gave up.

Back again the next day, we parked in a different field and puffed our way past a few thousand more cars to the ticket office. The woman behind the screen said, 'if you're expecting to see Prince Charles, he was here yesterday so you've missed him.' We bought our tickets and as we moved in the ticket woman was saying to the people behind us, 'if you're expecting to see Prince Charles...' Marigold said, 'what a helpful and informative ticket person.'

Through the entrance and the hordes of visitors, every one of them having come to terms with not being able to see Prince Charles today. There was a woman on a stand selling knitted farm animals and we thought she looked a bit like Camilla, plus she was puffing away at a Rothmans King Size, but it was a false alarm.

We wandered past a few hundred or so stands offering us things we didn't need, or even want, and found the dog show ring. Marigold got talking to one of the dog owners – one second prize for best of breed and a first prize in the obedience category – with a broad Black Country accent who told us she went to school with Frank Skinner. I wonder if Frank Skinner tells people he went to school with a woman who owned a dog awarded a rosette for being obedient. We didn't find out which of her three dogs had won this accolade, but I suspect the standard was pretty low as she was constantly telling the dogs to SIT and all three ignored her.

One of the judges, regulation bowler hat on his head, originally from Germany but has lived in Padstow for fifteen years, chose to engage us in conversation on the subject of Brexit negotiations. The gist of his diatribe was that 'the English' wanted 'Kuchen unt essen,' which roughly translates as 'cake and eat it.' We sought escape at the point he forgot to speak English and reverted to speaking German. We like visiting Germany, have several German friends, but I find it the most difficult of all the many languages I have attempted to learn in the past and I was struggling to contribute even the occasional word.

Arbeit Macht Frei – work will set you free – kept popping into my head, but the slogan attached to the gates of Auschwitz would not be very appropriate so I wisely decided to merely nod and look as if I were taking it all in. I do remember that sign being stolen from the gates of Auschwitz and the letter 'b' being deliberately formed upside down as an act of defiance by the prisoners who made it. I don't imagine a German dog judge, or indeed anyone else, would be very interested in the trivia that infests my brain.

When the conversation (a monologue, actually) turned to ontological speculation, Marigold called out 'coming' to a non existent friend and we dashed away. Marigold does not have much time for philosophical debate.

Many of the visitors are farmers, described by Marigold as people who looked like they had been dressed by their mum, and there were hordes around the tractor stands. Farm machinery seems to get bigger, flashier and brighter in colour every year and the gleaming monsters on display were much admired.

We had a few tastings, strawberries and Cornish ice cream for instance, walked the equivalent of a half marathon, saw sheep dog and police dog performances, cheered when a young lad on a quad bike jumped over a pick up truck and a couple of tractors and had several conversations with strangers. A young man from Newquay, a surfer not a farmer but having a day off from the waves to offer round food and drink 'tastings' told us he lived in the former home and birthplace of a famous, or infamous judge: Sir Melford Stevenson.

In a former life, or so it seems now after so many years, Marigold worked with several High Court Judges and Melford Stevenson's name was well known to both of us. I checked surf boy's claim later and Judge Melford Stevenson was indeed born in Newquay and lived there for many years. Before he became a judge, as a barrister he defended Ruth Ellis against the charge of murdering her lover. He opened the defence by saying: 'Let me make this abundantly plain: there is no question here but this woman shot this man ... You will not hear one word from me – or from the lady herself – questioning that.' No wonder the jury took only 23 minutes to find Ellis guilty and she was sentenced to be hanged, the last woman executed for murder in the United Kingdom.

After being appointed as a judge, one of his fellow judges, Sir Robin Dunn, described him as 'the worst judge since the war.' I particularly remember Judge Stevenson passing sentence on the Kray twins as in that year (1969) we left the surfing beaches of Newquay and moved to London where the trial was in progress. We were both working in different branches of 'law' at that time and I took a particular interest in Judge Melford Stevenson.

He sentenced the Kray twins, Reggie and Ronnie, to a minimum of 30 years in jail each, saying, 'In my view, society has earned a rest from your activities' and remarked that the Krays had only told the truth twice during the trial: when Reggie referred to a barrister as 'a fat slob' and when Ronnie accused the judge of being biased.

There are so many tales about Stevenson: when trying a manslaughter case in which a man who had run over a child pleaded, in extenuation, that he had thought the child was a dog; the judge, a great spaniel lover, promptly gave him the maximum sentence, him remarking when sentencing some presumed miscreant, 'I must confess I cannot tell whether you are innocent or guilty. I am giving you three years. If you are guilty you have got off lightly, if innocent let this be a lesson to you' and made at least two extremely biased remarks of geographic significance: on freeing a man accused of rape, he said 'I see you come from Slough, it is a terrible place. You can go back there' and telling a man involved in a divorce case that his decision to live in Manchester was 'a wholly incomprehensible choice for any free man to make.'

In fairness, those last two comments have a certain veracity about them!

We've had a good wander around Cornwall, between the showers, in the last week or so visiting Truro, Wadebridge, St Ives, Charlestown, Newquay, Mevagissey and many other delightful places. We also went to find a beach we last visited way back in 1969, known as either Gwenvor or Gwynver, depending on whether you're 'English' or 'Cornish.' However you describe it, it's the most exposed beach in Cornwall, meaning it's the best surfing beach in the whole county, therefore the best in Britain.

Locals say its name derives from Guinevere, wife of the legendary Cornish King Arthur, but they would say that, wouldn't they?

Access is by a steep path from the cliffs above and at low tide it joins up with the neighbouring beach at Sennen.

The very best surfers come here for guaranteed large waves, but it's no place for a novice. It's very hard to find too, adding to its appeal as holidaymakers don't know of its existence. We walked from the car park at Tregiffian Farm and the first glimpse of the sea along the narrow path is spellbinding. Of course, having gone to all this trouble, the sea was flat calm and apart from half a dozen sulking and frustrated surfers the whole beach was deserted.

We went to St Ives on a dull day, thinking this would deter the crowds, but of course St Ives was as busy as ever and it took ages to park the car. The harbour was picturesque as it always is, but we 'discovered' a real treat, the Fisherman's Lodge which we must have walked past many times without knowing its significance. It's a simple little place, just two small rooms with chairs, lots of pictures on the walls and a stove and it's a sort of sanctuary for the retired fishermen of St Ives directly overlooking the harbour. What an idyllic spot. It almost made me wish I had chosen the life of an offshore fisherman, but on reflection I amended this wish to being able to enjoy the perks of a retired offshore fisherman.

Barnoon Cemetery is another notable spot in St Ives that somehow or other we've never visited. Time to rectify that omission. We walked past the Barbara Hepworth museum, didn't go in, up Barnoon Hill and turned left onto Clodgy View West – wonderful road names – where we found the cemetery.

The cemetery itself has stunning views out to sea; almost but not quite compensating for the draconian entrance requirements for permanent residents. Marigold enjoys old graveyards and we wandered around, pointing out interesting names and exotically carved headstones. There are two small chapels, back to back, each with a single bell. This is such a delightful spot and yet we were the only visitors apart from a very old man and a very old dog.

We said hello to the old man and his dog and he offered to give us a guided tour. 'I bring this old boy here every day,' he said. 'We know the story behind every gravestone.'

I looked around at the hundreds of gravestones and thought that claim was perhaps a little exaggerated, but as we walked, slowly, around it turned out the old man certainly knew a great deal. He took us first to the burial place of Stephen Curnow, aged 32, who was one of the unfortunate victims of that night in 1912 when the Titanic hit an iceberg and sank. Another local man who died during that fatal voyage, William Carbines, is also buried here, but our 'guide' (Harold) couldn't quite remember where the grave was situated.

Another stone commemorated the crew of the SS Alba, which capsized and sank off St. Ives in1938 and an equally poignant memorial marked the last resting place of the seven crew members of the St Ives lifeboat who were drowned in St Ives Bay in 1939 while trying to reach a ship in distress. Two of the men were brothers, while a father and son also lost their lives.

Many artists are associated with St Ives and Harold took us the the grave of Alfred Wallis who died in 1942 and he said this grave is probably the most visited in the whole cemetery as Wallis was one of the most celebrated painters in St Ives history. We both nodded appreciatively, neither of us having any inkling who Alfred Wallis was. Quite shameful, this ignorance, as it turns out as I realised much later when I looked up the details of Alfred Wallis.

Wallis was originally a deep-sea fisherman sailing off to Newfoundland to find fish before switching to more local off shore fishing based in Penzance.

The family moved to St. Ives in 1890 where he established himself as a marine stores dealer, buying scrap iron, sails, rope and other items. Following his wife's death Wallis took up painting, 'for company'. He was self-taught, never had an art lesson, and painted on any scraps of paper or cardboard that were going spare using whatever paint he could find amongst the items in his shop. His art is now considered one of the earliest forms of 'primitism,' with scant regard being paid to perspective or scale – child-like would have been my description – but like so many artists he never achieved success in his own lifetime.

Wallis was penniless when he died in a local workhouse, but his friends bought a plot in the cemetery and arranged for a Salvation Army funeral. The grave is decorated in the style of his paintings with ceramic tiles made by Bernard Leach, which again would have meant very little at the time, but at least we both remembered admiring the tiles.

There's an old well in one corner which Harold said was named after a Saint, but was somewhat vague on detail at this point. Later, I discovered the well is called St La's Well, named after a 5th-century saint who is said to have arrived here from Ireland borne on a huge leaf. Ah well, maybe the actual detail of the tale is somewhat apocryphal, but there is a well there and it's evidently been there for many hundreds of year so why worry about details?

As we left Harold he told us he was 86 and his dog was 15. In all honesty, they both looked much, much older! He's still driving, just to take his neighbours to the shops and back, which prompted a mental note to be wary of cars driven by very old men on our way out of town. An equally old joke came to mind, but I kept it to myself.

I want to die peacefully in my sleep like Grandad. Not screaming in terror like his passengers.

See, there's a time and a place for jokes.

Hastings, Winchelsea and Spike Milligan

Marigold Says...

We decided to go and hunt for 3 pressies, including one for me as I am worth it, in Hastings Old Town. Grrhh, half of the favourite shops were closed and it was already 11.00am. We thought about going for food and drink and then trying again, but got waylaid by the few shops that were open.Firstly, we noticed the tattoo parlour had moved to smaller premises. Don't suppose you need much floor space for ink, needles and a chair. The new shop that replaced it was setting up and looked as if it was doing retro stuff. That should interest G as he still has clothes in his wardrobe which he covets and occasionally brings out, looks at, and says things like "this must be worth a fortune". Some of them are really trendy, as the moth holes are getting bigger by the minute.

There used to be an independent opticians. He had an old bike in the window covered in glasses which were really unusual. He is now in St Leonards I think. Never dared go in his shop, as it was so small, and being weak willed would have signed up for something not at all suitable, after parting with a few hundred pounds, and then hiding them forever.

Found our favourite Hastings coffee shop Hanushka. Full of books and lovely furniture and bits and pieces. The settees are so comfy, and they provide all the newspapers. On a Sunday, we could be in there for 2 hours. Can't bear it if someone beats us to the papers and are hogging the settees. Oh, and the toilets have loads more books and some lovely cloth flannels to wipe your hands.

The couple who run it are a delight and have two gorgeous children. The first time we went in the owner had just had a baby boy two weeks before and he was in a little pram. She had just opened up and was busy cooking, cleaning and serving. Success is a testimony to them, it is really popular and has a loyal following.

We set off looking for pressies again. They were for very special friends so my limit was £2 each. Couldn't find anything that cheap, so had to bite the bullet and get the plastic out. None of our friends are worth any more than £2 in my opinion. Saw lots of local characters, some great, some a bit whiffy. Walked our legs off.

Went to the organic, sourdough infested, whole grain and very expensive bakers. Several years ago we bought a small loaf and two very kind to pigs sausage rolls and it came to £7. I had already got a tenner to pay with readyin my hand, so couldn't get out of it. Lesson learned. We only

165

go in now for free tastings to try and recoup our money. So far we are well in by about £50.00. We were tempted by the organic spinach and asparagus quiche at 'only' £6 a slice, but were a bit full after the blueberry doughnut tastings, followed by organic chocolate brownies. Didn't give you much, but can't complain as suppose it was only supposed to be a tasting. G said you have a lot of chocolate on your face, and wiped it off with his hanky. What a waste of good chocolate, not to mention the state of his handkerchief. If he gets hay fever and starts sneezing, just imagine the looks he will get when he pulls out that brown smeared handkerchief.

We had a meander around a graveyard on the road to Rye, I like graveyards, and we chatted to an old and not very good artist and eventually found the grave of Spike Milligan. We must have been here about five times and we still have to wander around for ages before we find it. I am convinced they move all the gravestones around once a month. Apart from (probably) Prince Charles, G knows more about Spike Milligan than anyone else in the world so will let him tell you more.

G Says...

Hastings Old Town has to be one of our favourite places. Not the 'front' which has sold its soul to the day trippers, of which there are many, but the warren of narrow passageways known locally as twittens and the boutique shops and cafes that line both the street set back from the sea front and the old High Street with its exotic blend of antique shops and junk shops.

The Stade at the far end of the seafront is notable for the distinctive clapboard net huts which were built to store fishing gear in the seventeenth century for Europe's largest beach launched fishing fleet. There's a notable art gallery, the Jerwood Gallery, and the very last sailing lugger 'The Enterprise' which has been crammed inside Hasting Fishermen's Museum, plus a pair of funicular railways, one leading up to the top of East Hill Hastings Country Park and the other taking visitors from the heart of the old town to the West Hill. Hastings nestles between these two hillsides and there are glorious country walks to be had up there, but our destination of choice is the Old Town itself.

We meet a friend, by chance, outside 'the only bookshop and Thai Cafe in Great Britain or Europe' which is quite a claim and I have no way of refuting it. Despite living in the area for quite some time, we never ate here. The bookshop itself, second hand books of course, always seemed a little on the scruffy side even to me whenever I went inside and this undoubtedly gave rise to a predisposition that the food would be equally fusty in nature. No doubt, a completely false impression, but there you go. It seems popular and has been trading as a restaurant for quite a while although it's been a while since I saw it open for book selling business during the day. Our friend said 'someone will come if you ring the bell,' but we didn't bother.

We went just up the street to Hanushka, a café where the walls are crammed with books, they provide daily newspapers to read and even comfortable sofas for the weary. We love it there and the owners are delightful. Sitting outside was someone we know slightly who used to work as a waiter at a different restaurant, but would now have to be called a waitress. In these transgender times, it's a little confusing to meet someone who we last saw wearing waiter garb, black trousers, white shirt, black tie, and yet now wearing a garish floral dress. I just about managed to avoid saying my usual, 'hello, mate,' and gave a cheery nod of the head instead.

Marigold made her usual pilgrimage to browse some favourite shops and eventually we reached Judges Bakery. When we first came to live in this area we were delighted to find an artisan bakery in the High Street. We later discovered the owner was Craig Sams, a name we knew very well. Way back in the late 1960s we lived in Holland Park, Notting Hill and Bayswater in a succession of grim and dingy rented bedsits. We didn't care, this was the Swinging London era and we'd lived in a tent in Cornwall for six months before moving to London so just about anywhere was luxury by comparison and in our distant youth we weren't remotely concerned with creature comforts.

We loved the vibrancy of Portobello Road, within easy walking distance, and there we discovered Seed, the UK's first macrobiotic restaurant and shop, and later Ceres where the bread was baked on the premises and 'something from Ceres' became our Saturday morning treat. The owners were Craig Sams and his brother Gregory.

Nebraska-born, Craig Sams imported Afghan coats that he had spotted on his travels in Asia to sell on Chelsea's King's Road. Among his first customers were the Beatles and a fashion trend was born. Craig Sams was a pioneer of the 'organic' movement and without his influence the supermarkets and high street shops of today would be very different.

He later founded Green and Blacks organic chocolate and after he sold the chocolate company to Cadbury's came to Hastings to run a bakery shop. He no longer owns Judges, but is still very active in the area.

Leaving Hastings, heading for Rye, we stopped and browsed the churchyard at Winchelsea. This is a lovely spot, very peaceful, and we had the place to ourselves apart from an old lady painting a watercolour of the church. She told us she had been 'trying to get it right' for many years and this was about her fiftieth attempt. It was in its early stages, far too soon to make a judgement, but Marigold wasn't too impressed. The artist showed us a painting of the John Wesley house on the main road which she seemed pleased with. We weren't all that impressed with that either, but of course didn't say so.

The old lady, Edith, said she had lived abroad for many years but had returned to England 'for the sheer majesty of the scenery.' This we could wholeheartedly endorse. We've lived in several countries, visited a great many more, but few countries compare to the variety of scenery we find in England.

I was reminded of something that great Anglophile, Bill Bryson, said and looked it up later.

'Nothing, and I mean, absolutely nothing – is more extraordinary in Britain than the beauty of the countryside... the makers of Britain created the most superlatively park-like landscapes, the most orderly cities, the handsomest provincial towns, the quaintest seaside resorts, the stateliest homes, the most dreamily-spired, cathedral-rich, castle-strewn, abbey-bedecked, folly-scattered, green-wooded, winding-laned, sheep-dotted, plumply hedge-rowed, well-tended, sublimely decorated 50,318 square miles the world has ever known – almost none of it is undertaken with aesthetics in mind, but all of it adding up to something that is quite often, perfect.'

Well said, Mister Bryson.

After an unfeasibly long search – no excuse can be offered as it's in the same position it was last time we were here, despite Marigold protesting otherwise – we found the last resting place of Spike Milligan.

I've been a Milligan fan for many years. Genius and madness are closely intertwined and the man who wrote his own obituary, in which he stated that he 'wrote the Goon Show and died' was undoubtedly a genius yet suffered from severe depression for most of his later years.

Milligan's gravestone was intended to bear his own epitaph: 'I told you I was ill'. Regrettably, in my view, the Church refused to allow this inscription, but Milligan's coffin was draped in the Irish flag and the gravestone bears his exact words, but written in Gaelic as *'Duirt me leat go ruich me breoite.'* The headstone also bears the words, *'Gra mór ort Shelagh,'* which translates as 'Great love for you, Shelagh'.

(If any Gaelic speakers read this, I hope I copied it correctly- the words are somewhat faded).

That has to be the best ever epitaph, closely followed by one from another man with a great number of words at his disposal that I remember well: Winston Churchill's tombstone bears his own words: 'I'm ready to meet my maker. Whether my maker is prepared for the great ordeal of meeting me is another matter.'

A contemporary of Churchill, Charles de Gaulle, offered this wisdom: 'The graveyards are full of indispensable men'. On the same subject, Milligan famously said, 'I don't mind dying. I just don't want to be there when it happens'.

Better start working on my own epitaph; the bar is set pretty high.

Spike Milligan bought a house called Carpenter's Meadow, situated on the intriguingly named Dumbwoman's Lane, in the 1980s when he decided to escape the pace of life in London and lived there, with his (third) wife Shelagh from 1988 until his death. When appearing on the tv programme Room 101, Milligan offered up his own house, claiming it was a monstrosity. Further evidence of his dislike for the house was his removal of the house nameplate, Carpenter's Meadow, replacing it with one of his own, The Blind Architect.

'Nuff said!

Rod Hull also lived in Winchelsea. He was probably most famous for Emu, his puppet bird attacking Michael Parkinson. Comedy gold, even more so when Parkinson didn't find it even remotely amusing. Even so, he doesn't rate much of a mention here; genius being the entry level for inclusion in this graveyard.

Marigold Says...

We drove through Peasmarsh to see if Sir Paul McCartney was out and about, but didn't see him. Our friends in Rye used to see him quite often back when Linda was alive, but not so much since then. We had a meander through Rye and I nearly fell over on the cobbles (twice) but survived. Historic and charming they may be, but I think all cobblestones are a health and safety issue and something should be done!!! At least G managed not to stub his toe, which he seems to do quite often lately with gruesome results. He takes shoe size 12, but when he's been wearing sandals his big toes must be size 14.

Spike Milligan and a Beatle.

G Says...

We're wandering around Kent and Sussex just now, two counties brim full of history and with strong nautical affiliations. Way back in Pre-Norman conquest times; before William made the Sussex towns of Hastings and Battle synonymous with the year 1066, the perceived threat lay not across the Channel in Normandy but in Scandinavia where the fierce Norsemen were a constant threat.

For a time England even had a Danish king in the person of Cnut (who we now call Canute) but after his death the Anglo-Saxon Edward the Confessor was determined to keep the Norse threat at bay.

The security of England, Edward reasoned, depended on a successful control of the English Channel. To this end he granted the ports of Sandwich, Dover, and New Romney, all in Kent, certain taxation incentives in exchange for them agreeing to supply ships and sailors to defend the coasts when required. This was a valuable concession and the three towns prospered greatly as a result.

Later, Hastings in Sussex, and Hythe, in Kent were added and these five coastal towns made up the Five Ports (in Norman French they were termed the 'Cinque Ports'). In the 13th century Rye and Winchelsea also became affiliated with the Cinque Ports.

Defence was a major consideration in those uncertain times and other towns joined in including Tenterden becoming an ally of Rye, and Pevensey an ally of Hastings, reaching a total of 42 towns at its medieval peak.

A few hundred years saw some of the towns continue to prosper while others declined. Dover's harbour ensured its prosperity, but elsewhere the sea receded and rivers silted up, leaving Winchelsea and Tenterden totally isolated from the coast and Rye transformed from a former coastal port into a river one.

Walmer Castle near Deal in Kent is the official residence of the Warden of the Cinque Ports, a position little more than ceremonial today, but once of huge national importance and previous wardens have included the Queen Mother, Winston Churchill and the Duke of Wellington. I may apply for the post next time it becomes vacant.

We noted the black sludge in the river bed as we approached Rye, barely half a cup of water on show, but we know from previous visits the river will be brim full of water later in the day. Initially, we bypassed Rye and made the short trip to Peasmarsh to see if the French 'jam lady' was still around. Some years ago we met and became friendly with a French woman who was selling home made jam at a farmers' market and she also had a stall outside her cottage in Peasmarsh. We weren't looking to buy jam, just wanted to say hello while we were in the neighbourhood.

No sign of the jam lady, but we were flagged down by a woman wearing an outrageously large hat who appeared very agitated. She wanted to know if we had seen a horse on the road as one of her horses had 'escaped.'

We offered to drive around the area and report back and were barely out of sight before we found the escapee, safe and sound in the care of a young man who told us this was a regular occurrence as the owner of the horse kept forgetting to close the gate. We thought it unlikely the horse would have gone very far as it was very old and remarkably fat.

'She needs a bit of exercise, this one,' the young man said. 'Seems to enjoy escaping too. One time she went as far as Playden.'

I told him we didn't know where Playdon was and he looked astonished.

'Playdon was in the Domesday Book, you must know it.'

I've rarely felt so ignorant.

Retracing our steps, we reassured the horse owner that her escaped mare was on the way home and within a couple of minutes passed a sign informing us we were now in Playdon. Half a mile further on and we came to the far side of Playdon. No houses, no people, just a few fields, but there was a sign offering confirmation of the village being mentioned in the Domesday Book. Must have been a bit more lively back in the 11th century.

'We didn't even see Paul McCartney,' said Marigold. The former Beatle has lived in Peasmarsh for many years and when he was married to Linda they embraced the rural 'quiet life' and were often seen out and about in the village and in neighbouring Rye. He regularly popped over to visit Spike Milligan for breakfast, but as Milligan would never answer a knock on the door, would let himself in with the key Shelagh Milligan gave him and wake the sleeping Milligans by playing their piano, very loudly

McCartney hand-wrote a short lyric called 'The Poet of Dumbswoman Lane' (referring to Spike's address) on one side of a piece of paper and drew a cartoon titled 'The Nutters of Starvecrow Lane' on the reverse and it was sold for a large sum when Spike Milligan's effects were disposed of after his death. Starvecrow Lane is just one of many weird street names in this area.

We moved on to Rye, surely one of the most attractive and interesting towns in England and a place we visit often. The street names alone are worth the visit. We wandered down Cinque Street, Pope Walk, Love Lane, and Deadman's Lane, the latter believed to be the former site where many victims of the Black Death were buried. Rats came off the ships when they landed in port and spread the disease and most sea ports were overrun by the disease. It's also the lane going up the hill to where public hangings took place. No sign of a hanging today, but the house of one of the men who signed many death warrants, Thomas Lamb, is in Deadman's Lane. Thomas Lamb was Mayor of Rye twenty times and the Lamb family dominated the town for well over two hundred years. More about the Lamb family coming up! Many famous people have lived in Rye, plus a few surprises such as Bob Marley's great-grandfather, Frederick, being born in the town in 1820.

We walked up the hill as far as the castle, browsing the shop windows on our way, then retraced our steps and nipped into the Apothecary, a legendary café and very much a Rye institution, for a coffee and a quick chat with the staff. We've been frequent customers over a fair few years and they're always keen to find out where we've been and where we're going next.

Walking past the church and its graveyard, we reached a house with a remarkable history. Originally built in 1723 by yet another member of the Lamb family, James (who was Mayor a mere thirteen times), Lamb House is a brick-fronted Georgian house, but its classic simplicity is deceptive.

One of the most famous stories about Lamb House concerns George I. In 1726 the King was returning from Hanover to open Parliament when he was driven ashore by a terrible storm and made an emergency landing at Camber Sands. James Lamb escorted the King to his own house in Rye where the family entertained him for three days though George spoke very little English and the Lamb family didn't speak a word of German. (We can relate to this; even though Marigold seems to manage very well in countries where we don't speak the language. Romania, Lithuania, Ukraine? No problem at all).

On the very first night of the King's visit Mrs Lamb gave birth to a baby boy. The King agreed to act as godfather at the christening of the baby in St Mary's church; the boy was named George. Naturally.

The Lamb family eventually sold the house, leaving its name as a memento, but it came into its own when it was snapped up by the famous American writer, Henry James who spent most of the last eighteen years of his life here. Lamb House provided its owner with the inspiration for many of his most notable books, but it was as a host for other literary giants that the house has achieved such fame.

H.G. Wells, A.C.and E.F. Benson, Max Beerbohm. Hilaire Belloc, G.K. Chesterton, Joseph Conrad, Stephen Crane, Ford Maddox Ford, Edmund Gosse, Rudyard Kipling, Hugh Walpole and Edith Wharton all stayed here.

After Jame's death in 1916 the house became the home of brothers, A.C. and E.F. Benson.The view from the bow window of the Garden House was to give E.F. Benson the inspiration for his Mapp and Lucia novels and thrust the house and the town of Rye itself into the public eye. In Benson's stories Lamb House became Mallard House and Rye was renamed Tilling.

On a previous visit to Rye a few year's ago, with Marigold's sister in attendance, we discovered a large television crew filming a television adaptation of Mapp and Lucia for the BBC outside the house. Barring our further passage were two signs saying 'Quiet' and 'Please' respectively. Marigold's sister said, 'they surely don't expect us to walk all the way round' and set off between the two signs. Anna Chancellor, in mid speech, looked just a little confused at the sudden appearance of a random 'extra' and I wish I had taken a photo of the expression on the face of Miranda Richardson!

We missed the tv series, but I'm pretty certain they shot another take of that particular scene. Marigold and I, of course, walked the long way round.

Beyond Lamb House lies Mermaid Street, formerly the main road through Rye. Struggling to explain 'Ye Olde England' to a foreigner? Just bring them to Mermaid Street. Gorgeous old flower bedecked ancient houses, cobblestones underfoot and a pub where the original cellars date from 1156 and bearing a sign saying it was renovated as 'recently' as 1420.

The Mermaid Inn is fabulous. Dark beams, creaking oak floorboards, narrow passages, and winding staircases, it has many a tale to tell. Local smugglers, the Hawkhurst Gang, used this as their 'local' in the 1730s and no doubt made use of the secret passageways built into the fabric of the building. Today, it's a charming place to rest weary feet, have a drink, eat good food or even stay the night.

Back down on the quayside the river was now fully replenished with a pair of swans serving as backdrop to the stalls of a farmers' market.

Totnes, again. Delightful Devon.

G Says…

The Prime Ministers's attempts to hold a fissiparous Cabinet together having, possibly only temporarily, eclipsed the nations' obsession with the Ing-er-Land football teams' World Cup progress, it must be time to swan off for an adventure, we reasoned.

But, where to go? After minuscule debate, Marigold decided we would be heading for Devon, specifically to Brixham where we so very nearly bought a house a few years ago. Part of the triumvirate of towns making up Torbay, the region is widely known as the English Riviera. We've already lived on the French Riviera, so why not add the English version was a remark one of us made at the time of our putative house purchase. Sadly, in some ways although not in others, it was not to be, but we're due a return visit just to check out the area again and seek out the aspects of it we particularly liked.

So, a plan, but after setting off very early we almost immediately decided to make Totnes our first port of call. It's Friday, which means flea market day in Totnes, which was more than enough to relegate the English Riviera to later in the day.

We adore Totnes. We visit, often, and never fail to be charmed by its mixture of bohemian enchantment and the laid back pace of life. Time Magazine once declared Totnes to be the 'capital of New Age chic.' It's not a bad looking place either.

Totnes has the most listed buildings per head than any other town in the UK, there's a 10th century Motte and Bailey Castle perched at the very top and a Tudor arch straddles the Main Street right in the middle of town. What you don't get is a Waitrose or a Marks and Spencer and there's absolutely no chance of a Costa coffee after a petition to keep them out of the town made national news. Not that coffee aficionados like ourselves, just one short step away from addiction, are disappointed as there's a vast choice of alternatives on offer. There are quaint tea rooms with pure white tablecloths, resolutely in one's face vegetarian/vegan cafes/restaurants and any number of trendy organic coffee houses.

We parked topless Ruby in the car park alongside Steamer Quay and were immediately asked if we wanted to take a river boat to Dartmouth. 'Sorry, not today,' Marigold said.

'Well,' said the boatman, 'Dartmouth is always worth a visit and it's only 6 miles downstream taking the direct route. Takes a lot less time than it would take you by car.'

He's probably right, I thought. Summer traffic, narrow winding roads, every journey is fraught with possible delays and Dartmouth is one of the most difficult places around here to get into and find a parking space. Even so, we said no to the boat trip and set off across the bridge.

We'd already decided we'd visit the castle, but we stopped for breakfast at Seeds – a perennial favourite , '['seeds,' - 'perennial,' right? Oh, please yourselves] – before wandering around the market almost next door. In truth, we were flagging a little already after walking no more than three quarters of the way up the hill and were glad of a sit down. In mitigation, it was very, very warm, even early in the day.

Outside a couple of musicians were setting up. They looked interesting, but took so long 'tuning up' we decided we'd take them in on the way back. (By which time they'd gone).

The street market was fascinating, as it invariably is. Bread, cakes fruit and veg, jams, chutney, any amount of hippie-style clothing and hand made jewellery and in the car park a random mixture of junk and undiscovered treasures. A very smartly dressed stall holder, sitting in regal splendour with an old dog on his knee, told me everything there was to know about the breed in general and his own highly prized specimen in particular. Even down to measurements, from floor to shoulder for example. I listened, stroked the dog, said they both looked very smart and moved on.

By now Marigold was deep in conversation with one of her friends. We'd made a fairly tentative arrangement to meet today – I had actually forgotten - but were pleased to see them. They're French, we have known them for almost twenty years and we meet up every three or four years on an entirely ad hoc basis, much like today. They're visiting England, as tourists, and we wandered around together, chatting away. Marigold and Yvette were walking in front, laughing like loons, while I followed on 'chatting' to Bernard.

Yvette speaks very good English, even teaches English back home, but Bernard insists on speaking only French. Even though he knows a little English. 'It's good for you to practise,' he says. I should have pointed out it may have been a good time for him to practise his English as he was in England now, but the moment passed. So, I struggled. Just a bit.

We lived in France for ten years, but it was a while ago. I was never 'fluent' in the language, but 'rusty' does not even come close to my present ability to carry on a conversation with a Frenchman. Especially as Bernard seemed determined to thrash out each and every possible ramification of a no deal ending to the Brexit saga.

After ten minutes I was linguistically wilting and the heat was entirely blameless. Less of a polymath, rather a Jack of all trades. Even that description is stretching credulity. Linguistics have evidently tagged on to all my other faculties that are on the verge of extinction.

We caught up with our better halves, yes, still laughing like loons, and bartered fiercely with stall holders, ending up with very little, but proudly clutching a few disparate items we apparently want but can't in any sense of the word profess to 'need.' Hey ho, that's one of the joys of a flea market.

After a return trip to stroke the old dog, we walked up to the castle as our friends had already expressed an interest in seeing it. I hoped they weren't too disappointed by what little remains of what was the crowning glory of this prominent Saxon town.

Totnes was one of four Saxon fortified *burhs* in Devon, the others being Barnstaple, Exeter and Lydford and the original earth mound had a later stone keep added which makes it a pretty impressive sight. The arrow slits of the actual keep are still just about recognisable, the views from up here are magnificent and there were yet more buskers setting up to entertain picnickers in the 'Bailey' area surrounding the 'Motte.'

We parted company with our French friends as we were bound for the coast and Bernard wanted to see if the rumours that it was possible to make wine in England have any substance. We assured him it was not only possible to produce very good wine in England, we were even capable of making cheese. Both commodities, of course, in the opinion of every single Frenchman I've ever met, being impossible to find outside France.

Sharpham Wine and Cheese is both a vineyard and dairy and only just down the road so we sent them on their way. I read recently that Sharpham produces 100,000 bottles of wine a year, which Bernard may well regard as derisory but sounds pretty impressive to me. I see many similarities between Devon and one of our former homes in the Loire Valley and wine producers have obviously reached the same conclusion.

We strolled back down the hill, browsing and window shopping amongst the bustling crowds. On reflection, it was too hot to actually 'bustle' but there were certainly crowds doing whatever crowds do when it's hot.

We returned to Ruby, put the hood down and set off for the coast. Almost immediately, we discovered an essential diversion after spotting a sign for Berry Pomeroy Castle, which we've often heard mentioned, but never visited.

Buried, in almost every sense, in a valley just outside the town, it's 'only 15th Century' but the devastation of the centuries is as marked as that of the far older castle we just left behind.

Berry Pomeroy Castle is reputedly one of the most haunted buildings in the UK, but we always make allowance for such claims. Ghosts bring in visitors, although very few had made the journey so far today and we virtually had the place to ourselves.

The building of the castle began in 1460 by the Pomeroy family, who had been the most notable family in the area for hundreds of years, but almost immediately they found themselves short of cash and sold the castle to Edward Seymour, a brother of Jane Seymour, the third wife of Henry the 8th.

Jane Seymour died of postnatal complications less than two weeks after the birth of her only child who became King Edward VI. She was the only one of Henry's wives to receive a State funeral and the only one to be buried beside him in St George's Chapel at Windsor Castle.

The Seymour family were riding high in English society at the time and continued to prosper right up to the Elizabethan era when they decided to build a vast mansion to rival the likes of Longleat. Work started around 1600, but it was never finished – we've had building projects like that – and less than a century later the house was abandoned. It's a glorious ruin now, an abandoned masterpiece, and in its own way still rather magnificent. No, we didn't see any ghosts.

Much more to come of a very busy trip, but that will have to wait for another day.

The English Riviera.

G Says…

We drove away from Totnes with its wide range of individually owned shops and timeless charm with hedonistic Torbay as our next destination. Not quite candy-floss and kiss me quick hats, but this is July so anything goes.

The narrow lanes of Devon don't bother Mini Coopers so we only had to seek the shelter of a hedge twice – almost unheard of at this time of year - and made a brief stop in Babbacombe, home to what I've been told is the highest promenade in the country. There are stunning views over Lyme Bay and down to Oddicombe beach. It's a long way down, but we wisely decided we could make do with the view from the top of the cliffs. There's a model village here too, if you like that sort of thing.

We moved on to the ultimate retirees' destination, Torquay, with its palm trees, busy harbour and relentless desire to offer everything to the visitor, whatever their age. There's a theatre, a big wheel and any amount of tourist attractions to attract the summer trade while the mild climate keeps the very many elderly residents happy through the winter months. There's a gorgeous abbey too, Torre Abbey, just off the sea front and its lawns were packed with picnicking holidaymakers as we passed by. I remembered from a previous visit reading an information sheet saying that Torre Abbey was once the wealthiest Premonstratensian abbey in England. (Yes, I checked the spelling).

I reminded Marigold of this and she said, 'I was just going to say that.' Almost, but not quite, convincingly. On one of our many journeys around France we once visited Prémontré Abbey itself, where the Order was founded, and there are Premonstratensian abbeys or priories throughout the world.

We're not obsessed by abbeys, far from it, but we do like old buildings with character and I've yet to come across a 'boring' Abbey. As for this particular religious order; I just like the name Premonstatensian. Once remembered, it rolls off the tongue. Not the case with everyone, as Marigold pointed out, several times.

Torquay has been the birthplace of very many notable people: Agatha Christie, Peter Cook and Miranda Hart, for instance, while several sketches of "Monty Pythons Flying Circus" were filmed here and a hotel in the town was the inspiration for 'Fawlty Towers'. It's also the birthplace of two men whose exploits were a source of fascination to me as a young boy: Sir Richard Burton (not the one who married Elizabeth Taylor) and Colonel Percy Harrison Fawcett.

I looked up Sir Richard Burton to check his date of birth (1721) and he is described as a British explorer, geographer, translator, writer, soldier, orientalist, cartographer, ethnologist, spy, linguist, poet, fencer and diplomat.

Impressive!

He's also reputed to have been fluent in 29 European, Asian and African languages, which makes my difficulties earlier that day in Totnes with my rapidly failing command of the French language seem even more feeble.

Burton had visited Mecca, in disguise, at a time when Europeans were forbidden access on pain of death, translated the Arabian Nights and the Kama Sutra into English and with John Hanning Speke became the first Europeans to visit the Great Lakes of Africa in search of the source of the Nile. Explorers, the men who expanded my horizons and imagination at a very young age, still fascinate me.

Colonel Percy Harrison Fawcett was born in Torquay in 1867 and his exploits as an archaeologist and explorer in South America formed the basis of Sir Arthur Conan Doyle's novel The Lost World and, much later, as the inspiration for 'Indiana Jones'. Fawcett vanished, never to be seen again, searching for a 'lost city' he named Z somewhere in the uncharted, pretty much so even to this day, Mato Grosso region of Brazil.

We were bound for Brixham, at the far side of the bay, so we pressed on after deciding it was a bit too hot to wait an hour or more for a parking space to become available in Torquay.

Neighbouring Paignton has numerous brightly coloured beach huts, decent beaches, a cinema, railway station and the spectacular Oldway Mansion, built as a private house for Isaac Merritt Singer – the sewing machine inventor - and rebuilt by his third son Paris Singer in the style of the Palace of Versailles. (I'm grateful to a blue plaque for all this information). We didn't at first sight exclaim, 'it's just like Versailles,' but it's still an impressive house.

Onward then to Brixham. In fairness, we didn't immediately fall in love with the town when we were on the brink of buying a property here. Much of it is run down and a bit scruffy, but the harbour is attractive enough and boasts two remarkable features, only one of which attracts tourist interest, if today is any guide. Unless you have a 'historical bent', which a close friend once assured me I do possess. Sounds vaguely gynaecological, doesn't it?

The biggest attraction in the harbour is a replica of Sir Francis Drake's ship 'The Golden Hind'. Captain Drakes's original ship was the first to circumnavigate the world between 1577 and 1580. The 'copy' has been in the news recently with one of those great human interest stories that feed the tabloid press about a man who went for a day out with his children and ended up buying the Golden Hind.

Sean and Mary Twomey, who run the Torquay Backpackers international youth hostel, bought the replica of Sir Francis Drake's galleon and have guaranteed that it will stay in Brixham. The previous owner had one reputedly far larger offer from a group wishing to remove it to San Francisco harbour, but was insistent on it remaining in Brixham.

This 'version' of the Golden Hind replaced the 'original replica,' if that makes sense, which was a converted fishing boat that sank in 1987 while being towed to Dartmouth for restoration. The replacement replica, not full sized, was completed in 1988 and is not seaworthy, but attracts many admirers in the harbour.

Last time we were in London we saw another version of the Golden Hind. This is a full-size reconstruction of the ship, was built by traditional methods in Appledore, Devon and launched in 1973.

She sailed from Plymouth on her maiden voyage in late 1974 to San Francisco. In 1979, she sailed to Japan to make the movie Shogun, after which she returned to the UK having completed a circumnavigation of the globe to match the feat first achieved by Francis Drake. Obviously, there wasn't a great deal wrong with that original design and specification. Since 1996 she's been moored up in Southwark.

Quite evidently, as far as seaworthiness goes, the version we're looking at today is very much a poor relation. It would struggle to even leave the harbour. Even so, it looks good and nobody here appears disappointed.

The other attraction in the harbour area was attracting no interest whatsoever. Only Marigold and I could be bothered to go and look at a statue of a man with no nose, yet it represents the most important event in Brixham's entire history. In 1688, William of Orange made his claim to the English throne in Brixham Harbour stating to the apparently sparse crowd gathered in baffled attendance 'The Liberties of England and The Protestant Religion I will maintain'.

He had just landed with his Dutch army after being invited to come and take his place as ruler of England. He brought his entire army with him, evidently suspecting not everyone would be in agreement with this idea. The road leading from the harbour up a steep hill is called *Overgang* which I suspected was a Dutch word and later confirmed it was indeed so and meant 'crossing,' being the road up from where the Dutch army made their camp.

What became known as the Glorious Revolution followed. William of Orange became co-ruler with his wife and cousin, Mary II, daughter of James II, the monarch they succeeded who was destined to become the last Roman Catholic monarch of England.

On the statue, William's nose is absent, but there's no evidence to suggest the vandalism was the work of irate priests threatened with imminent redundancy.

Apparently, the modern fishing trawler was invented here in the nineteenth century and the town was also one of the places from which American troops bound for the D Day Landings left, but that's about it for Brixham.

If Torquay claims a whole host of famous people born in the town, sadly, Brixham falls short. Famous people born in Brixham? None that I could find. Apart from Hannah Harper a pornographic actress who once featured as Penthouse Pet of the Month in 2002. Apparently. Would-be parents living in Brixham should perhaps consider moving up the road to Torquay if they have any future expectations for their intended daughters.

The delightfully situated Berry Head Hotel was originally built as a military hospital in 1809 during the Napoleonic Wars, and was later the home of Reverend H F Lyte who wrote the famous hymn 'Abide With Me' here, reputedly on his deathbed.

We've been here before, several times, and decided we'd pay another visit after walking around the headland.

We drove up the hill, ignoring the hotel for now, to take another look at the area in which we almost became property owners a few years back.

The views of the sea are impressive, but the best aspect of the area is easy access to Berry Head nature reserve.

A sign says, 'Berry Hill, 400 Million Years in the Making' which is pretty impressive.

At one time there was an Iron Age Fort here – not exactly 400 million years ago, but worth a mention - but all remnants of it were destroyed when the building of Napoleonic War defences took precedence.

This place is exactly what a nature reserve should be: wild, untamed, peaceful and with stunning cliff top views to provide a 'wow factor.' We're perched on 200 feet high cliffs, surrounded by water on 3 sides and the views are breathtaking.

On the very far tip of Berry Head is a unique lighthouse. It is not only the shortest lighthouse in the United Kingdom it is also the highest. This apparent paradox comes about because the building housing the light itself is pretty insignificant, just about the height of a bungalow, hence the claim to being the UK's shortest, but perched on these high cliffs it is also higher above sea level than any other lighthouse.

A 'trainspotter' type in a tattered anorak turned up as I was taking a photo and started to tell Marigold all about the lighthouse. She was surreptitiously rolling her eyes so I rescued her, but I do remember the wise man of the cliffs saying this was not only the lowest and smallest lighthouse in Britain, but also the deepest. Apparently, a weight acting as a counterbalance that used to turn the light went down a shaft almost to sea level. I haven't checked this, but if it turns out to be nonsense, blame an anorak wearing know-all named Roger.

'Roger' – not a trainspotter but a bird spotter (same difference) – told us where to go to see 'one of the largest breeding colonies of guillemots you'll see anywhere' and also any number of birds we may or may not see on our walk. I can't possibly remember the whole list, but Marigold remembered him mentioning a razorbill and for the next hour any bird: thrush, seagull, whatever, she piped up with, 'is that a razorbill?'

Irritating? Yes, just a tad, after a while!

We did see a lot of guillemots though.

Roger the sage of Berry Head, assured us we would see both porpoise and dolphins out to sea from the cliff edge and that a humpback whale had been seen swimming around for a whole month last year. Did we see any of them?

Er, no.

We'd managed to avoid going into the 'award-winning' Guardhouse Café as we were set on going to the Berry Head Hotel, but it certainly seemed a popular stop. 'Award Winning' doesn't seem to mean anything special anywhere in Devon or Cornwall as it's very hard to find a café, pub or restaurant or buy an ice cream or pasty that doesn't boast of 'award winning' status.

We returned to the car and went to the award winning, of course, Berry Hill Hotel. Marigold will tell you all about it, coming up next.

Marigold Says...

Arrived at The Berry Head hotel. Been before and it is a magical setting. When we were in the throes of nearly buying in Brixham, we found the walk down from the top, through a wooded area and then onto a track to the hotel. Loved it, as it was a gorgeous day and it was a huge plus in the plus and minus sections. Again, today, the weather was absolutely gorgeous. The terrace was packed so we went inside. Found some lovely armchairs, ordered a pot of tea and some hand carved ham sandwiches, served with salad and crisps. Just the ticket and they didn't disappoint.

Just as I had taken a mouthful of grub, a couple sat opposite and the man said to me "you look as if you are enjoying that". Wanted to say, "well I was, until you turned up". I know my cheeks were bulging with food, but he didn't need to mention it. Ate the rest with little bites as he started talking about all sorts of random stuff, and quite frankly ruined my munching.

His wife was faffing about at the bar, ordering food. They must have been the fussiest people alive.

'Don't put any crisps on the plate, he won't eat them and if he did he'd only make a mess,'she shouted, loud enough to be heard on the outside terrace.

'You can put about half a dozen on mine, but I don't want any of the flavoured ones and definitely not if they're crinkle cut. We want butter on the bread, if I find margarine it's coming straight back and make sure there's nothing smothered in mayonnaise as well,' was the gist of what she was bellowing at the poor girl taking the order.

She sat down opposite us and started telling G she'd be 'giving this place a try but wasn't hopeful.' At the top of her voice.

Eventually, I said to G 'bring your plate and follow me as our friends are over there,' mumbled "goodbye" to the couple and scarpered to the library. Ecstasy, we finished our sandwiches in peace.with only us in there and I then had a 20 minute kip.

Had a walk around the gardens afterwards. Two teams of people were playing boules, rather noisily, and taking it ever so seriously. Said to G "they seem like show offs". They were measuring and gesticulating madly. Then we realised they were French. No wonder it was so precise. We weren't asked to join in. We have played boules when we lived in France, often with with plastic boules. It was always chaotic as our dog used to run off with them and they had all got chew holes in.

There were a lot of people sitting on the front of the hotel enjoying the spectacular views, and probably thinking like us " it doesn't get much better than this".

Dungeness.

Marigold Says...

We set off for Dungeness which we have been to before, and usually when we visit it is either foggy or raining. The weather didn't disappoint. The sea fog had come in, so everything looked eerie. It is like something out of Mad Max, with shed houses, some good, some bad. You can tell the ones which scream "I want to buy a shed house that will cost an arm and a leg, extend it and buy shabby-chic furniture, get bored and then sell it". You can also tell the old stagers who dress up like fishermen and collect stuff off the beach and decorate their shed houses with it.

The back drop for most of the inhabitants/nutters is the Nuclear Power Station. I just love it here. You can imagine them filming The Walking Dead, and maybe they have.

Apparently there are flowers and plants there, that are very unusual. Maybe it is the overflow from the power station that they water them with. I think I read something about an orchid found locally and its rarity. Only place in the world it grows. Better put back the one I just dug up then!

Not really. I don't carry a spade in my handbag. Or even a handbag very often.

What was really weird was watching the little steam train coming through the mist, full of holiday makers. All four of them. I said to G maybe it will drive into the power station and come out empty, and they will never be seen again. G ignored my imagination and carried on chuntering about the price of kit-kat (dark chocolate) in the petrol station. I like the milk chocolate ones. Talking of kit-kat, they are not the same without the silver paper. Enough confectionary related grumbling.

We visited Derek Jarman's garden, a lovely little wild fest. It is like a shrine to the great man, if indeed he was. Don't know much about him, but G does and will fill you in.

We had to leave all in a rush as a klaxon sounded at the nuclear reactor place and men in white suits came rushing out. Well, it could have happened.

Went off in search of Bovril to warm the cockles. As we left Dungeness the sun came out.

G Says...

Dungeness. Marigold really loves its wildness, its unworldly aspect. I just think it's a scruffy patch of unusable land with a shingle 'beach' bordered by a grey sea one one side and Romney Marsh on the other, blighted by

185

a dirty great, incredibly unattractive nuclear power station. We agree to differ, it's a rare event, but today the clouds are grey, there's rain in the air and in fact it's exactly what I call 'Dungeness weather'.

Marigold isn't daunted, of course. We approach from a different direction than our usual route, not that it's any more attractive. There's a bright pink Range Rover in someone's drive which we quite like, but certainly don't covet, and a fair few big houses which must have been even more impressive in their heyday.

We drive the coast road and are soon rewarded with our first glimpse of the power station, looming out of the mist. It's as hideous as ever. To be precise there are actually two power stations: a working one and its predecessor now decommissioned, but still remaining a liability for the next hundred thousand years or so. There are two lighthouses here as well. Show offs!

We'd just entered the scruffiest bit when we saw the little train approaching, so we parked up and went to get a closer look. It's travelled from Hythe, picking up passengers up along the way, there were four of them by now!

In fairness, in better weather and in the school holidays, we have seen it packed with passengers. A fellow train watcher, obviously a local resident as he greeted the train driver by name, decided we were in need of instruction and found an audience in Marigold. He had two visible teeth, one at the top, one at the bottom, which was a bit of a distraction as he talked. The Dungeness Estate, which we'd just entered covers over 6,000 acres and it's the only place in the UK which has been officially classified as a desert.

Marigold was obviously entranced by her new companion. I suspect she just wanted to watch those teeth waggling up and down as he answered her questions.

'How long have you lived here?'

'Oh, must be fifteen years, give or take. Just before the millennium.' (He didn't exactly say 'millennium,' but a garbled approximation of the word and if he arrived before the millennium he would have been living here rather more than fifteen years, but conversations of this nature are rarely an exact science)

'Is your house near here?'

'It's that one, over there,' the man replied. Unfortunately, for Marigold, he didn't add, 'would you like to look inside?'

The 'house' in question was a shack, constructed of corrugated iron sheets. We've seen refugee camps in Africa with better accommodation. There were three other houses in the vicinity, all equally shoddy: timber 'sheds,' old railway carriages and all adding to the general air of desolation. If this really is a desert, it's the scruffiest one we've ever encountered. The landscape has a 'lunar' quality, flat, bare apart from a few patches of scrub and looming out of the mist are that pair of nuclear power stations. Does Chernobyl look like this, I mused.

'I love it here,' two-tooth continued, 'especially in the winter when all the crowds have gone.'

Crowds? We were the only three people in sight, but I know what he meant. We've lived in areas frequented by tourists and the winter months are when we get our 'home' to ourselves. It's pretty bleak here though, even in June. In January it must be really grim.

'I do a bit of fishing, three of us have shares in a boat, and there's fish to be had out there, but we always go a bit further out, well away from the discharge point from the power station. That warm water, I don't reckon it's any good for fishing. There's plenty of 'em as do fish there, but not me. They say it's safe, but I don't know.'

Gulp! We both mentally crossed locally caught fish off the lunch menu. Nuclear power is efficient, does far less harm to the environment, in the short term at least, but even so, would we choose to eat fish caught within its shadow?

Marigold still needed to know more about the pleasures of living here.

'Are there many houses for sale?'

'If you want to live here, there's a long waiting list. The only one on the market just now is Sleepers Cottage. I heard they're asking £275,000, so it won't hang around for long. The last house that was sold has the removal men in today, so get your skates on if you're thinking of moving here.'

He wandered off, still without asking Marigold if she'd like to come and partake of a cup of tea in his kitchen.

We returned to our car, drove to the end of the railway line, right next to the power station, where there's a café, but as we were about to go inside for a drink, Marigold spotted a medium sized van and decided we should follow it as it was obviously a removal van. We followed the van, not a removal van, just a van, but soon saw the 'real' removal van outside a shack, not really a house, with actual furniture removing taking place.

I looked for 'Sleepers Cottage' on the web. It is indeed on the market for £275,000. It's a converted railway carriage, rather charming actually within its obvious limitations, one room and a cupboard, but I'll not be following up this opportunity.

Originally the home to several well established fishing families, today Dungeness resembles the shanty towns we've seen in the Nevada desert. It's become 'trendy' over the past decade or so; its out of the way simplicity an obvious attraction for those weary of the rat race. Assuming they have the financial resources to live here, of course. Many of the shacks purport to be art galleries, often with sculptures composed of driftwood and articles scavenged from the shore outside and there's an extensive nature reserve, still in the shadow of the power station, in the surrounding area.

I actually found myself liking the unreconstructed nature of the shingle beach with an occasional beached fishing boat lying askew and apparently abandoned. I also like the absolute randomness of the tin shacks, faded wooden sheds and former railway rolling stock that constitute home to those hardy souls that live here year round.

The serenity, the nonconformity, the proximity to the sea, I can relate to that. I could even live here. If only there weren't a vast and hideous nuclear power station stuck in the back garden! The phrase 'blot on the landscape' has never appeared so appropriate. Not that Dungeness would ever have the effrontery to regard itself as pretty. Not even attractive, but even a windswept landscape such as this deserves a better neighbour.

We went to look at Derek Jarman's house, Prospect Cottage, which we've been to view several times before. The former film maker bought the house many years ago and set about the task of making a garden from the scrubland that surrounded the cottage. The result is quite charming and Prospect Cottage receives many visitors who stand and admire the simplicity of his creation.

Jarman once said the Pilot Inn, nearby, provided 'Simply the finest fish and chips in all England,' the veracity of which claim we won't be checking out today in case they're 'locally caught fish.' I read an article yesterday describing Derek Jarman's garden as 'postmodern and highly context-sensitive, a complete rejection of modernist design theory.'

Hmm! Could you tell that was taken from The Guardian?

I like the scattered artefacts, the small circles of flint possibly intended as tiny versions of ancient dolmens or standing stones and the absolute and obviously intentional absence of any pretension. I also looked up a half remembered quote of Jarman, in relation to his garden.

'Paradise haunts gardens, and some gardens are paradises. Mine is one of them. Others are like bad children, spoilt by their parents, over-watered and covered with noxious chemicals.'

'Paradises,' as a word, grates with me, but there's no mistaking the desire for simplicity here. The cottage itself is equally unpretentious and somewhat more attractive in its intentional simplicity than most of its neighbours. (Neighbours being a relative term; we're not talking about a cheek by jowl traditional housing estate)

Mindful that this is someone else's property, I nevertheless was able to photograph the poem written on the black timber wall. It's taken from John Donne's poem The Sun Rising and reads:

'Busy old fool, unruly Sun,
Why dost thou thus,
Through windows, and through curtains, call on us ?
Must to thy motions lovers' seasons run ?
Saucy pedantic wretch, go chide
Late school-boys and sour prentices,
Go tell court-huntsmen that the king will ride,
Call country ants to harvest offices ;
Love, all alike, no season knows nor clime,
Nor hours, days, months, which are the rags of time.
In that the world's contracted thus ;
Thine age asks ease, and since thy duties be
To warm the world, that's done in warming us.
Shine here to us, and thou art everywhere ;
This bed thy centre is, these walls thy sphere.'

Derek Jarman died in 1994, but his former partner continues to spend time here and maintains the garden. Jarman was a confirmed and voluble atheist, but is nevertheless buried in the nearby graveyard at St. Clements Church in Old Romney.

We found the graveyard, quite easily. Finding the actual grave was somewhat more difficult but we managed it. It's a minimalist headstone; even an atheist buried in a churchyard would have approved of that.

Cornwall.

G Says...

We've been driving down narrow lanes, walking on beaches and cliff tops and taking advantage of some glorious weather to explore what is surely England's most photogenic county.

A Mini Convertible is the perfect antidote to those feelings of ennui that creep up on one when the weather is hot and Ruby has taken us far and wide in the last week or so. Cornwall is a big place, long and narrow, with the longest coastline in Great Britain.

A lot of coastline means a lot of beaches and we've walked on beaches in the past few days that are equal to any we've seen anywhere in the world and we've been almost everywhere! Blue sky and sunshine help, of course, but golden sand and a turquoise sea are an irresistible combination.

Cornwall, or Kernow as the locals call it, is one of the seven historic Celtic Nations – the other six being Alba (Scotland), Eire (Ireland), Breizh (Brittany), Mann (Isle of Man) Cymru (Wales) and Gallaeciea (Galicia, in Spain). Not a dud among them and we have personal experience of them all.

Poldark is back on tv, apparently, so there's fresh interest in Cornwall this summer and the remnants of the tin mining industry are doing brisk business with tourists. In the 1900s, half of the world's tin came from Cornwall. The tin miners of Cornwall once traded with the Phoenicians and at this time Cornwall was known as The Cassiterides or The Tin Islands. Later on Cornwall became known as The Stannaries – stannum being the Latin word for tin. (If I recall my school chemistry lessons correctly, the symbol for the chemical element tin is Sn).

Tin mining has long since ceased to be a viable industry in Cornwall and nowadays the only industries of note are the exporting of China clay and tourism. China clay is now Cornwall's largest export (apart than Cornish pasties!)

Cornwall has about half a million permanent residents, but more than five million tourists a year. Those tourists eat more than five million Cornish pasties every year, an average of 13,500 a day. No wonder the humble Cornish Pasty is worth £150 million a year to the Cornish economy.

We love Cornwall and have done ever since our first long-stay - seven months - visit in the late 1960s when Marigold worked in a boutique and I delivered custom built surfboards all over Cornwall and was a 'bouncer' in the Sailor's Arms in Newquay in the evenings. We lived in a very small tent, stored our meagre belongings in the back of our Austin A35 van, and our friends were itinerant surfers from Australia, New Zealand and California. These days, we don't 'rough it' to the same extent, but otherwise little has changed.

Visiting Padstow means going either early or late as the association with Rick Stein put Padstow on the map and now means this tiny fishing village is over run with visitors. We arrived in early evening and wandered around for an hour or so. We could have taken a trip around the bay, a ferry to Rock just over the way or a boat trip to visit the notorious Doom Bar.

Widely known as the brand name of the most popular beer in England, the flagship ale of the local Sharp's Brewery, the Doom Bar is a bank of sand at the estuary of the River Camel where it meets the Celtic Sea. It can be seen at low tide and appears innocuous enough, but many ships have been wrecked there.

Doom Bar dates back to the reign of Henry VIII and 60 percent of the sand is composed of crushed shells, making it an important source of agricultural lime, which has been collected for hundreds of years; an estimated 10 million tons of sand or more has been removed from the estuary since the early nineteenth century, mainly by dredging.

This evening we were invited to drink a Doom Bar over the Doom Bar by the crew of one of the many boats plying for custom.

The only cash we parted with went to a longtime Padstow 'attraction,' a busker who has been playing his guitar and singing on the quay for many years. Buskers divide opinion, but we've seen a fair few very talented performers in our time and at least they offer more than a beggar with his hand out.

As we sat on a bench, people watching, a dog came and sat right next to Marigold. We've met up with a two year old Newfoundland, two Saint Bernards, and a Dogue de Bordeaux on our recent travels. All of them eat and (possibly) weigh more than the average human. Today's offering, on the quay at Padstow, was not in the big dog league for height and weight, but was certainly impressive.

Dogs like me, I must smell like one, but Marigold is wary of those big enough to devour her in a single bite! The owner told us her dog was a Cane Corso - also known as Italian Mastiff – thought to be descendants of the Roman Molosser dogs.

Molossers were used to subdue wild boar, wolves and other predators in farming communities, but are best known for being used as attack dogs alongside infantry in Roman Legions. This one is not yet fully grown and turned out to be a playful puppy, albeit a very large one.

On our way out of Padstow, we drove through an ornate entrance gateway and discovered Prideaux Place, an Elizabethan Manor House, completed in 1592 by Sir Nicholas Prideaux and, over four hundred years later, still owned and lived in by members of the same family. We didn't go inside or opt for a guided tour as it was far too nice a day to go traipsing round an old house, admiring portraits of long since departed ancestors.

The grounds are superb, an extensive deer park especially, but the sight of a dozen 'detectorists' demanded our attention. Metal detector wielding enthusiasts were hard at work covering every inch of ground in search of buried artefacts. We watched for a while, but nobody uttered any shrieks of excitement as they unearthed a Saxon horde of precious metals so we gave up and left them to it.

Not been to the far tip of Cornwall for a while, so we decided to pay a visit. No, not Lands End which would be an over-commercialised waste of our time. We drove there, just in case it's improved, past the First and Last pub in England - depending which way you're heading – and could see at a glance it's still just a second rate theme park so we went to Sennon Cove instead.

Many years ago I remember this being one of the best places for surfing and there were surfers here aplenty today, all with glum faces as the strong wind was blowing straight out to sea and the waves were almost non existent. Marigold drove Ruby onto the cliffs, stopping a very long way from the edge, and we were lucky enough to see not one but four Cornish choughs, battling against the wind practically at eye level.

We went to look at, if not actually explore as security is understandably tight, the Goonhilly complex near Helston; the site of the world's first first parabolic satellite antenna. That disc, installed in 1962 and named 'Arthur', was built to monitor the ground breaking Telstar satellite and handled the first ever 'live' TV broadcast via satellite.

At one time the Goonhilly station was the largest of its kind on the planet with more than 60 dishes and it's still an impressive sight.

That first transmission using Telstar to bounce a tv signal around the curvature of the Earth transmitted its first image - a video of a wind blown flag outside a TV station in Andover, Maine - on July 11, 1962, but it was the historic broadcast that arrived 13 day's later that captivated my teenage imagination.

The Telstar satellite relayed the first ever live transatlantic broadcast. Walter Cronkite and Chet Huntley - newscasters on rival TV stations - and the BBC's Richard Dimbleby hosted the show. The program started with a picture of the Statue of Liberty and the Eiffel Tower side by side, each coming from different sides of the world.

 I can remember the quality being far from perfect, a fuzzy picture and a noticeable time lag, but everyone was talking about it for days afterwards. Now, we take this technology for granted, but back in 1962 this was truly astonishing and only the televised pictures of a Moon landing seven years later was deemed sufficiently remarkable to beat it.

Next stop was Lizard Point, complete with the Last Café in England. There's no 'first café' this time as the café is perched on the actual furthest point so to claim it as the 'first' would only be appropriate if approached from the sea.

The rocky coast of Cornwall has been the scene of many shipwrecks and Lizard Point was the scene of the greatest ever sea rescue by the RNLI.

There's a plaque commemorating the rescue of all the 456 passengers from The Sueric which ran ground on rocks while sailing from Australia to Liverpool in March 1907. Sixty volunteer crewmen from Cadgwith, Coverack, The Lizard and Porthleven rowed back and forth for 16 hours to rescue the passengers, battling huge waves and ferocious winds in open boats and saved 456 lives, including the 70 babies onboard, without a single life being lost.

Reading this account, we felt humbled beyond belief at the heroism of those volunteer lifeboat crews.

We chatted to a couple of well equipped hikers, with all the correct gear, who looked exhausted. Marigold asked how far they'd walked today and the lady walker looked a little surprised.

'We've just got here,' she said, 'not even started yet,' indicating their car parked right next to ours.

Oops!

We told them we were intending to go to Kynance Cove next and they told us it costs £5 at the National Trust car park, then a long hike, twenty minutes for 'walkers,' so that's half an hour for us, before reaching sea level.

'We're National Trust members so it's free for us.'

Yes, of course they are. We're not.

They suggested we left our car here, at no cost as car park ticket machine was out of order, and walk there along the coastal path. It's not far, they said, so that's what we did.

Not far? Well, maybe not if your name is Mo Farah, but it seemed a very long way to us. Much of the walk was along the cliff edge, no place for anyone even mildly acrophobic.

When we finally reached Kynance Cove, by now reduced to a weary 'trudge,' it was as glorious as we remembered from previous visits. Oddly, we don't remember the actual trek to reach the beach being so arduous on previous visits. The idea of ourselves having declined physically being so ludicrous as to be discounted we were forced to conclude that coastal erosion was responsible for the vastly increased level of difficulty.

'That wasn't too bad, really,' Marigold said after we'd recovered, a little.

'Still got to do it all again,' I pointed out, 'but this time it's mostly uphill.'

Hmm!

Of course we coped magnificently, even overtaking a few 'proper' walkers at one point. In fairness, they were carrying the equivalent of a sofa on their backs! Is it really necessary to carry so much 'stuff' in a vast rucksack?

Marigold pointed out one lad carrying all his worldly goods, plus a guitar, up the hill. Not that it seemed to bother him.

'I'd swap that guitar for a penny whistle if it were mine,' she said. 'Be a bit less to carry up this hill.'

'You should tell him" I replied.

'I would, if I had a bit more puff.'

We got back to Lizard Point, somehow, and made our second visit to the Last Café. On the way I noticed a sign saying 'Kynack Cove, two and a half miles.'

'Only five miles then, there and back' I said.

Marigold looked aghast. 'I thought we'd walked about twenty miles,' she said.

The sign helpfully told us it was a mere three and three quarter miles, one way, not there and back, obviously, if we took the coastal path in the opposite direction to Cadgwith. Or we could go there in the car.

We went by car. Cadgwith Cove is a pretty fishing village with a pub and not much else. About twelve years ago we came here over Christmas and the New Year, rented a cottage right on the harbour and we haven't been back since. Not that we didn't have a good time, far from it, but there's so much more of the world out there to see!

'Our' cottage wasn't very comfortable, as I recall, the bedroom was dark, dingy and a bit damp in the depths of winter, there was no tv, the oven didn't work, you get the picture? Christmas dinner, ingredients sourced from far, far away Marks and Spencer in Hayle, was a disaster, but when the tide came in, sea spray battered the windows, surf pounded on the rocks and it was glorious.

The whole village turned out to swim in the sea, in fancy dress, they suspended a galleon, decked out in coloured light, from one side of the harbour to the other to resemble a brightly coloured ship on the horizon and we still talk about the characters in the pub where dogs wandered around freely and a group of fishermen gave an impromptu recital of sea shanties. We missed out on food treats, but we enjoyed that Christmas immensely.

Today, it's more or less as we remembered. There are a few more new houses, almost certainly holiday homes, on the hillside and the fishing boats are drawn up on the beach. Not much to do here if you're young, I imagine, but we're not so we didn't mind.

We drove up the far side of the cove, somehow managed to get lost and, completely by accident came across Roskilly Farm where they make cheese, ice cream and many other delicacies. We parked up and were admiring a group of piglets, grubbing about in a field, when two old women turned up. 'Two mad old biddies' was Marigold's version. One said to the piglets, 'Guess what? I just had a bacon sandwich' and cackled energetically. Very energetically, which was pretty remarkable considering it was her 80th birthday today. She told us her name was Maud and her friend, aged 83, was Ursula. Perfectly suited names.

'If you go in the café, over there,' Flora advised, 'watch out for the cat, he'll have your arm off if you don't give him any milk.' She cackled wildly, again. It was relatively early in the day or I'd have suspected Maud and Ursula had been imbibing freely. Maybe they brought their own supplies.

Marigold asked Maud if she knew where to find the sculpture park above Coverack, our next destination.

Maud frowned. 'Ask them at Paris Hotel for best route to the sculpture park. I'm hopeless with directions.'

Ursula said, 'It's a nightmare. Up hill all the way, then there's just things sat in a field. Not what I call art. Had more fun in Sainsbury's.'

195

'Take no notice of my friend,' insisted Maud, 'she's got no appreciation of art at all. Ask at the Paris Hotel. They sort things out for me at the Paris, no problem. Nothing to do with France, the name, you know, but I'm saying no more.'

Ursula joined in. 'No, nothing to do with France. I should think not too. My late husband had a word for France and French people. I can't possibly repeat it.'

'Ursula's late husband was in the Diplomatic Service,' Maud confided. 'You get a rounded view of the world in the Service, but far too much association with foreigners for my liking. Don't you forget about that cat, now. Jumps on the tables, likes milk but prefers cream.'

They wandered off and we decided we'd risk the café, despite the grave expressions of concern about potentially lethal cats. We spotted the killer feline straight away and, as Maud had warned, he was perched on a table in the courtyard, sipping milk from a spoon offered by a customer. He looked too fat to be dangerous and so it proved. When we sat down for a moment, one of those stone in shoe problems, he waddled over, jumped up and began purring. We had no milk on offer, let alone cream, but he allowed us to live a little longer!

We moved on to Coverack, Another place we've been before and we actually stayed briefly in a cottage here a few years ago. We noted the Paris Hotel, set back from the road, on our way in.

We didn't bother to go in and ask for directions, but we did discover it was built by the Redruth Brewery in 1907 and named after the liner SS PARIS which ran aground on the headland on whit Monday 1899. So, the mad old biddies were right, no direct connection to France.

Marigold said she remembered a café on the right hand side from our previous visit, but the only one we found was the Harbour Lights café, which wasn't so familiar. It was waitress service, we were advised, and sat down and watched cars trying, in vain, to find a parking space. It appeared we had taken the last free space!

After ten minutes, no one had arrived to take an order so Marigold went inside. The waitress was talking to her friend, laughing like a drain as Marigold put it, and showing no inclination to attend to her VIP customers.

We left the car in its treasured parking space and walked on towards the harbour where we found the café we remembered from last time which also serves as a shop for locals. This isn't a 'beach' resort, there's very little actual beach, but it's a pretty village with a great deal of charm.

No actual beach as such, but the shoreline here is remarkable because of the rocks that form a narrow barrier twixt sea and shore. (Don't ever remember writing 'twixt' before, ever)

Back to the rocks; a proper geologist would doubtless have offered up a sesquipedalian account of their origin, but I'll try and keep it brief.

At the bottom of an ancient sea known as the Rheic Ocean, about 375 million years ago, the molten rock which would become the Lizard Peninsula of Cornwall was forced through the Earth's crust from about six miles below. The enormous pressure of these eruptions brought up a complete slice of all the rocks on the way up, from the mantle to the crust.

Rocks on this beach originate from the molten magma of the Earth's core, including the brightly coloured Serpentine rock unique to this area, the actual Earth's crust, and, even more rarely, rocks formed from the molten junction of the mantle and the core. This transitional section of the Earth's core is called a fossil Moho, the shortened version of Mohorovicic Discontinuity, normally found five miles or so beneath the ocean bed. Coverack is one of the few places in the world where it is seen at the Earth's surface.

Enough science, time for some culture. We set off to walk to the Terence Coventry sculpture park as Marigold had seen a reference to it in the Sunday Times. The article didn't tell us the only way to get there was up a steep hill from the harbour.

We struggled up the hill, wearing shoes not designed for fell walking, stopping every few minutes to appreciate those splendid coastal views. Otherwise known as getting our breath back. We passed a house on the left bearing a tablet in honour of Elizabeth Coad, who turned out to be a member of the ubiquitous Roskilly family whose wares we'd seen at the family farm.

Eventually, we reached the sculptures, in two fields, one to the left and one to the right of the path. The setting was spectacular and Marigold loved the sculptures.

Female Role Models.

Marigold Says...

We decided sort of last minute to have a bit of culture in our lives and set off early to visit the Minack theatre. We have been before and the journey there and the Romanesque theatre, had to look that one up, are really, well, theatrical.

We had to do a bit of a diversion to find Anne's Pasty garage which is attached to her house. We bought some years ago and I have never forgotten how good they were. They are hand made and the best ever.

Got horribly lost and we ended up in a very narrow lane with me driving. A huge lorry was in front of me and when it started to reverse there was nowhere left for me to go. I lost it completely. He was revving his engine, the revs making a noise like "move, move, move".

Red neck time and G took over with me covering my head with two wet wipes while he reversed for about half a mile, grumbling. As is usual at these times, I swear never to drive again. Last year I set off with the hood down and a farmer's muck lorry discharged a dollop inside the car. There is a stain there forever.

Anyway, I digress. I do that, a lot. We never did find Anne or her pasties. She has probably made so much money and lives in the Bahamas and writes about the history of the pasty.

We were one of the first to arrive at Minack and headed straight for the coffee shop. Priorities. There were a few tired looking scones on display there, as they were only just setting up. Views from the cafe are just incredible. Had our coffee and bought a packet of biscuits, 3 for me 1 for G. He wasn't looking. Two South Africans arrived with noisy shoes. I asked them what the shoes were. They were cleats on the shoes and they were cyclists. Looked too fat to be cyclists, I thought. Got a bit bored by this, so left G to chat about rugby with the members of the South African Fat Cyclists Club.

A lovely young woman who now lives in New Zealand arrived who was walking the coastal path. That's a very, very long way, but she's already walked from one end of New Zealand to the other, so this is just a stroll. She's quite well known as the Tiny Tramper or something like that. She had all her worldly possessions with her in a huge rucksack, bigger then her, and slept in a tent. She was coming back later to see the production. It is sold out well in advance and we always do things last minute, so only ourselves to blame. If it was Shakespeare I wouldn't be able to go as I am allergic.

We then went and looked at the wild gardens. A lot had died off over the winter as they had snow here for the first time in many, many years so they had re-planted.

The theatre is just amazing, stone tiered, and best of all is the setting. Can't imagine anywhere else like it. We sat down and took it all in. It is quite ethereal. Ooh, get me! If we were living nearer I would be a Volunteer. I would, obviously ,choose to be a meeter and greeter.

The production we should see is The Pirates of Penzance, because of the Cornwall links, but I'd rather go to a 'proper' musical.

We dragged ourselves to the top, and there was a bit of silliness on my part hiding behind the huge plants. Not like me at all. Tee hee.

The woman who was responsible for this huge, huge construction was called Rowena Cade, very tall, very skinny and virtually a one woman band for a lot of the time. I said to G, it makes you ashamed when we moan about watering the garden, but NOT with a hosepipe ban in effect I hasten to add.

They have restructured the gallery of her life, and last time there were pictures of famous people who have acted there. The pictures have gone, and I can only remember Judy Dench, but she is a biggy so will have to do.

Lots of people arriving, so we set back, and passed the new premises for Anne's Pasties. Bought two to be taken back, but pulled in and ate one while it was hot. Luscious. We went back and got six more as we have friends to cater for. G drove back as I was still traumatised from the reversing juggernaut while I had a kip. Yes, even with the hood down it's possible to sleep in a Mini Cooper.

G Says...

The only true wisdom is in knowing you know nothing.

Socrates.

We were deliberating where to go on a delightfully sunny day. Up with the lark so traffic would not be a significant consideration, at least on the outboard journey, I had just topped up the tank with petrol and Marigold decided we should have a coffee break.

'We've been on the road for less than ten minutes,' I pointed out. Marigold obviously decided this was not a consideration and set off for the attached café.

Very good coffee, newspapers to read and padded seats meant no more complaints from me. At the next table were a group of youngsters, twenty-somethings, engaged in a lively debate. One in particular was very agitated. Putting the world to rights doesn't even come close.

'How wonderful to have all that wisdom,' Marigold observed. 'What a prat.'

His three companions obviously agreed with Marigold as they soon departed leaving him morosely studying the remains of a blueberry muffin. Unfortunately, for us, he dragged his chair across, interrupted our important discussion of world events (unlikely) and set about cadging a lift.

'Any chance you guys are heading for St Ives?'

'No,' we replied in unison, even though we'd just agreed that's where we should go today.

Undeterred, our uninvited guest recommenced his previous conversation, seemingly unmindful that the previous recipients of his applied wisdom had speedily departed. A self termed anarchist, he said Jeremy Corbin had 'sold out' to the Right Wing and that only a revolution would bring about social justice.

'We're definitely not going to St Ives,' Marigold muttered. I was reminded of Citizen Smith, a television programme featuring Robert Lindsey as the wild eyed left wing agitator, Wolfie Smith. We lived through the 1960s, we've heard all this stuff before.

Marigold nudged me, obviously having heard enough. We hadn't finished our drinks, there were newspapers still unread and this was 'our' table, after all. I was spared the chore of having to tell the would-be anarchist to go away when he gave me the perfect opportunity.

'As Marx said, property is theft.'

'He may have done,' I replied, 'but as I'm sure you know, the words are not those of Karl Marx, but of Pierre-Joseph Proudhon. Marx merely plagiarised the sentiments of Proudhon.'

He looked at me blankly.

'Of course, without the existence of property the concept of theft would not even exist and, like Marx, Proudhon saw no problem with actual ownership, as long as it referred to the fruits of labour.'

Now I sound as big a prat as he does, I thought. One glance at Marigold revealed she was undoubtedly thinking the same thing.

'Maybe,' "Wolfie Smith" eventually conceded.

I suspect he had never heard of Pierre-Joseph Proudhon. Call yourself an anarchist? I stopped short of mentioning Fabianism or Revisionism. Why prolong our brief relationship? I'm pretty far removed from being a revolutionary Marxist, to put it mildly, but surely "Wolfie" should read up on his subject before inflicting it on complete strangers.

By now Wolfie was going on about Revolution, again.

'Russia, France, nothing was achieved without direct action,' he insisted.

He didn't mention the American Revolution. Unsurprisingly, given the US is the ultimate bastion of capitalism.

'Oh, go on then,' Marigold said as I turned towards her. She knows I'm reluctant to walk away when there's an ignoramus on a roll.

Given his obvious disregard for the United States, I could have quoted the section from the Declaration of Independence which I committed to memory in the Sixth Form and is one of the (few) remnants of my education that remains therein: -

'We hold these truths to be self-evident, that all men are created equal, that they are endowed by their Creator with certain unalienable Rights, that among these are Life, Liberty and the pursuit of Happiness.'

But I didn't.

(Just a brief digression: unalienable or inalienable? I've seen both versions, in print, many times, but have never bothered to check the precise wording of the original text. Does it matter? Of course not, in my view, but there are others out there of a far greater pedantic nature.)

Leaving Declarations aside, I offered instead something along the lines of:

'Surely you should be referencing Rousseau as without his influence Marx and Tolstoy would never have come to anyone's attention? Not to mention his being the philosophical voice that led to the French Revolution.'

Wolfie didn't respond. If he'd have been older, I may even have suspected he imagined I was referring to Demis Roussos. Having no knowledge of an overweight Greek crooner would be fair enough; never having heard of Jean-Jacques Rousseau while espousing Marxist ideology struck me as bizarre.

Rousseau directly influenced Karl Marx and Tolstoy, inspired both the Romantic movement and the French Revolution, massively influenced the philosophy of Kant and Schopenhauer and, in the 18th century, an era where great writers and philosophers changed ideas and beliefs throughout Europe, his was the preeminent voice.

Yes, Rousseau and his compatriots fascinated me at one time, enough to read up on the subject in some depth, but evidently Wolfie had gained what little he knew by reading the odd poorly printed pamphlet. Maybe ideation in his case had come about purely by garnering strands of conversation from others while under the influence of mind altering substances. I very much doubt the leaders of the G8 nations will be quaking in their collective boots.

Rousseau once said – yes, this time I did look it up - 'The first man who, having fenced in a piece of land, said 'This is mine', and found people naïve enough to believe him, that man was the true founder of civil society. From how many crimes, wars, and murders, from how many horrors and misfortunes might not any one have saved mankind, by pulling up the stakes, or filling up the ditch, and crying to his fellows: Beware of listening to this impostor; you are undone if you once forget that the fruits of the earth belong to us all, and the earth itself to nobody.'

That's powerful stuff, considering it was written in the 18th century. I bet Jeremy Corbin could quote it from memory, despite our idealist table-mate relegating him to 'sell out' status.

'I think I preferred him going on,' Marigold said as we walked back to the car. 'Almost made me wish for the days when I first met you. You didn't tolerate people like him then.'

She's right, but even so back then I was far more prone to threats of physical violence when offended by 'prats'. This must be progress.

St Ives having been postponed to another day, we decided one of our favourite places, the Minack Theatre, was due a visit as it would surely be glorious on a day like today.

Glorious is an understatement.

There's a famous quote from the Kevin Costner film Field of Dreams, relating to building a baseball stadium -

'If you build it, they will come'.

The rationale behind that quote could have been borrowed from the Minack Theatre.

In essence, it's an open-air theatre perched on steep cliffs above the sea, but the 'back story' as they would undoubtedly say in Hollywood, is where the appeal lies.

It resembles a scaled down Roman theatre, with its stone seats and the setting is simply magnificent. On a day like today with blue skies and a sparkling turquoise sea, the views are as good as anywhere in the

Mediterranean (and there are very few parts of the Mediterranean we haven't visited).

It looks old, but not much more than 80 years ago there was nothing here but rock strewn cliffs. A local resident, Rowena Cade, decided she would build a theatre, from scratch, to stage productions put on by her friends and family. With the assistance, on occasion, of two gardeners, Rowena Cade worked tirelessly on her project until in 1932, the Minack Theatre saw its first production – The Tempest. The setting could not have been more basic, the only stage lighting came from car headlights, but that first production was just the first of many.

Work could only be done in the winter, summers being reserved for performances, but this remarkable woman carried on working. It now seats 800 people and its reputation as one of the finest open air theatres in the world is well deserved.

Thinking back to our encounter with the alleged anarchist, Rowena Cade was by most definitions, a 'toff,' the daughter of a wealthy landowner, brought up in a privileged background, yet devoted most of her adult life to scrabbling about on a rocky hillside for the benefit of others. She carried enormous stones, hacked away with hammer and chisel, mixed cement and worked from dawn to dusk throughout every winter until well into her 80s. Still think 'toffs' lead an easy life?

We've often commented on the glorious scenery, the fields, the woods, the great houses and so on while travelling around England. In so many cases these marvels of nature have been preserved for us and subsequent generations by the landed gentry. The terminology often has pejorative connotations, but the people who own vast tracts of England have done so for countless generations. Their houses, their lands are not truly 'owned.' They are merely stewards of the land, taking care of it for the next generations.

Estates such as those of the Grosvenor family in Cheshire were formed immediately after the Norman invasion of 1066. Nowadays, the second largest landowner in Britain is the National Trust. These landowners have a vested interest in preserving the fabric of the countryside and offer far more benefit to our society as a whole than shouting slogans at visiting heads of state will ever do.

Back to Minack. In Cornish, Minack means rocky place and it's a perfect description. We walked around the site, took in the stunning views of the sea and the wonderful beach and marvelled at every step at the tenacity and work ethic of a remarkable woman, Rowena Cade.

At the end of a hard day's graft, she still had one more job to do: trekking down to the beach far below, filling a sack with sand to mix with cement on the following day, lugging it up the (very) steep hill and then go down and do it all again, and again and again. I stood at the top of the cliff, looking down at the beach, marvelling at the determination, the sheer bloody-mindedness of that remarkable woman. Her fitness levels must have been remarkable. I would have found that task daunting even in my youth and yet she was still doing well it into her 80s.

We met a young woman carrying a rucksack as big as herself who was walking the South West Coast Path, the longest National Trail in the UK. We've come across a few people who have done this walk - 630 miles from Minehead in Somerset, following the coast of Somerset, Cornwall and Devon to Poole Harbour in Dorset – and have never failed to be impressed.

This particular solo walker, Jules, lives in New Zealand now, but has returned to visit family and walk the trail.

'630 miles is a long way,' I said, without a great deal of originality.

'Well, I walked the Te Araroa trail in New Zealand so this should be okay.'
Blimey!

We've been just about everywhere in New Zealand, both islands, but we were in a camper van. Not walking with rucksacks on our backs. The Te Araroa Trail is over 1,800 miles long, from the top of North Island to the very bottom of South Island, taking in just about every type of terrain one could imagine.

Respect!

I'm looking down at that fabulous beach and thinking about whether we feel up to trekking down to get a closer look while standing next to a young woman half my size who thinks nothing of walking hundreds of miles, on her own. Do I feel inadequate? Oh yes.

Yes, I can soften the blow, a little, by factoring in our age, dodgy knees and our absence of tent or even a rucksack, but even so, it's a humbling moment.

If you're a young female seeking a role model, forget Kim Kardashian, think of Jules, the solo walker. Better still, consider the utterly remarkable woman who built the Minack Theatre, Rowena Cade.

Back to travelogues next time. Cue, sighs of relief.

Fowey.

Marigold Says...
They have just said on tv everybody must have regular drinks in this heatwave, well we didn't know about any of that new important advice, and in the future we must have better water regulations so we don't have to be told to drink when we're thirsty. AND by 2040 everybody will be living in caves with no clothes on, eating bats

Went and tried some sandals on as mine are falling apart and it's too hot to wear shoes, but because of far too many pesky holidaymakers, found nothing left in my size anywhere. Sent off for some off the internet, after looking at about 2 million or so. Used G's account so I set it up, put details in, and then he said 'why are you having these? Are you sure?' I reached over pressed the send button and said 'YES, because I want them.'

I then said 'why?'

He said, 'because they aren't coming for another five weeks and the reviews say they are awful and fall to pieces AND they are coming from China from a company called Ping Ping Yong which doesn't ring any bells as a fashion label'

Went out quick to walk Eddie the borrowed ugly dog and will never buy off Internet again, but no matter what the sandals are like when they eventually get here I will say they are wonderful. They were only £60. No, really £20. Why is life so difficult? I will have to wear wellingtons with the front cut out for the next five weeks.

Really LOUD Americans in supermarket yesterday. I interrogated them immediately. Rammed them into the yoghurts with my trolley so they couldn't escape. They are from California, staying with rellies, and of course LOVE the beaches, and the walks are just the BEST. If I had asked them where they were they wouldn't know, or perhaps say CORRRNWAAAL. Very, very loudly, or it it just me that does that?

Woman on TV has just said to check on old people. So will have to check G and get him hydrated. Wonder if he'll cut that bit out when he checks the spelling, punctuation and other things I don't bother with.

Some of my top tips on surviving a heat wave. I follow all these tips. Drink plenty of water, stay in the shade and don't put a 15 tog duvet on the bed or use a hot water bottle. Also drink your own wee.

We decided to go to Fowey, which is apparently pronounced Foy not Fow-ee, which I always find annoying. Why not call it Foy in the first place? Anyway, annoying name or not, it's one of the most expensive places to buy a house in England and only celebs can afford to live here.

I was chatting to a local - 'ow you today, my lovely?' – who told me I'd just missed Prince Charles and Richard and Judy had been seen in the paper shop. It turned out to be true as someone else told me the same thing half an hour later. That next person said Dawn French had been in town a lot recently, but they couldn't be certain what she had been buying. Gordon Ramsey and his wife visit Foy quite often as they have been renovating a former bank to use as a holiday home. Oh, Gloria Honeyford, don't forget her. She has a house just down the road.

So many celebrity visitors, it's odd that they even get a mention any more. I wonder if anyone says, 'do you know who I was talking to a bit ago? Marigold! Yes, really. She was moaning about the price of turnips.'

We parked about two miles away as Foy - I'm using phonetic spelling from now on - hates cars. (Last time I said I was using phonetic spelling I said 'philatelic' by mistake and everybody thought I was talking about stamps.)

It isn't really two miles out of town, but on a hot day like today it really seemed like it.

We had a cool drink, sitting inside as all the outdoor seats were taken, at a café on the quay and two lovely local girls were working as waitresses. The boss mustn't have been in today because they both stopped to chat every time they passed.

Someone had ordered breakfast for six people earlier on, then walked away two minutes later so the kitchen had cooked six full breakfasts and the customers had gone when the girls took it to the table. It made everybody very cross, then twenty minutes later one of the party of six came inside and said, 'how much longer will our breakfast be?' They had only moved round the corner, into the shade!

G found a different way to get to the top of the town and we went to look up there, in the car, later. We could have walked up there, but that's a well known symptom of madness locally. There are some lovely houses up on the hill, we parked outside Dawn French's house, which isn't one of the lovely ones, it's very big though, but she didn't invite us in. It's a gorgeous area around here. No wonder houses cost so much, but the roads in Foy are very, very narrow. I wouldn't ever want to drive through it. Even G wasn't keen when we did drive through once and he's driven through, London, Paris, Florence, Rome, Marrakesh, Tesco's car park in Heswall, all those places where I close my eyes for the whole journey.

Even without going through the centre today we were glad we were in Ruby as she's much thinner than our other car and every car we met going the other way seemed to be a Range Rover, which are not thin at all.

Over to G who knows lots of things about Foy, mostly to do with famous writers and I've never read anything any of them wrote. If they didn't used to be in Vicar of Dibley, the names mean nothing to me.

G Says...

We parked the car in one of the few places in Fowey where we could access the town itself, more or less on the level. There's another car park high above the town, but it was a very hot day and neither of us fancied the trek up the Cornish Version of the Eiger that the return trip would entail. Fowey is best approached as a pedestrian as the roads are narrow. How narrow an unwary driver will soon discover when meeting a procession of commercial vehicles heading in the opposite direction with sides scraping against the buildings on both sides after supplying shops and restaurants. That was our experience the first time I drove into town and as I'm not a fan of constantly engaging reverse gear, we were happy enough to park on the outskirts and walk in.

The houses are mainly Georgian – architectural shorthand for impressive – with many grand properties on the hillside and an assortment of pastel coloured cottages overlooking the river.

Fowey has always been a pretty place. Queen Victoria referred to 'some of the narrowest streets I ever saw in England' and the 'perpendicular hills,' but readily acknowledged Fowey was 'very pretty'. The poet Robert Bridges said Fowey was 'the most poetic-looking place in England' and J M Barrie, who wrote Peter Pan, said 'it is but a toy town to look at, on a bay so small, hemmed in so picturesquely by cliffs and ruins, that of a moonlight night, it might pass for a scene in a theatre'.

Quite a lot to live up to then.

In front of us as we walked in was a little girl, aged about three, walking alongside her mum as she wheeled two babies in a push chair. This was their conversation:

Mum: 'Lucy, stop answering back.'

Lucy: 'I'm not.'

Mum: 'You're still doing it.'

Lucy: 'But, I can't help it'.

We laughed, along with Lucy's mum.

We passed Fowey Harbour Offices and the quay where Queen Victoria and Prince Albert landed on their visit to the town. Alongside is a striking sculpture, Rook with a Book, inspired by local author, Daphne du Maurier's book The Birds and transposed into a memorable film by Alfred Hitchcock.

Fowey and Daphne du Maurier are irretrievably linked and across the river we see the blue and white house, Ferryside, the holiday home where she wrote her first novel. She lived for most of her life at nearby Menabilly, a relatively isolated grand house in the countryside which was the inspiration for Manderley in her best-selling novel Rebecca.

Daphne du Maurier died in 1969, but a du Maurier Festival is now an annual event in Fowey. From her first days in Fowey, Du Maurier felt that 'the place has taken hold of me,' writing 'ships anchored, looming up through blackness ... the splash of muffled oars' in her diary. (I read this extract in the local bookshop and committed it to memory).

Looking across at Ferryside I can easily see the appeal of the setting for a writer. Relative solitude but with a soothing background of sound from the river. As the author herself put it, 'Here was the freedom I desired. Freedom to write, to walk, to wander, freedom to climb hills, to pull a boat, to be alone. The lights of Polruan and Fowey. Ships anchored, looking up through blackness. The jetties, white with clay. Mysterious shrouded trees, owls hooting, the splash of muffled oars in lumpy water... All I want is to be at Fowey. Nothing and no one else. This, now, is my life.'

She should have been a writer!

Fowey is very much a 'boat town;' dozens of craft in view today, ranging from tiny skiffs to larger yachts and the odd freighter bound for the china clay wharfs being manoeuvred into place by tug boats.

Ships left from here to join battle against the Spanish Armada and supplied boats for the D-Day landings; its maritime history spans the centuries. Nowadays, ferries shuttle to and fro across the water, carrying cars between Caffa Mill, near where we are parked, and Bodinnick, and foot passengers between Fowey and Polruan, the village on the opposite headland.

We reach the main quay in the town centre and decide to have a cool drink then wander the narrow streets to look at the shops. It's only a small town, easily walked around, but the hill looms above and we congratulate ourselves on not having to make the journey up to the top car park. We passed Fowey's oldest building, the Well House, which was built in 1430 and is now a B&B and a hand painted sign on a wall reading 'oh, how lovely,' - Jeremy Irons', the derivation of which I am unable to reference, but I like it.

The cafes on the Quay are packed with customers, but we find a spare table inside. Our waitress immediately decides Marigold has just come in for a chat – an easy assumption most days – as they instantly start up a conversation. The girl is 17, Marigold, er, isn't 17, but there's no sign of an age barrier.

When I could get a word in, I asked the waitress what they had in the way of a cool drink.

'We've got a perfectly cromulent elderflower cordial,' she replied, 'that's yummy on a day like today.'

'Cromulent? Is that a Cornish word?'

'Nah, someone said it in The Simpsons. It means something's pretty good. I say it all the time.'

Fascinating, this example of the constant evolution of language; this latest word, like so many other new words, emanating from popular culture. I approve.

After our walk around the town, we set off back to the car park, with a quick stop at the intriguingly named Pinky Murphy's café for yet another cold drink. We then drove to the top of the hill, glorious views over the estuary and paused to admire the scene from the terrace of the Fowey Hall Hotel, formerly Fowey Hall and an inspiration for Kenneth Grahame's The Wind in the Willows – he is said to have modelled Toad Hall on Fowey Hall and the town of Fowey is depicted as 'The Little Grey Seaport.'

I've no particularly fond childhood memories of The Wind in The Willows, but Kenneth Grahame formed a great attachment to Fowey, even celebrating his marriage there, during frequent visits to his great friend Sir Arthur Quiller-Couch. Quiller-Couch, usually referred to as simply Q, was apparently the inspiration for the talkative Ratty in Wind in the Willows.

Q was a remarkable man of letters. Without intentionally disparaging Kenneth Grahame or Daphne du Maurer, we're talking chalk and cheese here.

'Q' was appointed King Edward VII Professor of English Literature at Cambridge University in 1912, and retained the chair for the rest of his life. Simultaneously he was elected to a Fellowship of Jesus College, which he held until his death. I recently read a biography of the late Alistair Cooke, a former student of Quiller-Couch, whom Cooke described as 'rather eccentric.'

'Q' is perhaps best known for producing not one but two remarkable anthologies: The Oxford Book of English Verse and The Oxford Book of English Prose. On his death an unfinished novel, Castle Dor, was discovered and subsequently completed many years later, by Daphne du Maurier.

Keep it in the Fowey family!

My interest in Q is derived from a fragment of his advice to authors, 'kill your darlings.' Basically, he's suggesting if a writer becomes self indulgent, reads a passage back and is then overly pleased by it, cut it out, immediately. 'Darlings' are those words or phrases that give the writer pleasure, but may add little to the eventual reader. Cut them out. Kill them.

The hardest task for any writer and the most important.

We drove on and parked outside some rather splendid gates. Behind that solid barrier stood the home of Dawn French. She didn't invite us in. The gates came from the du Maurier family's former country home a few miles away, her inspiration for Manderley in Rebecca and the opening lines of her most famous novel came to mind, 'Last night I dreamt I went to Manderley again. It seemed to me I stood by the iron gate leading to the drive, and for a while I could not enter...'

Port Neptune was bought by Dawn French and Lenny Henry in 2006 and although they are no longer together, she still lives there. A vulgar reader would doubtless ask the price. Okay, £2.8 million, but don't expect a repetition of this descent into Hello territory. A lot of money in 2006, especially as it needed a total 'refurb,' but you get 40 bedrooms so it's not pokey.

A local woman in the bookshop had already told me of the property being advertised at the time it went up for sale as being, 'next door to the house where Daphne du Maurier once lived,' Readymoney Cottage being much more famous than the estate house on the hill to which it once belonged.

We then found Readymoney Cove and the former coach house to Point Neptune where Daphne du Maurer once lived, if only for a short time. It was recently sold, for over £2 million which puts the price of the far larger, but substantially less pretty Port Neptune looming above it into perspective. This is a pricey area and no mistake.

We were in the company of some people the other day who I can best describe as being not our first choice as conversational companions, but some things are unavoidable. One of the youngest members of the group was particularly tiresome: rising inflections at the end of every sentence, constantly flicking at her hair, laughing loudly in an attention seeking manner, you get the general idea?

One of the many annoyances, right up there with fingers either side of the head indicating quotation marks when no quotation was involved, yes she did that too, was an apparent compulsion to add 'hashtag (add random word, usually one without any relevance to the previous words) at the end of every sentence.

I took to adding octothorpe plus an unrelated word or word combination at the end of a sentence, octothorpe being the word that describes the symbol #. Nobody even noticed.

Pearls before swine.

Cultural St Ives.

G Says...

We've been doing a fair bit of walking lately – I blame the sunshine – so it wasn't a great surprise on leaping from my bed this morning (leaping? Yeah, right) to discover my knees had been removed during the night and replaced by a vastly inferior pair, completely unfit for purpose.

We had already arranged to go to St Ives today, driving as far as the splendidly named Lelant Saltings and taking the scenic route train into town.

'We could try the Barbara Hepworth exhibition again', Marigold said, 'or even the Tate. They don't know we're coming as we only decided last night so it might be open.'

We've been to St Ives several times in the past couple of years and each time have seen our hopes of cultural enlightenment dashed as both the Barbara Hepworth museum and the Tate Gallery were closed. This happened so often we had started to take it as a personal slight, but this time we may foil them as they may not be expecting us.

They don't muck about in St Ives; when an attraction closes its doors they stay closed for six months or so. Marigold and I have renovated entire ruined houses in less time than that.

We reached the roundabout leading to the Park and Ride at Lelant Saltings, only to miss the exit and had to stay on the roundabout for another circuit. Marigold was driving but was most insistent the fault lay elsewhere as her navigator had failed to say 'it's the next exit' the required five times. On our second trip around the roundabout Marigold decided unilaterally to take the previous exit.

'I decided we'd drive in, not go on the train,' Marigold explained, not entirely convincingly.

'Oh, right.'

'I also decided the traffic might be bad so you can drive.'

We swapped over at the next lay-by. Marigold has not yet fully recovered from a juggernaut she was following down a narrow lane suddenly deciding to reverse. No idea what the technical term is for juggernaut induced trauma but it's chiefly manifested by an acute dislike of narrow roads, traffic cones and most other road users.

We try and refine our parking options on the way into town. Even if we'd come on the train it's a bit of a hike down the hill – hard work for knees –

so we find a space (phew!) in the same car park we used on our last visit; the one with the big mural on the wall.

As I'm taking a photo of aforementioned mural, a man in a people carrier decides it is a good idea to reverse his car into a space at least a foot too narrow for his car, right at the car park entrance, thus blocking the road for everyone else. I can see his car won't fit into the space, as can Marigold and a couple of local residents who offer the driver the benefit of their advice in colourful terms. Undeterred, the driver keeps trying every possible angle, seemingly without any concern for the traffic behind him now blocking the road completely.

One of the locals, morbidly obese and wearing an off white vest and very tight trousers, decides he has seen enough, walks over to the deluded would be parker and bangs a meaty hand on the bonnet.

'Oy,' he shouts, 'it 'ain't gonna go in that space. Go away.' (He doesn't actually say 'go away' but words to that effect, one of which ends in 'off.') The driver looks at him calmly, winds down the window and says 'I always park in that space.'

We can only assume the space between the two neighbouring cars must have been wider on every other occasion.

We leave them to it as the overweight local seems to be getting even more agitated and could be having a seizure at any moment Fortunately, there's a funeral home over the road.

We walk down the hill, well aware that at some stage we will have to head uphill again to reach the Barbara Hepworth Museum. My knees are protesting at every single step, but courageously I utter not one word of complaint. Well, hardly any! I am well aware such symptoms of caducity, allied to increased hearing loss, are unlikely to gain much sympathy as I had mentioned my intention to strap my knees before leaving this morning, but forgot.

Better add short term memory loss to the decrepitude list.

The Hepworth Museum is great and the sculptures in the garden look fabulous in the sunshine. The artist said she 'loathed' seeing her work exhibited in art galleries with only blank walls as a backdrop, and seeing them here, surrounded by flowers intermingling with tall bamboo it's hard to disagree.

I recently read a biography of the artist and one sentence stayed with me:

Hepworth wrote: 'Perhaps what one wants to say is formed in childhood and the rest of one's life is spent trying to say it.'

Profoundly thought provoking I felt at the time and reading that sentence back after writing it now I still feel the same.

Hepworth was a leading figure in the colony of artists who resided in St Ives during the Second World War, but her work as a sculpture first came to my attention in my teens when I made my first of many visits to Twickenham to watch a rugby international.

On the morning of the match me and a group of others found ourselves in Central London, sightseeing, and I noticed a metal sculpture on the wall of the John Lewis department store. I was interested in art, but what fixed the occasion in my mind was having recently seen another metal sculpture recently installed over the main entrance of Lewis's store in my home city. The 'tin man' as the locals called it, wasn't particularly well received but I liked it and liked this London version, bigger, more stylish and stunningly impressive, even more.

I read up on that John Lewis sculpture. 19 feet high and called simply 'Winged Figure' it had been created here in St Ives, first as a wooden prototype, then constructed at actual size from sheet aluminium.

The main body of the final work was cast in aluminium by the founders Morris Singer in Walthamstow, with supporting rods of stainless steel. It was installed on the John Lewis building on Sunday, 21 April 1963, (so I saw it soon after it made its first appearance) on a plinth 13 feet above the pavement. It was refurbished for its 50th anniversary in 2013.

I've no idea how much Barbara Hepworth received for her work of genius, still attracting attention 55 years later, but a brass maquette – a small scale model of the intended sculpture - for Winged Figure made in 1957, i.e. six years prior to the finished article, sold at Christie's in November 2012 for 422,500 dollars, round about £325,000. Just for the rough draft scale model.

Jocelyn Barbara Hepworth was born in 1903 in Yorkshire and moved to St Ives with her second husband in 1939, never to leave again. She had a son from her first marriage and five year old triplets in tow, but from reading her autobiography it appears work took precedence for most of the time. The triplets were farmed out to nursery and boarding school and were never allowed in Hepworth's studio when she was working. She told an interviewer in 1966 that 'we lived a life of work and it is taxing if the children fall ill. That becomes a strain.'

Trewyn Studio appeared to satisfy her every wish: 'Here was a studio, a yard, and a garden where I could work in open air and space.' She increased her studio space when she purchased the Palais de Danse, a cinema and dance studio, across the street from Trewyn in 1960 and used this new space to work on larger commissions.

Barbara Hepworth's studio and garden remain as they were when she lived and worked here for 26 years until her death in a fire on the premises in 1975. I was particularly taken by her workshop; untidy, full of tools and dusty old working clothes. I have a shed very like it.

Her sudden death at the age of 72 was not a complete surprise. Hepworth had cancer and much preferred whisky and cigarettes to food, but her lifestyle at that time was only the indirect cause of her death. She died in a fire while working in her studio, undoubtedly while drunk as she was for much of the time, according to her biographer, Sally Festing.

A remarkable woman and a great talent. We enjoyed our visit here so much. Hepworth was a slender, rather small woman yet defied the assumption that carving vast pieces of stone required brute strength. A woman in what had long been considered a man's world she certainly was, but decried any attempts by others to label her a feminist.

'I hadn't much patience with women artists trying to be women artists,' she once said. 'At no point do I wish to be in conflict with any man or masculine thought … Art is anonymous. It is not competition with men. It's a complementary contribution.'

We walked down to the harbour, not with any great expectations of seeing the nine-foot shark that had visited the harbour yesterday. We probably won't be swimming here today, just in case. He'd have been welcome to bite a chunk out of my knees, as that's what my various surgeries have amounted to, but that's about as far as I'm prepared to go.

The tide was almost completely out as we reached the harbour with fishing boats and pleasure craft canted at unnatural angles on the sand, but by the time we reached the end of the harbour wall an hour later they were all bobbing around in the briny.

We called in for a cool drink at the Sloop Inn, a St Ives institution since 1312. It's a real pub, dark and a bit dingy inside and pretty noisy and I love the drawings on the walls,

Before we went back up the hill to our car, we walked the crowded tangle of narrow cobbled streets leading from the port known as The Downalong. Is there a season when St Ives isn't busy? We've been here at all times of the year and it's never 'empty.' I love the street names: Teetotal Street, Virgin Street, Fish Street to name a few favourites and stopped, as we invariably do, to look at the battered old green door at the rear of The Bakers at number 1, Virgin Street. A passer-by told us the door was 200 years old (it looks even older) and it has its own site on Social Media. I don't doubt it.

We also passed a plaque on a cottage where Daphne du Maurier once stayed in the 1840s. After our previous trip around Fowey, awash with references to the author, we both groaned and said, 'Not her again.'

Back at the car park we were relieved to see no sign of the man who we'd last seen attempting the car parking equivalent of squeezing a quart into a pint pot.

Salisbury.

Marigold Says...

I'm very tough. Nothing frightens me. Well, not much. Just the odd thing. Such as G saying 'let's go to Salisbury,' on our way to somewhere or other.

We like Salisbury, have been there several times. The difference now is ever since that former Russian spy and his daughter were poisoned by Novichok and only recently somebody else died there from the same thing it's a bit of a scary place to visit. G was very calm. He promised he would taste everything we ate first.

We found a hotel in Salisbury where the man on Reception was very bossy and pretended to be busy, but one of the cleaners said the hotel was nearly empty and bookings had gone 'through the floor' since the nerve agent was discovered.

We walked into the centre, which has an enormous open square right in the middle and two buskers were playing Simon and Garfunkel songs. They were terrible. Really, really awful. I gave them 20 pence hoping they would decide that was enough for the day, but no such luck.

We walked around the shops for a bit, with me shouting 'don't touch it' every time we passed a door knob and went to the cathedral to seek sanctuary. I liked the street names of the smaller streets such as Oatmeal Row, Fish Row and Silver Street, all of them named after whatever trades used to be carried on there.

As for the cathedral, it's impressive. I read this bit in a leaflet inside so it must be true: 'The cathedral spire is 404 feet high, so it is the tallest surviving pre-1400 spire in the world'. A bit selective on dates, but still very high. There's also the best preserved copy of the Magna Carta in existence on display, but visitors can't really get near it and it's in a dark area and photos are 'forbidden' so it didn't impress me very much.

What did impress G was the oldest 'modern' working clock which dates from 1386 and does not have a 'face' as in those days clocks only rang out the hours on a bell and didn't have a face as there were no hands. I didn't think much of a clock that didn't even say the time, but every time I said so G answered, 'it was made in 1386, Marigold.'

Edward Heath, former PM, is buried in the cathedral and used to live here. In Salisbury, not in the cathedral. G said the cathedral used to be at Old Sarum and was rebuilt here so we agreed we'd go there later, maybe tomorrow if we survived the night.

Back at the half empty hotel we decided, well, I decided, not to eat anything that might be a nerve agent so we had bananas, peeled while wearing two pairs of gloves, and some stale bread I found in the car boot next to the spare wheel.

Obviously, that isn't entirely accurate as we don't have a spare wheel just a can of glorified air freshener or whatever it is the car makers provide in place of a spare wheel these days.

Next day we went to look at Old Sarum which always fascinates me as you can walk around an Iron Age hill fort where people lived thousands of years ago. The site survived many invaders, even the Romans, until it was finally flattened and burned by Vikings led by a king who has the best name, ever, Sweyn Forkbeard in 1003.

Trying not to give dates, but G will check this and tut tut if I don't try and do the history part properly, so in 1226 the cathedral was moved from here to Salisbury. A man in a brown shirt, who may or not have worked there, told us the site for the new cathedral and the new city around it was chosen by shooting an arrow from Old Sarum.

We could see the cathedral spire from here and G said, 'I don't think so, it's about two miles away.'

'Ah,' the man said in a know-all voice so I decided he definitely worked here, 'the arrow struck a white deer, which continued to run and run and eventually died on the spot where the cathedral now rests.' G sniffed, but didn't say anything. Like most legends of long ago it got more and more unlikely with every added detail.

The brown shirt man wasn't finished though, rambling on and on like the worst history teacher I ever had, but I can't remember any of what he said. G said, 'that last bit was interesting,' when we were going back to the car park and so it might have been if I could have been bothered to listen.

We found what might have been a fossil on the way back to the car so I took a photo of it in case it was an unknown species of dinosaur.

We went past Stonehenge, which was full of tourists and we've been before so we just just had a quick look from a distance. Anyway, it's £14 to go in these days which is a lot. Unless you're American which almost everybody else seemed to be. They were all wearing garish golfing clothes and saying 'gee, this is so OLD' to one another.

Later on, we were heading for Bournemouth for no particular reason when I said 'can we stop at Ringwood to see if that fruit and veg shop is still there?'

G understands my occasional silliness and said 'okay.'

Ringwood is a sort of gentile, rather old fashioned place and, best of all the fruit shop was still there. We bought an orchard's worth of fruit, had a wander round and sat in or on the tree sculptures at the far end of the car park.

We also went into a Meeting House, very old with wooden pews and a gallery all around it where I got talking to a very odd couple who said they came here twice a week for coffee and a chat. The woman was a chronic giggler and the man had loose false teeth so I found them very entertaining.

As we're chatting G came back from where he had been lurking in an attempt to not start laughing at the poor man's loose teeth and the man said to him, 'don't let them rope you in as a helper; they're all a bit mental.'

His wife shouted out 'Mental, mental, chicken oriental' at the top of her voice and they both collapsed with laughing.

'I think they're a comedy double act at weekends,' G whispered. I was getting ready to avoid the false teeth which looked as if they were ready to shoot out at any moment.

I asked them if they lived in Ringwood or were just visiting and should have guessed what was coming next when the man said, 'go on then' to his wife.

She said, ''we live just outside, but we just sold our house and now we're renting.'

They looked at each other and both shouted out, 'Rental, rental, chicken oriental' before howling with laughter.

'Time to go, Zebedee,' G said to me and we left them to it.

The teeth were still in place.

Just about.

We looked in an estate agents window, as we do often, and saw immediately this is a pricey town. Not far from the sea, not far from the New Forest, so that explains it. Oh, and it has a Waitrose so that's the clincher.

We drove on a bit further and ended up in Wareham which I can't remember visiting before although G insisted we had. After we parked the car a woman driving out said, 'there's nearly two hours left on that' and gave us her parking ticket. Very nice of her.

We went into a pub and by then I had remembered we had been here before. Everywhere we went I remembered and tried quite hard not to keep saying 'I remember this bit' every two minutes, but not always successfully.

The local beer was wonderful. I didn't actually drink any of it, but I loved the names on the pumps. The brewery is called Dorset Piddle. Jimmy Riddle is a brown ale, then there's Silent Slasher and Amber Piddle. The barmaid said they brought out a beer called Santa's Potty at Christmas and the same company make wine called 'oui, oui.'

Brilliant. Yes, childish, but brilliant.

We looked round a museum and G got very interested as it was almost all related to Lawrence of Arabia and he has just finished reading Seven Pillars of Wisdom for about the twentieth time.

When Lawrence finally retired he went to live in Clouds Hill just outside Wareham and was killed in a motorbike accident in 1935 on his way home. The man who ran the museum, (curator?) told us a 'mysterious black car' had been seen in the area and this gave rise to dozens of conspiracy theories. 'More theories than arose from Princess Diana's death,' he said.

Winston Churchill attended the funeral and described him as 'one of the greatest beings alive in this time,' which sounded a bit odd to me as he wasn't actually alive at the time!

The curator man told us where to find a stone effigy of Lawrence in the local church and we went to look at it on the way back to the car. He also told us there was a memorial by the road side at Clouds Hill marking the scene of the accident, but we realised we had come in that way and missed it. We didn't go back. Trying to avoid accident black spots. Even if the last one happened in 1935.

When we reached the car I noticed there was still seven minutes left on our 'free' ticket. I didn't think anyone just arriving would be very grateful if I offered it to them so didn't bother.

We went to a vintage car rally on the weekend. Lots of old cars, which I like, and strange people, who I like even more. We were talking to an old man with an MG older than himself who said he only used it in cooler weather as the seats smelt of urine in hot weather. I don't know whether he meant his own urine or a previous owner, but I stopped stroking the leather upholstery very quickly.

Next to him were a biker couple with a bull terrier who were lovely and we chatted to them for ages. The dog loved riding in the sidecar and they have been all over the country with her.

I found a 1930s caravan, made for a travelling family, and spent a while trying to persuade the owner to sell it to me. 'Where would we put it?' G asked. I don't bother with such unimportant details, it was fab. Anyway, he wouldn't sell it to me.

Three women were screeching on a stage, we couldn't make out the tune or the words as the speakers were so crackly. They were middle aged, very keen, unsuitably dressed and couldn't dance in step or sing a note. Some people were clapping. Must have been the local deaf association on an outing.

There were some really odd people around and they all seemed to have some connection to steam engines. One man said he had spent thousands of pounds restoring a sort of little train over many years and it was now finished.

'So, what do you do with it now?' I asked.

He gave me a funny look and said, ' I look at it. Sometimes I start it up and listen to it.' I don't think I am suited to restoring little steam engines. I went and got an ice cream instead.

Sunny Stoke.

Marigold Says...

We're in Middleport, an offshoot of one of the six towns* that make up the Potteries, Stoke-on-Trent to see an exhibition first installed at the Tower of London three years ago - Blood Swept Lands and Seas of Red - represented by ceramic poppies.

Yes, I know all about Anna of the Five Towns, but Arnold Bennett would have to change his title now as Fenton was added to Stoke, Hanley, Longton, Burslem and Tunstall quite a while ago, making Stoke-on-Trent a city made up of six towns.

We are obliged to park in a specific car park as the exhibition is bringing in a couple of thousand or so visitors a day and there are traffic wardens out in force to stop anyone paring in side streets. We pay our £3 and the girl who takes the money tells us there is a courtesy bus to the exhibition, 'but the driver's just having a brew and a ciggie so he'll be a while.'

Hmm!

We park next to only about a dozen or so cars, it's still early, reversing into a free space when asked to by one of the three attendants. The next car to arrive is driven by a rather fierce woman who flatly refuses to reverse 'because I'm crap at it' and tells the young man if he wants her car reversing into a space he can do it himself.

Which he does. Not very well. It took him three attempts and he had to face the scorn of his two colleagues and the expression on the face of the car's owner said, 'well, I'm not very good at reversing, but neither are you.'

No sign of a courtesy bus, so we decided to walk and were glad we did. The walking route took us through a pretty scruffy area, despite a local couple assuring us many thousands of pounds had been spent on upgrading the area, and then across a canal bridge. On the canal were several barges/narrowboats, one was set up as a floating pub and another was called 'the oatcake barge.' Bet that's the only oatcake barge in the world.

Staffordshire oatcakes, best served hot with bacon or cheese but there are hundreds of other possible uses, are not widely known outside Staffordshire and Derbyshire, but we love them and the rest of the world doesn't know what it's missing.

One of the barges was parked (moored?) next to the bridge and and a man fiddling with a rope said 'hello.' It turned out he is a water bailiff, which sounds impressive and we got the impression he was a sort of Canal Sheriff. He certainly knew a lot about canals.

He said, 'We get about 60,000 craft, mostly barges a year on this stretch of canal and we've made mooring here as attractive as possible which will only be to the benefit to Middleport.' Yes, he did talk like a press release!

He was very believable, but we couldn't see the attraction of this particular stretch of canal. It's a very run down area with many derelict buildings lining the banks, but the oatcake barge is an attraction, I suppose.

We crossed the bridge and walked past a metal shutter set into a wall which had been decorated as a Secret Garden. The 'secret' is that there's nothing behind the shutter, the shutter itself is the garden. Nice idea.

We reached the entrance to the Pot Bank as they call a pottery works in Stoke-on-Trent, and joined a queue. It's free to go in, but you have to get a ticket online. The man checking the tickets didn't look very closely. We could have shown him a shopping list and been waved through. As we went in, the courtesy bus finally arrived, packed with people looking very fed up.

The poppy display was very impressive, with them coming out of the top and then tumbling down the side of an old bottle kiln and spreading out as a huge puddle of red at the bottom. I talked with the man who had organised the display who was very interesting.

He told me it's been almost three years since the original display was set up at the Tower of London and since then Weeping Window has been sent 'on tour' around the country. Over half the ceramic flowers were made in Stoke, at Johnson Tiles, and the rest were made in Derby.

I wrote down what he told me, so this is from the horse's mouth! 888,246 ceramic red poppies were made, one for every British or Colonial serviceman killed in the First World War. The artist was a man named Paul Cummins, who got the idea from the first lines of a poem by an unknown World War I soldier.

The poem begins:

'The blood-swept lands and seas of red,

Where angels dare to tread.'

(Hope I got that right, but I did my best, scribbling away, standing up, on a scruffy bit of paper.)

'How many did you break?' I asked him.

He looked a bit cross, but I thought that was a good question as they're made of pottery and look very fragile.

'Only one,' he said, 'but that caused us a problem as there has to be exactly 888,246 poppies as every one presents a human life so we had to report the loss of a poppy so a replacement could be made. We only used 11,000 poppies here.'

They used 497,000 kg of Marl-based Etruscan red earthenware to make the poppies (Obviously, I wrote this bit down as well) and he also told me about a crow who used to perch on top of the bottle kiln and got very cross when these men turned up to fix poppies all over his favourite perching place, which was much more interesting than knowing how much clay was needed to make 888,246 poppies. This 'pot bank' was chosen to host the display as it is the last working Victorian pottery in the U.K.

G had been talking to a man who used to work at Wedgwood and now makes his own pottery items on these premises. He was giving a demo with clay and a potters' wheel and was very good. He was also very funny and G and the Jolly Potter were in fits of laughter when I joined them.

They had been talking about the Prince of Wales opening a section of the factory about four years ago and how his friend, a fellow potter, had slipped on a patch of wet clay, fallen over and regained his feet, covered in wet slime just as Prince Charles walked through the door. Charles shook hands with the man and said, 'you look like you're having fun.'

I found a friend there, (not saying an 'old friend' as she's still gorgeous, like me) not seen each other for many years, and we had a good laugh and chat. I recognised her straight away and we had one of those really weird conversations that seemed as if we had been interrupted and just carried on as if the interruption happened five minutes ago. She said G needs to grow his beard, moustache and hair back, but the hair part is easier said than done.

Later on, we drove past a couple of our many former houses, one in Longsdon and one in Rudyard, and stopped for a cool drink at a canal side pub that used to be our 'local.'

The cottage in Lake Road, Rudyard, looks exactly the same as when we left it, in 1984. Rudyard Lake is a local beauty spot, as they say, and we walked its banks with our dogs many a time. It's much smarter than it used to be and there were lots of people in boats even though the lake is pretty low after such a dry summer.

There's a statue, carved out of a tree, of a tightrope walker who walked across the lake in 1878 and the feat was repeated in 2016 by a man called Steve Bull. There's a steam train line running alongside the far shore as this used to be a working railway line, but now it's just for tourists. We had just missed the train but as we walked away we heard it whistling.

There was a little village fete going on near where we used to live and of course we went in for a look around. I got talking to a woman who lived next door to our old house and she said if we came back later she would find the people who bought our house and still lived there.

We went for another walk, there isn't a village shop now, or a post office, and the trees lining the road are much bigger than we remember, but otherwise it was all very familiar. The War Memorial for the 1st World War says 1914–1921 not 1914–18. G will pop in later and explain that.

The woman who had bought our house turned up and said they hadn't changed the garden, the fish pond or anything else we had left behind, even the original bathroom suite was still there. Did she offer to walk about twenty yards to show us round? No, she didn't.

G Says…

Those dates on the War Memorial took my eye when used to live in the village. 1921 was the date that Parliament finally recognised the end of the war as after 1918 there were still soldiers on active service left in various other countries, right up to 1921. I've also seen Memorials saying 1914-1919 elsewhere in the country, so there's evidently quite some leeway given to the commissioning local authorities.

Many communities considered the First World War to be over when the Armistice was agreed (11 November 1918), or when the Peace Treaty of Versailles was signed (28 June 1919) or when Parliament officially declared the war ended (31 August 1921).

Very confusing. It seems the 1914-18 War, dates everybody associates with the First World War are not 'set in stone,' so to speak. Apparently, British troops continued to serve during the 1920s in the Army of Occupation in Germany, in Palestine or in Russia and so some war memorials use other dates that are relevant to their own communities, as is the case with Rudyard.

We were in Fowey recently, battling the crowds who flock to Cornwall, and I noticed a plaque on a wall reading 'on this date, September 5, 1752, nothing happened.'

Intriguing!

I looked it up, then kicked myself for not recognising that date!

'Give us our eleven days back!' was the rallying cry behind the English calendar riots of 1752. The eleven days referred to are the 'lost' 11 days of September 1752, skipped when Britain changed over from the Julian calendar to the Gregorian calendar, bringing Britain into line with most of Europe.

The Gregorian calendar is today's international calendar, named after the man who first introduced it in February 1582, Pope Gregory XIII.

Before 1752, Britain and the entire British Empire followed the Julian calendar, first implemented by Julius Caesar in 46 B.C. However this calendar had an inbuilt error of 1 day every 128 years, due to a miscalculation of the solar year by 11 minutes. This affected the date of Easter, traditionally observed on March 21, as it began to move further away from the spring equinox with each passing year.

To get over this problem, the Gregorian calendar was introduced, based on a 365-day year divided into 12 months. Each month consists of either 30 or 31 days with one month, February, consisting of 28 days. A leap year every 4 years adds an extra day to February making it 29 days long. First to adopt the new calendar, in 1582, were France, Italy, Poland, Portugal and Spain, so Britain didn't exactly rush to fall into line. Turkey was the last country to officially switch to the new system on January 1st, 1927.

The Calendar Act of 1750 introduced the Gregorian calendar to the British Empire, bringing Britain into line with most of Western Europe, but brought a few teething problems. It meant that the year 1751 would be a short year, lasting just 282 days from 25th March (New Year in the Julian calendar) to 31st December. The year 1752 would then began on 1st January.

There remained the problem of aligning the calendar in use in England with that in use in Europe. It was necessary to correct it by 11 days: the famous 'lost days'. It was decided that Wednesday 2nd September 1752 would be followed by Thursday 14th September 1752.

This prompted nationwide alarm and the rise of the 'give us our eleven days back' movement.

I thought back to this as we drove through Endon Village, across the stream that's now barely a trickle in this dry summer, and the well that is bedecked with flowers every year in one of North Staffordshire's longest running and most charming ceremonies.

One 18th Century Endon resident, William Willett, was evidently alert to the possibility of turning the new calendar into a business opportunity. He went all around the village taking bets that he could dance non-stop for 12 whole days and 12 nights. On the evening of September 2nd 1752, he started to jig around the village and continued all through the night. The next morning, September 14th by the new calendar, he stopped dancing and claimed his bets!

Absolutely no relation, but on the same theme, another William Willett was responsible another landmark piece of 'time shifting,' not eleven days, just an hour, but we now take it for granted.

William Willett was responsible for the introduction of daylight saving, campaigning over several years at the beginning of the twentieth century almost single-handedly. He did not live to see his success as he died in 1915, a year before the measure was first introduced during the First World War.

As a house builder, he became conscious of the many hours of daylight wasted in the mornings, when his men could be working, and came up with the idea that more could be made of daylight by adjusting the clock. He put his ideas in a pamphlet, 'Waste of Daylight', and campaigned ceaselessly to win over influential people in government.

It was a slow process and his ideas suffered much opposition – people habitually resist change- but he also attracted support from many prominent people such as Winston Churchill, then President of the Board of Trade and Sir Arthur Conan Doyle.

When the measure did eventually come in it was intended purely as an emergency measure during the First World War as a means of saving fuel in munitions factories. The Summer Time Act of 1925 finally made daylight saving a permanent feature.

That's far too much 'history,' far too much guff about people named William Willett. Even if one of them did change the way we live, possibly for ever.

One more thing and yes it's William Willett related (the daylight saving one, not the dancer) and this time it's interesting! Willett's great-great-grandson is Chris Martin, lead singer in Coldplay.

Trying to write a Travel Themed Blog when Travel 'Ain't Possible.

G Says...
Listening to My Achy, Breaky Heart by Billy Ray Cyrus. No idea why.
Ah, they don't write songs like that anymore. Here's a section from the second verse,
'You can tell your ma I moved to Arkansas
You can tell your dog to bite my leg
Or tell your brother Cliff whose fist can can tell my lip
He never really liked me anyway.'
Never hear much about line dancing these days and poor old Billy Ray, who apparently released 12 albums and 44 singles since 1992 yet I've only heard of one of them, is now best known for being Miley Cyrus' dad.
I woke up (always a good start to the day), with My Achy Breaky Heart running through my head the other morning. Everything in my world is now heart related.
"It was a terrible shock to me when I realised I was getting too old to die young anymore.'"
The marvellous quintet of autobiographical novels by Edward St Aubyn have been mainstays of my 'books I can happily re-read' group of old favourites for many years and the above quote has never failed to delight on reading it again. I read Book 3, 'Some Hope,' the other day and for the first time that particular quote had more than usual impact.
Much more.
This poor blog has been languishing for a while now, unattended and seemingly abandoned. Even some of our readers have noticed! The reasons owe less to my habitual dilatory nature, but rather more to recent events. A blog devoted mainly to travel finds its raison d'être called into question after a couple of months spent rooted to an armchair with only hospital trips and visits to the GP as light relief.
A 'significant' heart attack – aren't all heart attacks 'significant?' – is the culprit. A tad more serious than a stubbed toe, my excuse last time I was this inactive.
Even so, after weeks and weeks of blood tests, scans, trailing wires and bleeping machines, the various remedies have so far been the greatest inconvenience. Beta blockers, blood thinners and various examples of chemically induced 'downers,' they all conspire to induce a zombie state. The new regime is working. Blood pressure is practically at minus levels

and I now have the resting heart rate of an Olympic athlete, without the accompanying fitness.

Going out requires a prodigious act of will, even getting out of the chair requires careful planning, but life must go on, so we go out. We don't go far, at times I am forbidden to drive anyway, but with Marigold taking the wheel we visit a couple of nearby hotels for morning coffee.

Very civilised.

It's a bit of a novelty being a passenger. I still find myself stretching out one or other leg to operate a phantom clutch or brake pedal, but as I mentioned in the company of a complete stranger sat alongside us in a hospital waiting room the other day, it's rather nice to have one's own chauffeur. I certainly wasn't expecting the response to such a trivial remark to be quite so impassioned from a fellow heart attack victim.

'Of course, the word is of French origin,' the man seated next to Marigold declaimed. Yes, we did know that, but we're British, we're reserved and a hospital waiting room rivals a great cathedral for its obligatory imposition of hushed speech.

My fellow patient was a step ahead of me in the process, clad in one of those one size fits all gowns that gape open at the back. Alarmingly so in his case. More than sufficient to reveal the absolutely pointless nature of the disposable modesty pants he wore under the gown.

Imagine a bank robbery where the miscreants' faces are disguised, supposedly, by the addition of a stocking 'mask.' Now, take that image of a distorted and flattened nose dominating an otherwise perfectly recognisable face and transpose it to the vision of (un)loveliness on open display beneath the gaping folds of a floral hospital gown. I resolved to request a plastic bag from Tesco as an additional aid to modesty when my gown donning turn came. Or a duffel bag.

'Yes,' our informant continued, shifting on his chair slightly to afford passers by a further glimpse of his undercarriage, 'The term chauffeur comes from the French term for stoker because the earliest cars were steam-powered and required the driver to stoke the engine, heating it up, before it would start. Chaud means hot in French, you know?'

Yes, we did know, but were spared a continuation of the lecture by the welcome sight of a nurse beckoning to him. He leapt to his feet, far too swiftly, in my opinion, for a man attending a coronary heart disease clinic and, more pertinently, revealing in full frontal display everything below his navel to the rest of us.

Marigold began to visibly shake, a familiar precursor to full blown hysterics, but a man seated opposite beat her to it. Within moments we were all bellowing with laughter.

It's supposedly the best medicine, isn't it?

One of the most glorious beaches in Europe is just down the road from us and we regularly visit one or other of the two hotels that directly overlook the beach. They're popular places, but every hotel worth its salt, especially out of season, welcomes non residents to swell the takings. In our case, a couple of mugs of coffee isn't perhaps their idea of the ideal customer, but you win some, you lose some in the hotel business.

The hotel we patronise least, our second choice, is just down the road from our 'favourite' and is very swish indeed. Three different people told us on our first visit that local Cornish celebrity resident Dawn French held her wedding reception here. I remain unsure of the correct response to such information.

It's adults only there, no children, no dogs and, oddly, no staff. A notice greets the newly arrived, saying in effect, we know you are here and someone will come to attend to you very soon. The Big Brother connotation, we are being watched, I find a tad unsettling. The residents are mostly couples and either very young, in their 20s, or old codgers like ourselves.

They appear to like lounging about on the terrace overlooking the beach, visiting the spa areas or sipping cocktails at the bar. I spoke to a rarely spotted member of staff who said hardly anyone walks down to the beach or even leaves the hotel after they arrive.

'It's cool to chill,' she said. Oh, okay, we can chill with the best of them, but surely not for a whole week? Apparently, that's what most people do here.

The other hotel, slightly further along, is far more laid back. There are children here, not always a reason for rejoicing, and dogs are welcome, which we invariably like to see. They make excellent toast, the staff, not the dogs, – no, toast is not toast wherever one goes, there are infinite varieties of toast – and provide ginger biscuits to accompany coffee.

Even better, there are free newspapers for patrons and various areas with views of the beach for quiet enjoyment of our morning coffee. Our favourite place is the 'Tranquillity Space.'

We were in there the other day and the only other person was a man standing by the window looking down at the beach. Presumably imagining himself alone as the chairs we were seated upon had very high backs the recently breakfasted guest gave vent to a thunderous fart. I couldn't resist from saying 'well, that wasn't very tranquil,' and as the poor devil rushed out Marigold erupted into hysterics that were even louder than our recent companion's contribution.

We walk our local beaches, within the limits of what a barely functioning heart will permit. Fistral, Mawgan Porth, Watergate Bay, they're all gloriously empty apart from the odd dog walker in Autumn, although surfers are still out in force atop the waves.

We first walked these beaches in the 1960s when Cornish beaches and surfing encapsulated the spirit of the age.

Zeitgeist.

A relatively new addition to Watergate Bay is a gigantic, well fifteen foot high, sculpture of a surfer, apparently made from recycled milk bottle plastic. As our oceans are increasingly blighted by plastic debris, the choice of material is especially appropriate.

Alaska and the Canadian Rockies.

G Says...

Circumstances have put our travel plans on hold, just as the cold weather arrives, so nothing 'fresh' to report. Cognitive dissonance theory has been much discussed in our household lately. A heart attack brings many aspects of what we have hitherto regarded as 'normal' life into sharp focus.

In particular, it's the balance between risk and reward that dominates our lives. I'm told exercise will assist recovery, yet in the next sentence given dire warnings about over exertion. If I get breathless or experience chest pain I now have a spray for use under my tongue. If this doesn't relieve symptoms within five minutes, I have to ring 999 and be carted off to hospital in an ambulance.

Gulp!

Easy paced walking, for short periods a few days a week, interspersed with 'rest.' That's the plan. Unfortunately, the drug regime I'm on makes me so lethargic I can barely walk across the room at times. The drugs are helping by lowering my heart rate to a crawl, yet I am also expected to exercise at a time when I already feel as if I have just completed a marathon.

A drug enhanced sedentary life will not help me to lose weight, as recommended, yet vigorous fat burning exercise is ruled out. Risk/reward again. The cognitive dissonance aspect comes into play as I rationalise that my close attention to diet has already brought about some weight loss, ergo it's fine to slob around the house for days on end as I am dealing with weight loss by other means. Then there's the weather. It's barely above freezing out there today and we just had a sleet shower, so vigorous walking in these arctic conditions is likely to hinder more than help. That's my considered opinion, anyway. Marigold agrees. Cognitive dissonance theory again.

Back in the day when I wrote novels to earn a crust, as is I'm sure the case with most writers who achieve a modicum of success, I had the odd critic. One American gentleman decided he needed to tell me in a long and virtually incomprehensible email, 'your a crap writer.' I replied in what I considered to be a helpful fashion, offering a few grammatical tips and introducing him to the concept of the apostrophe. Hence, 'your a crap writer' would have far greater resonance if written as, 'you're a crap writer.' A critical comment acquires greater likelihood of acceptance if the writer's words are lucid and rational.

I was reminded of this very recently when debating the respective virtues of 'real' books and ebooks. I was formerly devoted to traditional books, but have over the passage of time come to enjoy reading on my trusty Kindle. I'm reading three books, contemporaneously, at present. I can multitask. Kindle on the bedside cabinet, a paperback book alongside my armchair and a fairly weighty tome in the shed reserved for fine weather 'sitting out' sessions. Reading is reading, whether through the medium of traditional paper or via electronic gadgetry, right?

I forget the exact circumstances by which a calm and rational chat about our respective reading habits between myself and a man I'd never met before denigrated into World War Three, but denigrate it did.

My fellow debater was a visiting Canadian, from Whistler, and we'd initially found common ground in a mutual liking of his home town. Marigold and I went there eight years ago during an extended trip taking in Alaska, by sea, and transversing the Canadian side of the Rockies. I should have guessed he'd be difficult when taking issue with Vancouver, Banff, Lake Louise and indeed everywhere else we had visited on that trip, apart from Whistler.

'A wise traveler never despises his own country,' is a quotation attributed to Carlo Goldoni and it's as relevant to Canadians abroad as it is to expat Brits with barely a civil word to say about the country of their birth. We've met a great many U.K. knockers on our travels and find the practise quite baffling. Many people have remarked on the recent resurgence of racism and xenophobia in the world at large, but an uninformed prejudice against people from other countries is still far more easily explained than a virulent and minacious dislike of one's home nation.

My new Canadian 'friend,' when the subject turned to books, favoured an aphoristic style. I don't. Inevitably, I found it necessary to say so. An aphorism is a short sentence expressing a point of view in the fewest possible words and a great many authors choose to write using short, snappy sentences, usually choosing words of very few syllables.

Yes, that's a ridiculous generalisation, I know. Lee Child doesn't go in for long sentences and the thriller genre in general favours the vibrancy that short, snappy sentences engender and I'm a big fan of Mister Child. In general, though, I like a little more depth in my reading material. I can even cope with what some others may regard as pedestrian writing if the quality is there. It's simple personal preference.

Not according to Dan the sage of Whistler it isn't. No, indeed, I am wrong about the way I choose a book to read, wrong to even possess a Kindle, let alone read one, wrong about the writing style I prefer, wrong about my appreciation of many areas of Canada and so on. It's a wonder I have survived this long with such erroneous views of life.

'That's you told,' Marigold said as we were leaving. Indeed it was. I was just glad we didn't meet Whistler Dan before we set off on that Canadian trip as we'd almost certainly not have bothered going!

Of course, we should all take criticism and the opinions of others with a generous pinch of salt. Especially when it comes to travel. 'Better to see something once than to hear about it a hundred times' is an expression I often say to myself when planning a trip.

I don't know who was the first person to say that, but the man I first heard it from was a car park attendant in the Ukraine. We were in Yalta and standing beneath a vast statue of Lenin, one of many in Yalta. The car park attendant spoke very good English - we wondered what he must have done wrong as he was so obviously overqualified for his job - and told us many tales of Vladimir Putin's foibles, likes and dislikes garnered from the Russian President's frequent visits to this rather underwhelming resort on the Black Sea.

He left us with the words, 'I am now going where the Tsar goes on foot.' Marigold called him back for an explanation. The expression, a common one in former satellites of the USSR, means simply 'I am going to the toilet.' Apparently, it was the only place the Tsar wasn't carried to by flunkies. At home we now use the phrase quite often. Just one of the many benefits of foreign travel.

We loved our Canada trip. The mountains, the scenery, the wildlife. Bears, moose, killer whales, we were fortunate enough to see them all at close quarters.

One night in a log cabin in the mountains we heard a scuffling sound on the decking just outside the entrance door. 'I suppose you think that's a bear,' I said to Marigold, opening the door to investigate. I closed it again pretty swiftly on finding it was indeed a bear. A big one. In the morning we discovered we'd left both windows and the (passenger) door of the car open all night. There was a large moose outside the next cabin, but the bear had at least moved far enough away for us to make our getaway.

We liked Alaska too. Well, some of it. Our overall view may have been somewhat tarnished by this leg of the trip involving about three thousand other people. Our first cruise and after only one night our previous reservations about cruising had been confirmed. We boarded in Seattle, which we liked, and after being herded into a mass introductory meeting to tell us what to do in the event of a Titanic style incident we were both already wishing we could get off again.

'Hell is other people' is a line from a 1944 'existentialist' play by French philosopher Jean-Paul Sartre called Huis Clos, or No Exit. In the play itself, the meaning of the words is very different from the way most people interpret them today, in common with much of Sartre's works. Unfortunately, we didn't enjoy our first experience of cruising. Mainly due to the proximity of our fellow passengers.

As the only 'Brits' on board, as far as we could determine after a week long stay, we couldn't even blame our own citizens, but we both found the constant feeding frenzy, where even 24 hour availability of food still involved a dash for first choice on the menu, best seats and a compulsion to load one's plate with enough food for six people rather more than disconcerting. Just one of many 'issues.'

As far as scenery goes, however, Alaska by ship is the very best way to see the country. Glacier Bay, for example, was spectacular, the towns we stopped off at along the way rather less so. Juneau, the capital of Alaska, must be one of the strangest 'important' cities we have ever visited. Did I just write 'city' – it's barely more than a village. A small town at best. Or so we thought after walking around all of it in about twenty minutes. There's a few saloons, reminiscent of the Wild West, a Russian Orthodox Church and that's more or less it.

We'd also visited Anchorage, which did look as if it should have been the capital, but even then, 'capital city' seemed a bit of a stretch. Juneau, however, despite its relatively tiny population (31,000), has a surprise up its sleeve, being the second largest city in the United States by area. The four largest are all in Alaska, Anchorage being the fourth largest and the former Alaskan capital, Sitka, being the largest of all at over 12,400 square miles. Los Angeles, which when we were there last year, appeared to go on for ever, boasts a mere 1,300 square miles.

So, Juneau is a tardis city. Its municipal area is vast, but hardly anyone lives there and we easily walked all round the 'city centre' in next to no time. Juneau is almost unique among U.S. state capitals – the only other comparable city being Honolulu, Hawaii - in that there are no roads connecting the city to the rest of Alaska or indeed to the rest of North

America. Visitors arrive by air or by sea as the outskirts are an unrelentingly vast wilderness.

A very, very strange place, but we did like the incongruity of the Russian Orthodox Church. We've visited a fair few in our travels and this tiny little church is a true gem. In every sense, given the amount of gold leaf and jewelled decorative fixtures inside.

Ketchikan - The Salmon Capital of the World – was lovely. Another relatively modest town, but in a spectacular 'nature in the wild' setting it contains the largest collection of totem poles in the world. Local residents were easily distinguished from the loud, vulgar, bloated specimens who'd recently waddled down cruise ships' gangplanks; we found them polite, charming and very good company. Even so, we could only imagine the privations of living here all year round. Pretty scenery and totem poles apart, in the depths of an Alaskan winter, as Marigold often remarks, 'and then what do you do?'

Released at last from the floating gin palace, we hired a car and drove first of all across the border to Vancouver and after a couple of days straight up the hill towards Whistler – we didn't come across Dan, fortunately – and into the gloriously scenic Rocky Mountains. Apart from a thumping headache in Banff (altitude sickness) we loved the whole trip. Even getting a speeding ticket was memorable. I'd spotted a police patrol car on the opposite side of a dual carriage way and watched in my mirror as it bumped over the central reservation and came hurtling down the road behind me with lights flashing and siren screeching. 'Someone's in trouble,' I said to Marigold, just before the patrol car forced me off the road and onto the hard shoulder.

The officer showed me a barely legible print out taken from a contraption in his car revealing my speed at the time taken as 61 mph, the speed limit being 56 mph. I hadn't noticed; it was a completely empty road with no other cars for comparison, but was intrigued by the technology: my speed being recorded on the dashboard of a police car going the other way on the opposite carriageway.

As the officer was, politely, taking details of my (unblemished) driving licence, Marigold decided she would get out of the car to 'stretch her legs.' Officer Friendly immediately drew his gun and bellowed, 'get back in the car, Ma'am, or I will arrest you or shoot you.'

Blimey!

Marigold got back in the car. We got a ticket, the fine to be paid within 24 hours, and were sent on our way with 'you folks have a nice day' or whatever the Canadian version was. After a great deal of searching we found the office where fines had to be paid, handed over 40 dollars and the man behind the counter said, 'you needn't have bothered, we never chase up foreign nationals anyway.'

(Un) Happy New Year.

Marigold Says...

Some proper writing from G later on, but I get to say my piece first. Only fair.

Been to Asda yet AGAIN as the bargains were too great to ignore. Have bought yet another pair of warm trousers, virtually the same as the previous pair but at £8 a pop had to have them. I am of the mindset that if you don't double up on a bargain it will never be repeated. I think supermarket music is indoctrinated with words that seep into your brain like "buy two".

We are using the boot of the car for things like huge packs of toilet rolls and a bargain duvet, plus various tins of stuff which we might have needed over the Xmas period but never did, like tinned chestnuts. We call the car boot our "larder" which sounds most pretentious to anyone listening. WHY did I buy tinned chestnuts, all I did was sage and onion stuffing with a bit of holly on the top. We have also got three jars of pickled walnuts.

I had intended making 4 different stuffings but plans changed after spending the morning and part of the afternoon guzzling wine and cake. The hotel visit on Xmas day was a brilliant idea. They had huge fat settees in front of a real fire, drinks and snack type food on offer and lots of hotel guests, some with dogs to look at. The funniest thing was a black lab, who devoured in one gulp a plate of sandwiches, luckily it belonged to his owners. There was a lot of screaming, but having owned a very greedy lab, I think they got away lightly.

After I had a kip, and not started cooking till 4, and only after G suggested we just have a sandwich as he was starving, we sat down to eat at 8 pm. We'd tested the turkey at half time, cut a chunk off and rammed it between 2 slices of frozen bread, microwaved it in case we got salmonella and lavished cranberry sauce on it. Does anybody want the Recipe?

We then had 2 cooked sausages and a piece of cake. I was so glad we didn't have guests as it was not very Christmassy. We still ate a huge plateful of Xmas feast later and I must say, when not given any attention or much thought, food tastes better. It was so late we put all the dirty pots in the washing basket and left it in the shed till the next day. Brilliant suggestion by G.

Boxing Day was spent with friends who were organised, fed us royally, and it was wonderful. They are very well brought up, so included in the presents we gave them were the tinned chestnuts and pickled walnuts out of the car boot larder. Xmas is all about re-cycling. I am brill at it.

We both have Fitbits bought in a weak moment on Black Friday, or Monday, whatever. I never wanted one as I thought you had to divulge your weight. G wears his like a Patek Philippe watch, checking his heart, pulse rate and steps. He is on a fitness regime doing road circuits at a very fast pace, so we no longer have a leisurely "stroll", chatting, remarking on superior houses, peoples' sheds and passing the time of day with neighbours. Now it has become a nightmare with his heart rate being measured up hill and down dale, and me being shouted at to 'hurry up" when he can breathe and speak. Of course, this only ever happened once and now we are divorced from enjoyable walking and my Fitbit is back in its box ready to return and join the mountain of others at Amazon.

I racked my brains for 30 seconds for a surprise extra pressie and came up with the idea of a different dark chocolate selection from Asda. They have Peruvian, Madagascar and others. He was thrilled and so was I. Our place was like Hotel Chocolat, with me handing out samples and G had to guess which country they were from. He didn't get one right. I did but knew in advance, so I won.

My absolute favourite present over Xmas, was a necklace made of zips. It doesn't measure or track anything it doesn't even count steps. I love it. We are now getting back to normal after G's heart scare and are already looking at travel. I don't think about the scare anymore and have stopped poking him in the night to see if he is still breathing, shocking him out of his slumbers with a start, not a good idea. We have practised mouth to mouth resuscitation, but in the circumstances probably not a good idea.

Anyway enough of that, he will be around till he is 100, with all my care and attention. He fares better than the Christmas dinner did anyway.

G Says...

2019. A New Year. How exciting! Hmm! 2018 has gone and as it marked the year I suffered a heart attack, good riddance to it. Even so, I'm struggling to find much enthusiasm for the latest one. Next year, 2020, may be better as it at least has the virtue of being easier to say. Twenty-Twenty has a certain style about it; Twenty-Nineteen does not and Two Thousand and Nineteen is even worse.

It doesn't stop others from propagating their relentless positivity, but that's nothing new. Here's what Henry Ward Beecher had to say:

'Every man should be born again on the first day of January. Start with a fresh page. Take up one hole more in the buckle if necessary, or let down one, according to circumstances; but on the first day of January let every man gird himself once more, with his face to the front, and take no interest in the things that were and are past.'

Edward Payson Powell got in on the act as well:

'The Old Year has gone. Let the dead past bury its own dead. The New Year has taken possession of the clock of time. All hail the duties and possibilities of the coming twelve months!'

All a bit much? It is for me. I'm not a habitual curmudgeon, far from it, but with Brexit, an extremely odd word that didn't even exist until very recently still dominating the media and my wretched heart restricting our movements we're spending the winter months in England for the first time in many, many years.

Dead of winter.

Now is the winter of our discontent.

Left out in the cold.

Just a few seasonal phrases that come to mind. Are there any cheerful expressions invoking winter? Probably not. The weather hasn't even been particularly bad, but we're missing blue skies, we're missing warmth, we're missing sunshine and it's all my fault. If I were a car I could cope with a dented bonnet or a loose wiper blade. I couldn't cope with a major engine malfunction. The automotive version of a heart attack.

A heartbeat, Even though it's necessary, constantly happening, and, hopefully will continue to do so, being as aware of it as I now am can become highly irritating. It gives rise to a condition known as rubatosis, the unsettling awareness of one's own heartbeat. A condition that often manifests itself at three in the morning. Oh, it's still working, that's good. If it were not the case, I would have long since been unaware of the fact, but rational thought does not often flourish in the wee, small hours.

A broken arm, leg, collarbone, you name it I've broken it, does not engender nocturnal fretting. You accept your limitations and put up with them. Maybe it's the underlying uncertainty that makes the difference. Broken bones heal, usually without any significant long term consequences. My heart attack has been and gone, I'm in drug assisted recovery, just deal with it.

Ah, if only it were that simple. I never expected my heart to cause a problem. Big surprise all round. The aftermath is proving a tad more problematic than I anticipated. I know I can cope pretty well with pain; I've had lots of that over the years. Dealing with a heart that isn't working very well turns out to be much more difficult. Regular exercise, sensible diet, keep taking the tablets, that's about it.

Easy. Well, not so easy, as it turns out. Brisk walking, raising the heart rate to sensible levels without over exerting the poor old thing: that should be easy enough. I walk, far too quickly for Marigold to even contemplate joining me, along a route involving both uphill and downhill sections. Even on a brumous January morning, I'm out there.

English winters aren't ideally suited to the recovery process. I'm a heliophile by nature. Bring me sunshine, as Morecambe and Wise used to say. Not very likely, not in England, in January. It's weather to delight a pluviophile, to send sales of wooly hats soaring and those legions of Lycra clad skeletal figures that used to pound pavements a few months ago are conspicuous by their absence.

Even so, I'm out there. Almost every day. Grumbling, cold, wet, miserable, but out there. Doing what needs to be done. A ship in harbour is safe, but that is not what ships are for – can't remember who originally said that, but it fits the bill. A dog would be handy and provide a bit of company, but dogs like to stop and sniff and I need to keep pressing on, so that's no good.

As for human companionship, after the first circuit I don't have enough breath left to carry on a conversation anyway so my regime is necessarily a solitary one. It's not even fear of sententious health professionals that sends me out in the wind and the rain. The cardiac staff I've come across are unfailingly helpful and supportive. It's just one more chore that has to be done. Even in January. So I do it.

What's the use of January anyway? A time for rejoicing? Hardly. Start the New Year dieting, giving up smoking, stop drinking, resolve to be a better person? All very laudable, yet all induce misery in some degree or other.

Anything good about the winter months? Well, the beaches around here are empty just now, gloriously so, for those willing to brave the elements. Most of them are 'dog friendly' and in the winter months there's not the same concern over whether funds set aside to buy lunch will have to be diverted to pay for car parking. We've seen more basking seals than we've ever seen in England before – 'basking' obviously being a relative term for seals in January – and friends who live near St Ives and

Brixham have sent videos of schools of dolphins, knowing we are both pining for the Mediterranean.

On Christmas morning we went to visit friends staying at the legendary Headland Hotel in Newquay. It wasn't exactly beach weather, but Fistral Beach was far from deserted and a few surfers were out on the water. We wandered around the various lounging areas, exchanged Happy Christmas greetings with strangers – no 'happy holidays' here – stroked a few dogs and finally found our friends in the attached conservatory, knocking back cocktails for 'elevenses.'

After hastily rearranging our judgemental facial expressions (!) we joined them and ordered coffee. Marigold added a slice of cake to the order on seeing what was being delivered to a neighbouring table. We were directly overlooking the beach and managed to convince the others we had already been for a Christmas Day swim. Many of our friends are extremely gullible, possibly why they have remained as friends for such long periods.

I was fascinated by a conversation between two women, obviously mother and daughter, at the next table and conversation at 'our' table died away completely as we all tuned our ears in the direction of the next table.

The older woman, the mother, said 'did I tell you I'm having a shed?'

'No,' replied the daughter, 'where will you put it?'

'Outside.'

Long pause.

'Whereabouts?'

Long pause.

'In the garden.'

'Oh!'

The daughter took out her knitting, fiddled around in her bag and produced an unwrapped boiled sweet. She offered it to her mother who shook her head.

'It's got fluff all over it.'

'It's not too bad, only bits of wool. Natural fibres.'

Her mother pursed her lips.

'How's your Jane getting on with the diabetic nurse?'

'Oh, not very well. She's very strict, keeps saying Jane eats too many sweets.'

'She's only eight, though.'

'She's nine, mum.'

'No, She's eight. I know how old my own grand daughter is.'

'Mum, she's my child and she's nine. She's getting better about sweets anyway. Last night, after she'd finished her meal, I asked her if she wanted that bag of palma violets you left for her and she said no.' 'That's good, isn't it?' 'Yeah. She said she was full up, but that doesn't normally stop her wanting sweets.'

The old woman looked pleased.

'I'll bring her something from the pick and mix next time I come over as a reward for being a good girl.'

One conversational Christmas present I shall treasure!

Marigold recounted an account of another overheard conversation from a few days previously, in a different hotel. Two other women, one carrying a clip board, the other with briefcase and bulging leather bags were leaving as we arrived.

The woman with all the bags was saying, 'would you like to smell anything else before I go?'

The other woman said, 'No, thank you, that's plenty' and they both left.

Our waitress arrived as we were still shaking our heads in bewilderment and said, 'Glad she's gone, stinking the place out.'

She explained the 'bag lady' had turned up with samples of fragrant oils to be offered for sale in the Spa shop.

In the opinion of the waitress, 'the downstairs staff toilets smell better and that's a clothes peg on nose area if there ever was one.'

If my hearing continues to decline I shall soon miss out on these snippets of overheard conversations, but I can rely on Marigold to carry on the work. She misses nothing.

Our coffee arrived, along with a gargantuan slice of cake and surfers, beach walkers, the conversations of others and the company of old friends took second place to the fair division of cake. Our friends had already had their breakfast at the hotel so slicing into unequal portions, loosely based on two to one ratio, was easy enough. I throughly enjoyed my sliver of cake.

I've chatted to a few postmen lately on my exercise route. Fellow purposeful walkers, seemingly impervious to wind, rain and winter's chill. I still have to fully master the postman's cheerful whistling. The whistling isn't the problem; it's the presumed jollity I'm struggling with.

The period leading up to Christmas usually brings a few new faces behind the wheel of the Royal Mail Van. Shorts are still in evidence. Our regular postman told me shorts are best in heavy rain as bare legs are easier to get dry than trousers! Makes sense. They're out there, whatever the weather, delivering our mail. Bless 'em.

We are still in touch by email with a married couple we met on our US Road Trip, they're both proud servants of the US Mail Service and so we had very many postal service related conversations. Yes, we did converse on other subjects as well, but we found greater congruence in that area of their expertise than with topics like the most efficient way to skin a deer. You need a sturdy trestle and a well honed blade was the gist of that, if you're interested, which we weren't.

The words 'Neither snow nor rain nor heat nor gloom of night stays these couriers from the swift completion of their appointed rounds' - while not an official motto of the United States Postal Service - are inscribed on New York's James Farley Post Office, but have no official status.

Our American 'posties' didn't know about that, but thanks to my lifelong compulsion to read everything and anything, I did.

The English Patient, a Hollywood film based on a very fine book by Michael Ondaatje has as its central character a badly injured burns victim who is presumed to be English, hence the title, but who turns out to be Hungarian and Ondaatje gives the character a book as his sole possession. The book is The Histories by Herodotus which I had never read prior to reading The English Patient but has now become one of my established favourites.

The phrase written on that building in New York is taken from Herodotus' description of the ancient Persian precursors of the Pony Express around 500 BC. The actual quotation, yes of course I had to look it up, is: 'It is said that as many days as there are in the whole journey, so many are the men and horses that stand along the road, each horse and man at the interval of a day's journey; and these are stayed neither by snow nor rain nor heat nor darkness from accomplishing their appointed course with all speed.'

Royal Mail operate at a slightly reduced level from the ancient Persian model, but their staff are still out there, rain or shine, disproving the common assumption that all communication is now screen based. Somebody has to deliver all those online purchases.

I am indebted to the latest issue of Proceedings of the National Academy of Sciences - surely everyone else out there reads this – for further enlightenment. The quite splendidly named English Longitudinal Study of Ageing, and their equally splendidly named lead author, Andrew Steptoe, interviewed 7,000 adults aged over 50 to gain insight into 'teasing out better ways to promote a good life in middle and older age.'

The questioning focussed on peoples' perception of to what extent they regarded their daily routine as being 'worthwhile,' on a scale of 1 to 10. Those rated as 9 or 10 walked, on average, 18% faster than those rating their lives in a less positive fashion.

The smug brigade, my term not that proffered by Mister Steptoe, were claimed to sleep better, be less susceptible to illness, have more friends and (possibly) be far more likely to be invited to the Steptoe household's next soirée than those with a degree less self worth.

That's me told, then. No more grumbling, cast aside my recent captious outlook on life, grasp the future with two frail hands and rejoice at the dawn of a New Year. If my lap times don't drop by 18% as a result, the editor of Proceedings of the National Academy of Sciences can expect a stern letter of rebuke for propagating 'duff gen.'

It's only just 2019 after all. Early doors as the licensed victualler trade would have it. A bifurcated point, maybe, so I will indeed put away gloomy thoughts of the unlamented version gone by and enter the far more convivial glass half full era that awaits. That's somewhat excessive alcohol related symbolism from the view point of a man who's had barely a sip of wine since last March, but, as with trudging up hills in winter, abstinence is not necessarily a first choice.

Parties for Grownups.

G Says...

Back in 2010 Health minister Simon once described Speaker John Bercow as "a stupid, sanctimonious dwarf". Pretty tame, really, unless you're a dwarf in which case it's very insulting. Mister Bercow, very unlikely to become Lord Bercow after leaving office in contrast to just about every other former Speaker in recent times, dominates the news bulletins lately.

I'm not a great fan, to say the least, even though Marigold says he is her guilty crush. She likes his loud, hectoring voice and garish ties. Hmm!

Anyway, I met a man recently who could have been Mister Bercow's body double. The resemblance was not just confined to his physical appearance. Short of stature, big on opinions, he was holding forth at great length on a variety of subjects about which he knew very little. It was a social gathering, at a friend's house, so my retaliatory options were limited.

'Odious little cockalorum,' I muttered to Marigold, secretly relishing the opportunity to use one of my all time favourite words in the appropriate context. The 'cock' aspect, perhaps a little disappointingly, is linked to a brash, crowing rooster rather than the more vulgar yet even more appropriate attribution, but the addition of 'alorum,' being a version of the Latin genitive plural ending 'orum,' allows the word cockalorum to mean the cock of all cocks. In essence the word describes a little man with an exaggerated idea of his own importance.

Or Bercow for short then.

In every respect.

The one boring me rigid at that recent 'gathering' of friends and neighbours obligated to attend so as not to offend the hosts didn't even have a flamboyant tie on. A suit jacket, denim shirt and jeans: a mode of dress that only Jeremy Clarkson imagines still looks good, actually.

I felt well dressed, smart and even a tad trendy in comparison. This is pretty rare.

'Bercow' had cornered me, although I'd never even clapped eyes on him before, giving off the air of a man who had by some serendipitous means located his soul mate and was seemingly bent on setting a new world record for speaking without drawing breath. There wasn't a subject about which he didn't have an opinion. A very strong opinion.

Ignorance of the subject was no barrier. I recently finished a book, Archipelago, by Saif Rahman, and at one point a character says, 'Never procrastinate, never ultradecrepidate'.

Ultradecrepidate?

I looked it up

I'm glad I did as the word means, 'to criticise beyond the sphere of one's knowledge.'

In an ancient Roman story, a cobbler criticised the sandals in a painting by the painter Apelles, and then complained about further parts of the work, to which Apelles is said to have replied, "Ne sutor ultra crepidam", which roughly translates as 'The cobbler must not go beyond the sandal'. As true today as it was then, stick to what you know when indulging in criticism.

Yes, my Bercow impersonating and definitely unwanted companion, you're an ultracrepidate alright.

He was now informing me he hadn't had the benefit of my education, but was 'street smart.' In my experience, street smart is an alternative form of 'imaginary smart,' but I was here on a three line whip as regards best behaviour so I let it go.

Marigold was way over the other side of the room, but we managed a mutual eye roll. She was trying to reassure a woman we've only met twice before that the seventeen successive bad experiences, really, really bad experiences, the woman had suffered on 'dates' arranged on a dating site were just bad luck.

Maybe she should try somewhere else as desperate.com* doesn't seem to be finding her the man of her dreams.

*Not necessarily the real site name.

Marigold is awash with prescience and was seemingly making a good fist of predicting future happiness for the concerned woman.

'Don't get me wrong,' the woman said as they parted, 'I'm not asking for the Earth. I just want someone with a nice house, a decent car, no kids, who is good at DIY and likes lots of holidays.'

As Marigold made her escape the woman added – I heard this from across the room – 'oh, and I want lots of sex, but no dressing up or filthy stuff.'

Even theJohn Bercow impersonator couldn't compete with that.

I managed to get to Marigold and we made our way to the kitchen where the promised 'nibbles' were laid out. I've seen less impressive buffets in five star hotel. If this is what our hosts class as nibbles I want an invite to Sunday lunch!

'All home made,' a bright young woman told us, standing next to an overflowing Brabantia bin stuffed with the outer wrappings of Marks and Spencer pies and cakes. 'Help yourself to stuff.'

We crammed some 'stuff' onto plates, real plates, not plastic or cardboard, and tried to find a safe haven to munch in peace. We're not great mixers, not remotely antisocial as such, but 'parties for grown ups' can be purgatory. Getting a cross-section of people under one roof for whatever reason is a risky enterprise, but there do appear to be certain unwritten rules governing the clientele.

There are the quiet ones, badgered into attending, the party animals who want to get hammered on drink they didn't have to shell out on, the opinionated ones relishing the chance to drone on all night to strangers too polite to walk away and the select band of guests who fall into the 'weird' category.

So far tonight, we've only met the weirdos.

They gravitate to us.

Marigold is naturally gregarious, yet abhors evenings like this. I am even less tolerant, yet cursed with a modicum of manners so tend to suffer in silence the attention of people I would otherwise avoid at all costs.

'You must be Marigold,' a faintly scary woman wearing a lilac trouser suit says. Her make up makes her look like a manikin in Debenhams window. The lips are black, the soaring eyebrows were presumably drawn on with a child's crayons and her eyelashes were miniature wind turbines. If chaos theory has any validity, every time they flutter a hotel roof blows off in Taiwan.

Marigold confessed to being Marigold, looking a tad disconcerted at the woman's intense scrutiny. Only four words, but containing hints of disbelief, adoration, scorn, active dislike and others yet to be determined.

'I somehow imagined you would have been more, oh what's the word?' The manikin woman says, screwing up her bizarre features with even greater contortions.

I can think of appropriate descriptive words to fill the gap, but decide against voicing any of them.

'Exotic, is that the one I mean?' She asks, eventually.

Marigold looks at her, then at me. How would we know?

'Yes, exotic. Not that you look ordinary, but you're just not how I imagined from reading your blog.'

'Ah!' The blog is packed with photos of Marigold, so quite how this strange creature imagined her to look escapes us both.

'All that travelling, so much gadding about, why do you do it all and how do you find the time?'

'Well,' says Marigold, 'of course we don't do anything else. We don't work apart from a bit of modelling for Chanel.'

'And we manage to fit our travelling around our ambassadorial duties for Poundland,' I add.

In adversity we move swiftly to flippancy.

'Goodness, I never knew. Well, good for you, I say,' says the manikin.

Worse than we thought, dim and gullible, a difficult combination.

We're about to make our excuses, an imminent Skype call from our good friend Kim Jong-un perhaps, when the manikin asks a sensible question.

'Where had the biggest instant effect on you, which country?'

Hmm, interesting.

We've been to over 100 countries now and seen many places that had an instant impact. Some of our favourite places are not too dissimilar from England, some of their citizens even speak English, but others were an instant shock to the senses.

Morocco, for instance, a country we have visited many times, we even lived there for a while. We both adore the bustle of the Imperial cities, the sheer relentlessness of the many sights, sounds and smells of Fez or Marrakesh, but Cairo, for example, while also teeming with be-robed figures and exotic aromas, never had the same appeal.

Istanbul, that ancient juxtaposition of Europe and Asia was fascinating. We drove through great swathes of Turkey, but crossing the Bosporus, by car over the spectacular bridge or by boat, we did both, was incredible.

The ultimate divided city; the Western side is all bustling traffic, minarets and domes but affording scant preparation for the much more simple and yet equally awe inspiring portal to the vastness of Asia.

We will never forget the Blue Mosque and so many other magnificent landmarks, but it was that sharply delineated contrast between East and West that stuck in our memory.

Oh, and the traffic!

I have driven through Rome, London, Paris, Fez, Marrakesh, deep into the Sahara, up precipitous mountain tracks and many less well known but even more daunting expeditions into the unknown, risking imminent collision at every turn of the wheel, but Istanbul was at a whole new level.

Driving tests? Rules of the road? Don't be ridiculous!

Marigold was ready with an answer before me.

Not unusual.

'Ukraine,' she said.

Of course.

We drove through the entire country a few years ago. We'd already traversed Romania, not a great deal to see in most of rural Romania, ie most of Romania, the road system is best described as 'challenging' but the people were incredibly welcoming. Moldova was an even further step back in time and then we were in Ukraine.

First impressions, Ukraine is a very big country. I'd intended to drive to Sebastopol, but there's a great deal of not very much between Moldova and Sebastopol. Don't imagine we found the absence of landmarks boring; far from it. It was like going back in time to when life was simpler, self-sufficient farms, animals grazing peacefully and virtually no evidence of modern life. I'm not against progress, far from it, but the absence of pylons, factories and tower block housing was very soothing.

We got to Sebastopol in the end, but I knew Marigold was thinking about Yalta when she singled out Ukraine from the myriad places we have visited.

Yalta was wonderful. Statues of long dead Communist leaders were everywhere in a bustling street scene where the young women were mostly six footers, slim and haughty and the older women, at least a foot shorter and weighed three times as much as their younger versions. The weight gain with advancing years I could readily understand, but not the reduction in height.

Very odd.

Yalta is President Putin's holiday venue of choice. He swims in the Black Sea so his fabled toughness is obviously not an act. I waded in to mid thigh level and decided I didn't actually 'need' to go for a swim that day.

A bit nippy!

After much wandering around, looking at the wares on offer in the many kiosks, there are very few supermarkets in Ukraine, admiring the longevity of elderly and much battered Lada taxis, and trying to spot the head honcho of Russia wearing his Speedos, we were exhausted.

Marigold spied a bench with two middle aged and obviously prosperous ladies already in residence and decided we needed to sit down and try to listen to their conversation.

A very short lived plan.

Marigold produced a flask containing lukewarm coffee, a drink made about seven hours previously. The flask had been a free gift from a German supermarket and was intended to resemble a bottle of German beer. As a beer bottle the resemblance was reasonably accurate, as a vacuum flask it was rather less successful. But, hey, it didn't leak and the coffee was still, just about drinkable so not bad for a free promotion gift.

As we were taking our ease, sipping what was once supposed to be coffee and taking in the sights, we were approached by a uniformed man wearing an enormous peaked cap and an unpleasant expression.

Confession time, I don't speak or understand Ukrainian very well. That may be a slight exaggeration, but 'not at all' reflects badly on my renowned facility with all foreign languages(!)

If I tell you 'Good morning' is 'Dobroho ranku' in Ukrainian, you may understand my difficulty. If you were to write Good morning' you would write it as Доброго ранку! Not many linguistic clues there.

Whatever the officious man, who turned out to be a policeman, was saying, it certainly wasn't 'good morning.' I tried to explain my inability to understand as he was in danger of a burst blood vessel or two by this stage.

As I stood up he shouted something very loudly and gave every impression of wanting to machine gun everyone in the vicinity. One of the 'matrons' began shouting and we soon drew a sizeable crowd. Handcuffs were now being brandished and I thought it advisable to sit down again.

For reasons that I have yet to fully comprehend, Marigold has a tendency to laugh at the most inappropriate times and this was one of the least appropriate imaginable.

The policeman by now was on the verge of apoplexy. He took the coffee container from Marigold and poured the contents on the ground before stalking off to shout at someone else.

'This is forbidden,' one of the onlookers said, pointing at the wretched flask.

'Coffee is forbidden here?'

'Alcohol.'

'Ah!'

'Why were you laughing?' I asked which set Marigold off all over again.

'That cap, every time he shouted it wobbled up and down,' she replied. Fair enough. Whoever designed the headgear for Ukrainian policemen had obviously never considered the complete absence of dignity inflicted on the wearer.

We eventually found out that Ukrainian law frowns on public consumption of alcohol. Smoking too. We found this rather surprising after traversing the whole country where booze consumption appeared compulsory and even toddlers chain-smoked.

Draconian measures are being taken in Yalta as Putin was due to visit, possibly today, and a zero tolerance approach to such antisocial behaviour was in effect.

We still bellow 'this is forbidden' to each other, the more trivial the presumed offence, the louder the admonition.

We never met Putin, but the policeman in the ridiculous cap was much more fun.

As we left our host and hostess to walk home from the 'party' we exchanged views on our fellow guests.

Mostly unfavourable.

'We're crap at parties, aren't we?' Said Marigold.

Indeed we are.

'Did you like anything about tonight?'

I thought about this. Not really was the honest answer, but most of the evening had been monopolised by strange people.

'The food was good,' Marigold offered. Yes, it was, and I'd even enjoyed the background music, soft jazz, very soothing, up until the point someone decided we all needed to stop chatting and should instead dance to loud music on a thick shag pile carpet that made any sudden movement a torn ligament in waiting.

I showed Marigold a photo I'd taken on my phone while visiting what our hostess called 'the facilities.'

No, not that sort of photo!

I am incapable of visiting any building containing books without looking at the titles. This often involves contorting my head at an unnatural angle to read the spines of books, but the 'facilities' featured a number of books deemed suitable for browsing whilst otherwise engaged.

I noted 'Driving over Lemons,' 'Bleak House' and 'Scouting for Boys', a fairly eclectic mix, but it was the weightiest tome that took my attention: 'Psychopathia Sexualis' the legendary treatise by Richard von Krafft-Ebing.

Browsing? Well, why not?

If the choice is only Bleak House, Kraft-Ebing gets my vote.

I opened the book at random, laughed aloud for the first time in an hour and took a photo of the couple of sentences that opening the book had revealed.

Here it is:

'One subtype of olfactophilia is eproctophilia. This is a paraphilia in which people are sexually aroused by flatulence.'

Come on, Charles Dickens never wrote anything like that.

Brexit and The Beatles.

G Says...

Someone asked me today how many toilet rolls I have stockpiled. How intrusive! Answer, none, but I felt almost ashamed to confess I was not in panic mode over the seemingly limitless conjecture inspired by Brexit. This provoked my unwanted interrogator into a frenzy of instruction aimed at my woeful and inadequately briefed self.

Rather a lot of it.

She went on and on, barely pausing for breath. Such passion, I thought. Why pick on me, i thought. In the face of this verbal assault thoughts were all I had to offer.

The gist of this diatribe was, more or less: If Brexit turns out to be a dystopian nightmare, the polar opposite of a utopian ideal world we were promised but now revealed once and for all as being exclusive to dreamland and a few deluded politicians, what should we do about it?

What indeed?

I confess I didn't get as far as the conclusion; I'd long since switched my attention span elsewhere. Obviously, I retained my expression of rapt interest and boundless gratitude for her efforts to explain how best I should adapt to inevitable catastrophe. Or triumph. Whichever conclusion she reached.

Assuming she did.

Eventually.

The same woman said, greeting me in the manner of one finding a war zone refugee long since given up as dead by all who knew him, 'not seen you for a while'. To the best of my knowledge, I'd never met the woman before.

'You're very zen, aren't you?' She added at one point. Accusingly. I must have still been paying attention at that point as I remember it clearly. Well, if by that she meant I have a tendency to appear relaxed and relatively unconcerned about things that I cannot change - surely the essence of 'zen' - then I suppose I am.

I try to reserve my capacity for getting actively involved to aspects of life where I have some prospect of actually influencing events. Having one's attitude to life diminished in such a fashion can be disconcerting. This no doubt well intentioned woman appeared bent in converting me to her point of view and was evidently concerned at my apparent indifference.

A tad harshly, I thought, she'd seen overwhelming evidence of existential nihilism: a belief that life has no intrinsic meaning or value where every aspect of humanity is insignificant, without purpose and unlikely ever to change.

All this from a passioned diatribe on the subject of Brexit with minimal imput from me.

Conversing with strangers can be hard work. Enduring a monologue even harder. When what amounts to verbal assault is accompanied by pedantry, one of the many irritants that assail me on a daily basis, I sometimes marvel at my own capacity to avoid spontaneous combustion.

A classic example: this tiresome creature said at one point, 'I would say I should reiterate, but of course the word iterate is perfectly adequate for the purpose.' This made me grind my teeth.

Yes, of course, reiterate is merely a hyper correction tagged onto a perfectly adequate word that already means to repeat or perform again an action, but is there any need to point this out other than as a means of demonstrating some imagined intellectual superiority?

A psychologist would term this aspect of human behaviour as the Dunning–Kruger Effect: in essence being ignorant of one's own failings and offering up a version of oneself at variance with actuality. Most of us fail to acknowledge we're not as clever as we imagine.

I certainly do.

It's tiresome when a presumption of self worth is so widely removed from how others view us. I offer in evidence the woman making it her duty to inform and instruct me today on subjects about which her actual knowledge was vastly less than my own.

Sometimes, being 'British' and striving to maintain a façade of 'good manners' is a curse. I referenced psychology as the woman bending my ear with relentless zeal digressed from Brexit for a moment to tell me she was addicted to painkillers prescribed for MDD. My understanding of MDD, major depressive disorder, is that painkillers would be an unlikely remedy for what is in layman's term, depression.

Having spent what seemed many days listening to the lady's various 'issues' I suspect anhedonia, a complete inability to experience pleasure while participating in what others regard as pleasurable activities to be a specific diagnosis.

I read about anhedonia earlier this morning in a magazine article and am now expert on the subject. That's the Dunning–Kruger Effect in action.

Fortunately, I have no medical qualifications at all, therefore I am unlikely to offer such insightful diagnosis assistance to everyone I meet.

One has to occupy one's mind in some way while a complete stranger is sounding off with such vigour. I wished Marigold had been there to witness my monumental fortitude.

'That's you told,' Marigold said as we walked swiftly away. She'd disappeared just after our toilet roll stocks had been questioned, abandoning me to twenty minutes of purgatory. 'You're getting better at pretending to look interested though. Didn't fool me for a minute, but she's got you down as a convert now, so one of you was happy at least.'

This whole Brexit debate is wearisome. I hold fairly strong opinions on the subject, as I do with many others, but prefer to keep my views to myself. Others with deeply entrenched viewpoints elect to offer up their perceived wisdom to everyone they meet.

The recent EU elections have only increased the level of intensity. Everyone has an opinion, everyone is an amateur psephologist. If only they would refrain from sounding off at me. I must have features that suggest extreme gullibility or an apparent burning desire to learn from others far wiser than myself. In reality, neither of these presumed qualities have ever been present.

I read in the paper today, in one of those 'on this day' sections commonly used to pad out newspaper content, that The Beatles Album, Sergeant Pepper's Lonely Hearts Club Band, was released 52 years ago on 26 May 1967.

Fifty-two years!

Not an early offering either, their eighth album in fact, and The Beatles had long since become a world wide phenomenon by the time Sergeant Pepper came along.

Even so, fifty two years is a very long time. I put down the newspaper and went rummaging.

I kept a diary for two years in that period of adolescence where irrational and pointless acts were the norm. That was a very long time ago. I found them while clearing out my dad's loft, diaries dating back to 1961 and 1962. After a quick glance, they were put on one side. I recently found them again.

Pure gold!

We're in Newquay today. We lived here in the far off 1960s. Life was very different then. I had long hair, a spectacular moustache and a view of the world best described as relaxed. Marigold was the same, only without the moustache.

On Towan Headland, with the Atlantic Hotel as a backdrop, is a plaque commemorating the visit to Newquay of The Beatles in 1967. They were filming what I remember as a pretty dreadful and self indulgent film, Magical Mystery Tour, and spent several days in the area.

We met a couple recently who were 'extras' in the film, only their mothers would have even noticed them, who told us about a hilarious segment involving Ivor Cutler only a very small section of which ever made the final cut.

I would class Ivor Cutler among the most idiosyncratic people I ever met. At that time I was playing Sunday League football for a pub team in Twickenham and surrounded by very odd people. Eric Sykes, Jimmy Edwards and Bill Oddie were pub 'regulars' and Ivor Cutler made occasional appearances, especially on Burns Night as the landlord was a fellow Scot.

For many years Marigold and I quoted some of his sayings. 'Never knowingly understood' was a favourite and for many years I kept a sticky label he handed to me in the bar one night bearing the legend 'to remove this label take it off.'

Okay, maybe you had to be there.

Our goalkeeper, when not off on the road touring, was Jake Thackray. As a goalkeeper he was a very fine poet and songwriter! If you get the chance to read the words of a Jake Thackray song you may appreciate the influence he had on an entire generation of songwriters. As a writer of verse or prose he broke all known 'rules' and yet the end result was nothing short of genius.

Far later in life, as a writer myself by then, I was told I 'broke too many rules' by the esteemed Literary Editor of a major publishing house. I disregarded her advice and never regretted it. What did a mere Editor know compared to the wisdom of a not very good goalkeeper?

My first public snog with a complete stranger was in Liverpool. In the Cavern Club, no less. She was a fair bit older than me, 25 or so and I would have been 15, she was well supplied with alcohol, it was very crowded, hot, smoky and very, very loud. Matters did not progress as the main attractions were just coming on stage and not even snogging a precocious 15 year old could compete with the Beatles.

I remember that night so well. December 23rd 1961 as recorded in my diary, an 'All-Nighter' at the Cavern Club, the original one not the recent mock-up, in Matthew Street, Liverpool. I was still at school, stayed until dawn was about to break, had to walk seven miles to get home as there were no buses running and had spent all my money anyway, got into massive trouble when I finally got back.

It was worth it.

The Cavern Club was mainly a jazz club in those days, but there were a couple of guest bands that the whole city was talking about. The jazz was dire, just old people's music, but there were these other bands who were LOUD and exciting. The place was packed, it always was, and I can't remember anything that had happened in my life until then that even came close to those nights.

The bands – we'd only just started to use the word 'groups' – oh yeah, there were Gerry and the Pacemakers, Johnny Sandon and the Searchers and a scruffy bunch who'd recently changed their name to The Beatles.

I worshipped John Winston Lennon from the start, as did everybody else in my class at school. Paul McCartney looked young enough to still be in my class, Stuart Sutcliffe was the epitome of cool and all the girls screamed over Pete Best.

Gerry Marsden was a proper singer, even then I remember thinking he had a great voice, while Johnny Sandon – always Johnny Sandon AND the Searchers – was a tosser. He left the Searchers shortly before they went on to fame and fortune.

I saw the Beatles several times in those early days, still well before they achieved global fame. At New Brighton Tower Ballroom and at the Cavern Club. During this time Stu Sutcliffe died of a brain haemorrhage and Ringo replaced Pete Best as drummer. Both events were major talking points in Liverpool even if the wider world remained largely disinterested.

Stu Sutcliffe wasn't destined to be a musician and had already returned to his first love, art, by the time of his untimely death, but I can still remember how well audiences reacted when he sang Love me Tender, Elvis reborn with a Scouse accent. As for Pete Best, lets just say Ringo's arrival as his replacement wasn't well received and the chants for 'Pete' were still ringing out months after Ringo took his place behind the drum kit.

I put stars around 1st July 1962, it marked the date the music world was finally handed over to my generation; the first night at the Cavern Club without a jazz element. The Beatles, The Swinging Blue Jeans (I drew a turd next to their name – its recognisable nature serving as both critical opinion of their performance and precursor of the 'surely there has been some mistake' O Level Art qualification I would gain within the next year) were the performers on stage along with Sounds Incorporated about whom I remember nothing and, oh joy, the one man who out-shone even John Lennon for an impressionable youth, Gene Vincent.

Clad in black leather, mike stand swinging around within inches of the audience, I remember it as if it were yesterday. Magical and I'm feeling the goose bumps as I write this.

We drove along the promenade at New Brighton a while ago, so much a part of my youth, along with so many of my generation. The magnificent art deco outdoor baths, where I'd learnt to swim and first plucked up the courage to hurl myself into space from the high board, have long since gone, along with the outdoor fun fair. Fort Perch Rock still looks impressive, but the other crowning glory, the pier, is no more.

Amongst the clutter abandoned in my dad's loft was a scruffy programme, dated 21st June 1962, from the Tower Ballroom, New Brighton. In its heyday, long before my time, the Tower Ballroom was a real landmark as it originally featured a huge Tower modelled on the Eiffel Tower in Paris, completed in 1900. The Tower, at that time, was the highest structure in Britain, 567 feet high. NB. I looked this up – not even my ability to retain vast numbers of useless facts is up to the task of remembering the precise details of high buildings. I do have a faint recollection that George Harrison's grandfather had been employed as a doorman at the original Tower, but don't quote me on that!

One of the largest ballroom facilities on Merseyside, able to accommodate many thousands, I knew The Tower Ballroom best as a venue for that new phenomenon of the early sixties, 'groups.'

Brian Epstein was the promoter of the event on 21 June 1962. Top of the bill was Bruce Channel – 'Hey Baby' for those with long memories – backed by Delbert McLinton and the Barons. The Beatles, second billing in those early days, were advertised as 'Parlophone recording artistes.'

A Bolton group,The Statesmen were next on the bill, followed by the Big Three and the Four Jays. I remember The Big Three very well – until that point they'd ranked just below Rory Storm & the Hurricanes as my second favourite group; The Beatles having been my favourites from the first day I saw them at The Cavern Club.

The Big Three were pretty terrible that night. I know this because I wrote 'rubbish' next to their name in the programme. Nothing else, just that one word – 'rubbish.' Sad, really. They may have had an off night, perhaps the equipment was playing up, all that remains is my verdict, 'rubbish.' I was very evidently a stern critic, yet inclined to brevity.

Many years later I read that Delbert McLinton encouraged John Lennon to play the harmonica by teaching him the passage from 'Hey Baby.' When the Beatles came to record 'Love Me Do', their first record to hit the charts, John Lennon played the harmonica riff. The harmonica lesson must have happened that evening.

History in the making.

I was there.

The bus to the Pier Head, the ferry cross the Mersey - to coin a phrase – the excitement mounting with every step along New Brighton Pier, then the bright lights of the Tower ballroom, the milling crowds. I remember it all so well.

It's all gone now. TheTower Ballroom burnt down in 1969, the outdoor funfair I remembered chiefly for the Ghost Train, Hall of Mirrors and lime green cream soda in a glass bottle sealed with a marble gone too, replaced by a housing estate.

End of an era. Gone, but not forgotten.

There's a commemorative stone on Tower Promenade which celebrates the fact that The Beatles played at the Tower Ballroom on 27 occasions in the early 1960's but it's so insignificant as to be easily ignored by visitors.

As for Sergeant Pepper, no I hadn't forgotten, I still have a copy. One of three albums, we called them LPs back then, I kept for posterity, including another Beatles album, Please Please Me. I used to have the White Album too, but it's vanished.

I'm not trendy enough to have reverted to vinyl and bought a turntable so the actual records are useless. What prompted the retention of Sergeant Pepper for over 52 years was the cover. It was the most expensive album cover ever. The final cost for the artwork was nearly £3,000, a huge sum back in 1967 when the average cost of artwork was around £75.

The figures chosen for the cover are a weird mix. Of musicians, Bob Dylan is the only contemporary. I was pleased to see Stu Sutcliffe made it, just about and was baffled by the inclusion of Sonny Liston, but not Mohammed Ali who the Beatles met on several occasions.

Anyway, life's too short to count how many people I recognise. Maybe, one rainy day, I'll have a go at naming them all.

Oop North.

G Says...

We're 'oop North' for an all too brief visit. Recent heart related nonsense involving various invasive hospital procedures have necessitated numerous trips to my GP to try and make sense of the frequently contradictory conclusions being drawn by a plethora of hospital Consultants.

The GP I usually try to see is not the best advert for health. He's a big chap, weighs about half as much again as me and after getting up to insert fresh paper into the printer on the other side of his desk was quite out of breath. This apparent disregard for his own well being may be one of the reasons I like him.

The main reason though is his bleak sense of humour. I told him I was hoping to drive 350 miles or so tomorrow and did he feel it was 'safe' to go. He indicated the numerous letters concerning recent tests of my heart function on the computer screen and said, 'well, as the great minds of the medical profession appear convinced you could peg out any time I can't see the relatively trivial matter of a trip to the north of England being a problem. Pop your clogs in Cornwall or somewhere else, the effect's the same.'

Hmm!

That's what I want from a doctor: a bit of light relief in the midst of recent stress.

We are staying on The Wirral, where we lived for many years, and it's a real joy to be back here where complete strangers chat away and find humour at every turn. We were in a supermarket, Morrison's if you're sufficiently anally retentive as to require absolute disclosure, where an elderly granny was supervising three young children.

'Sit on that bench until I get back with the shopping and don't move a muscle or I'll batter you' she ordered.

They all giggled but were still there twenty minutes later, not having 'moved a muscle' when we left the store. Nowt wrong with a bit of traditional discipline!

The next day we were all set for an expedition. The Albert Dock is home to the largest group of Grade I listed buildings in the country. It had fallen into dereliction before it was rescued in the 1980s and transformed into very smart and desirable waterfront apartments and numerous shops and restaurants.

We've visited many times over the years, but today's visit was all about culture. We drove through the Mersey Tunnel from the Wirral and I remembered, just in time, to take the Docks exit.

The sun was shining and the Liver Birds looked as magnificent as ever perched atop the clock towers of the Royal Liver Building. These world famous copper-green symbols of the city each weigh around four tonnes and were designed to watch over the city of Liverpool, one guarding the population, the other the source of city's 'prosperity,' the sea.

My Grandma, a ferociously fierce if tiny woman and as 'Scouse' as anyone I ever met once told me the 'female' bird looks out to sea, awaiting the safe return of the sailors, while the male bird faced inland waiting for the pubs to open!

So, there you have it, the real story behind the Liver Birds.

If my grandma had threatened to batter me, a battering would inevitably follow. I would never dare argue with my grandma – she once threatened to put my head through the mangle for talking during The Archers, the only threat that wasn't carried out.

'Put your hand on that door,' she once told my four year old self, pointing at the metal door to the kitchen range. I did as I was told and received a burnt hand as a result, the coal fired kitchen range being alight at the time.

'That'll teach you,' she said, 'oven doors are hot when there's a fire in the grate.'

I'm sure she meant well but that was just one of many painful lessons I learnt in that little house in Liverpool. Being instructed to place your fingers under a rocking chair when someone's sitting in it, yes it's not an act ever likely to be repeated.

Tough love my mum said. She was scared of the old lady too.

We were bound for The Tate. There are four Tate galleries in the UK. There are two in London: Tate Britain and the new Tate Modern; one in Liverpool; and one in St Ives, Cornwall.

We recently visited The Tate Gallery in St Ives, have been to both London galleries several times, but today was the turn of Liverpool, my particular favourite.

In the 1980s Alan Bowness, then director of Tate, decided to create a 'Tate of the North', as the project became known. This would be a gallery with a distinct identity, dedicated to showing modern art and encouraging a new, younger audience through an active education programme. A warehouse at the disused Albert Dock in Liverpool was chosen as the site for the new gallery.

The dock, once the hub of unloading cargos from Asia, mainly tea, silk, tobacco and spirits, was derelict. In 1981 the dockyard underwent a massive rejuvenation and as 'locals' at that time we followed the development with interest.

In 1985, James Stirling was commissioned to design the new Tate Gallery at Liverpool. His designs left the exterior of the brick and stone building built over a colonnade of sturdy Doric columns almost untouched, but transformed the interior into an arrangement of simple, elegant galleries suitable for the display of modern art. It opened to the public in May 1988.

2008 marked the year Liverpool was named European Capital of Culture. To celebrate this in 2007 the gallery hosted the Turner Prize, the first time the competition was held outside London. More than 600,000 visitors a year visit Tate Liverpool and today we were there to swell the numbers even more.

We were there for the first major exhibition in the UK of American artist Keith Haring. Haring came to prominence in 1980s New York with his immediately recognisable style, somewhat childlike in form but politically charged and motivated by a number of 'causes.'. As an openly gay man, Haring's work as an AIDS activist remains his most essential legacy but he also made quite significant contributions to nuclear disarmament campaigns.

Keith Haring's career was brief, and on 16 February 1990 he died of AIDS-related complications at the age of 31. He frequently collaborated with Andy Warhol and Jean-Michel Basquiat but it was through his street art that I first became a fan.

Haring's chalk drawings on the New York subway and his collaborations with the likes of Madonna, Grace Jones, Vivienne Westwood, and Malcolm McLaren, making sets and designs for videos and performances were early influences and this current exhibition didn't disappoint.

We started, as we invariably do, on the 4th floor and worked our way down. By its very nature art appreciation is subjective and we found 'pieces' we would happily take home with us juxtaposed with objects or images we happily rushed past. My low point was an exhibit set against a backdrop of flashing fluorescent lights and a thumping hip hop sound track.

A couple we briefly chatted to, one floor down, said that piece had been their favourite. Subjective appreciation or were they operating on a higher cultural level?

Surely not the latter.

Does art appreciation become ossified in the same manner as our musical taste remains ever so slightly rooted in the past? Asking for a friend...

On one of the lower floors Marigold was admiring a picture – Orthodox Boys by Bernard Pellin- and said to the man standing nearby, assuming it was me, 'I really like this.'

Oh dear. Art galleries are a risky setting to engage a total stranger in what they perceive to be a conversation and this was no exception.

I kept my distance as Marigold's new acquaintance unleashed a passionate dithyramb on the merits of Orthodox Boys. Art and wine appreciation are surely the ultimate refuge of those sententious and pompous individuals who crave a captive audience in order to propound their perceived wisdom.

Marigold is afflicted with the double whammy of a butterfly mind, unable to concentrate on any subject for any length of time and chronic politeness. I watched her eyes glaze over even as her nodding head and adopted expression of rapt attention assured her 'instructor' of her total engagement.

I am not unkind. I interceded on Marigold's behalf after not much more than ten minutes!

'Sorry to interrupt, but you really must come and see Venus of the Rags' I said, taking Marigold by the arm and steering her to safety.

'Ah, a fine example of arte povera,' Liverpool's resident art bore shouted after us. 'Yes,' I called back, 'so typical of Michelangelo Pistoletto's work.'

I'd only just read the information card alongside Venus of the Rags; naturally this made me an expert on the subject. Obviously so as we were allowed to depart without further delay.

The Gallery is housed in a former warehouse and I had noticed the grimy nature of the windows as we walked around. Finding a reliable window cleaner is tricky these days. I took a couple of photographs of the distant Liver Buildings and a passing ferry crossing the Mersey and, given the surroundings, decided only an arty farty black and white photo would be appropriate.

A vast expanse of floor space was devoted to Jim Lambie's Zobop 1999, a psychedelic melange of brightly coloured stripes producing weird images that changed with ever step. Marigold refused to even look at it, never mind actually set foot on it. The power of art to repel is obviously as well founded as its capacity to attract attention.

Liverpool, according to the museum curator, a lovely man we spoke to at some length in the Tate Café, has more public sculptures than any other UK location, outside of Westminster.

Thus reminded we diverted to find a few of our favourites, The Beatles at the Pier Head, Billy Fury just up the road and Eleanor Rigby in Stanley Street.

Billy Fury, back when he was plain old Ronald Wycherley, worked as a docker alongside one of my uncles and I met 'Ron' several times. When he was 'discovered' and a new stage name chosen I saw him live on a couple of occasions and was very impressed with his singing and his brilliant backing group, Georgie Fame and the Blue Flames especially Georgie Fame who was a fabulous pianist.

What did I know? Poor talented Georgie got the boot but turned out to be reasonably successful, especially after teaming up with a former member of The Animals, Alan Price.

I was lucky enough to watch an audition by my favourite local band, known back in their early days as The Silver Beetles (note the different spelling of beetles, the more familiar 'Beatles' came along later). They were offered the job of backing group to Billy Fury, a major star by then, for £20 a week on the condition that they sacked their bassist Stuart Sutcliffe.

John Lennon refused as the decision had been already taken to see if they could make a go of it as a stand-alone group. A pretty sound decision as it turned out.

There's a statue consisting of brightly coloured cubes perched one atop another outside. I forget the artist's name but we saw the original version of this exhibit, many similar stacks of coloured 'blocks' in the Nevada Desert outside Las Vegas.

If you read our blog posts relating to that US Road Trip you may recall our vehemently expressed dislike of Las Vegas, but without doubt the piles of coloured blocks in the desert were vastly more interesting than that tawdry city of a million broken dreams.

The statue of Eleanor Rigby, the subject of the Beatles song, was designed and commissioned by an entertainer from a previous generation, Tommy Steele, as an act of homage to the Beatles and the city of Liverpool.

Pretty impressive generosity for a boy from Bermondsey.

Not long after the statue was installed I used to collect Marigold from her place of work, a barristers' Chambers in Stanley Street and invariably sat on the bench next to 'Eleanor' while I waited. No chance of perching there today as the queue of tourists waiting their turn on the bench was daunting.

More culture tomorrow if the weather stays fine. The Lady Lever Art Gallery at Port Sunlight is on our list and another trip out to see Anthony Gormley's magnificent Another Place collection of Iron Men.

Lady Lever.

G Says...

We're not content until we're awash with culture, so off we go to yet another Art Gallery our second in less than a week. Two art gallery visits in a week sounds rather more impressive than the wider context of two Art Gallery visits this year.

Our very good friend Sheila accompanied us. She claims to be extremely cultured and her wisdom is, apparently, legendary. The Lady Lever Art Gallery is delightfully situated in one of the most beautiful villages we have ever visited and we have been here many times. The Gallery and Port Sunlight Village were both founded on soap.

William Hesketh Lever was born in Bolton and started out working in the family grocery business. One of the products they sold was soap, which, at that time, was poor quality stuff that was cut off a large block in the shop. He hit on the idea of selling a pre-packaged, good quality product. Initially he had it manufactured for him but as demand grew in 1888 he set up Lever Brothers with his brother James to produce the soap themselves in a new factory on the Wirral.

The village was built alongside the soap factory to house his workforce and the name Port Sunlight came from after the main product, Sunlight Soap. Please indulge the subsequent lavish encomium, but I really love visiting here.

Lever was heavily influenced by William Morris and the Arts and Crafts movement, who looked back to a golden age of "Merrie England" where happy peasants lived and worked in a "green and pleasant land".

Lever's stated aims were 'to socialise and Christianise business relations and get back to that close family brotherhood that existed in the good old days of hand labour' and build a rural environment with green spaces and allotments where his workers would be able to grow their own food.

This alliance of what would, much later, be called Socialist ideals with hard headed business acumen was not uncommon at the time – George Cadbury's Bourneville village also comes to mind – but William Lever was a forerunner of Prince Charles being so passionately interested in architecture. Hence Port Sunlight is a mixture of many different styles of buildings with over thirty architects given licence to design their own versions of 'vernacular' English style. Over time a war memorial and the Lady Lever art gallery, which opened in 1922, were built, adding to the splendour.

The village now contains over 900 houses - more than two thousand lucky people live here - all set amidst a flower bedecked expanse of open landscaping. This was probably the first purpose-built garden village and on a sunny day like today it looked gorgeous. Over 300,000 visitors come every year to marvel as we did.

We decided to enter the Art Gallery by the side entrance rather than climb the steps. This route took us through the gift shop and the café, thus catering for both my favourite and least favourite areas of any public building. The main reason behind our visit was the Rembrandt in Print exhibition of fifty outstanding prints imported from the Ashmolean Museum and displayed together for the first time to mark 350 years since his, (Rembrandt's), death in 1669.

I have been to the Ashmolean in Oxford a few years ago, but don't recall Rembrandt's work being displayed on that occasion. Better late than never, here it was in Port Sunlight.

We know Rembrandt's reputation as the greatest painter of the Dutch Golden Age, but he was also one of the most innovative and experimental printmakers of the 17th century. It was fascinating to view these prints at close quarters, especially as magnifying glasses were made available to view the fine detail.

Rembrandt's epigones are legion, but having now seen the works of the Master Artist himself at close quarters I realise their efforts are light years removed from his genius.

When I returned my borrowed magnifying glass I asked one of the museum staff what I thought to be a very intelligent question. Not related to Rembrandt at all, strangely enough, but merely an enquiry concerning the whereabouts of the Adam Room having read in the Museum Guide about best collection of Wedgwood jasperware anywhere in the world.

'Just go out there, turn left, left again, go straight on and it's the third room on the left' she said. I followed the instructions exactly and emerged on the far side of the same room I had recently vacated. Marigold was busily pointing out the finer points of a nude sculpture of Antinous, a young man immortalised in marble for being the lover of the Roman Emperor Hadrian. I got the impression my two companions were lowering the cultural tone by remarking on the manner in which the sculptor had economised in the use of marble in certain areas!

A woman out of my sight behind another statue said, very clearly, 'You can't miss her, she's wearing a commode.'

What?

Kimono? Possibly. A camisole perhaps? But, she said 'commode' very clearly. I sometimes fear for my sanity as I do seem to concern myself unduly with overheard snippets taken wildly out of context.

The museum guide passed by and asked if I had enjoyed the Adam Room. I was reluctant to confess my failure to find it, fearing another barrage of go left, right, then left instructions, but she offered to escort me. There are times when looking slightly vague is helpful.

'Pity my confrère isn't in today,' she said as we walked left, then right, then left again, 'she is a real Adam expert.'

My confrère! You don't get to hear that in the check out queue in Lidl. I doubt you'd hear it in Waitrose actually.

Culture done for the day we drove around for a bit admiring the houses. Sadly, the original *raison d'être* of Port Sunlight's existence: housing employees skilled at making soap, is no more. The factory remains, but actual soap is no longer made here. My friend Peter was one of the very last soap makers. His final months at work were spent training his replacements in a factory in Prague.

Nowadays actual bars of soap are rarely found in our supermarkets as people are switching to shower gels, moisturisers, liquid soaps and body washes.

The first Lord Leverhulme, William Hesketh Lever, conceived the idea of manufacturing sweet-smelling soap at the end of the 19th century after seeing the repulsive offerings available in his father's store in Bolton.

He called his first product Sunlight, the advertising slogan being: 'Why does a woman look old so much sooner than a man? Answer: Because she doesn't use Sunlight.'

Personally, I think his advertising agency weren't up to much.

Lifebuoy was added to the production line in 1894 and Lux in 1929. All gone now but the 'soap factory ' at Port Sunlight is still going strong. Port Sunlight has been the centre for the soap industry's Research and Development programme for over 100 years. Think of brands like Dove, Sunsilk, Domestos, Comfort, Surf and Signal; they all have Port Sunlight technology inside. I know you're all wondering where polymer deposition technology, used in 2-in-1 shampoos and conditioners was invented. Yes, of course it was at Port Sunlight.

My mate Peter knew everything there was to know about making soap, it was his life's work, but unfortunately he wasn't able to transfer his skills on site. Port Sunlight today employs a multi-national community of over

750 scientists who have 200 PhDs between them. If you're thinking of a science based career, give Unilever a call.

May Contain Frivolity.

G Says...

The previous post, Mainly about Soap, received a modicum of criticism, not that I care about the opinions of the misguided ones, for its perceived emphasis on factual comment. 'Not your usual mucking about stuff' was one comment from a regular reader.

As you can tell all sorts read this blog, they're not all of an intellectual bent or seekers after enlightenment! Even so, I vow to please everybody so here's a blog entry containing more than a little frivolity.

I must be looking even rougher than usual this morning as the chatty couple we met in passing last night have only one topic of conversation. Hard to ignore them while retaining my legendary courtesy (!) so I grin and bear it.

Last evening they were celebrating their 25 years of marriage with a renewal of vows shindig in the hotel we're staying in. Lots of overdressed revellers, dozens of discarded stiletto heeled shoes abandoned on the lawn outside by their foot blistered owners and assorted children ignoring the wedding buffet to feed pound coins into the machine dispensing crisps and chocolate.

We arrived as it was all winding down and the happy couple interrupted their blazing argument to come over and sit next to us.

'Don't let him start talking,' the 'wife' cautioned, 'he never shuts up.'

Her spouse appeared to have imbibed rather freely at the bar and also managed to reveal the nature of most of the buffet items by decorating his suit jacket in food stains.

'Twenty five years of this,' he said, jerking his thumb in the direction of his beloved. I waited for the inevitable next sentence, oh here it came...

'Twenty five years, you don't get that for murder.'

Laugh? Well, we made a token effort at acknowledging his massively unoriginal remark. It wasn't even much of a token effort.

The centrepiece couple weren't the only ones engaged in relationship trauma. Just about all their guests seemed to have been invited solely for their fissiparous tendencies.

Everywhere we looked there was a squabble.

We made the wise decision to take our matrimonial harmony demonstration off to our own room as it was so obviously alien to the ambience of the downstairs lounge.

This morning the dining room was deserted as we arrived to do battle with the breakfast buffet. No sooner had I demonstrated my mastery of high end culinary skills: adding hot water to an instant pot of porridge - Marigold is hard to impress - than we heard the uneven clatter of high heels on the floor tiles and recognised this presaged the imminent arrival of a woman with severe foot blisters but no spare footwear.

'Hello, you two,' the woman bellowed, no longer wearing last evening's dress made for a much smaller person, but instead mostly but not entirely confined in a Lycra outfit that revealed most of the areas it was supposed to cover.

Her husband had similarly abandoned his food stained wedding suit for a pair of flared jeans the like of which I last saw being worn by a member of Slade and a tee shirt bearing the legend 'Size Matters.'

Keeping a man from his morning porridge is pretty bad form, but today's infraction was even worse than we had imagined. Ignoring the buffet the couple wanted to talk about dying.

Do I look like a person with one foot in the grave, I muttered to Marigold. Her lack of a response was a tad worrying.

'The Silver Wedding done and dusted,' Mister Fashion Catwalk of 1973 announced, 'now we've got to go and sort out a piggin' funeral. It's the wife's brother, he's on his last legs.'

'Oh, right.'

'Yeah,' the Lycra goddess said, 'as if we haven't had enough to do with organising our wedding vows thingie.'

Marigold looked as concerned as it is possible to do while stifling hysterical laughter.

'Percy,' the woman continued, prompting the arrival of a red rash on Marigold's neck, 'my brother, he's been set to croak for years and now it looks like he's gonna do it.'

'I'm so sorry,' I said, 'you're obviously upset.'

'Well, yeah, but it's not a surprise, you know? Muggins here got lumbered with making the arrangements.'

Her husband stood up abruptly and said, 'my belly thinks my throats been cut' and set off at a rapid waddle for the breakfast buffet.

His wife looked up and sighed. 'No use at all, him. Like everything else this funeral will be all left to me. Either of you ever planned a funeral?'

'Not really,' Marigold said, vaguely.

'I just don't know where to start and Percy may still be alive but he's useless. He's not religious, don't want no hymns, but he said he won't mind what we do as long as everybody gets a good drink down 'em.'

The husband returned with a tray containing a selection of every item on the buffet table and sat at a table about twenty feet away.

'I thought a song or two, perhaps a poem, but no hymns. Will that be okay do you think?'

I was tempted to say, 'do what you like, it's your funeral,' but of course, strictly speaking, it was the still breathing Percy's send off she was planning.

'There's that one about breaking the clocks from Four Weddings and a Funeral, do you know it?'

I nodded and glanced at Marigold who appeared to have been suddenly struck dumb.

'Yes,' I said, 'The Funeral Blues by W H Auden.

Stop all the clocks, cut off the telephone,

Prevent the dog from barking with a juicy bone,

Silence the pianos and with muffled drum,

Bring out the coffin, let the mourners come.

and so on.'

The chief funeral planner looked astonished.

'Wow, you must have watched the Four Weddings DVD a hundred times.'

Marigold snorted.

'I just remember the poem,' I offered. WH Auden was part of my A level syllabus and even after what seems like 100 years later that poem has obviously stuck in my memory. I even remember WH Auden's full name, Wystan Hugh Auden, but thought it wiser not to mention it. Even though I frequently can't remember what I had for dinner last night dredging up poems learnt at school could be termed showing off.

In fairness, Auden wrote about four hundred poems yet The Funeral Blues is probably the only one I can recall with any clarity.

Romantic Comedies notwithstanding, it's a common enough choice as an alternative to the more austere threnodies of a traditional funeral.

The woman - we'd never bothered with actual introductions - was looking more cheerful.

'Yes, that one and I thought of having something by Leonard Cohen as well.'

'Leonard Cohen? Perfect,' Marigold said, brightly. I agreed Well, he didn't write anything upbeat or cheerful, ever.

Our companion smiled. 'The roving one, that's the one I was thinking of.'

I looked at Marigold, she looked as perplexed as me.

'I don't know that one,' I said.

'Oh? It's very good. Anyway, I must get back to Malcolm. He's diabetic and has to be watched.'

She lowered her voice and spoke to us from behind her hand. 'He's a right greedy so and so, I can't relax for a minute, have to watch him 24/7.'

We all looked at Malcolm, busily tucking in to a vast Full English with buttered toast and jam on hand ready for the next course.

'Yes,' Marigold said, 'you can't be too careful.'

We returned to our own meagre fare, my porridge long since congealed to the consistency of cement, and tried to avoid listening to the raised voices from the distant table as Malcolm received both health advice and censure at maximum volume.

That evening Marigold announced 'found it,' holding her iPad aloft.

'Oh good,' I replied having absolutely no idea to what she was referring.

'The Leonard Cohen song. The roving one is actually 'So we'll go no more a-roving' and it's on the Dear Heather album. I think we've got that, or used to have it anyway.'

We did once own that album and I remember the 'song' – actually more of a poem – spoken but not sung, although with Leonard Cohen the difference is minuscule.

I remembered the provenance of the actual poem as well; one dashed off by Lord Byron during his many perambulations around Europe. I looked it up and the second verse caught my attention.

'For the sword outwears its sheath,

And the soul wears out the breast,

And the heart must pause to breathe,

And Love itself have rest.'

In a letter to Thomas Moore, the poem is preceded by Byron's account of its genesis.

'At present, I am on the invalid regimen myself. The Carnival - that is, the latter part of it, and sitting up late o' nights - had knocked me up a little. But it is over - and it is now Lent, with all its abstinence and sacred music... Though I did not dissipate much upon the whole, yet I find 'the sword wearing out the scabbard,' though I have but just turned the corner of twenty nine.'

Good grief, if he felt like that at the age of 29 no wonder he died when he was 36.

We set off the next morning, having been first to appear for breakfast at 06.30, and made it through the Wallasey Tunnel without mishap – the last time we crossed under the Mersey there was a multi car collision at the midpoint and we spent many an unhappy hour playing I Spy in the gloom as wrecking trucks prised vehicles apart.

We drove past a mural of Liverpool scenes including the Titanic, the much missed, by me anyway, Overhead Railway, a tram, a cormorant invoking the origins of the Liver Birds and much more painted on a cocoa bean storage shed at Seaforth Docks.

There's so much on that mural to invoke a Liverpool childhood.

No, not the Titanic, I aren't that ancient, but the overhead railway and the trams were integral parts of my childhood.

Rattling along the cobbles, getting off in Church Street to shop at the new C and A (some people insisted it stood for 'caps and 'ats' – I believed them) or going all the way to the Pier Head, 'for the ride.'

As for the Titanic, it may have been built in Belfast and sailed from Southampton on its only voyage, but it's very much a Liverpool ship. Titanic was registered in Liverpool, its managing company, White Star Line has its headquarters in James Street and Titanic carried the city's name on her stern.

My Uncle Fred, who worked on the docks, told me about a long passageway that connected crew quarters deep below decks on Titanic was named Scotland Road in honour of the road where he, my mother and their other siblings were born and grew up.

We drove along Scotland Road on leaving the Tunnel today. It has changed beyond all recognition since my childhood. The rows of narrow streets flanked by grimy terrace houses where I played football and cowboys and Indians as a child are long gone.

Those post war slums are no more but nobody is claiming it as a shining example of urban gentrification just yet.

The Overhead Railway appears on the mural as it operated all along the docks, almost seven miles of them, between Liverpool and Seaforth between March 1893 to December 1956.

I rode the 'overhead' many times as a child, many years ahead of its time as the first electrically-operated elevated railway in the world and was devastated when it finally closed in 1956.

There's one of the original carriages in Liverpool Museum. We sat in it and it was certainly evident the intention was to carry a workforce to and from their place of work, not as travellers expecting to be pampered.

At its peak over 20 million passengers travelled on it every year. I miss it so much.

The shore at Crosby was our destination today. The car parking has become more formal since our last visit a few years back and I eventually parked at a gym and outdoor activities centre where an earnest young man implored me to go and look at the plans for Everton's proposed new stadium.

We didn't bother.

We were here for art, pure and simple: Anthony Gormley's superb creation, Another Place. Gormley is well known for his iconic Angel of the North sculpture alongside the A1 at Gateshead and we've visited a fair few 'Gormley's' over the years, most memorably a suspended installation in the National Portrait Gallery entitled 'Object' which was breathtaking.

As with 'Object,' Gormley's statues of iron men at Crosby, 100 of them in all, are casts of the artist's own body and are spread out along a 2 mile stretch of the Mersey just north of Liverpool.

The serried ranks of iron men are situated looking out to sea along set lines reaching up to half a mile from the entry point of the beach, which means that as the tide comes in many of the figures gradually become engulfed by the waves.

We took some photos but film cannot capture the sense of awe at viewing these naked figures forever fixating on the seascape before them. Every new day, every tidal surge, brings a fresh viewpoint as the more advanced figures gradually succumb to the advancing waves.

We could have stayed there all day.

Anthony Gormley's Art is found all over the world, but perhaps the most striking of all is The Angel of the North.

We've passed that in sunshine, in rain, in a snowstorm and, memorably, on a misty day. It's truly spectacular.

No Angel this trip, but it cropped up in recent conversation with an old friend who declared he would avoid passing by the statue at all costs due to its Nazi connotations.

I know, I know, but he's an old friend and not all my friends are rational human beings. Very few of them meet the criteria in truth.

I did offer up a rejoinder to the effect that Brian Sewell would doubtless agree with my friend as the late art critic, never one to hold back when there was spleen to be vented, affirmed the Angel to be 'not a work of art, a monstrosity'.

I looked up this next quote, the words of Brian Sewell written ten years after the Angel's installation: 'It is a monstrous ugly object and God knows why it got planning permission... If you are talking about it as art, it's nought out of ten. It's about as engaging as the gigantic arms of Saddam Hussein on the way into Baghdad. I can't understand how people don't realise it is like a statue from almost every undemocratic regime you care to mention.

Still not keen then, Brian.

Shame as it never ceases to inspire Marigold and I. We are evidently descended from Philistines.

Not that the Philistines deserve their unfortunate reputation being a rather cultured and erudite people on the whole.

The Angel's wingspan is often compared to a Jumbo jet. I garnered some facts, its wings actually span 54 metres (that's 175 feet) and it stands over 65 feet in height, the same as a five storey building or four double decker buses.

While ensuring the accuracy of these measurements I came across a reference to a comparison between the proposed artwork and a figure, complete with almost identical stance and with outstretched wings, commissioned by Albert Speer as a symbol of German air superiority for Adolph Hitler and a statue was erected outside Berlin in 1935.

Hitler, apparently, liked the design very much.

Oops, now I shall have to upgrade my opinion of my old friend. At the very least I now have something to place in the credit column to partially offset all the debits he has accumulated over the years.

Emmets. Farewell to Cornwall.

G Says…

We're in a rather swish hotel overlooking the beach at Mawgan Porth, one of our favourite coffee stops, watching a drama unfold. In the adjoining dining room a waitress had been standing, pencil poised over her pad, for quite some time now alongside a group of three 'yummy mummies' waiting for them to abandon checking their emails to give her a breakfast order. It had been a long wait.

Eventually one of the women looked up and said imperiously, 'we'll have what we had yesterday' and then resumed her animated tapping on her phone.

The waitress, obviously having no idea what the group had ordered yesterday, looked flustered.

A different woman looked around the room for her child and eventually located him on the outside terrace where the railings overlooking the sea provided an enticing challenge to an active toddler. We'd already noted the absence of adult presence in an area where several young children were running unsupervised, the game of the day being upturning all the outside furniture.

'Theodore, do you want smoked salmon or eggs Benedict?'

Theodore, a hefty three year old, was too busy lobbing gravel at the plate glass window behind which I was sitting to reply. His mother said, 'could you check again in a few minutes?' The waitress nodded politely and walked back to the kitchen, her expressionless face a perfect example of the well honed forbearance ingrained in the very fabric of Service Industries. The visage cracked as she muttered to Marigold in passing, 'Theodore needs his backside tanning.'

We didn't disagree.

Two young (ish) women are carrying on a loud conversation behind us. It clearly says Tranquility Area on the entrance door, but they must have misunderstood the meaning. Marigold nudges me and we do that mutual eye rolling thing. From where I'm sitting I can't see the protagonists but their conversation reveals a great deal. (You know you're entering your cantankerous phase when a few simple sentences uttered by complete strangers is sufficient to set your teeth on edge.)

Here's a section of that conversation.

'I brought 36 tops.'

'36? For a week?'

'Yeah, a week's holiday, that's loads of selfies. Can't be in the photos always wearing the same stuff can I?'

'Yes, but 36 tops? Don't reckon I brought more than twenty.'

'Couldn't get any more in the cases. I can always buy some more if we go clothes shopping.'

'Oh, we will, we will.'

As the unseen couple dissolve into raucous laughter, our regular waitress, the one who spoils us rotten due to our regular attendance as locals as distinct from transitory hotel residents, turns up with our coffee, toast and three newspapers intended for residents but intercepted in transit.

'This lot,' she mutters, jabbing a thumb in the direction of the dining room crammed with breakfasting guests, 'they're worse than the August crowd. We lose the school age crowd now and they were bad enough, but this mob with a granny or nanny in tow and pre-school kids left to run riot are even worse.'

'Hotel looks busy,' Marigold said.

'We're packed. When aren't we? This place costs an arm and a leg to stay in and there's never a free room. I haven't had a day off for weeks. Give us our Cornwall back I say.'

It's a recurring theme, this resentment of visitors. We hear it all the time. I have my sympathies. And yet, and yet…

'He told him that he saw a vast multitude and a promiscuous, their habitations like molehills, the men as emmets.'
Robert Burton, The Anatomy of Melancholy.

'Once a dream did weave a shade
O'er my angel-guarded bed
That an emmet lost its way
Where on grass methought I lay.'
William Blake, Songs of Innocence, A Dream.

Derived from the Cornish language word for "ant," the 'emmet' is an analogy for the way in which both tourists and ants are often burnt to a vivid red colour and appear to mill around aimlessly. Emmets, the summer visitors, if you're 'Cornish,' are a bit of a nuisance, blocking the roads with their cars and caravans, thronging the narrow streets of picturesque Cornish villages and most of the locals would rather they weren't there at all. In Devon they feel the same way, but their summer influx are termed 'grockles.'

It makes a change from arguing about the correct way to present a Cream Tea which has been raging for generations. In simple terms a 'proper job Cornish cream tea' has the scone coated with jam, then and only then is the clotted cream applied. Mix them up at your peril. It's cream on scone with a jam topping in Devon and better to be termed an emmet than being confirmed as Devonian.

Of course, without the despised emmets Cornwall would be a virtual Third World Country - I say 'Country' not 'County' as every Cornish born and bred local knows Cornwall is not part of England and never has been. Cornwall, even whilst still seeking, or even demanding, separate nation status could not survive without tourists.

Part of the trouble, of course, is that Cornwall has never been rich in anything much except fish and tin. Fishing stocks have dwindled and tin mining exists only on the set of 'Poldark'.

Tourism, mass tourism, long since became the only game in town. The beaches are glorious, 400 of them dotted around a vast coastline - the ramblers' path around the coast of Cornwall is 300 miles long – and wherever you are in Cornwall you're never more than 20 miles from the sea.

We've lived in close proximity to Mediterranean beaches, wandered along the shorelines of Australia, New Zealand, California and many other exotic locations and can honestly say nowhere we've ever been exceeds the sheer beauty of many of the beaches and sparkling blue waters we found in Cornwall.

Add in the Eden Project, the Tate Gallery in St Ives and many more 'attractions' of that ilk and it's easy to see why the tourists come.

They come every year, in vast numbers, despite a woefully inadequate road network and the environmental damage caused by far too many seasonal visitors. Pubs, restaurants, hotels and car parking spaces are deluged with trade every summer. When the visitors leave there's virtually nothing left. No jobs, that's for sure, the locals can't afford a house as the outsiders have bought up most of the housing stock to use as holiday homes and the beaches revert to one man and his dog status until next Easter.

We pop into Newquay every now and then, it's only just up the road but in July and August it's a madhouse. On our last visit we went for an early morning walk on Fistral Beach, not a very strenuous walk but glorious in the early morning with just a dozen or so surfers on the water.

We intended to wander up to the Headland Hotel for a coffee, but on the spur of the moment decided to go to the Atlantic Hotel instead. They're both Newquay icons and while we prefer the rambling splendour of the Headland it's never a bad thing to act on a whim. The Atlantic it would be then.

The uniformed man guarding the revolving doors welcomed us inside and then asked if we were here for the party. Marigold was looking lovely as usual, but I had dressed for a wander along a beach and was looking fairly dishevelled even by my lamentably low standards.

We said we weren't here for a party and he grinned and waved a hand at the selection of high end limousines in the car park.

'Wall to wall toffs today,' he confided, 'there's a party getting set up to celebrate the end of the season but I reckon they're a bit premature. We're booked chock a block for October and my mate at the Headland Hotel says they're the same. Looks like we're stuck with the emmets for even longer this year.'

We walked into the lobby, both a tad pleased to be so readily taken for Cornish 'natives' and almost immediately saw what the planned party was all about. There were tables being laid, flowers placed in vases and a group of women dressed up to the nines bustling about with place cards.

'Hello,' one woman called out and we turned to see the owner of an artisan bakery we occasionally chat to when our paths cross. We went over to say hello and received news of a celebratory party to mark the official end of summer.

'Last day in September,' our informant said, 'from tomorrow all the beaches revert to being dog friendly, not just some of them, and the visitors vanish until Easter.'

Behind her the dining room was packed with hotel guests and we'd just been told of buoyant bookings for the following month, but we're far too well mannered to argue the point.

'Newquay becomes our town again. We can park our cars, get a table in a restaurant, walk on the beaches, isn't it marvellous?'

We agreed it was indeed marvellous and went in search of a restorative coffee. Our waiter wasn't slow in putting an alternative view.

'My last shift,' he muttered, 'only told me yesterday there'd be nothing doing here after today. I'm summer relief, see, not permanent, but most of them will be off at the end of next month as well.'

'What will you do?' Marigold asked. She's a worrier, usually on other peoples' behalf.

'Dunno. Might have to go back on the dole. There's loads of us being laid off and every other place will be the same I reckon.'

There's the conundrum. Locals begrudge the influx of visitors but without them, what's left? Very little I fear.

The beach is getting busier we see from our vantage point as we sip our coffee. Fistral Beach has become synonymous with surfing and now looks very different to the stark beauty of the bay we first glimpsed in the 1960s when there was a beach, the Headland Hotel at the far end and behind the beach just sand dunes and the Newquay Golf Club. Now there are surf schools, restaurants and all manner of stuff, but the beach and the waves are what everyone comes here for.

I learnt recently the name 'Fistral is derived from the Cornish word meaning foul water. The sea here is almost translucent blue so it's obviously not a reference to water quality, but to the ferocity of the breaking waves making it an unsuitable landing site. A sailors' misery is a surfers' delight.

Almost every day here is good surfing conditions and there's also a 'secret' breaking point called the Cribbar where under certain conditions of wind and tide 30 foot waves can occur. It's every surfers dream to rock up on the beach at dawn and find The Cribbar in full spate.

A while ago we did a road trip through the Western USA and one of the highlights for me was visiting Huntington Beach. On entering Huntington Beach a big road sign proclaims this is 'Surf City, USA.' Huntington is surfing. Almost every shop sells surfing gear and the cafes and restaurants are surfing themed as well.

There's a statue of Duke Kahanamoku there too. He's the man credited with introducing the sport of surfing to California and also, later, to Sydney, Australia.

Originally from Hawaii, he was a great swimmer, winning gold medals at three Olympic Games, eventually beaten by no less than Johnny Weissmuller who became the first Tarzan.

In Britain the first person to surf the waves in Britain was a man of far less exotic origins. He was a dentist from Nuneaton named Jimmy Dix who wrote to Duke Kahanamoku asking for details of how to build a surfboard. Instead of a specification Duke sent back a 13-foot Tom Blake surfboard as a gift!

Jimmy Dix strapped the huge board to the roof of his car and drove down to Newquay to try it out. I imagine he received many baffled looks, but when three Aussie lifeguards arrived in Newquay with their fibreglass performance surfboards, they changed the face of the town forever and the Cornish surfing craze was born.

Three local residents set up a surfboard manufacturing company, Bilbo Surfboards, one of them being a man named Doug Wilson, formerly a beach photographer.

At this point our association with Cornwall began.

In early 1969 Marigold and I arrived in Newquay in a decrepit Austin A35 Van containing all our worldly goods and a leaky ridge tent.

Marigold worked for Doug Wilson at the Bilbo Surf Boutique and I abandoned academia to work as a 'bouncer' at The Sailors Arms directly opposite the boutique and in the day time delivered custom built surf boards to customers all across Cornwall and Devon.

Back then the road which leads down to Great Western Beach was known as The Slope and the bottom of The Slope was the meeting point for a cosmopolitan group of surfers. The Sailors Arms was the epicentre of Newquay nightlife, seemingly it still is, and the bar staff worked flat out every night to satisfy the throngs of thirsty customers.

In the day time they went surfing. Our friends were Aussies and Kiwis, following the waves around the world. It was a special era and set us irretrievably on our quest to see and do as much as possible in the time allotted to us.

I've just had the news we've been waiting for – the blood clot floating around in the region of my ailing heart has now, apparently, 'stabilised' and is no longer posing an imminent threat – so this will mark the end of our long enforced sojourn in England, for a while at least.

Eudaimonia expresses the contented happy state of a traveller. That's us then.

A Berber friend in the High Atlas Mountains of Morocco once told me I was a musafir. I wasn't too sure about that until he told me it was the Arabic word for traveller. Fair enough.

We're off to find sunshine, blue skies and contentment. Much better than sitting in Doctors' waiting rooms and traipsing hospital corridors.

Travelling.

G Says…

A few years ago we were wandering, fairly aimlessly, through the arid countryside of Algeria in our scruffy, venerable no-mod-cons camper van and found ourselves in Souk Ahras, formerly known as Thagaste. A man stopped his car- an ancient Mercedes saloon they had stopped making about forty years ago - to come over and welcome us to his country – it wasn't a region that saw many tourists.

In a conversation mainly notable for being one of the rare occasions (unique, maybe?) that my command of the French language, our only means of communication, exceeded that of the other party, he referenced Saint Augustine of Hippo who was born in the town.

Having some interest in Philosophy I had heard of Saint Augustine as a devotee of Cicero and subsequently discovered his interest in philosophy derived from the long lost 'discussion paper' Hortensius in which Cicero and some others pondered on the best use of one's leisure time. At the conclusion of the work, Cicero apparently argued that the pursuit of philosophy is the most important endeavour in life.

I don't necessarily agree with him, sorry Cicero, but as he wrote this in 45 BC I imagine alternative leisure time options were rather less widely available.

Saint Augustine became and remains the Patron Saint of Brewers. I came across an extremely pious account inferring this was 'because of his conversion from a former life of loose living, which included parties, entertainment, and worldly ambitions. His complete turnaround and conversion has been an inspiration to many who struggle with a particular vice or habit they long to break.'

Parties, entertainment and worldly ambitions, eh? Who knew they were bad things?

A quotation attributed to Saint Augustine struck a chord.

'The world is a book and those who do not travel read only one page.'

Well said, Augustine. All that loose living must have inspired you.

Meandering around France must be one of the best ways of passing one's time, but not without its pitfalls. We had spent the day on the coastal strip between Narbonne and Beziers, on back to back sandy beaches bathed in glorious sunshine. When it became apparent we needed to sort out accommodation for the night, typically neither of us had given the matter much thought.

We found an Internet connection and Marigold announced, 'leave this to me.' After ten minutes searching she claimed success and we set off for a reasonably priced seafront luxury hotel 'just up the road.'

Ten miles of winding, very narrow roads later we'd passed through an assortment of seemingly deserted villages, but still not found the hotel in question. Marigold questioned a couple of villagers who looked at her in baffled amazement. It was only when Marigold wrote down the name of the town where the hotel could be found that enlightenment dawned.

'Oh, but that is many, many kilometres from here,' one woman said with an expression suggesting it would be wise to give up our quest.

We set off again and after no more than an hour, although it seemed like a week, reached the town we sought. I have blotted its name from my memory, something something sur mer is the best I can do, as the elusive hotel continued to elude us. Finally we reached journey's end, an aparthotel said to be on the seafront and very popular with French clients who returned year after year.

The hotel was incredibly dingy, peeling paintwork, rusted downspouts – shabby but not remotely chic. There were a dozen or so Frenchmen, in their 70s, on the verge of rioting on a boules court where rules had evidently been flouted. Noisy, excitable and most certainly threatening their blood pressure levels, so we tip-toed past and found a door saying Reception.

After the grim exterior I wasn't expecting anything fancy in our room. Amazingly, it exceeded all expectations. Not in a good way.

'Only one night,' said Marigold, by now in open denial of this hotel having been her choice.

I opened the curtains and discovered the recommended sea view. Of sorts. The 'sea front' claim was technically correct, albeit with a fair degree of license. There were no buildings between our balcony and the sea. There were, however, vast tracts of swampy mudflats and boasting a sea view would be a struggle for even the most creative estate agent's 'glimpse of the sea' description to pass without complaint.

Ah well, only one night.

It was a long night as the boules contingent found many opportunities to continue their argument in neighbouring rooms, but at least it became relatively quiet at three in the morning. At four am the local bin men turned up and bashed skips around below our window for a good half hour. We didn't bother with breakfast even though it was included in the price. You win some, you lose some.

We drove into town. It was closed. Until Easter. The hotel receptionist had whispered the news that the day of our arrival would mark the end of the season and forty five other guests would have to travel several miles away for a place to sleep tonight as the hotel owners had unilaterally decided to close down for renovations. Nobody had yet told the guests who were booked in for another three days.

Marigold barely uttered a word of complain in the hour and ten minutes it took us to find a café that was open for business. When they say it is the end of the season around here they really mean it. What would probably be termed a road side diner in other countries was open and almost as pleased to see us as we were to be fed and watered.

We were in a French supermarket the other day trying to find an 'adapteur' to connect one of our English plugs to a French socket. Yes, of course we took some with us, probably a dozen of them at least, but I'd forensically reduced the car to its component parts and still couldn't find one anywhere. Unfortunately, locating one in a big French hypermarket was proving equally fractious. Marigold's whoops of triumph when she finally struck gold may have been heard in the next town.

We were on our way to the till area when we were accosted by two (obviously British) women waving their arms excitedly. When it became apparent we were fellow Brits they looked relieved.

'Finally, someone who isn't foreign' one declared. Hmm!

There are rather a lot of French people in here, not surprisingly as we're in France, but we've only come across two 'foreigners' apart from ourselves and we're talking to them now.

What burning issue of the day demands our attention, I wonder. Brexit, climate change, can it be true that John Bercow has really gone, what will it be?

The answer is a massive let down.

'Have you tried any of these French ready meals?'

The question is presented in a manner suggesting the future of mankind depends on our answer.

We glance at the selection of meals merely requiring a microwave oven to be transformed into a gourmet feast. We don't tend to shop in this aisle, but managed to say so in a resolutely non judgemental fashion.

'Only, we've got guests arriving at the weekend and they're dedicated foodies. Do you think I can make this look homemade?'

The stouter lady, it's a close call between them but I'm still trying to be non judgemental, holds up a cardboard box promising the consumer all manner of delights. I look at the photograph on the box and decide this is a question worthy of Marigold's attention. I wander off as if my presence is urgently required in the tinned preserves aisle.

As incurable hodophiles we often go 'abroad' and many of the Brits we meet on our travels come across as a breed apart.

I can make allowance for holidaymakers; they're usually focussed on spending one or two weeks trying to get as bronzed as possible in the shortest time. Yes, their version of 'bronzed' would be three pages removed from 'tan,' way out there next to fire engine red, in a Dulux paint colour chart, but they always seem happy enough with the result.

The Brits who offend us, mightily, are expats. Namely the 'we live here' brigade. Now, we've been part of that group over many years and a vast number of our fellow long stayers have been wonderful people so please don't imagine I'm venting out of simple residual grumpiness.

Simply put there are many Brits scattered across Europe in particular with whom we have no common ground other than a shared country of birth. If I met these people in England I would avoid them so why imagine I should have the slightest interest in their lives merely because they're 'British?'

A case in point. We were sitting in the lobby of a French budget hotel the other evening, simply because there were two armchairs near Reception and only a bed in our room, no chairs. Catching up with emails after a few days on the road can be a fraught process. Friends/relatives/fans, (okay forget the last one), find it hard to accept access to the Internet can be patchy 'on the road.' Marigold is replying to her third 'where are you, are you dead?' email when a middle aged couple arrive at the front desk looking very annoyed.

'Took me twenty minutes to find this hotel yet your information clearly states it is only two minutes off the motorway' the man bellowed at the receptionist. In English. I took notice as I had also followed those two minutes from the motorway directions. It took me two minutes!

The reception was a delightful young woman, originally from Ukraine but married to a Frenchman, and we had been chatting earlier for quite a while. She spoke a little English, but as English was her fifth language we cut her some slack!

'There's no point in even talking to her,' the shouty man's wife said, 'she's only going to speak French, they don't bother to learn English.'

The Receptionist did indeed speak fluent French. She was also fluent in her native language as well as Russian and Polish. When the woman started shouting I decided enough was enough.

'What's the problem?' I asked, trying hard to be civil.

'They want us to pay double, that's the problem.'

I looked at the paperwork she was brandishing.

'You've booked two rooms,' I said.

'Well, obviously, that was a mistake. I probably pressed the key twice by mistake when I booked online. Now this stupid girl expects us to pay for two rooms.'

I had a brief conversation, in my sadly inadequate French, with the Receptionist. She does not have the authority to cancel a booking as it was made through a third party site. I told Mr and Mrs Harvey the situation. Mister Harvey was not easily pacified.

'Now look here,' he shouted, 'and do not interrupt when I am speaking. I have lived in France for the best part of ten years so don't imagine you can put one over on me. We booked a room with this hotel for tonight. I expect a key to that room at once and a refund for the other room.'

The Receptionist shrank back. 'I cannot refund,' she said, 'not booked with hotel.'

'See, she speaks English,' Mrs Harvey snarled, 'she's just trying it on. We want our money back.'

Bitterly regretting my involvement I made further enquiries and passed on the information that a refund could only be obtained from the booking agency, not the hotel.

'Oh, this is ridiculous, give us the keys to both rooms if we're expected to pay for them.'

'Well, you won't get a refund from the agency if you use both rooms,' Marigold piped up. Ever practical.

This sensible advice was not what they wanted to hear and it all kicked off again with the wretched Harvey couple bellowing abuse at all and sundry. 'Foreigners ' was the term most in use, seemingly oblivious to the fact they were the only actual foreigners involved in the argument.

The next morning we were about to leave when we heard Mrs Harvey complaining, loudly, about 'not even a rasher of bacon on offer' in the five euro 'Continental breakfast.' We scarpered before they started demanding a copy of this morning's Daily Mail.

Outside two van drivers were chatting prior to setting out on their day. One very obviously French, the other speaking French in an evidently

Eastern European accent. The subject under discussion was the wretched Harvey couple. We got the impression they hadn't been impressed. The Polish/Romanian/Bulgarian driver summed up his opinion of our fellow Brits with much arm waving. 'Les Anglais, jank,' he said.

I used to have fairly regular contact with many members of the gypsy community and the Romani word he used was familiar. In English we'd probably substitute another four letter word, one starting with sh and ending in t.

Who needs the Brexit debate when so many of our our expat citizens are doing such a splendid job of offending the nationals of the country in which they've been allowed to remain?

We resolve to attempt to conceal our immigrant status for the rest of this trip.

Solitary Confinement.

Marigold Says...
About time I added some wisdom to this blog. I'll start with something you don't get from Delia.
Secret family recipe for using up old food.
Manky bread and butter pudding, I call it.
Cut green bits off bread and any fluff, disregard.
Put in any fruit lying about and soak everything in dregs of alcohol collected from bottom of glasses and any empty bottles
Sweeten. Or not . Doesn't make much difference.
Milk and 2 eggs.
Leave overnight.
Cook till crispy.
No actual cooking skills required. Present nicely and say 'enjoy' while smiling in a weird way.
We're able to sit out in our tiny patch of what only an estate agent would dare to call a lawn. It's peaceful enough, but we're ducking down behind a bush every time we hear footsteps in case it's a neighbour who wants to talk. They should be forced to ring a bell and shout unclean every time they go wandering.
It's not as big a 'garden' as our last house, nowhere near, but no embarrassments so far.
Not like the last place we lived.
We were sitting outside minding our own business. I was downing a large G and T, guffawing whilst reading Adrian Mole. G wasn't guffawing as he was trying to mend the sun umbrella with wire, pliers, gorilla tape and super glue. It wasn't looking good so far. I had been trying to curl my short locks with some home made rollers. Do not try this at home. Cut up a bath sponge into quite long shapes, then dampen them and sellotape them onto hair. Getting them off was more painful than any operation. I think I may have a curly bald patch.
Suddenly a voice from behind the bushy tree at the back, said "You two OK?"
I felt as though I had been rumbled as the local alcoholic and hid my glass. "Fine thanks, we are coping". Then wanted to laugh as G came out of the shed, as usual oblivious to what is going on saying some very rude words and throwing the tools down, just as the umbrella went on the tilt. I then said "well, must get on".

290

We found a dead bird on the lawn this morning, and I very gingerly moved it, with a garden rake, just in case its cause of death was questionable.

Chucked it over next door about 8 metres away. No idea how far eight metres is really, but good to have a bit of detail included.

Can't stop thinking about food lately. Said to G they will have to lift us out with a crane at the end of this. We never used to have "treats all the time". Ginger biscuits are now a staple of our diets morning, afternoon and night. We bought some from Tesco at 25p a packet called Mollys. Whoever Molly is 'ain't making much profit. I had G blind test the Mollys against McVities. He bit his tongue, so will have to do it again, when it has healed. I think it was the excitement of the task.

Over the road a neighbour has set up a stall with free second hand books. In former times would have rushed across and pillaged. We will not cross the threshold.

Went inside and found the binoculars. Marvellous, can pick out most of the titles. There are 3 books I definitely want. G asks what on Earth I am doing so I said "looking at the naked man running past". He just said ok and went off again.

G Says...

'You can observe a lot by just watching.'

That's a quote attributed to Yogi Berra, a legendary figure in basketball, both as a player and later as a manager, whose often bizarre post match utterances have been passed down through the ages. As with such comments as 'it's déjà vu all over again' we sort of know what he means.

Our observational patterns have been much changed of late. Our ability to watch, to observe, has been manifestly affected.

Just a few short weeks ago the world swivelled on its axis. With lavatory paper replacing bitcoin as an alternative currency, people were forced to confront the terrifying reality of a new world order. Will every economy collapse? Can a cure be found for what everyone seems to suggest is an incurable disease? Certainly there's no shortage of effort going into the eventual production of what appears the Holy Grail on which all our futures depend – a viable and effective vaccine. How far away this is, who knows? We're dealing with the unknown. In the words of Albert Einstein, 'If we knew what we were doing, it wouldn't be called research.'

Imminent peril from a pestilence bringing mortal danger across entire continents is bad enough, but many people appear to find their greatest worry is an inability to carry on doing exactly what they want to do. I overheard a remark recently, back in my going outside the door days, which came back to me yesterday while watching journalists and politicians squabbling over something so trivial I've actually forgotten what it was. The words uttered by one stranger to another were, 'everybody wants to go to heaven, but nobody wants to die.' As with almost every overheard remark, context is all, but that simple phrase resonates now far more than it did when I first heard it.

We revisited Cheltenham a short time ago. The famous spa town with its white Georgian styled buildings used to be a regular haunt back when we lived in the Cotswolds and this return trip was prompted by an offer of two nights for the price of one at a Malmaison hotel. Mal Maison – Bad House in French - that's a name to make anyone wonder if the person who came up with that idea for a hotel chain remained in the job for very long.

The hotel was full and there was a riotous party going on in the cocktail lounge. Alcohol did not appear in short supply and it was with some trepidation we wandered across to snaffle the last remaining armchairs. As so often happens, a woman seated close by immediately engaged Marigold in conversation. I can usually manage to avoid eye contact with garrulous strangers, but on this occasion it wasn't possible. The most dreary man in Europe decided his air of accrue boredom could only be elevated by telling me his life history. He was in his mid seventies so it looked like being a lengthy topic.

As I was hearing far more than I needed to know about his troubled adolescence and the consequent ramifications that haunt him to this day, a woman came over, perched on the arm of my chair and snapped, 'Gavin, shut up, this gentleman isn't interested.'

Give him his due, Gavin not only 'shut up,' he stood up and walked away. My rescuer made profuse apologies for Gavin, who turned out to be her husband of 'far too many years.'

'Gavin can't help it,' she said, 'it's supposed to be a party, but he can't bring himself to find enjoyment anywhere. He suffers from anhedonia. Do you know what that is?'

Actually, I did, it's the inability to experience pleasure even while taking part in what other people regard as pleasurable activities, but I didn't say so. I received a rather lengthy explanation of poor Gavin's condition only for his wife of 'far too many years' to add the rider, 'well, that's what his doctor says is Gavin's problem, but I think he's just a right miserable old bugger and always has been.'

As my new companion dashed off to join a drunken conga Marigold got my attention. 'He looked good fun,' she said. I gave a shortened version of Gavin, his wife and their very different outlooks on life. She didn't appear to find the topic fascinating so we did what we should have done in the first place and tagged onto the end of the conga line.

I find myself 'lurking' online far more these days. I rarely contribute on the vast range of opinions expressed. My reluctance perhaps stems from a similar disinclination to watch television during the day. Am I missing anything that will advance my knowledge or enjoyment of life? I think not.

The Internet is a fabulous source of knowledge. The same applies to its propagation of fake news and crackpot conspiracy theories. In my former incarnation as a 'writer' I felt an obligation to respond to a few of the many people who were variously kind or disparaging about my novels. I very soon realised to gain entry to this new medium and pass muster therein I must forget everything I'd ever learned about grammar, the use of witticisms, spelling, good manners and any valid pretence of acceptable literary appreciation.

Boredom has now replaced Brexit as the chief topic of conversation. Marigold and I are baffled. What is this boredom of which they speak? We're more restricted than most. The NHS, in its wisdom, after careful study of my recent medical records has seen fit to enter me into the register of seriously vulnerable citizens. I can see their point and under different circumstances being judged 'special' could be something to take pride in, but being considered seriously vulnerable, as my letter goes on to say, means I am considered unlikely to survive infection with Corona Virus.

Lockdown for twelve weeks, confined to the house, no contact with anyone apart from Marigold, that's what I'm faced with.

So, where's the problem? I can't see any. I get to spend the next four months with only Marigold for company? Bring it on.

The word which best describes a man who dotes on and adores his wife is uxorious. Uxorious is almost always used in a pejorative manner, as a negative action references a man who allows his spouse to 'control' him.

I can find no corresponding adjective relating to the far more common practise of a wife 'controlled' by her husband. Not that such a system exists in our household.

In the days preceding the great lockdown Marigold nipped out to buy a paper from a corner shop where she was being served by a woman in her thirties.

'Sorry, love, that'll be £2.70 'cos The Telegraph is dead expensive, but I'll make sure you get a receipt. Do you have to claim the money back or prove how much you spent?'

Obviously the inference being only a 'boss' would buy the Daily Telegraph and sending a 'girl' out to buy his morning paper for him is exactly what a 'boss' would do. I approve of my new found presumptive status almost as much as Marigold accepted 'girl' status, but as for expecting Marigold to go and fetch the newspapers as part of her job description - never going to happen.

I read a very serious, worthy and doubtless well intentioned article the other day containing advice in spending all this extra leisure time 'gifted' to us by COVID- 19. Not so sure everyone will see it as a 'gift,' but let's not quibble. Develop a hobby, learn to speak a foreign language, immerse yourself in house cleaning and home improvements, just a few of the suggestions.

Oh, come on. Be reasonable. Where will I possibly find the time for this stuff?

I climb out of bed, pad to the bathroom and – absolute priority - wash my hands for twenty seconds, following Government advice to the letter. I've tried singing Happy Birthday, more or less silently. That didn't avoid the scrutiny of Marigold's exceptional hearing. Isn't it odd what some people find unbearably irritating? I moved on to God Save the Queen - who could possibly take issue with our National Anthem? Well, I found one.

I considered reciting a poem, no singing involved. I swiftly ruled out Eskimo Nell and then the Rubaiyat of Omar Khayyam – far too many verses.

At one stage of my life, certainly not recently, I could recite Kubla Khan by Samuel Taylor Coleridge in its entirety. Alas, yet one more example of former abilities vanishing for ever. I did surprise myself by remembering the first verse.

'In Xanadu did Kubla Khan
A stately pleasure-dome decree:
Where Alph, the sacred river, ran
Through caverns measureless to man
 Down to a sunless sea.
So twice five miles of fertile ground

With walls and towers were girdled round;
And there were gardens bright with sinuous rills,
Where blossomed many an incense-bearing tree;
And here were forests ancient as the hills,
Enfolding sunny spots of greenery.'

As for that last line, it grated when I first read it and it still does. Even Coleridge must have read back 'Enfolding sunny spots of greenery' and thought to himself, 'that'll have to go.' Maybe he was interrupted before he could get around to it. I know that feeling.

I reported back to Marigold, having timed the opening verse when spoken out loud at just a tad over the twenty second recommendation. She didn't offer praise or congratulate my endeavours.

Her response was, 'why can't you just wash your hands like a normal person?'

I have now reluctantly switched to silent hand laundry, even amidst my ongoing concern that the required twenty second rule may be at risk.

After hand washing and other necessary bathroom functions I'll gloss over for now, I move to the kitchen where my morning feast of medication awaits. Having swallowed half of a Boots dispensary stock, I make coffee and ask Marigold if she'd like me to make her tea or coffee. I can't abide tea so my choices are much simpler.

'I'll make it myself,' she invariably replies. This implied slur on my culinary expertise doesn't become any easier with repetition. Marigold is a far better cook, no argument there, but surely even a ham fisted buffoon like me can be trusted to make instant coffee or pour boiling water onto a tea bag?

Apparently not.

I make my coffee, well up to Barista standard in my view, munch a banana and go back to wash my hands again. The chance of viral infection since I last washed my hands is somewhat less than zero, but I do it anyway. I don't go out, I don't see anyone else, I am living in a virus free bubble, but I wash my hands. Again. For twenty seconds. Give or take.

Exhausted by my efforts I allow myself to be sent off to a specific armchair where previous experience indicates porridge will be delivered at this time of the morning. After that, back for a much needed hand washing and then I'm ready to start the day.

Every morning, on rising, I mutter 'exercise' to myself and every morning I remember I should have got that out of the way before the arrival of breakfast. Oh well, I can do it later.

In fairness, despite my chaotic organisational skills, I do exercise. Indoors. I cycle, feebly, on an exercise bike I bought off Gumtree. I got it home and almost immediately realised why the previous owner wanted to get rid of it. It has two settings, well there are many settings but only two of them are working. Setting number one is virtually freewheeling, a gust of wind could turn the pedals, while the only other viable option is set at the equivalent of ascending the really, really steep section of Alpe D'huez.

I settle for the easier setting and pedal away for five minutes or so while keeping a wary eye on my heart rate. The smart watch, so called, I am wearing tells me my heart rate at any given moment, how many steps I walk, the depth and quality of my sleep and many other things I have absolutely no interest in knowing.

Stress level readings, for the day, for the week? Theoretical calories used up by my cycling efforts? I'm happy to remain ignorant of all this, but my inability to work out how to reduce this flow of information means I'm stuck with it. It took me half an hour to reset the time when the clocks changed recently and I only noticed later this action had already been done as part of the 'smart' watch's pre programmed tasks.

For the rest of the day I chat with Marigold, write the occasional email, read the newspapers online and do 'jobs.' This could be tidying out my bedside drawer, arranging pants and socks into neat piles, rearranging the clothes in my wardrobe – sweaters, tee shirts, trousers, polo shirts – in order of likelihood of ever getting worn, it's pretty full on this lockdown lark.

As I'm not venturing forth I must confess I have lowered my previous dress standards. Yes, even more. This may surprise people who know me who are surely wondering how it could be possible to drop down from such a lamentable lack of style. My three pairs of track suit trousers, all suitable only for wearing when putting the bins out at midnight, have found a new lease of life. I wear them in strict rotation to preserve their lifespan. Add a sweater rescued from a bag of stuff intended to go to the tip and that's my look du jour. Fortunately, Marigold does not have a judgemental nature. Or has finally given up with trying to make me look 'smart.'

Pause to wash hands.

I learnt a new word today. I was wondering if there was a means of expressing my only real concern about being confined to three small rooms for at least the next four months: a fear of running out of things to read. The word I was seeking is abibliophobia. It's not in the Oxford dictionary, yet, but it's a recognised word all the same. I have a few hundred 'old style' books here and many, many more on Kindle, but I do have a pretty prodigious reading habit to indulge. I'm okay for now, but in four months time I may have resorted to re-reading last week's newspapers or, unlikely as it seems just now, even plodding through the local free paper's recommendations for non surgical beauty treatments available in our area.

Several friends have suggested this imposed isolation may provide the impetus to write another novel. It's about time. Apparently. There's reasons aplenty in favour, but I'm still not yet prepared to devote another entire year to a book project. Been there, done that. I wrote a Young Adult novel recently, far less taxing than writing in my usual genre, with a storyline centred on a viral outbreak becoming a pandemic. Yes, pretty spooky as this was all done and dusted way before any indication from the Far East that there was a new virus raging out of control.

Given the subject matter I sent the manuscript to a couple of publishers. The last time I grovelled at the feet of a publisher I said 'never again.' Older, but no wiser I wait with barely concealed excitement for their reply. In other words, I haven't given it a moment's thought.

Que sera, sera.

What will be, will be.

I did spend an hour or so composing an author biography, as requested by one publisher. It's been a while since I did one of these and I still find it hard to treat the subject, namely myself, seriously. The preferred format is to refer to oneself in the Third Person which is in itself hardly conducive to taking a serious approach. Here's a typical sample:

'Since attaining adult status he's never been a financial burden to his parents or the State. This may be his only redeeming feature. Even so, he frequently regrets scorning those lost opportunities.'

Anyway, that will have to do for now. These hands won't wash themselves.

Lockdown Musings. In Solitary.

Marigold Says…

Not been out for seven weeks. Eek!

We last ventured out to do our last public pandemic shop a week before lockdown. As G and I were at odds as to what we needed I said you take a trolley and get what you need, and I will do the same. Will meet you at the tills.

First of all the most important thing toilet rolls, none to be had. People were apparently stocking up on serviettes to use instead. Gave up on that one. Headed next for Marmite, nobody wanted that yet. No chance of G adding any to his trolley. He always says he's been around the factory where it's made and taps the side of his nose three times. I assume this means something. I still like Marmite though.

Then of course, rich tea biscuits. Then I headed off for the meat aisle where everything seemed to be in short supply too and everybody was grabbing. I wanted to study what was what but was getting pushed around.

A horrible woman dressed like an extra from Game of Thrones was shoving everybody. She had got a trolley full of crisps, about 20 Pringles, chocolate and toilet rolls, about 8 packets of 9, followed by her daughter who was busy on her phone who had even more.

As quick as a flash I lifted a packet of 9 toilet rolls off her trolley when she turned around to shout 'shurrup' at her daughter.

Marv.

Think they might still have had well over 200, but with all the garbage going down their gullets might have needed them.

Got the rest of tins we needed, thinking we would need enough for a few weeks, at the most. Beans loomed large. I haven't eaten tinned beans and sausage forever, not since we spent six months in a tent in 1969.

Anyway now we have 10 tins. No tinned tomatoes on the shelves. WHY? Got some Italian tomato stuff in a jar, that will do. I seem to want to buy stuff we used to eat whilst camping like Smash. Managed to get 4. Need to get a grip.

Think the fact people are running about and grabbing is making me stressed. Can see G with a trolley full. Meet up. His pandemic shop consists of wine gums, ginger biscuits, huge packets of Twix, Shiphams paste and tinned steak. His family used to love tinned steak and he considers it a treat. Oh yes 6 packets of liquorice. Good job I got the toilet rolls.

When we got to the till it said only 3 packets of toilet rolls per order. Tee hee I thought.

Now let me tell you something, I am well practised at lockdown. Spent most of my childhood being sent to my room sometimes for most of the day. Depending on the crime it could be an hour or sometimes a whole morning or afternoon.

I can remember aged about 9 setting off with the family to a caravan park in April. We were in an A35, hand painted green by the whole family. We were going for a week and only the minimum of clothes could be taken, as we had to take all the bedding.

It rained all the way there and every day for a week. The only time we went out was to go to the toilet block and as they didn't provide anything there, we had to take our own toilet paper. The question was 'are you going for number 1 or 2?' I got one sheet of toilet paper for number 1 and four sheets for number 2. I did notice that when adults went they took the whole roll.

Early 'life isn't fair' lesson from childhood.

We lived on toast with jam. As the cooking facilities were minimal and the cooker gave off fumes, not much cooking was done. I can remember soup featured regularly, particularly tomato, again served with toast.

We never saw the sea as it was a car ride away, and the smell of damp clothing travelled with you. Showers were not taken all week as the season hadn't started, so we had to have a strip wash. Loved that. We played games, drank lots of tea and can remember loving the fact we were on a holiday in a different place. Think it was Cromer.

This is so much better. A roll of toilet paper, comfort and so far even the weather has been brill. We can't go out because G is the World's most at risk man, yes he really is, but we're still ticking over nicely.

Food delivery hasn't been easy to arrange and as we can't go to the shops we're not exactly blessed with a great variety of food. Just as well G eats anything.

The local butcher and veg man deliver, bless 'em. We have got a glut of potatoes as the veg man gets everything wrong. I asked for a pepper. He said they hadn't got any but he was sending a cucumber instead. We asked for a small bag of new potatoes and this is the 3rd time he has sent a huge bag of giant spuds instead. We also asked for some onions and he sent beetroot. We won't say anything in case he gets the hump.

G says he is glad the veg man doesn't work in the dispensing area at Boots.

G Says...

'Thou art a boil, a plague-sore, an embossed carbuncle...'

Not very nice is it? King Lear letting rip at his daughter, Goneril.

In fairness the tragedy of King Lear is not renowned as one of Shakespeare's rib ticklers, but no wonder as he wrote it during lockdown. In the Tudor era in an attempt to 'flatten the curve', 'the 1603 plague outbreak brought a directive from the privy council that all theatres and playhouses had to close when 'more than thirty disease-related deaths were recorded in a week.'

Thirty? In a week? Call that a plague?

Be that as it may, it forced Shakespeare to close his theatre, The Globe. As an actor without access to YouTube, Shakespeare couldn't work from home but as a playwright and a poet he could get on with some serious writing.

During the 1606 outbreak Shakespeare wrote three of his most famous tragedies, King Lear, Macbeth and Anthony and Cleopatra. Not many laughs in those three and no wonder. Lockdown isn't the ideal backdrop to comedy.

'All of humanity's problems stem from man's inability to sit quietly in a room alone' - Blaise Pascal.

In the era of COV-19, many would argue that the last thing any of us need is more time for self-reflection but Pascal may have been onto something in his praise of solitude as a means of unlocking creativity.

In the autumn of 1830, Russia's most famous poet, Alexander Pushkin found himself stuck at Boldino, his family's estate due to a cholera outbreak. Russians now use the phrase 'Boldino Autumn' to signify a period of great productivity during isolation as those three months, Pushkin stayed in Boldino proved to be the most productive period in his writing career.

I don't claim an encyclopaedic familiarity with the works of Pushkin, far from it, but glancing at a biography recently struck a chord with our present situation. He's a writer, he can work anywhere, so surely the same should apply to me. Ah, but Pushkin was a young idealist in confinement, eager to get his thoughts down on paper.

As for me, I aren't even Russian!

I did find this in a letter from Pushkin to his fiancé, a thousand miles away in Moscow and discovered a certain kinship between myself and the great man of letters – 'I wake up at seven o'clock, drink coffee and lie till three o'clock. I have been writing a lot recently and have already written a heap of things. At three o'clock I go riding, at five I take a bath and then dine on potatoes and buckwheat porridge. Then I read till nine o'clock.'

As for me, I miss out on the horse riding, but everything else…

Writing requires elements of detachment. Writers live inside the confines of their heads, peopled by random characters who don't exist in reality. I doubt I will ever have a greater opportunity to write another novel. And yet… Several full length novels to my name and what I remember most vividly from the process is the sheer amount of time each one takes. Time is too precious to waste on just writing another book.

In 'normal' times Marigold can more easily put up with my periods of navel gazing introspection while I ponder the plausibility of plot twists, but not now there's just the two of us, most of the time in one room.

No man is an island, as John Donne said. I wish I could remember the rest of this, I used to know it, but it's being elusive. (Yes of course I could look it up but I'm far too busy. Only so many hours in the day, you know?) I still remember the last line, 'never send to know for whom the bells tolls; it tolls for thee.'

If all poetry was restricted to just first and last lines, No Man is an Island would take some beating.

I was thinking the other day that people who smile, pull faces and talk aloud when they are alone used to be taken away to a padded room before smartphones and iPads made this behaviour acceptable.

Just now, for example, far more important matters are afoot as we sit here trying to divide a Twix bar into 14 sections, one piece each for a week. Rationing days are back.

We may even eat the apple core I was saving for Sunday lunch at this rate.

The only post we're getting delivered consists of letters from the NHS telling me I am Britain's most vulnerable man. I had the original 'vulnerable person' letter back in March and got another one this week telling me I am likely to die if I even peak through the curtains at the world outside.

I must immediately exfiltrate from the world and stay indoors until it's deemed safe for me to go out.

Allowing for a reasonable period as ruler in the prescribed succession from Elizabeth to Charles, and then William I suspect I will be given the all clear in the reign of King George 4th.

Meanwhile, I linger indoors in semi solitary confinement, constantly washing hands that have had no contact with the outside world and treating every possible fomite with acute suspicion.

A cardboard box from amazon left on the doorstep? Don three pairs of gloves and a balaclava, poke the box well away from the house with a yard brush, leave it there for three weeks. Meanwhile burn yard brush, gloves and balaclava before rushing back to bathe in neat bleach.

Can't be too careful.

I always follow orders and the furthest I have travelled in the past two months has been the end of the path, very private, that leads from our front door to the entrance road.

I've been quite energetic today after a leisurely start. 15 mins on exercise bike, then 15 mins on the path doing brisk walking. Glad nobody watches me as I have my phone open in one hand checking my heart rate stays under 90. Would hate to be mistaken for a teenager as I toddle to and fro adding to my daily 'steps.'

Marigold's 'steps' are very different from mine. Yes, I'm a foot taller with longer legs as a consequence, but even so…

What I've decided to call my 'caged tiger' walk, along the path leading from entrance road to our front door is a mere 25 'steps,' faithfully counted on a far too clever for my liking 'smart' watch and relayed as if by magic to my even smarter cell phone.

Tendons that refuse to reattach from whence they were torn away have left me with a left foot that is no longer fit for purpose. But, a heart takes precedence over a foot and I need to persuade an underperforming heart to carry on pumping so I walk.

Backwards and forwards, 25 steps, turn and repeat. The painful foot grumbles away, but I am a true stoic and I press on.

Four 'lengths' make up 100 steps and I'm aiming for at least 5,000, every one performed at a level roughly equivalent to an equine canter. A fast walk but way short of a gallop.

Marigold maintains, nay insists, that two lengths equate to 100 steps for her minuscule legs.

Hmm!

I press on. It's only painful at every other step and pain is an aberration that affect only the weak. There's nobody making me do this after all. Footsore and fancy free, as opposed to footloose.

When we began our travels the world was a very different place. It certainly seemed larger than it does now. No mobile phones to keep in touch with friends or relatives, no tablets or laptops with the ability to email just about everyone on the planet and of course no access to Internet search engines.

Primitive times indeed, yet somehow far more liberating. When we left, we vanished, free to explore where fancy took us. One huge advantage we had over travellers of today was the element of surprise.

'The traveler sees what he sees, the tourist sees what he has come to see.' G. K. Chesterton said that and it's even more appropriate today with the option to research just about every aspect of a place you intend to visit.

Such a change from our early meanderings where we turned up somewhere different and it was a step into the unknown.

Even a prolonged journey such as a gap year – what's that we would have said at the relevant time of our youth, sounds like something spoiled rich kids do to avoid looking for a job - isn't likely to reveal much that is unexpected and new.

Every 'new' place has been researched, attention paid to Trip Advisor ratings, it's not 'new' at all.

I understand the gap year idea. What could be better than an extended holiday, a last taste of freedom, postponing entering the job market and becoming a wage slave beset with responsibilities? Nothing prepares you for this. If they knew what awaited them, these young people would just stay on the beach for ever.

Marigold is clearing out her wardrobe, I heard her say 'I bought this over 20 years ago and it still fits perfectly.'

'Yes,' I said, 'it's a very nice scarf.'

On that note…

*Only the Lonely. Solitary Confinement - It's Not All Fun and Party Games.

*This blog post won a rather prestigious U.K. award as 'best blog post about lockdown.'

Marigold Says...

I have decided my hair needs cutting. I actually said to G, 'my hair needs cutting badly' and he of course jumped straight in with, 'that sounds the perfect job for me.'

I have two styles to choose from. It can either be Boris post virus locks or Michael Fabricant. To actually wear a wig like that needs an award. Love it. I haven't decided yet. It all depends on G's patience, and nifty use of a rather large pair of kitchen scissors. As their use is varied from cutting up a chicken, cardboard or old clothes for dusters, am sure they will be up to the task.

As my hair is not a favourite asset it doesn't really matter. In fact I can't think of an asset I have got. Anyway need to work up to it when G isn't on his exercise bike or wandering up and down the path.

Have started to think about waste a lot. Had loads of peelings yesterday and thought about making our own potcheen. Anyway, I thought about it and then put them in the bin. We have made all sorts of strange and varied things in the past.

We had a spell making Kombucha when we lived in France. It was very successful. In fact too successful and we were left with lots of Mother pancake things and didn't know what to do with them. It was suggested you fry them and eat them. We in fact buried them in the garden. I wonder if any have grown into something that can't be identified.

I also added cheese to olive oil and herbs. It went rancid. Buried that as well. Tried rhubarb wine. Awful. It would have been great as a toilet cleaner. We had grape vines, lots of them and the wine we made was a success thankfully. We had vineyard owning friends who were good teachers and we ended up with a quaffable product.

I was in charge of labels and my only instruction was "put them on straight". Did they think I was going to put them on upside down? Why do people get bossy when they know more than you? We even had a wine bottle hedgehog. Look it up. Surprise, surprise.

We have been walking up and down the path and G counts his steps. As I was borrowing his Fitbit and he claimed I was pinching his steps he bought me one. No stopping me now. Onwards and upwards. As it is a narrow path G starts one end with me at the other. We meet halfway and do a dozie-doe circle as in Scottish dancing to liven us up a bit.

Marv.

I have walked to Lands End and back. G said you would be better in shoes and not your slippers, but comfort is really important for athletes.

Have had requests from family, friends, debt collectors and people I have never heard of to do a video something or other called Boom, Zoom or something or other. Can't think of anything worse.

What does it involve? Do you have to wear make up, remove any rogue hairs, have an interesting backdrop? It all sounds very stressful and have had to decline. What if we came on their screen and they screamed, or we screamed? Our conversation could be over in 3 seconds and then you have to revert to "somebody is at the door" while G can clearly be heard shouting "I don't want to talk to them". Then you are trapped in a cycle of daily non goings on.

I imagine it is like visiting someone in hospital and saying "what did you have for lunch" or "are you sleeping ok". I would rather people imagine we are having lockdown parties and doing handstands.

A friend said she started to do a diary. Day 1. Got up, had breakfast. Had a walk for an hour. Had lunch. Had tea. Had shower. Went to bed.

Day 2 - ditto-. She won't be doing it anymore.

On the Thursday night clap session a woman over the way from us was clapping in an upstairs window, well actually a bit more energetic than that; she hangs out of the bathroom window with a large saucepan and a plastic veg drainer. Anyway, saucepan went flying and would have killed the old geezer underneath if he'd been there at the time.

It is still on the lawn. I have got my eye on it, as it looks better than mine. G said she could be lying on the floor having fell off backwards off the stool shouting "the clap has killed me".

Just off to do steps and catch up with G. I need to win.

After I made such a brill job of cutting his hair G came at me with large wallpaper scissors, a tin basin and said "put your legs in the stirrups" and guffawed. He is not taking it seriously so can bog off.

More to come from G in a bit. Don't expect any more sense from him either. We're both going a bit doolally.

G Says…

I don't go in for Zoom or any other type of video conferencing malarkey. Quite apart from having to make a bit of an effort with my appearance there's the absolute certainty I would be miles away, both literally and figuratively, when faced with the distraction of someone else's living room in the background. If there's a bookcase in view, forget conversation, my attention is elsewhere.

Even television presenters work from home now and I find it hard to listen to anything they're saying as their furniture, fixtures and fittings become my main focus.

Actually, I prefer it like this. Something to occupy the mind while they waffle inanely on, just like they always did, but now I have a valid excuse for tuning them out.

Even in real life situations, whatever they used to be, I constantly found myself contorting my head and neck to read, sideways on, any books on a shelf. Talking to me under these conditions is a waste of breath. Oh, and no, of course I can't concentrate on more than one thing at a time. Multitasking is not in my DNA. I struggle to cope with one task at a time.

I messaged a friend a week ago, just to say hello, and asked 'what are you up to anyway?' She hasn't replied. I can't believe it requires so much thought. A simple question, surely?

Is overthinking yet another byproduct of our recent isolation? Or am I reading too much into this? Did she just forget to reply? Even worse, is she ignoring me and my fatuous remarks? I wish I hadn't mentioned this now. I may not sleep tonight for worrying...

The same friend moved house 18 months ago and she's still got numerous taped up boxes in the 'spare' room. Getting sorted out after a move, that's just asking for an onset of prevarication, isn't it? Some 'stuff' gets unpacked and put away virtually straight away. By which I mean, within the very first week. Or so. After that, it's bye bye box, see you whenever.

I find the best removal system (and we've moved house many, many times) is to incorporate the science of random selection. Obviously, one should never write on a box what it contains - where's the fun in that? When its time comes to be opened, possibly far into the future, there's a frisson of excitement about the process.

There's about an equal balance I find between, 'oh, finally, there you are' and 'why did we ever imagine we'd need that?'

Best of all are things you really needed, couldn't find and so went out and bought a new one. Now, inside the box you finally got around to opening is that most precious of all items, 'a spare.'

I see Marigold has just referred to our 'French' period when we grew, nurtured and cherished the many grape vines on our land. We became confirmed oenophiles in the process, but not everything went smoothly all the time. I developed a condition related to tennis elbow, namely secateur wrist through pruning about a million vines.

The vast wine press in the cellar of our isolated farmhouse took all our combined strength to operate - we only learnt later that the previous owner used a mule to provide the muscle power - and Marigold, for all her many virtues, having briefly and unsuccessfully tried every other aspect of the wine making process was finally relegated to sticking labels onto the bottles.

Easy? Not as I recall. Getting a wine label to attach to a bottle and look anywhere near level must be harder than it looks. Perhaps the major chateaux have a ready supply of spirit levels to hand as our finished wine bottles would never be snapped up by the head buyer of Majestic Wine.

I heard someone on the News this morning saying how much they're missing their grandchildren. They come over to wave and shout hello occasionally and the proud grandparents throw them down a Magnum each as a treat.

'Sorry we can't come down to give you a cuddle,' they shout.

'Don't worry,' the kids reply, 'we'd rather have the Magnums anyway.'

Marigold has now started saying 'I'd rather have a Magnum' to me every time I give her a kiss or a squeeze in passing. It ceased to be funny five hours ago.

In retaliation I have threatened to withhold all future aspects of intimacy, but that strategy seems to have backfired. Oh well, as long as she's happy.

The modified sheep dip pit I ordered to protect us from people calling at the house hasn't been entirely successful. Our postman wears shorts, winter and summer, and yet is still insistent on blaming me for the full body rash he claims to have contracted by his very brief immersion.

Yes, I fully accept I made an error in not realising he was relatively short of stature before filling it to the brim with Domestos, but if he carries on complaining for much longer he'll be risking missing out on the usual 50 pence tip come next Christmas.

Marigold was dead against the plan from the start and continues to complain about my choice of Domestos when Tesco's own brand bleach is so much cheaper.

'Have you even glanced at the comparative efficiency ratings in this Which? Report,' I ask, but Marigold has always shown very little interest in my extensive research material.

I suppose I shall have to just carry on digging the moat as a back up now the Council have taken up such an unreasonably antagonistic stance to my outline planning request for a minefield.

'High explosive devices not allowed on domestic dwelling units within the Borough' indeed.

If they had bothered to read all 96 pages of my dossier they should have realised the mines would be concealed underground and therefore not visible at any time.

It's bureaucracy gone mad in my view.

The news flash along the bottom of the television screen just said, 'Greater Manchester Police attended 500 house parties last weekend.'

Well, that's not setting a very good example, is it?

My latest NHS letter, my third since the decision was made, presumably at Cabinet level that my life expectancy if exposed to 'other people' or other equally dangerous entities starts off by saying… 'Persons like you in the clinically extremely vulnerable cohort will continue to be advised to shield themselves for some time yet, and the Government recognises the difficulties this brings for those affected.'

Wow! Last time I was classified as being in the 'clinically extremely vulnerable group.' Now it's the 'clinically extremely vulnerable cohort.' Is a cohort better than a group? More selective? Even more special?

Who writes this stuff?

Pubs, bars, nightclubs, snooker halls, Burger King and gyms are all closed. Hordes of people have apparently had their lives ruined by the enforced absence of these recently deprived pleasures.

But, even allowing for this devastation, it appears my own routine will be completely unaffected.

That can't be right.

It's now day something or other since we entered the deep hibernation of lockdown. Not every day is a bundle of laughs. I'm finding it a bit upsetting to see Marigold with her nose pressed against the window, tears streaming down her face making whimpering noises.

It's heart breaking, it really is.

I've even considered letting her come back inside, but after she went out and collected that Amazon parcel left on the path we'll need to wait a few days yet to see if she starts coughing.

Oh, I know it seems harsh but rules are rules.

Just hope those Midget Gems in the Amazon box are okay out there. It's getting a bit nippy at night.

Marigold has decided to cut my hair. No fastidious micro examination of a stray hair, none of that two mirrors malarkey or inane chatter about inconsequential trivia, it's sit down, keep still and don't distract me.

As a result I have a haircut that will last several months without even seeing a brush or a comb, that takes moments to wash in the shower, is economical with shampoo and yet only took three minutes to create.

Salons of Britain, you can learn much from Marigold. Seat customer, switch on clippers, three minutes later shout 'next.'

I suspect Marigold watched a training video from the United States Marine Corps Induction Centre when honing her technique.

Oddly, my offer to return the favour and cut Marigold's hair has not yet been accepted.

Some say we need social interactions to maintain good mental health. Aristotle said, 'man is by nature a social animal.'

I yield to no one in my admiration for Aristotle. More than 2300 years after his death, he remains one of the most influential people who ever lived. He contributed to almost every aspect of human knowledge then in existence, and he was the spark, the founder of many new fields.

According to the philosopher Bryan Magee, 'it is doubtful whether any human being has ever known as much as he did.'

Even so, and far be it from me to offer an alternative view to old clever clogs, I know several people who are positively relishing lockdown.

There's a couple living behind our place - there's a ten foot hedge between us so I've never actually seen them and their entrance road is 'around the back, somewhere'– but they're obviously elderly and a bit deaf as I used to clearly hear snippets of their conversation on days when we were both engaged in that idyllic activity usually confined to warm, sunny afternoons known as 'sitting out'.

I only learnt the name of the unseen neighbour yesterday as I limped along my 25 step exercise path.

'Malcolm, are you coming in? I've got the thingie all set up to zoom the family.'

The enquirer was female, seemingly not in the first flush of youth, and with more than a hint of exasperation in her tone.

'No, 'I'm stopping here,' replied the unseen Malcolm. 'I've just got to a good bit.'

'The book can wait. Your grandchildren will want to see you.'

Malcolm was obviously having none of it.

'No, they won't, they're as fed up as I am of these wretched video things. Quite frankly I don't miss seeing any of them and if you're honest, neither do you.'

'No, I know, it's been lovely having time to ourselves and no need to pretend we enjoy having the whole tribe turn up on the doorstep, but they think we're lonely. They think we're at risk.'

Silence, then a deep sigh from Malcolm.

'Tell them I've croaked,' he shouted. 'I'm not coming in.'

Another long pause and then the woman said 'I'll say you're on the lavatory.'

I really want to meet this pair one day. Malcolm and I would get on very well. Imagine having to leave your place in a book just as you get to 'a good bit.'

It's just not on, is it, Malcolm?

Lockdown Layabouts.

G Says…

I am not a Number. I am a free man.

The expression 'I am not a number' was a regular feature of The Prisoner, a television series about an unnamed intelligence agent abducted and imprisoned in a mysterious coastal village, actually it was Portmeirion in Wales. I had to look up the dates, but filming took place from 1966 to 1968 with Patrick McGoohan playing the imprisoned 'number 6.'

We've been to Portmeirion several times and it's hard to imagine a more interesting place to be imprisoned in. Number 6 didn't know when he was on to a good thing. We don't get to whiz around a beautiful deserted village in a Mini Moke and keeping an award winning travel blog afloat when we're not travelling isn't easy, but here's some random musings from Cell Block B. Don't expect much wisdom and, this week in particular, you should drastically scale back on any foolish hopes that this long running travel blog will contain anything to do with, er, travel.

If it's reports from afar you're craving, it's just not possible to say when, or indeed if, our nomadic lifestyle will restart.

Marigold Says…

We were at one of the London airports a long time ago, and a woman asked if she could sit opposite and was carrying a pot of tea. We had got a coffee each and a packet of rich tea biscuits as a treat.

There was nowhere else for her to sit, so of course we said "yes". It was Raine Spencer. She was a bit chatty and had been there all day as they were installing a Harrods Shop in the airport concourse and she was overseeing it. Think she worked for Harrods for a bit, probably when Al Fayed was there. I offered her a biscuit. She took two and rather spoiled our biscuit dunking by giving us dirty looks of disapproval.

Anyway she seemed very nice in a hoity-toity sort of way. I would have loved it if her mother had been with her, but unfortunately she was dead. Unfortunately for me, but even more so for her I suppose.

People were looking and commenting as she was newsworthy back then. I kept smiling, thinking they were looking at ME.

She got up to go as she was being collected, fiddled in her pocket and I thought she was leaving us a tip. She was looking for her hanky.

The only thing she left was a huge smudge of plum lipstick on her cup. She had got very nice hands. I didn't know if I should curtsy and G click his heels.

G just said who was that overdressed woman pulling faces at us? He's never been up to speed on public figures or the nobility.

That was the nearest I ever got to a royal connection.

Me: 'Alexa, what's the weather going to be like tomorrow?'

Alexa: 'Why should you care, you're not going anywhere.'

I hate Alexa. She annoys me so much. Ignores me, yet whatever G says to her she dashes to obey. G says it must be because I am using what he calls my 'telephone voice' and it's obviously not being interpreted as the English language. I could get very cross with Alexa if she doesn't buck her ideas up. I suspect she doesn't like my taste in music. It's hard, being judged by a machine.

G and I were saying how much money we were saving. No shopping expedition treats like coffee, lunch, cinema, charity shops, book shops with coffee shops attached, petrol, finding lovely b and b's to book and stay in. We must be quids in.

Lipstick is another one, I now only apply it when going to the bin. We were also wondering how long it will take to not say to people "stop there and leave it on the step". Will we still be thinking, you're too close, go away? Mind you I did think that with some people before.

A friend e-mailed yesterday. You would have to know her husband to believe this. He thought he had got piles, but as he is a hypochondriac, maybe not. Anyway, he had a video consultation with their doctor. Asked him a few questions, the final one being are your stools hard. He answered, "no because they have got cushions on". I can believe it all.

He had been very frightened in case he had to show his bottom on the big screen. It certainly puts me off the idea of video health screening. My doctor will be relieved by that.

G Says...

We're still here under strict lockdown conditions, unlike those with a death wish still hankering after treats such as a trip to the tip. It said on the television regional news - that's the one where the presenters appear far better suited to working in radio broadcasting than television, adopt experimental hairstyles and bizarre mode of dress and usually have indecipherable regional accents – there are two hour queues at our recently reopened local 'tip' – it's not all fun and games out there then.

A recent Government pronouncement invited us all to take part in unlimited exercise. Former Prime Minister Winston Churchill had very clear views on the subject of exercise.

'Never stand up when you can sit down and never sit down when you can lie down.'

It didn't take long for that advice to permeate down to the majority of British people and yet now we're told we need to exercise more. Exercise can even be 'unlimited.'

Blimey!

It's a suggestion, not an enforceable edict, but even so I can think of many people I know who will have to look up the meaning of the word 'exercise' in a dictionary. Not Marigold or I, obviously, as we're both physically unchanged by lockdown.

My somewhat unfit for purpose heart requires exercise. It's a muscle after all and quite an important one. The regular bumf I get from Cardiac Bloke* at Hospital - *not sure that's his proper title – always refers to my 'Myocardial Ischemia' which certainly sounds impressive, but it basically means an inefficient pump - the heart version of 'leaves on the line' - hence its only working at about 30% of capacity.

A part time heart in layman's terms, so I put it to work.

I have my (pathetic) 25 step walking routine, access to a (even more pathetic and useless) exercise bike dominating our 'spare' room and a pair of hand weights (roughly equivalent to lifting a bag of spuds) which take up a minuscule part of my day. As every aspect of my life is governed now by heart rate I have to constantly check my pulse at every stage on a very clever app on my phone.

I vaguely remember being considered rather fit once. It was a while ago now, but as Lee Trevino once said about his golf prowess, 'The older I get, the better I used to be.'

I read about top sportsmen worrying about their fitness levels since Covid–19 took effect and fretting about resuming competition in less than perfect shape. 'I'd be ready,' I mutter to myself, self delusion being just one of the effects of increasing age.

Now 'free time' has become the norm I find I can get an immense sense of accomplishment from doing nothing for a whole hour. Doing as little as possible is okay, at a pinch, but it's not right up there in top spot.

In this period of tremendous upheaval it's obvious changes will have to be made to what was once regarded as 'normal life.' Gloves, masks, social distancing and so much more. Life as we used to know it will soon be a forgotten memory. Marigold said this to me the other day, but I insisted we are made of the right stuff and will still remember the olden times.

'I even remember a time when pesto and squashed avocado weren't classed as essential to a balanced diet,' I said.

She just looked flummoxed. Maybe I'm just imagining life existed in the pre pesto era.

Earlier today there was an ice cream van in the road, playing March of the Mods very loudly. No idea if there were any customers but there were three deafening bursts of his 'music' so he's pretty eager to sell his wares. Does hearing March of the Mods - hardly cutting edge music – convey the idea of 'Ooh, ice cream' to Millennials? I doubt it.

I wonder if there's a shortage of ice cream van jingles. Are they the 'third wave' of shortages following on from toilet rolls and then self raising flour? Very odd mixture if true.

I'm reading a book set in Russia, (Moskva   by Jack Grimwood if you really need to know) as today's contribution to my 'One a Day' regime – books may not have as many vitamins as fruit but provide longer lasting enjoyment.

The Russian word for 'solitude' means 'being with everybody.' Russians called poustinikki would withdraw to the desert (poustinia) and live in solitude, but not actually in isolation. Poustinikki relished living alone, but turned up in the nearest settlement from time to time for a brief dose of wine, women and song and then toddled off back into the desert wastes to recuperate. That sounds a fair life balance.

Marigold is not too keen on my latest suggestion for keeping Corona virus at bay. They're telling us the inability to detect smells is a symptom, but my new health check method obviously needs a bit more work. I blame those beans on toast for giving me the idea.

Now we can't go out to shop, ordering food – better make that 'requesting' – to be delivered requires great tactical planning. We need a list, an approved strategy and hitherto untouched levels of organisation. None of these actions is easy for us.

Marigold writes a long list of all the meals we're going to eat and the ingredients each one needs. Then she rips it up, laughing in a rather unsettling fashion. We just don't function like this.

We end up with a list for the butcher and another for the greengrocer. How simply marvellous, I hear you say, supporting local tradesmen. Well, yes, but there is also the matter of the sheer impossibility of getting a delivery 'slot' from the major supermarkets. Frustrated in my hunter gatherer prime, I tried the 'locals' and they've been as good as gold. Fruit, veg, meat, bread, milk, we can get it all.

Okay, we don't always get what we asked for but it seems churlish to mention that the substitution of a cucumber for a pack of oranges, for example, is even remotely close to what was requested so we just get on with it.

A supermarket delivery would be cheaper, no doubt, but ordering online would deprive Marigold of an opportunity to have a laugh with the veg man when she phones in our order. Order? Better make that a wish list. They've never met, but what would for anyone else be a quick two minute phone call takes at least a quarter of an hour and Marigold gets to hear all about the veg man's ingrowing toenail. Even Waitrose don't offer that service.

Friedrich Nietzsche, amongst many other pearls of wisdom said, 'the most common form of human stupidity is forgetting what one is trying to do.'

Freddie, you got that right.

Incidentally, I do try to check any quotes I use here that pop into my head as being deemed relevant to what I'm writing at the time. It's someone's actual words after all; better get the words in the right order. The Nietzsche quote I wrote down then went to check on it. Nailed it, exactly word for word. Gold star.

I do find it a little alarming how accurately I can still recall quotations, snatches of poetry, obscure facts hoarded in my memory many, many years previously yet struggle to write today's date and month with any degree of accuracy. Years? I'm not too bad on years. It's 2020 and has been for quite a while now. I've got that bit sussed. Months are a struggle lately and as for knowing what day it is, one of them will have to do. They all seem the same now anyway.

Anyway, back to Friedrich, I was attempting to trim my wilderness man beard into something bearing an approximate resemblance to 'smart' the other day while pondering on matters of great importance. No idea what those were, but when I reconnected with reality I noticed I now had a bushy left sided visage and a bare right side.

It's easier to subtract than add in situations such as this, so I was forced to complete the job and am now clean shaven. It's been a while since I looked at this fresh faced, apple cheeked youngster in the mirror so it was with a sense of expectation I wandered into the kitchen to find Marigold.

'You look awful,' she said. 'How long before you can hide all that away again?'

If beauty really is in the eye of the beholder it's a most unfair system. I almost wish I'd retained the option of retaining a stub of moustache. I don't imagine Adolf Hitler was ever banished and told not to reappear until his face was once again covered in a three day stubble at the very least.

Of course, this isolation situation, it's nothing new to us. Quite a while ago now I wrote in this blog about the year we spent living in a ruin, at that stage not even worthy of being called a house, in a gloriously remote region of Southern France.

That year in the Corbieres was true solitude, we didn't see anyone at all as there was nobody there to see. Birds, snakes, scorpions and the occasional wild boar, that was it. We both agree, it was the best year of our lives.

Touch Me Not.

M Says…

G was saying he had been reading that we all wash and shower too often and once a week was plenty, as people are suffering from itchy skin, etc. So guessing where this was going, I said "well shall we get a tin bath which we can keep outside, boil a kettle of water and share a splash each". He said "aye, Sunday nights like when I were a lad," in a very common northern accent.

I pointed out to him he could do what he wanted but we don't have a caravan in the drive he can sleep in. Anyway it could be construed as a second home and have tax implications.

We need an old shed, as we shall be social distancing for 6 days of the week and he can sleep on a camp bed with a chemical toilet. He said it sounds a lovely idea, but will I be joining him. I said "only on Sundays, after the bathing".

Had a delivery from the veg man, who had been boasting he had got flour. Ordered a packet as he phoned to ask if I wanted any. It said on the invoice when delivered "no flour left so have sent you some crackers." I phoned him and asked about promised flour. He said he had only got 20 bags and the first two orders were for 10 each, you have to be quick. I thought no that's just greedy. No wonder he runs out. He said "bananas are hard to get as they have got a fungus". We will not be ordering any, put me right off.

We have had an infestation of woodlouse spiders, well to tell you the truth, two of them on separate nights. Surely anything over one is an infestation. I got out my I Spy books but no good, so had to rely on internet. G picked one up and said "what are they"? I said they are the only venomous spider in U.K. He quickly dropped it, and put a mug over its body. He then realised I was having him on.

Am scared of them and sit with my feet off the floor, whilst wearing thick socks. It says they are coming in to breed. They were both lethargic so imagine the act had taken place. Yuk.

They are now in next doors garden after flinging them 6ft over the fence.

As a kid I used to keep all insects in various jars usually till they died of hunger. Loved ladybirds, but all I had to feed them on was grass and the occasional corner of a biscuit. My longest living insect was a wasp. Loved him, but he got crosser by the day. Was difficult to go to sleep with all that buzzing. He lasted a week and I let him go. He was still angry. I was able to observe him with my plastic magnifier. Bet he was thinking "If I get out of here". I think he quite liked me as he didn't do a U turn and sting me. I fed him on fresh dandelions and honey sandwiches.

Was reading that people were queuing for 5 hrs to get into Ikea. It sounds like something in a horror film. Wonder if they all made for the beds to have a kip. Why oh why?

We have been there in the past to see what all the hype was. G has got an illness called Queuing-never and it can strike at any time. He gets a cross look on his face if there is more than 2 people in front. I on the other hand love it. Being a born chatterbox comes in handy and I have found the common denominator is moaning about the queue which we have chosen to join.

Getting back to Ikea we went ages ago to look at the Billy Bookcases. G's first impressions were not favourable and we were both getting fed up after half an hour. It seemed we couldn't get out unless we went through the rest of the stuff, round and round departments which we didn't want to do.

We were trapped. The glazed expression came over Gs face. He found an assistant, "my wife feels ill, can we get out quickly?" This should work he thought, hoping we weren't taken to First Aid.

"Follow me," she said and off we went through secret doors and were back to the car in minutes by which time I felt much better and G's contorted expression was gone. Can imagine the queues now are for cupboards and Billy Bookcases to house toilet rolls and sacks of flour which will probably have weevils crawling in by now.

Hope all the public toilets were open in Ikea otherwise the fake display bathrooms will be smelly and they won't be selling many.

Wonder if people will be wearing masks forever and we never get to see people's mouths again. The fashion for plump lips will be no more and maybe people will want plump foreheads or ears and a whole new look will be announced. Elastic sales have gone through the roof and will become the new must have at all times.

G is desperate for a dentist. Do they exist anymore in this far removed from Utopian world? If they do who are they practising on? He has had toothache off and on for a bit. I got very worried when I saw string round the door handle and then realised it was the shed key, or maybe he will just fetch some rusty pliers from the shed. Dentists are opening again in a week. Presumably we will have to queue in the street, in the rain, or if you are not quick enough, in the snow in winter. He said he would like it done by Xmas as we do enjoy Thornton's toffee with a hammer.

The dentists already wore masks, will they now wear two, and two sets of goggles. Will they be able to see? It is all very worrying.

We could never understand anything our dentist said before. What if he is double masked and says are you ok and you are not and he can't hear you screaming because he is wearing ear protectors, in case you spit in his ear?

What if the toilet is locked? What if there are not enough Perspex screens to go round the dental chair? Is he going to poke the drill through a hole? What if he puts the drill up your nose and does not realise?

We are now looking at on line dental remedies. G is no longer moaning about it, just the odd squeak when he eats nuts.

A friend of mine has a very large old door, not a euphemism. There was somebody outside ringing the bell. What to do. She can always think on her feet, well that's what she says, and donned her paisley mask, well she does live in the Cotswolds, and opened the letterbox, shouting at the top of her voice "step back and say what you want." It was her husband who had locked himself out. Apparently, he called her something not very nice so she still didn't let him in.

Am very worried about everybody being allowed to pee in the open. Mr Macron we think has made this suggestion. Can you imagine what Thomas Crapper would think after all these years of civilisation? Are they going to start selling huge poo bags, like the ones for dogs but for humans? Will they be sold like bin bags in different colours and sizes? You would have to say a small adult pack and an extra large for my friend. Can you imagine them hanging from trees or bins marked "Drop your faeces in here?" People could get very muddled. Signs saying "No dumping here" will take on a new meaning. We will all be very confused. I can't bear to think about it.

And another thing what is R rate? Don't understand it all but find it worrying when mentioned. It is like getting exam results. G has tried to explain it and all I could think about was we hadn't got any tea bags. Usually in very important matters G asks me to repeat it. Luckily phone went. Was never any good at maths.

And another thing. There has been an ice cream van going up and down playing jingles. People have been buying cornets, no doubt touched by a man with no access to a toilet, handling money. They are all wearing masks. How will they eat them?

G in a weak moment last week suggested we buy a chess set. I said "don't be ridiculous". It hasn't been mentioned again.

Had Scottish bloody Power on regarding a long running saga about tariffs. Like talking to the Krankies.

Don't want to brag, but we have a letter from our MP on House of Commons paper, also one from Ombudsman. Everything was going swimmingly with Scottish Power on phone but then I couldn't say ombudsman. Had to have three goes. G was smirking. Anyway put my best voice on and said our treatment at your hands has left us feeling ill. At the time I was eating a bacon butty. Was feeling better by the minute.

G Says...

Don't stand, don't stand so, don't stand so close to me'
The Police

When Sting wrote that song, way back in 1980, he surely didn't intend it as an advance warning of life as we know it today.

Actually, as revealed in an interview he gave in 1981, as a former teacher his reasons were very different. Here's part of that interview:

'I wanted to write a song about sexuality in the classroom. I'd done teaching practice at secondary schools and been through the business of having 15-year-old girls fancying me – and me really fancying them! How I kept my hands off them I don't know... Then there was my love for Lolita which I think is a brilliant novel. But I was looking for the key for eighteen months and suddenly there it was. That opened the gates and out it came: the teacher, the open page, the virgin, the rape in the car, getting the sack, Nabakov, all that.'

Hmm! Different times, different viewpoints, different impressions of 'acceptability' eh?

How about *Noli me Tangere* then as an applicable message for the pandemic?

A Latin motto that translates as Touch me not - is the title of a novel written by José Rizal, one of the national heroes of the Philippines, during the somewhat unwelcome colonisation of the country by Spain to describe perceived inequities between Spanish Catholic priests and the ruling government.

The expression didn't originate with José Rizal as I discovered recently when re-reading one of my fall back authors, Pliny the Elder who referenced vast herds of deer belonging solely to Caesar for hunting purposes which bore a tag on their collars stating, 'Noli me tangere, for Caesar's I am.'

A derivation of the original phrase, in this case 'Don't tread on me,' is the motto of the US Army's oldest infantry regiment, the 3rd U.S. Infantry Regiment (The Old Guard), located at Fort Myer, Virginia and also Number 103 (Bomber) Squadron of the Royal Air Force.

Touch me not should be inscribed on all our collars just now. Not needed on mine as I have no intention of going anywhere until the All Clear is sounded. The dire warnings I get from the NHS continue to arrive regularly and a very pleasant young woman has taken to ringing me up every week to 'see if I am managing.'

She always sounds a little startled when I answer the phone as if she expected an unanswered ringing tone to forlornly continue until she moved on to the next poor unfortunate on her list. I always reassure her of my continued if tenuous grasp on life, but in view of her continued air of astonishment that her call has been answered I do rather worry what aspects of my medical records she's regarding in such a pessimistic manner.

It may be totally unrelated, but I've recently been targeted by adverts for affordable funerals. By 'affordable', do they mean 'cheap?' if so, why not say so? Even more importantly, why are they focusing on me? What do these funeral firms know that I don't? Life is one worry after another lately.

I'm still ticking along nicely, thanks for asking. I still do my daily walks, albeit they're not what most people would call 'walking' restricted as I am to a mere 25 paces along my entrance path. A house on one side, a high hedge on the other I walk, turn, walk again up and down this slim corridor of what we mockingly call 'outside.'

Recent warm weather means I can wear shorts again, the effect marred somewhat by an ancient, utterly repulsive but effective knee bandage holding together yet another defective body part. Marigold suggests, often, it's just as well my walks are hidden from public view.

When we left England for distant shores many years ago – not all that distant actually, the Loire Valley being not exactly Outer Mongolia – we had our first taste of solitude. We knew nobody at all in France, didn't speak the language, there was no telephone and of course this pre dated mobile phones and the Internet by many years.

It didn't bother us much. We coped. We had enough to fill our days after taking on the renovation of a much neglected and vast French farmhouse without funds to pay tradesmen and only rudimentary building skills. In the first six months or so we were too exhausted at the end of the day to even think about a world outside our gates.

Our nearest neighbour, about a mile away, was everything we'd imagined a French peasant farmer to be. Hard working, just getting by, no 'plan' for the future. We had a number of chats about farming when my French language skills finally got up to speed.

For Bernard, living one day at a time was the norm. All he had ever known. Plowing, sowing, harvesting, that's it. In a rare lucid moment after several glasses of his lethal home brewed and completely illegal *eau de vie*, 90% proof, he once confided that if he ever stopped to think beyond the set routine of planting and harvesting he would become so depressed he would not be able to function.

'This has been my life. It is my life. It will be my life until I die.' It was a bleak moment. I compared my availability of choice to those of that son of the soil and realised how lucky I was. Even now, still in lockdown with a modern day version of the Plague unleashed on the world we have so much to be grateful for.

This may be 'our' pandemic, but terrifying diseases are hardly new. Here's what Samuel Pepys had to say about 'his' plague:

"The taverns are fair full of gadabouts making merry this eve. Though I may press my face against the window like an urchin at a confectioner's, I am tempted not by the sweetmeats within. A dram in exchange for the pox is an ill bargain indeed."

Samuel Pepys may or may not have written this in his celebrated diary as there are suggestions it was tagged on a few years later. I certainly can't find it in my copy, but in style and attitude it's a fair representation of the great diarist's views.

Maybe it has been mischievously tagged on or maybe some long dead scholar just adding in a section of his writing discovered elsewhere, it was so long ago it would be easier to confirm the authorship of all Shakespeare's plays.

However, Pepys did certainly write this next passage in his journal and it caught my eye when reading a section of Pepys' Diary late one evening. Yes, I know that may make me sound weird, but I have very broad tastes in literature and Samual Pepys is not even listed in the top fifty unlikely authors I continue to read and re-read

'On hearing ill rumour that Londoners may soon be urged into their lodgings by Her Majesty's men, I looked upon the street to see a gaggle of striplings making fair merry, and no doubt spreading the plague well about. Not a care had these rogues for the health of their elders!'

Oh Samuel, you could easily get a job as a roving tv reporter nowadays. Just dig out some of your old scribblings and stick them on autocue.

Lockdown, isolation, it has advantages. In times of peril it's not a bad idea to establish priorities. A time to connect, or reconnect, with people we like and an ideal opportunity to let the ones we've never been all that keen on drift away.

I have hidden Marigold's latest toy, the hair clippers. Even though the few remaining areas of what I used to call 'hair' have been surgically removed by this wild eyed woman wielding clippers she's still got the idea my eyebrows are too bushy and could do with a 'trim'.

Me, on the morning after Marigold scalped me. 'Why have you put a picture of an old man in the bathroom?'

Marigold, 'I haven't, that's a mirror.'

I'm not hugely impressed by the new 'hairstyle' and no amount of talk about the money we've saved on barbers will change that. Marigold said, 'women find bald men sexy,' then looked at me, rather unkindly I thought, and added, 'not all women and not all bald men though.'

Glancing into the communal bin the other day – old habits die hard – I noticed half a dozen bread crusts. We've gone back to the 1950s at our house, nothing is wasted. What's wrong with crusts? A bread crust is still bread, just slightly firmer. I eat everything, crusts and all. No, it doesn't always taste as good, but it's still food. Even Marigold has a strange aversion to eating some crusts. I told her yesterday she could at least make an effort. After all she really liked the middle part of that water melon…

Tales from the Crypt.

Marigold Says...

Talking of Ikea. Weren't we? Doesn't matter. When we had one of our French houses which sounds a bit grand but they were dumps we did up, we bought a self assembly cupboard for the side of the guest room, yes we do have friends, to house books and treasures which look interesting. Great excitement as we opened the box. Many parts and packages fell out.

Usually at these times I excuse myself quickly as I can feel boredom coming on. It took us 2 days to sort it all out and we lived with a cupboard on the tilt with additional superglue to support it. We had to tell visitors not to put anything heavy on it, in fact don't put anything on it. I wouldn't like to think that by now it has fallen on some unsuspecting Frenchman who was using it to store his winter cabbages.

They do that in France, i am sure, everything is stored in the bedroom.

I once went into a Frenchman's bedroom, always wanted to say that, and there were apples, green things and tomatoes in jars all stored at one end, and of course wine. Also at the side of his bed was a piece of cheese and a knife. Thought we were going to have a picnic. Must add he was a granddad and wanted to show me some heirloom which was quite horrible. It was a carved piece of wood in the shape of a cow, or a pig or a dog.

Don't know what significance it had as I couldn't tell a word he said. There was also a cat up the corner eating a mouse. Have gone full circle, cheese, mouse, cat.

Our postman called George was due to retire before virus but has had to stay on as they are not training anyone at the mo. He is too old for shorts. I asked him why the other postmen wear shorts even in the cold. He said 'they are just show offs. Anyway nobody wants to see my hairy legs.'

His instructions from metres away are very questionable and not very politically correct.

'Its a big one, do you want it on the mat?'

or

'Shall I poke it through the letterbox?'

He has got a problem with his eyes. Sounded like a cereal name, think it was something like Cornflakes. Will ask him again. No wonder we keep getting everybody else's post.

Had the usual lucky dip veg box. Ended up with lots of green stringy cabbage. Thought we need to turn it into soup. Cut all the stringy bits off and piled it in a cauldron with old veg on the turn. Boiled it up, and whisked it to a pulp. The colour was amazing. G said it looked like a cow pat and he wasn't eating it. He also said send it to the Scientists as it could end the virus. He said something else which I can't print.

He then said he would do us a hearty and healthy tea. Marvellous I thought and was presented with banana sandwiches with a side order of ginger biscuits. He tried to glam it up by claiming this was Elvis's favourite food. Well, we all know what happened to him! G certainly knows how to slice a banana.

G Says…

'Do what you can, with what you have, where you are.'
Theodore (Teddy) Roosevelt

Marigold has just been reminiscing about a woman she used to work with whose husband came up with one of the most memorable adverts of the television age. No, not saying which one. Despite this the Advertising Agency 'let him go' six months later after his creativity dried up. Marigold asked why and was told, 'because he's a tosser that nobody else can work with. They should try living with him.'

There's loyalty for you.

In fairness, he was a seriously weird bloke. We went round to their huge house one evening for drinks. Eight bedrooms, but they hadn't a hope of keeping it up to scratch so lived on the ground floor with the two upper storeys being virtually derelict.

When we'd chatted for five minutes he toddled off into the kitchen to fetch some what he called 'nibbles' and his wife called 'bits.'

Whether they resembled nibbles or bits we never discovered as we didn't see him again for two hours. His wife said 'oh, he does that, forgets what he goes for and walks around for a bit until he remembers.'

When he turned up again, two hours later, he ignored the three of us and put a record on, very loudly, in the next room. It was 'I'm a wanker' by Ivor Biggun and the Red Nosed Burglars. Isn't it odd how some things stick in your memory?

As we left Marigold muttered to me, 'No wonder they gave him the push,' but I thought they must be a pretty stuffy lot in those top advertising agencies. Never a dull moment working with that bloke.

If you're not familiar with the work of Ivor Biggun, it's the stage name of Robert Cox, a former sound engineer at the BBC who adopted the prefix

'Doc' when spending ten years performing on That's Life. It's pretty clear Esther Rantzen has distinctly low-brow musical tastes!

He's about the same age as me, but there the similarity ends. I do admire the names of his various bands, notably Nurk Wildebeest and the Mutations and he still performs occasionally, apparently, in a Suffolk based band The Trembling Wheelbarrows.

Without the guiding musical talents of Ivor Biggun the world may never have even heard of Screaming Lord Sutch.

Somebody was just being interviewed on the BBC, complaining that they've driven nearly 200 miles to go to the beach and when they got there everything was closed. 'Even Poundland!'

Leaving aside the rationale of people who drive 200 miles for a day trip to Cornwall – in the midst of a pandemic - passing numerous beaches along the way, the closed and shuttered Poundland was enough to sustain a rant for several minutes.

As the, frankly useless, interviewer finally butted in to say 'back to the studio' the woman who'd been rabbiting on for ages decided she needed yet more air time. Jabbing a finger at the reporter she bellowed, 'where are the toilets? What am I supposed to do when...'

Just in time the video feed died and we were safely 'back to the studio.'

I'm a Poundland fan myself, tat appeals to me and the spirit level I lavished my hard earned pound on about five years ago has recently confirmed to Marigold that the picture I could clearly see was out of alignment was indeed 'skew-wiff' after she'd insisted it was level. A bitter row that could have rumbled on for days averted because I invested £1 five years ago. Bargain.

No, of course we don't have rows. Ever. Even our very occasional disagreements are swiftly rectified by me apologising for whatever it was I was alleged to have done wrong.

As for the absence of lavatory facilities I'm nobody's idea of a public lavatory maven, but can fully understand the reasons for their closure at this time. Even so, as it's pretty obvious there's been no drastic change in human physiology, what went in must at some stage come out.

The World Health Organisation has spent decades trying to solve the 'sewage' problems of the Third World yet we've managed to inflict on the UK the same sanitation conditions that are common amongst those living in an Amazonian rain forest. I even suspect this temporary deprivation could cause greater stress to most people than an inability to buy four rolls of fruit pastilles for a pound.

I made a list yesterday. I don't write lists. Ever. But, yesterday I did. It was a list of various 'jobs' that needed doing. Quite a long list.

House maintenance, organisational tasks, clerical matters, personal grooming. No, not that last one.

There are so many jobs I have been putting off until I had some 'spare time.' Such as now. There are even jobs that have been on the back burner for what seems like forever. Like writing another book. Even getting the last book project into print. I need to decide on a cover and the layout, organise and set out the formatting for both Kindle and paperback platforms and a myriad other tasks.

I've done all this seven times now and that's my problem.I know how laborious and soul sapping it is to do all the tidying up bits necessary to prepare a novel for publication. Even so, I surely will not have so much free time again. Have I done it yet? No. Have I even started? Well, I have given it some thought. I'm not just sitting here doing nothing, you know? This is valuable thinking and planning time.

As for the other jobs on my list, I just need to find someone to do them now as it's clearly not going to be me. Maybe next week. When I have a bit more free time.

I'm beginning to hate the Internet. Everywhere I look there are virtue signalling people boasting about their newly acquired beach bodies and new skills. I watched some irksome young woman yesterday whose latest accomplishment, allegedly one of many, was playing her own composition on the violin. I thought she was, quite frankly rubbish, both as a composer and also as a violinist and I speak as someone who would struggle to make an acceptable sound from a tambourine.

I haven't used my free time profitably. Not at all. Does the Internet now only offer up people whose days are spent in making a scale model of the Taj Mahal out of All Bran in their front room or becoming fluent in Mandarin inside three days? Are there none out there like me? The undisciplined/bone idle silent majority? I find this all pervading aura of presumed worthy activity quite exhausting. I shall go and relax by tuning in to my yoga class on YouTube.

No, of course I don't actually do any of the poses. I wouldn't even if I could persuade my limbs to even attempt such ludicrous contortions, but it all takes place on a very nice beach and I like watching the waves rolling in with the sound turned off. It's very soothing.

We've been chatting a lot lately to one of our lovely friends, by which I mean she's actually lovely and not just one of our friends who are all lovely. Some of our friends are neither lovely nor lovable, but we keep them around anyway.

The lovely friend in question, just picking a name at random here let's call her Sheila, is sporting a trim almost as drastic as my own 'haircut.' The difference is, her hair looks great. The skill of the stylist can only be appreciated by knowing she managed the whole performance from the house next door, peeping through a knot hole in the fence and snipping away with long handled garden shears to preserve social distancing. Afterwards she trimmed the privet hedge into a representation of Windsor Castle viewed from the school cricket pavilion at Eton. Knowing Sheila as I do I doubt she got much of a tip!

Interestingly, having more closely examined my head following Marigold setting about it with hair clippers I tentatively mentioned, 'it still looks as if there's a couple of grey patches.'

'Oh, don't worry, it's not hair,' Marigold explained. 'That's where the clippers dug in a bit. I think what you can see are bits of brain.'*

*I hope nobody thinks much of what I ramble on about in here has any basis in reality.

With my skull having barely any skin left on which a hair follicle could thrive at last the rest of me remains untouched by the resident barber. I can at least retain ownership of the unkempt jungle I laughably refer to as my beard.

Facial hair. What's going on in the real world so far removed from us now and only glimpsed on television screens? It's gone way beyond the absurd tokenism of 'Movember.' It's no longer a fad, it's here to stay. The lockdown/isolation beard as they're calling it because its devotees obviously all stopped shaving on day one of the lockdown.

Even our tv weathermen look less pristine lately. Verging on scruffy. Celebrities, well obviously they're never going to miss out. Madonna would be sporting a full set of whiskers if she could.

These days beards I see on tv all look the same, which is to say pretty rough. They are always patchy, uneven, unkempt and usually have grey bits included.

But, they're not so much just beards grown in isolation, as evidence of what happens when men stop shaving. They stop caring what they look like, or maybe it's as simple as just not caring when there's nobody else to see or sit in judgement.

The avoidance of grooming, in spite of having the same access to shaving materials they've always had, not to mention more leisure for shaving than ever before. It's a gesture promoted by this pandemic.

Rules? What rules? We're all survivalists now, or trying to be. Not Fancy Dans with designer haircuts and precisely calibrated facial adornment any longer. No, we're hunters, we're warriors, we're MEN.

Real men don't waste time primping and preening, we've gone back to basics now. Nature in the raw.

Even so, after much reasoned debate I recently removed what was referred to in my inner circle - ie Marigold - as my 'hideous' beard. The clean shaven look was deemed even worse. I have compromised by cultivating a half way point between naked flesh and an actual beard; a sort of benign neglect appearance stopping just short of vagrancy.

The Plague Year.

Marigold Says...
Now we're finally getting home deliveries, after only ten weeks of banging our heads against the wall, not really, I can now mark the supermarkets by helpfulness to us personally.

Number 1.
Asda. We don't normally shop with them, not for snobby reasons but think it is a bit of a mess, well suppose that is a bit snobby. Just saying. Plus points, two deliveries now.

Number 2
Tesco. Finally managed to book deliveries a few times. Was a favourite because of the sturdy carrier bags but didn't keep up with promised slots and two deliveries we had booked never happened.

Number 3.
Sainsburys. Absolutely useless. Couldn't get a slot and we are long life customers. Wrote to Mr Sainsbury, or was it someone called James in Customer Services. He sounded about 10 as his voice hadn't broken, and said he was head of Customer Liaison, Mathematical Genius and Research Analysts on why people liked Jigsaws. There was also a lot of rustling, so he could have been on his break and crunched when I was explaining our trauma.

He might have been Mr Sainsburys great, great grandson doing a holiday job. He said we would get a slot and we never did. Told him we were ancient, living in the cold with just a candle and were down to our last tin of economy beans. I think he started to cry or was it just a fit of giggling?

Number 4
Waitrose. Well, was really looking forward to their more than splendid big van arriving. I would have shouted "here we are" at the top of my voice so everybody could hear, as I think in these times you are judged by your deliveries. It was hopeless. No staples of life like wine gums or liquorice. They hadn't got any tinned peaches but had tinned kumquats. No thank you, I thought, but we never got a delivery slot anyway.

So ASDA win hands down. Hoorah for them. We also discovered a Polish section and ordered some weird and wonderful things, to be honest am too frightened to open a couple of them. I am now learning Polish as I think it will be a culinary expeditious holiday. Who doesn't like a dumpling? Guess what, dumpling in Polish is the same word. Will say it a lot, in a Polish accent.

Well it seems we can now enter a bubble or a tunnel. How big is the bubble? We can bubble with people in the park, up to six. As we have never met six people in the park who I would want to spend an afternoon with that's out. I wouldn't mind bubbling with six Labrador puppies. What if it is raining and everybody has got an umbrella, do they count as extra bubbling? If you take sandwiches is there a limit as to how many you can eat? Are pickled onions allowed? Wish somebody would explain it all.

The triple RRR rate I still don't understand, or is that the size of my trousers. My friend said her bra was very tight and had sent off for some bra extenders. She said one wasn't enough, so she somehow fashioned two together. The fit was better but the cups were under her armpits.

Talking of trousers, the elastic I bought to make masks is now being used for my expanding waistline. I have never made a mask yet. I am getting very good at knots. It actually looks as if I have three belly buttons through my jumper. Hugging is not allowed so nobody can wonder what the sticking out bits are.

G does lists of food we need, and says he feels like a hunter gatherer, then we lose the list.

Things seem to be at last getting better.

The new rules say you still can't go near the postman but you can touch each other with a tickling stick.

I can imagine there will be new signs in the laundrettes: You have to form an orderly queue and if you are washing your husband's underpants you have to keep your mask on at all times whilst handling them.

If you are washing the dog basket you have to doubly check the dog isn't in it.

The toilets are closed but if you go round the corner there are several plastic buckets. Be careful about positioning yourself as they are visible from the window.

I said to G will we ever do the Hokey Cokey ever again.

He said we never really did it before. I said, but at the end of the war everybody did the Hokey Cokey

I wonder if people will look different at the end of lockdown. Will women have hairy legs and faces.

I asked G if my legs were hairy. He said I thought you had been knitting yourself some mohair trousers.

Thank you and have a nice day.

G Says…

While my concept of time in isolation has blurred into a psychedelic haze, all I know for sure is that there are now just three days of the week: yesterday, today and tomorrow. Much easier.

I still have daylight and darkness as an aide memoire so it's easy enough to mark the point at which yesterday segues into today. That aside this is the era of endless day where nothing much changes.

Marigold asked me (sounds better than 'ordered') to take the mat from inside the front door outside and shake it. I did so and about three feeble dust grains dropped almost apologetically to the ground. Nobody comes and goes any more. Nobody traipsing in half a pound of dust and muck at every entry is some consolation I suppose.

As must be evident by now, according to those wise bods who write newspaper columns and talk to us from television screens all of the 'over-70s' are frail, feeble minded, vulnerable creatures with creaking hips and gigantic hearing aids. If they happen to be male better I had better add they will have big ears with sprouting hairs and enough nasal hair to stuff a single mattress. Oh, hang on, the hairy ears and noses bit does strike a chord.

I'm getting weekly calls from my local council to check if I'm still alive. It may be the onset of paranoia, but it's hard to shake the impression I get that the council's representative sounds a tad miffed when I somehow manage to pick up the phone. Is there a quota system? Perhaps a target that has to be met? I feel I should be apologising to her for spoiling the anticipated mortality figures.

Although I have 'health related conditions' that seemingly elevate me into a high risk group, I don't feel remotely 'vulnerable.' Yesterday wasn't a good day, but in general I feel fitter than I have for years.

Doctors? They know nothing.

The first letter from the NHS told me my 'underlying conditions' made me especially vulnerable to Covid-19 – and infection would result in very serious illness with a strong likelihood of death. To stand even a slim chance of survival I must immediately go into complete isolation for 12 weeks.

Gulp!

'Well,' said Marigold in her Florence Nightingale voice, 'that's you told, oh sickly one. Go and hide in the wardrobe for 12 weeks and try not to make a racket.'

It turns out the reality of isolation is no problem at all. I have now had three letters from the NHS/Government each more scary than the last. 'How are you still able to even get out of bed in the morning?' Marigold asked after reading the third letter.

We haven't seen a recognisable human for almost three months. People drop boxes or letters on the mat, bang on the door and run off like naughty schoolboys, but even they are masked, gloved and look like extras from a remake of Invasion of the Body Snatchers.

Yesterday not a good day? Oh yes, but just one of those occasional energy sapped days from 'doing too much' the day before. I am somewhat mollified by reading in an email from a friend whose legendary (frequently self proclaimed) fitness is widely known that he has the occasional 'off day' as well.

I woke up yesterday feeling more weary than when I went to bed the previous evening. My ever so annoyingly 'smart' watch recorded my 'deep sleep' as zero - not unusual - 'light sleep' as 48 minutes and REM (Rapid Eye Movement) as 5 hours and 53 minutes. Good grief, no wonder I woke up knackered; my eyes go disco dancing every night.

I said to Marigold, 'I have written off today completely. Let me know when it's tomorrow.'

Marigold says I am in terminal decline. I think she recognises the symptoms from when the guppies died in a fish tank she was supposedly looking after. I'd better keep her away from the well meaning 'better see if the vulnerable brigade are still above ground' people from the Council next time they ring up.

Making assumptions based on mere age is ridiculous and those one-dimensional definitions of the 'at risk' generation, even in this one size fits all Covid-90 context are more ridiculous still.

As if we haven't got enough to fret about, does anyone else suffer from Internet related malady or is it just me?

'Password is incorrect' is the message on the screen when logging on to same web site I log onto every single day.

Okay, fat finger syndrome I say to myself and type it again.

'Password is incorrect.'

Double check, no, it's the same one I used yesterday and the day before. I try again

'Password is incorrect.'

Reset password - quite a laborious procedure involving typing in a number sent to my mobile phone, which as usual took five minutes to locate and proving three times I am not a robot by identifying traffic lights and fire hydrants on fuzzy photographs and typing in letters and numbers designed to be deliberately unidentifiable.

When prompted to do so I type in my old 'unrecognised' previous password

Message on screen 'Cannot use same password as previous password'

Throw iPad at the wall and go in search of 'The Peoples' Valium' - Midget Gems – to calm down.

Incidentally, the chief virtue of a land line phone in our disorganised home environment is its ability to locate a missing mobile phone. This saves time and avoids the blame culture of, 'well you had it last.'

Floccinaucinihilipilification. Now there's an icebreaker at parties or a chat up line for nerds. No charge for this service.

It's a word I shall never actually speak in a conversation and, hopefully, never write again. I came across it recently as an example of one of the longest words in the English language. Big deal I thought at the time and almost didn't bother to find out its meaning. If you are so desperate as not being able to sleep tonight without this information I can reveal it means the estimation of something as valueless. About as valueless as the word itself then.

On our US road trip, (yes, we used to actually travel at some time in the dim and distant past), we came across quite a lot of Mormons. Every single one being polite, respectable and friendly to us 'foreigners' with our strange customs and funny way of talking. From the conversations we had, discounting the subject of their impressively restrictive underwear which so fascinated Marigold, it was the manner in which they prepared for possible social problems that stood out. In particular the laying up of food stocks which we've thought about quite a lot recently.

When the pandemic struck we were pathetically behind the times. Many eminently sensible folk insisted those people rumoured to be stripping the supermarket shelves were a media invention. Others thought it was a temporary phase and everything would be back to normal in a week or so.

We ended up without a plan of campaign – food buying having become like military manoeuvres by the time we cottoned on – and our only response when friends got in touch to gleefully report their ownership of enough Andrex to last a family with incurable incontinence a hundred years was to mutter 'we're very short of storage space.'

Every disaster is an opportunity for some and Covid-19 is no exception. Among the advertisers pestering me to increase the size of my manhood (thanks but no thanks) or invest in Bitcoin as 'it's value will only rise unless something goes wrong' – hardly an enticing pitch – I came across a reference to the UK Preppers Guide who have all the answers in regard to 'Survival, Bushcraft and Prepping.' They continue with, 'How do you prepare and could you survive a doomsday disaster? Are you ready for when the SHTF.?'

Well, if the S really does HTF, if it hasn't already, I fear I shall be woefully unprepared.

As for U.K. Preppers – '...when the SHTF.?' You don't need the full stop as well as the question mark, either will suffice.

Pedantic? Well, maybe but I have lots of free time lately. Just don't get me started on the excruciating misuse of apostrophes!

In response to expressions of sheer disbelief from those fortunate people who don't get to meet me in person very often, yes I really do read 'weird books written by dead people' on a regular basis. In particular, as I mentioned in the last blog post, I possess 'analogue' versions of the works of Pliny the Elder and Samuel Pepys – what we used to call 'books' in the olden days – but even for a fairly recently deconstructed Luddite it's much easier to read Pliny on a Kindle. Digital versions of two thousand year old books are free as authors' copyright issues are never going to be a hindrance.

Human remains recently found near Pompeii can be directly attributed to Pliny the Elder according to unimpeachable scientific data. The cranium really does belong to the Roman admiral who died leading a rescue mission after Vesuvius erupted, even if the provenance of the jaw found nearby is less certain.

Gaius Plinius Secundus, usually called Pliny the Elder, was a Roman author, a naturalist and a natural philosopher, a naval and army commander of the early Roman Empire, and a close personal friend of the Emperor Vespasian.

Vespasian? Nowhere near as important as the group who ruled Rome during his lifetime. We all know of his predecessors, Julius Caesar, Augustus, Tiberius, Caligula, Claudius and Nero, but Vespasianus was a notable soldier in his own right. In his early career he played a major part in establishing Roman rule in Britain and as Emperor began the construction of The Colosseum

Pliny, as his friends will almost certainly not have called him wrote Naturalis Historia, which became the accepted model for all future encyclopedias and markedly improves the scholastic tone of my bookshelves. Yes, to a casual observer it may seem obvious I prefer Lee Child, but I can only plead the availability of a greater body of work from Mister Child when set against an author who inconveniently died two thousand years ago.

In my browsing I rediscovered several quotes by Pliny which have stood the test of time.

'Home is where the heart is.'

'The only certainty is that nothing is certain.'

'Bears when first born are shapeless masses of white flesh a little larger than mice, their claws alone being prominent. The mother then licks them gradually into proper shape.'

'Our youth and manhood are due to our country, but our declining years are due to ourselves.'

Addito salis grano - With a grain (or pinch) of salt.'

I'm not fixated on Pliny the Elder. Pliny the Younger was a pretty perspicacious chap as well. His remark 'Fortes fortuna iuvat - Fortune favours the brave' – to his uncle during the eruption of Mount Vesuvius was the catalyst for Pliny the Elder to set off with his fleet to investigate in the hope of helping a friend. As a consequence Old Uncle Pliny lost his life when sailing too close to shore during the apocalyptic height of the eruption.

Parkinson's Law accurately describes the manner in which work always increases to fill the time available for finishing it. So, why bother? Young Pliny agrees with me on this subject.

'That indolent but agreeable condition of doing nothing' is a phrase attributed to Pliny the Younger. Doing very little whilst giving the appearance of being busy is my own modified version and has stood me in good stead for most of this lockdown period. Some would doubtless venture to suggest I have applied this system for rather longer than the last two or three months.

Good news from the Front. We're getting supermarket deliveries now. Today's has been our second after a major battle to get anyone to acknowledge out there in the real world that we even exist. We got what we asked for, minus the items that seem to have universally vanished from shelves; just now it's flour, but before that it was pasta and toilet rolls. We're not bothered by that or 'substitutes' being supplied for two or three other things we wanted. All in all a very efficient process.

Where's the fun in that?

Our local fruit and veg man has been delivering to us for a while. He's not regular, not remotely efficient, but he gives us what a supermarket will try hard never to include in a home delivery – the gift of randomness. If we ask for parsnips, he may have bushels of them when we ring in our order but none at all when the actual order goes on the van. So, 'no parsnips, I'll send them some satsumas instead'.

No need for the customer to be disappointed at the sudden emergence of parsnips on the endangered species list. Here's my imagined version of the thought processes of our greengrocer.

'I bet they like a satsuma of an evening. I always think when she rings in the order, that Marigold sounds like someone who enjoys a satsuma. Maybe even two. I'll chuck a coconut in as well. They didn't ask for one, but I just noticed there's two broken eggs in that box so I'll put in a coconut to make up for them.'

A supermarket would just replace the broken eggs. What dullards.

Housebound Traveller.

Marigold Says...

Here we are again happy as can be all good friends and jolly good company.

Whoo hoo, some people are now allowed to sort of mingle, but with all sorts of conditions. You still can't have a bath with the next door neighbour or look over a high wall.

We have expanded our walk and now go around the block. Very strange at first as we walked with a sort of reticence in case people popped up like hobbits trying to blow venom at us. None of this happened, as it was very early, six o'clock in the morning and the only person about was a twelve year old paperboy, who was managing to ride a bike with his bag on his back, do a wheelie and smoke a fag at the same time.

Rattling along as well was the milkman. He had obviously got a good lockdown business going on selling cake, bread, biscuits and what looked like potatoes, everything but milk. It was either that or his weekly shopping. We ran away and hid when they came into sight.

The walking is showing results. I have built it up to such a speed I nearly overtake myself. I suspected someone next to me was clapping, but G was only batting away a fly.

We are starting to eat from our meagre pandemic larder, including tinned steak. I think it's just about ok. G thought it delish, mince mixture, yuk, again G liked it. Shiphams sardine paste, why oh why? Next door's cat likes it. G said we could put it on a baked potato. I said and then what, throw it away? Nothing will ever be thrown away in this house. I have got some more pandemic staples which I will not admit to. Remember we were in a heightened state of confusion, and thought we were going to starve and be found in a cave.

G Says...

Not much to offer you from Marigold today. She's far too busy. Apparently. This isn't laziness. Perish the thought. Even so, I don't think temporary indolence is an unkind description. Mondays are difficult, aren't they?

Pause to check what day it is. Yes! It's Monday. Phew!

I'm in occasional contact by the miracle of email with an old friend who tells me he's about to croak any day now. He says that every time we speak, so a panic attack isn't called for, but he's been in bed for a very long time now.

'We're in the same boat,' he says. Well, not really. It's not like comparing my personal version of lockdown with most other people who can go shopping or have a beach stroll. They're wearing an ankle tag, I'm in house arrest. The difference is one of degree. My friend can't go out and almost certainly never will.

I won't even attempt to begin to equate chronic illness with lockdown. One occurs because sickness has already come, the other is an attempt to avoid it. One is usually permanent, the other is temporary – even if sometimes it doesn't feel like it. Of course the lines between health and sickness seem more blurred than they used to. Recently most of us were housebound. Some of us still are. But for some of us, this is a permanent state. Time for the rest of us to count our blessings.

I was reading recently about a Nasa astronaut Andy Thomas, who has been on four space flights, including twenty weeks onboard the Mir space station in 1998. After 141 days in space he must know a bit about dealing with isolation. He couldn't even go outside to bring a parcel off the doorstep.

This section of what he had to say made a lot of sense. 'When you're in isolation, you get the opportunity for a lot of introspective thought. You get a chance to think about your life. What are the things you do that you like and what are the things you do that you don't particularly like, but you do them merely out of obligation.'

There must be something about space travel that gives you insight. We all do things we don't really want to do, but we do them anyway out of a sense of obligation, of duty. Don't we? Surely it's not just me and that astronaut bloke. Recognition of a situation is all well and good but doing something about it can be a big step. As another man from NASA said way back in 1969, 'one small step for man, one giant leap for mankind.'

I've been engaging in a bit of a dispute with our electricity supplier. I can't write a letter as I'm forbidden to go within five miles of a post box. I may be slightly overstating the stern conditions attached to my enforced house arrest regime since lockdown began, but better safe than pushing up daisies.

My grandma used to say that, 'I'll be pushing up daisies next week if you don't mend your ways.' I should point out I was only about five at the time. Our next door neighbour was called Daisy and on one occasion I asked 'pushing up Daisy's what?'

'You'll be the death of me, lad,' she snapped which left me still feeling slightly confused.

So, postal service out of the question, It's impossible to email them as all of their emails to us are marked 'do not reply' and there's a direct message service which I tried several times and the best response I ever had was 'your call is important to us. The current waiting time to connect to one of our helpline staff is 37 minutes. Please try later.'

It's a similar story on the Customer Services Helpline. 'Is your call in connection with Covid-19? If so please press 1 on your handset.' There are no other options.

Eventually I pressed 1 on my handset and waited for 17 minutes while someone with no musical taste whatsoever ran through their 'I think I'll kill myself now' playlist.

Eventually I got in touch with Karen. Why Karen was ever considered suitable for the job of answering the telephone is a matter for Human Resources to consider at their next staff appraisal meeting, but I will say she was very polite.

Well, her tone was polite. I couldn't actually hear what she was saying which I have noticed in the past tends to restrict normal conversation. Okay, I'm a bit deaf, but when I passed the call on to Marigold, who can, and often does, listen to conversations being carried on fifty yards away, she said she couldn't understand anything Karen was saying either.

I'm quite used by now to still not hearing something repeated to me for the third time, normally dealt with by laughing inanely, saying 'oh yes' and hoping for the best. We're no further forward, but being at home all day does give ample opportunity to keep trying the help line and hoping Karen is on her lunch break.

Being stuck at home can make you rethink how much 'stuff' we really need. I made a very casual enquiry to Marigold this morning.

'Do you really need all those clothes stopping your wardrobe door from closing?'

I couldn't possibly write down her reply. I decided to set an example and set out on a marathon trying on session of my own sartorial splendour. We have downsized as regards property, but not so much when it comes to clothes. I have tried to set aside the outfits, winter and summer versions, I had reserved as suitable only for 'out side jobs' involving dirt, dust and the likelihood of the clothing becoming swiftly unfit for purpose.

I told Marigold but she claimed to be unable to distinguish between the 'only fit for clearing out a septic tank' clothing and the pile I had reserved for 'going out.'

I discarded any items that don't fit perfectly. Quite a few of them, surprisingly. Alterations are not on the horizon. Then there are the shirts or sweaters that, apparently, 'don't suit me.' Sadly I had to agree with Marigold that her opinion should take precedence. She decided the pile of 'mucky outside jobs' clothing should be significantly enhanced.

A stressful episode, not to be repeated any time soon. It's not easy maintaining a reputation as a dandy and snappy dresser in the face of such brutal scrutiny.

One of our arty-Farty friends has been rabbiting on about an online art course she 'just adores' run by Ivy Newport. If you want more info it's called Flight and Feather and it's an online mixed media and encaustic workshop.

Discounting, for now, a wise remark made by Alexei Sayle – 'anyone who uses the word workshop who isn't an engineer is a self abuser (or words to that effect) – I just said, 'oh, that sounds good.'

Isn't it great when the person at the other end of the phone says, 'do you want me to explain about encaustic painting?' and you're able to say 'no thanks?'

Wax encaustic painting technique was described by Pliny the Elder in his Natural History, written in the 1st Century AD. See, I knew reading weird books would come in handy.

Elvis Presley, The King, wasn't just a great singer he was a notable gourmet and way ahead of his time as a nutritionist.

I suspect there will be people who disagree. Well, hang on a minute. Leaving aside for now the Cheeseburger addiction, a well known medical condition and may even be an actual 'syndrome' which is the Gold Standard for medical issues, what about his favourite sandwich? If you're not yet serving up peanut butter, bacon, and banana sandwiches, you're missing out on the fodder that kept Elvis ticking over in between burgers. Try one. Do you want to live for ever?

I love sandwiches. It started early in life. Sugar butties were a treat I can still taste even now. The joy of a crisp sandwich only really took flight when I opened a bag of crisps and the little blue bag of salt was missing. Smiths made very good crisps but their quality control system was notoriously unreliable. Missing out the salt should have been on the statute book as a crime against humanity.

After rummaging in vain I laid the crisps between two slices of bread and made what I imagined to be a unique feast. I was only five so the realisation I wasn't the first to experiment in this way was hard to take.

Smiths crisps received a body blow quite early in my childhood when rival firms sprang up offering the hitherto unthinkable: ready salted crisps. Walkers set up in business in 1948 and now has not only the biggest crisp factory in the world in Leicester, but by employing Gary Linekar has enabled the poor fellow to make ends meet and accept a mere pittance* from the BBC for his media 'work.'

*If you're American, this sentence contains irony. Yes, I know, it's a concept you will find almost as hard to understand as the Laws of cricket. Getting back to crisps, I must mention Golden Wonder. By the mid 60s they'd blown away the rest and were the biggest crisp makers by far. With a proliferation of crisp makers adding a new and even more irrational flavour about every twenty minutes and expanding into designer crisps, organic crisps, fat free, potato free and bizarrely named 'healthy' crisps I'm getting rather bewildered.

I prefer the original, plain crisps to most of the fancy ones. I think asking for a packet of 'plain' crisps sounds slightly tacky. I much prefer requesting a packet of 'regular' crisps. A small point, maybe.

Arranging crisps on a sandwich is an art form, but the degree of difficulty is worth it. A decent sandwich needs careful preparation. Banana sandwiches are delightful, filling and nutritious with the option of choosing cross cut slices or for the purist longitudinal strips. Chip sandwiches, sheer delight, must be on white bread for perfection and vinegar usage should be minimal. My personal favourite has to be the fish finger sandwich. Even writing about it makes me want one.

Today I'll be eating mashed potato blended with brown sauce in my sandwich because there are no rules anymore. If that sounds boring, why not mix in a few processed peas as well? Pre-squashed obviously.

I wonder if I'm considered sufficiently a la mode to write a food blog. Probably not. As with art appreciation, I like what I like and that's good enough for me.

I like breakfast buffets in hotels. It's my naturally greedy nature. I wander around with my bowl or plate, spoilt for choice but loving it. My only complaint is my fellow diners. A man we came across in a rather dingy hotel in Ukraine springs to mind. I think it was in Yalta, but can't be sure.

The wretch who irritated me was hogging the toaster. One of those where you lay a slice of bread on a revolving grill and it turns up again about thirty seconds later transformed into golden toast. While we were waiting for the man to load up the contraption with a dozen slices of the local dark, dense and almost black bread, I made the mistake of saying to Marigold, 'this bread may not be up to being toasted. Each slice weighs half a pound.'

The irritatingly slow toaster hogger whipped round and launched into a 'well, that's just where you're wrong, matey' type of retort. Not at all what I'd expected. He was obviously not a local as the Ukrainian version of spoken English was by now pretty familiar to us after a week or so spent traversing this vast country.

I didn't exactly argue the point of whether Ukrainian bread made good toast as my knowledge base was pretty low, but my expression must have spoken volumes as the man seized his toast and stormed off.

I had to make a full circuit of the room to find our table, Marigold always claims the most remote section as she hates anyone chatting to her when we're trying to fuel up for the day. Any other meal is fine – in fact we both rabbit away pretty much nonstop at every other time of the day - but breakfast is sacrosanct. I once thought a Trappist Monastery breakfast would be perfect, but we stayed in a monastery in Spain once and the monks were a very chatty bunch. That was in Caravaca de la Cruz, one of only five places designated as Holy Cities by the Vatican. If you want to know the others, (we've visited four out of five without being regarded as remotely saintly), you're welcome to look up the details in one of our earlier blog posts entitled No Dirty Habits.

We'd barely taken a mouthful when 'toaster man' appeared and took a seat at 'our' table. There were half a dozen other empty table nearby, but our worst fears were confirmed: he had come for a chat.

It turned out he wasn't Ukrainian, as we'd already surmised, but had moved here from Poland a few years ago to raise the intellectual level of Ukrainian university students. He didn't use those exact words but that was the gist of it.

Despite surreptitious nudges from Marigold that came close to overturning the table I made the mistake of joining in with his 'chat.' After about a minute I thought to myself, 'I'm getting in over my head here' and lapsed into silence as our unwanted dining companion reeled off a stream of inconsequential advice and instruction.

Did you know a funambulist was a name for a tightrope walker? No, neither did I. If I ever have to say or write the word again I suspect I shall just say 'tightrope walker.

Our new friend, self proclaimed, had a name I could neither spell nor pronounce. Marigold insists it was Dettolfungious. It wasn't, but I think she's on to something as it was a very long name and certainly began with 'Dettol.'

Unfortunately he spoke almost entirely in the third person so he repeated the name about twenty times in the next ten minutes.

'Dettol is surprised at the low level of knowledge in this country. Dettol is particularly surprised at how few people have any interest in molecular gastronomy.'

'Well, better add me to the list,' I thought, laying my prune stones around the rim of my plate in an artistic fashion. Had I really eaten 14 prunes?

(Having looked it up later, an annoying habit I sometimes wish I could break, I now know molecular gastronomy is a sub discipline of food science that investigates the physical and chemical transformations of ingredients that occur in cooking).

'Dettol is concerned about the lack of knowledge he finds everywhere he goes. You would be surprised how few people Dettol meets are even aware the process by which bread toasts is called the 'Maillard Reaction'.

He paused, possibly expecting a nod of agreement or appreciation from me. I missed my cue.

'Dettol reminds you the process is a variant on caramelisation, a chemical reaction between the amino acids and sugar contained in bread. It's a non-enzymatic version of browning bringing out furanones to create a different   flavour in the same way heated sugar gives rise to caramel, as far removed in texture and taste from sugar as toast is from bread.'*

He sat back in his chair again as if waiting for applause. Marigold looked momentarily concerned when he looked directly at her, but relaxed when he switched his attention back to me.

*No, of course I didn't remember all this stuff verbatim, but the 'Maillard Reaction' is now glued into my memory banks, along with a load of other unusable nonsense and I was able to 'remind' myself of Dettol's wisdom when writing this.

My plate was empty by now, Dettol's toast, cheese, ham and large pile of what looked like cat sick remained untouched. He was the only one talking. This was a lecture, not a conversation. After expounding on the inadequacies and inconstancy of Ukrainian lifestyle, customs and educational standards for a further five minutes or so, Dettol pushed back his chair, said an abrupt 'goodbye' and strode away with his untouched tray of food.

We watched as he sat down at another table containing two weary young people apparently still in recovery mode from a prolonged and exhaustively gymnastic sex session. I mentioned this to Marigold who appeared not to have reached the same conclusion.

'That was fun,' Marigold said. 'I don't know why you encourage people like that to start talking while we're having breakfast.'

The unfairness and inappropriate nature of that accusation still lingers. Marigold says...

G said he feels like a hunter gatherer now. I said you are only ordering bacon and 4 chicken fillets from the butcher. The only thing you hunt is your glasses and then gather three pairs of rubber gloves to bring the delivery in off the step.

The role of ordering delivery food he has nominated to himself. Just as well as I aren't very organised. I have never had such weird food and treats.

I have noticed he has emptied his sock drawer which now contains lots of liquorice, dark chocolate and very cheap midget gems which he says are the best.

I really can't imagine enjoying a meal in a restaurant surrounded by Perspex. It would be much easier and cheaper to get a takeaway and sit in the car which would be a similar experience. You could even have a conversation with non-existent people in the back or an imaginary dog. Think we will manage with neither of those options.

G Says...

"I've heard that hard work never killed anyone, but I say why take the chance?"

— Ronald Reagan.

People I know only through social media - ie not 'real' friends and for all I know not even real people – do seem to have some very strange misconceptions about me in the Lockdown Era.

Surely you're lonely? No, I'm not and never have been.

Marigold and I must be getting on each other's nerves? Oh, come on. We only ever fall out on those very rare occasions I am slow to realise my culpability in a dispute. I apologise, order is restored. Marigold adopts the Queen's motto: never apologise, never explain, and who am I to argue with either of those redoubtable ladies?

I suppose you're busy learning a new skill with all that free time? Another language, perhaps?

Oh dear. These strangers who've surreptitiously invaded my life know nothing. After moving to France, on a whim, the whole process took about three weeks from Marigold asking 'do you fancy living in France' to turning up with our entire possessions inside a van I soon suspected to have been an MOT failure parked in the wrong slot by the Van Hire company.

The house was vast with equally massive outbuildings, the nearest neighbours were a mile away, the house was unliveable having been abandoned for the past thirteen years and we lacked both construction skills and the ability to speak French.

Learning the language by association only with the staff of builders' merchants isn't recommended, but we managed and after ten years I reckoned I'd 'cracked' one language and was ready for a fresh challenge when we moved to Spain.

I genuinely thought learning Spanish would be a doddle. It wasn't. Learning a language requires tremendous feats of memory and there's the first problem. I know 'lots of stuff,' but dredging it from the bottomless pit of my memory when an instant response is required, that's not as facile as it used to be.

I could win Mastermind, I keep telling myself, if only they'd relax the rules a little. Instead of relentlessly firing questions at the contestants, why not allow a reasonable period of grace to allow those contestants who 'know' the answer, but need a little longer to come up with it. About twenty minutes between questions sounds about right. No, I wouldn't watch it in that format either, but at least I'd stand a chance of winning.

Learning Spanish, as with any language, isn't all that difficult. Learn a thousand words and you're in business. Leaving aside the inconvenient niceties of grammar and perceived pronunciation for now, that thousand words will get you well past the 'me Tarzan, you Jane' stage, but won't ever get you presumed to be a native speaker. Fluency is reserved for the very few.

Add in my slight deafness, bad enough in English but seriously limiting in another language and I knew I'd got problems. Our only neighbour on the remote goat track that formed the access road to our ruined finca was an elderly man named Candido. He spoke to us every single time we saw him. We never understood a word he said.

He was often the worse for wear after an afternoon sampling the (vile) spirit he distilled in his bodega/shed, which didn't help our understanding as his Andalusian dialect was already pretty much indecipherable.

Marigold never sees the absence of linguistic skills as a barrier. She can ask for and receive food, drinks, directions anywhere in the world without using any words at all. I remember making an utter fool of myself in a Chemist shop in Croatia, or may have been Romania, floundering around with phrase book in hand while asking if they stocked knee bandages. When the woman produced a packet of Viagra I gave up and handed over to Marigold. She rolled up my trouser leg, pointed to the swollen knee and within seconds an elastic bandage was offered. I really don't know why I bother.

So, no I haven't learnt a new language during lockdown. Just one more opportunity scorned.

When we first hit Lockdown I realised I would be forced to find a substitute for the daily exercise routine my ailing, substandard and barely fit for purpose heart demands. No more ten mile hikes, yomping across moorland with a rucksack full of bricks on my back, no more pre dawn plunges into the ocean and absolutely no chance of ever breaking a world weightlifting record for the clean and jerk.

When I broached the subject to Marigold she looked a tad bemused. 'I didn't know you'd actually started an exercise routine,' she said. 'I remember you saying you were intending to start one. Sometime.'

'I need to exercise,' I said. 'The Health Minister and Boris himself are worried about me' and proffered in evidence my first 'vulnerable person at death's door' letter advising me to avoid people, places and impure air at all costs to try and ensure my survival for another week or so.

Marigold was actually quite supportive of my plans. I can walk outside, up and down the path, without ever coming into contact with anyone else. It's not much of a path, a return trip, there and back, takes about thirty seconds, but the only other alternative is to repeatedly walk up and down the hall which I can't imagine is beneficial to either heart or floor coverings.

I have an exercise bike housed in what an estate agent would try and persuade a putative buyer was a second bedroom. With the bike in situ there's not very much room for anything else. Marigold saw the bike for sale on Gumtree a while ago, long before the onset of a pandemic, and noticed its listing dated back eight months.

'They'll take an offer after all this time,' she announced and we set off for a viewing. On arrival at the house, with Marigold navigating this took quite a while, my initial impression of the bike was one of surprise. I hadn't expected it to be so big.

'It cost £450,' the seller informed us as we crammed together in his hallway with the enormous orange contraption taking up most of the space, 'but I'll take £25.'

The owner (verbally) demonstrated its ability to record times, duration and, most importantly in his view, cadence by pointing at the large dial mounted on the handlebars. 'I don't think it's working just now,' he said, 'Probably needs a battery.'

Marigold offered him £20, he was happy to accept, and we carted it back home. Did I mention it weighs about as much as three fridge freezers? The magic dial didn't work and still doesn't. I doubt it ever will now as I knocked it off its mounting on getting it through the front door so my 'cadence' will be forever a mystery.

There are eight settings, varied by turning a knob on the frame. Setting number one is virtually free wheeling - a gust of wind would set the pedals spinning – while setting number five requires the rider to have thighs like Sir Chris Hoy to budge the pedals. I have no idea what the other settings are supposed to do as the knob only works on setting number one and setting number five.

'Twenty quid, eh?' I said.

'He wanted twenty-five,' Marigold pointed out, 'until I beat him down.'

Hmm!

I use it, not every day but most days, pedalling away furiously (high cadence) until exhaustion point or five minutes, whichever comes first. Usually the former. As with my walking regime the key to success has been a smart watch, busily recording steps and heart rate. I need to keep an eye on my heart rate – enough to do good but not so high as to risk harm – so having a contemporaneous record is vital.

Knowing how many steps I take is of little value as I walk for a set time, twenty minutes brisk walking up and down the path at a time is all anyone could reasonably stand, but Marigold expressed an interest in the data so she bought a wrist band to record her own steps. Now it's a competition. A one sided one as even someone as highly competitive as me draws the line at step counting. It's 24 paces, end to end, along my marching route, 25 if I concentrate, while Marigold takes about 85 steps to cover the same distance. Or so it seems. Does she really walk like a gheisha? I hadn't noticed it in the past.

'Eight thousand, three hundred and seven,' Marigold announces, flopping red faced into her chair. I nod and try to look impressed. I hadn't even noticed she'd been out. For all I know she's only been out there for ten minutes. I try not to look at my wrist, but just have to do it. It's only half eight in the morning, I've not even got my shoes on yet, not even considered going out for a 'walk.'

'How many?'

'Two hundred and eight,' I say.

Marigold doesn't say anything. She doesn't need to. It's another crushing victory.

Another of the many treats I'm missing out on (allegedly) is researching my Family Tree. I suspect my family tree has diseased roots, but ignorance is bliss on this subject. The likelihood of turning up landed gentry – gentry of any kind is unlikely – and as for Royal connections, forget it. I don't even have a Hapsburg lip. No, I'm from a long line of undistinguished, utterly benighted riffraff and I know my place.

I was glancing through a copy of The Spectator published on 15 October 1954 recently. What, you mean everyone else doesn't hang on to their 'stuff' like me? Okay, it's a fair cop, I found it while doing what some people call online research, but Marigold calls just being nosy.

The subject of my far from prurient interest was Compton Mackenzie. Let's be fair to him, Sir Edward Montague Compton Mackenzie. I was convinced he founded the Scottish National Party - even though he wasn't Scottish he identified as Scottish – and it turns out he did. Result!

I knew he'd been a prolific author, about 100 books, even though Whisky Galore and Monarch of the Glen are the only ones most people will have heard of and only then because of the film tie in. I didn't know he had been President of both the Croquet Association and the Siamese Cat Club. Now, that's much more interesting than founding a Nationalist Movement.

Getting to the point, finally, I'll offer up this quote from the great man of letters taken from his correspondence with Sir Harold Nicolson who had 'declared recently that the novel was dead.' Compton Mackenzie wondered if if this were indeed the case 'I should presently be called as a witness in a murder trial' and took issue with Nicholson's conclusion. He did add, however, 'While I would not say that the novel is dead yet, I often wonder whether anybody will be writing novels fifty years from now.'

This was written in 1954, remember, and novels are still being written. More than ever before. We will always need forms of escapism. In the present day, however, newspapers and magazines are in decline and the written word, if not doomed to extinction, shows every signs of morphing into very different means of communication.

Marshall McLuhan prophesied in the 1960s that people would eventually stop reading paper based print completely and henceforth communicate instead through electronic media. I was just one of the multitudes who mocked this sacrilegious subversion. His words back then, 'the medium is the message' resonate rather more vividly today.

McLuhan's chief concerns were radio, telephone and television. If he'd foreseen the arrival of the Internet Age he'd have spontaneously combusted.

As avid travellers we've occasionally been asked, 'what's the point?' The enquiry is invariably genuine. A woman said to me recently in response to a remark I made to someone else about the joy I find in the solitude of a desert landscape, 'why do you have to actually go there and put up with the heat, the discomfort, all of that when you could just watch someone else show a video of a desert on YouTube?'

Would there be any common ground if I bothered to take issue with remarks like that? No, so I didn't bother. Marigold thinks I'm mellowing.

Jack Kerouac would never have bothered to inspire the Beat Generation with 'On the Road' if he had been content to stay cooped up in his bedroom forming a view of what the world had to offer him by watching television.

Lavoisier was guillotined in the French Revolution on May 8th 1794. I know this because my diary, yes I do have a diary not that I use it to record events for future generations to marvel over, it's just so I can remember when my car insurance is due or how much I weighed in 1975, told me so last month in the 'on this day' tailpiece at the bottom of the page.

This is the man who discovered the existence and properties of Oxygen and Hydrogen, neither of which were known about until 1778 and 1783 respectively. His major contribution to Science didn't save him from a populist mob baying for an end to elitism and his head was chopped off, number 4 among 28 prominent citizens of Paris deemed to be surplus to the Revolutionary ideals on that day.

The eminent mathematician, LaGrange, commented, 'a whole century could not produce another head the like of that one they have made to fall in a second.'

Marie Curie died in 1934 from prolonged exposure to radiation, specifically Radium-226, and was buried in a lead lined coffin directly alongside a matching one containing her husband. Her name lives on, but maybe not for for as long as her contaminated laboratory equipment, furniture, clothes, books and everything she ever came into contact with will remain lethal. Those ordinary objects will be dangerously radioactive for another 1,600 years.

If people of their stature die before their time the World notices. It's thoughts like this that get me through the day. I've done nothing of note and won't ever rate an 'on this day' entry, but I'm already way beyond the 'taken too soon' threshold so am winning hands down over Marie Curie and Lavoisier.

This period of theoretically enforced lockdown has affected people differently. Some can't wait to get out there into the big, wide world again; some are (often understandably) nervous nellies who have lost all self confidence.

It's not dissimilar to people who have spent time in controlled environments. I'm thinking of the armed forces, prison, even boarding school. Some people blossom when they leave, others struggle to acclimatise to a newly unrestricted world. Of course it's all a lot more complicated, just as the threat of the virus is still out there. Throwing open the door, casting off the (hopefully) metaphorical shackles and dashing to freedom isn't quite so easy.

The acceptance of routines can be very important for many people because they offer a safety net, safety, security, an impression of predictability. The outside world shrinks, becomes less of a challenge. Bad things happen, but only on television. Yes, burying one's head in the sand is a massive con job, but reality is much harder to live with. I decided I need to keep busy.

After a week's thought the best I could come up with was to take another look at a book I 'finished writing' about a year ago. When I say 'finished'...

Editing, formatting, all the technical fiddling that's involved in taking a scribbled manuscript and knocking it into shape takes up a lot of time. Far too much time. Once the laborious, tedious, seemingly Sisyphean task has begun it takes over one's life. Everything else stops, but as I remind myself every day now, I have plenty of free time for a 'project.' Of course my project had to be connected to the written word.

I came across this passage a few days ago. Nothing to do with Covid-19, but it encapsulates the current lifestyle of many people.

'The nights were long...The innkeeper could not travel to his village, but he was well supplied. He made soups and stews. He sat by the fire and read books he had been meaning to read...He drank whiskey and wine. He read more books.'
— Erin Morgenstern, The Starless Sea.

Recently I sent that rough draft manuscript out into the scary world of agents and publishers, a world I imagined I would never again allow to concern me. It's a novel aimed at a teenage readership, a very different genre to everything I have written before, but I realised its time may have come as the central theme of the narrative is surviving a world wide pandemic. I wrote it long before coronavirus was ever heard of so it turns out to have become topical by entirely serendipitous means.

It's not been snapped up and I've allowed the publishing world an entire month to dash in with offers of a hefty advance and suggestions of film rights to follow. Four weeks, nearly five actually, is a mere nanosecond in the glacial publishing industry, but I wasn't bothered about tying myself down to a publisher again anyway.

'How long is a nanosecond anyway?' replied Marigold, reading over my shoulder like an annoying commuter.

Other than being aware it was not very long at all, I hadn't the faintest idea. I looked it up.

I'll be with you in two seconds,' in our house is a pretty inaccurate measurement of elapsed time. It can mean anything from a couple of minutes to half an hour. The next time I am accused of offering misleading information as to how long it would take me to finish the (undoubtedly) vital task in which I was engaged and sprint off to do something mind-blowingly trivial instead I will offer up, 'if I'd said I would be there in a nanosecond, would that have been soon enough?'

A nanosecond, apparently, is one-billionth of a second, but time can be measured by increments far shorter. A picosecond is three orders of magnitude shorter, one-trillionth of a second, and a femtosecond is shorter still at one-quadrillionth of a second. It's pretty unlikely any of these measurements will ever find a place in my daily routine.

Getting back to the book project I'll publish it myself. This time around I will have zero expectations and thus avoid disappointment if (when) it sinks without trace.

Leaving it unpublished, however, written but not sent out to a wider audience, has a bizarre attraction. The concept of being unpublished has perhaps been understated and undervalued. As a writer, my work is done. The book is written. Does it really matter if anyone other than Marigold ever reads it? It mattered once. It mattered a great deal. But, maybe no longer. There's a certain kudos in being a deliberately unpublished writer. I may set a trend.

I really liked being an ex writer. So much more interesting than just being a writer. I never said 'I'm a writer' anyway if asked how I spent my days. Much easier now when asked 'what do you actually do' to say 'I don't do anything. Nothing at all' or if the enquirer is a tiresome stranger I mutter, 'I don't do nuffink.' That keeps supplementary questions at bay.

Once a book is published, it cannot ever really become unpublished. I think occasionally about my previous books. If I were writing them now, would they be different? Better? Well, I'd hope they'd be better. I imagine most writers would like to go back and rewrite their own published novels. I know I would.

A friend who is an artist – not in the urine sense, but an actual painter – faces the same dilemma as does a novelist: when to say 'enough.' One more brush stroke, one more edit, there has to be a time to say, 'that's it, finished.' A painted canvas or a novel, they're never really 'finished' in the eye of the painter or author, but there has to be a completion point.

My artist friend says she doesn't regard her pictures that leave to go and hang on gallery walls as a 'finished project' but as an 'abandoned project.' It's a fine distinction but encapsulates perfectly my own feelings when I declare a work 'finished.' I know only too well how much any subsequent re-readings of any of my published novels have irritated and annoyed me. I could have described that scene better, made a better fist of that section of dialogue, but it's far too late now.

In a sense, after allowing a period of contemplation, I have already done this. Taken some of my old books in hand, tidied them up, changed any style elements that subsequently irritated me and reissued them under a new identity in one of my many different pen names.

Unheralded, different author name, different title, amended content, they won't take off and become best sellers again as once I imagined was the be all and end all of being a writer, but I'm happier with them now and that's all I wanted.

Writing a novel is rather like climbing Everest; much better as something that's already been done, or even better claimed to have been done, than on a list of things still to do. Achievement is so much better in hindsight. Better still in plausible absentia, I imagine.

I walked the walk so can safely talk the talk as a writer, but hypergraphia, the overwhelming compulsion to write has never been much in evidence with me. Overwhelming compulsion to eat, that's very different.

This last book isn't what I call a novel. It's certainly been easier to write. Shorter, that helps, lighter in tone and content, the Young Adult readership make far less demands on a writer so I thought it would be a good idea to make life as difficult as possible for myself. .

I'm not, never have been and (unless there's more to reincarnation than I think) I suspect I never will be a fifteen year old female. That's a difficulty I could have avoided by choosing a male lead character, so why then compound the problem by writing the book as a First Person narrative? This compels the writer to include the narrator in every 'scene' with all the plot restrictions that brings to bear and I try to avoid using First Person narratives from choice.

Evelyn Waugh once wrote 'the writing of novels in the first person is a contemptible practice'. The fact he later wrote his most popular novel, Brideshead Revisited, in the first person still doesn't mean he was wrong.

So, why make life difficult?

Well, I can't speak for Evelyn, but with me it's the challenge, you see? If I am to escape accusations of 'dumbing down' for a more youthful audience, no swearing, no graphic violence, no torrid sex*, I need an escape route. The alternative is succumbing to a mind numbing sense of ennui which is bad enough in normal times but in lockdown would be unbearable.

*Although several of my previous books contained all these elements, I have never been asked if the sexual content is prompted by personal experience. Gruesome murders, yes, but gymnastic sex never. I'm rather offended by that presumption of those activities being entirely imaginary.

Obviously, the sex scenes are just like the actions and thought processes of serial killers which people so readily attribute to my nature, I make it all up.

Amazon know me as Gulliver Smith in this latest incarnation. I've been known by many different names, been called a good many more uncomplimentary ones as well, over the years and Gulliver Smith is as good a substitute as any.

Summer 'ain't what it used to be.

Marigold Says...

There's more than a faint hint of smoke and the scent of charred sausages in the air. Summer barbecue season is here. Only, without the summer. I could write a book about barbecues we have had and been to. Every year we would get out our rusty lump of scrap metal and hopefully it hadn't still got a bit of last year's sausage impaled in it, decide it was probably the start of Ebola and taken it to the tip. Then a quick trip to B and Q for another. We looked enviously at the stainless steel ones with an attached kitchen unit. Just what we've always needed, we said. Then we went away and bought another cheapo.

France were the best for expensive bbqs and kit. We went to a French neighbours once for a bbq. He had one of the huge gas models with burners etc. He then served up chips cooked in the oven and some of the thinnest, saddest burgers I've ever seen. I was very surprised as we were expecting a Roman feast with fireworks.

Over the years we have had all shapes and sizes of bbqs, the most useless was a cast iron bucket shaped one which we always took away with us in our various camper-vans and never used, as there were even more substantial ones on the camp sites and it just got more and more rusty. Touring around Australia and New Zealand in tiny camper-vans we had lots of barbecues as Kiwis and Aussies love to cook outdoors. Even when we 'rough camped' we were often invited to join in with someone else's feast. That's one of the best things about living 'on the road' and it's also one of the things we miss most about being confined to barracks. I well remember for all the wrong reasons having a huge barbecue gathering at our place, well only 12 people actually, but some of them were very big so it seemed like more. It was a disaster from start to finish. Our dog, a Labrador, ran off with a string of sausages, with everybody screaming "stop him" and he ate them raw under the bed. Then G who for some reason has to take over cooking duties at these times and flounce about with a glass of wine like Keith Floyd, kept shouting "won't be long" and faffing about all night. He was making a very good bonfire, but was supposed to be to cook food on, not to sit around and admire. I asked him what he had put on the pork chops as they were a funny colour. He said 'I have mixed up brown sauce and tomato sauce as a marinade. It's my own invention.' I had another drink and left him to it.

We sat down to pork chops, no sausages which were 'in the dog' and left the chicken pieces, which we had forgotten about, still cooking. There were a few funny looks. I tasted my chop. It tasted like petrol. I suspect G had hurried up the lighting process with firefighters. Luckily there was lots of bread and other stuff to fill up on, and am sure the effort was appreciated if not the final result. We did finish off the night with bacon butties, not bbq'd.

After that we bought an electric bbq which was brill. It had fake coals over an electric element which fooled nobody, and I never heard a comment of "must get one of those". We used it at our first house in France and it always blew the electrics, so entailed a lot of running in and out, jumping over the extension lead. The two goats we were fostering, Thelma and Louise, arrived one evening, attracted by the smell of charred meat, dragging the tractor tyres they were tethered to behind them and one of our friends started screaming and running around like a mad woman as if a pride of lions had turned up.

The funniest bbq we went to was given by somebody we didn't know too well and we hardly knew anybody there either. Food was served and mine host took his pinny off and sat down revealing out of his short shorts a portion of his anatomy which is usually kept private. I got hiccups from laughing and went and sat round the corner as I couldn't concentrate on my food. G nudged me and said, 'I see we're only getting chipolatas' and I choked on my wine.

Maybe it was their idea of "Get to know your neighbour". Hope he bbq'd those shorts. Think somebody had told him as he appeared later with trousers on. Very glad G always wears long shorts on these occasions. I always check by looking closely and rummaging, which he seems to enjoy.

We have now progressed to an electric hotplate from Ikea, bought three years ago. It is still in the box.

I remember when we first had a fondue in the 70's at the house of one of our trendy 'London' friends. Loved it. Of course I bought one. What a terrible idea, boiling oil in the middle of the table. People poking pieces of spitting steak and reaching over each other, trying to retrieve their particular piece. Good fun but ridiculously dangerous. A cheese fondue with dipped bread - disgusting. We were served up a three cheese fondue. Of course we said it was delicious and went home to swig from a bottle of Gaviscon.

What about those hot brick things, where they served minuscule slices of meat which you fry yourself? In fact you virtually do your own dinner. That trend didn't last long. Luckily we didn't buy any bricks which would have only been used once and stored on top of the dusty fondue.

Fortunately Covid doesn't encourage gatherings and maybe in the future all barbecuing will be illegal because of emissions or lack of charcoal, meat and vegetables will also be illegal and all barbecues will be collected up and made into a giant sculpture of a burnt hamburger with a dill pickle on the side.

Our neighbours have had three barbecues in a fortnight. It's not even barbecue weather. The smoke only ever seems to blow in our direction. It's like Paris when the *gilets jaunes* protests were going on (I had to look up the French bit).

I thought the loud screaming was out of control children, but G is convinced it is coming from drunken women. He says he has wide experience of females making a racket like that every time they've had three glasses of wine and someone mentions sausages. He gave me a meaningful look which I ignored.

I assume the pandemic means everyone has to bring their own chair, cutlery, plates, wine glasses and probably their own charcoal as well so that should cut down the fun a bit.

G Says…

People who think they know everything are a great annoyance to those of us who do.

Isaac Asimov

'How old are you anyway?' That's a question only a person only just out of their teens would ask. I've been 'chatting' to the grandchild of a friend. Only on the phone, obviously, so I missed seeing the expression of disbelief that my reply may have produced.

Age is just a number. Yeah, right. I'll grant you it's not all that important. Unless you're a cheese or a bottle of wine when the process is beneficial. I suspect I'm more inclined to resemble a bottle of milk than a bottle of wine where the ageing process is significantly less rewarding.

'It must be wonderful, being retired,' she said with the absolute certainty of youth. 'All that free time and no stress.'

Ah, bless! Such innocence. I didn't argue as I am no longer young enough to know everything.

I'm feeling more than usually enervated today. Weak, feeble, listless, it's the weather, isn't it? Overcast, dull, damp, it's such a change from that brief sunny interlude when I was running around like a spring lamb.

Marigold scoffed at this description at the time, but has no problem in ignoring my 'woe is me' protestations on the very rare occasions I fail to leap out of bed announcing a flurry of tasks I intend to complete with the next hour or two.

I eventually made a start on clearing out what I call the Folderol Drawer. We've always had one wherever we lived and this one is both wide, deep and capacious. Or it was until we started chucking things into it. It's full to the brim with 'stuff' we don't need, don't want, may never need. The perfect easy start to the day. No heavy lifting involved.

I abandoned the task after a brief rummage uncovered a long lost favourite pen I'd long since given up for lost. Best not be too rash, the rest of this clutter may yet 'come in handy.' This isn't   a generational descent into hoarding – it's only one drawer after all – but an example of future recycling, even though I'm pretty sure none of these items serves any useful purpose. Maybe in a year or two, who knows? Best not take any risks with potential future treasures.

The favourite pen, with which I wrote out early drafts of books while still in my computer denial phrase, doesn't work. Ah well. I'll just keep it for sentimental reasons. I popped it back in the drawer. I've done an extensive inventory of our pandemic hoarding stocks. It's not impressive. As Marigold says, 'beans and peas are essential items.' As for variety, well there's peas, beans and er, not much else.' I busied myself for arranging them in use by date order. Life's pretty full on these days; it's just one treat after another.

A couple of hours flew by, as they do in lockdown, (ha!) and I was looking out of my window at the wind and the rain as Marigold said, brightly, 'Almost at the end of July already and we haven't been out since the middle of March. We're not missing much today.'

No, we're not. It makes us appreciate those who are out in all weathers because it's their job. The bin men for a start. They came even earlier today, banging and clattering. The continuation of their early morning calls is a boon even now most of the rest of us are either restricted to four walls or on furlough, the extra holiday with pay treat that keeps on giving. Bin men help us all, gently reminding us another day has dawned, or is about to dawn, and giving us the opportunity to throw off the covers and embrace life again.

Our post lady isn't a ray of sunshine even on a nice day so she'll be even grumpier today. We don't get much post lately, unless it's from Matt Hancock who has become a pretty regular correspondent. I'm touched that a Minister of State finds time to write to me even in the midst of a National Emergency. (I thought a national emergency rated capitalisation)

One of the people we know – I won't say 'friends' as that's a very exclusive club – emailed us recently to say she's 'invested' in a luxury kitchen and has 'got the builders in.'

How lovely for her. What's a luxury kitchen and how will it differ from the (immaculate and fully kitted out) kitchen that was already in the house when they moved in six months ago? Nobody calls those labour saving appliances that so bewitched previous generations: washing machines, dishwashers and the like, luxury items any more and while everyone, including us, still calls it a Hoover we love our cordless Dyson. Is it a 'luxury' though? Surely not.

Luxury items continue to proliferate, even if only words on the packaging. Luxury toilet rolls, bit of a stretch that, champagne truffles, bath oil, even smoked salmon. Are there tins of 'luxury' baked beans out there yet?

It all seems far removed from the days when the word luxury meant just that. My parents, suckers for slick advertising, went into raptures over the newest invention: a 'fitted' carpet. Wall to wall floor covering. It didn't actually 'fit' very well, not after my dad realised the 'fitting' part was extra so decided it was a job he could easily do himself.

All prompted by an advert that seemed to be on Britain's television screens twenty times a day: 'This is luxury you can afford — by Cyril Lord.'

It's been a while since we had any luxury in our life. Better make that never. We don't crave five star experiences. Our happiest times while travelling were spent 'roughing it,' either in a distinctly minimalist camper van or flitting from place to place choosing our overnight accommodation on a whim with luxury not even being at the bottom of the list of requirements.

We lived in a tent for six months, just outside Newquay and this marked the start of our love affair with Cornwall. Not a fancy 'glamping' style tent, this was a basic, two person ridge pole effort from Millets' bargain range. We did allow ourselves the luxury of a mattress – a piece of foam, a whole inch thick – a rolled up towel each for pillows and that was it. It's hard to carry anything other than basic essentials when your entire belongings have to fit in an Austin A35.

We found work easily enough, just as well as we had no money at all on arrival. Marigold got a job in the Bilbo Surf Shop and I reinforced my decision to abandon the academic life of Oxford in great style by obtaining work as a doorman at the town's busiest and most notorious pub which was just over the road from where Marigold toiled away.

We used to say 'bouncer' not 'doorman' in those days, back when rodent control operatives were still rat catchers. I hear the term du jour is door supervisor now, but whatever the nomenclature the role is that of a 'chucker out of undesirables.' Being occasionally undesirable myself at the time it was a classic case of poacher turned gamekeeper.

In many ways it was a dream job. I was usually able to persuade unruly or especially truculent customers to go outside for a breath of air without resorting to the violent laying on of hands and almost everyone was in happy, holiday mood.

I was provided with liquid refreshment 'on tap' as required and a staff meal, usually either pie and mash or the latest craze in the pub trade, a Ploughmans' Lunch.

If you managed to locate a ploughman in Newquay, never easy, he'd surely decline the offer of a chunk of hard cheese, some person's misjudged version of half a 'French Stick' and a dollop of pickle where I suspected (with good reason) some of the dark lumpy bits were actually dead flies trapped in the glutinous mixture. That French stick may have had the correct shape, but there ended any resemblance to the genuine Continental article, but we weren't to know that back then.

Even so, this was the 1960s, the British back then were an ill informed bunch at the best of times, ever eager to pounce on the latest offerings dreamed up by advertising men in smoke filled rooms. Not that much has changed in the interim, apart from smokers becoming workplace pariahs.

The Sailors' Arms is still there, apparently still thriving, and still a Mecca for the young. I don't imagine current regulations allow quite so many to be crammed inside, customers took it in turns to breathe back then, and I very much doubt it will be to my taste nowadays, but back then we loved it. The bar staff were mostly itinerant surfers from Australia and New Zealand, following the waves around the world and the regular after hours lock ins were legendary.

We rarely came across anyone there with much of a plan in their heads. The next big wave, that was about as far as a surfer's imagination stretched and none of our circle possessed much in the way of a prescient nature. Which suited us very well.

Morocco and its Atlantic coast surfing beaches was to be the next stop for most of us. Long haired, free spirited hippies without structured lifestyle plans, we fitted in perfectly back in 1969 and there have been many subsequent occasions when we've stepped back from the brink of complete respectability just in time to avoid being considered 'normal.'

Marigold and I often think of those wild, carefree days and often the catalyst for memory is a song we associate with the Sailors's Arms juke box, full volume and free play settings applied after hours. I can precisely date certain songs by their association with that jukebox. Honky Tonk Women from the Rolling Stones alternating with Get Back from The Beatles. Elvis offering up In the Ghetto and so many more. Give Peace a Chance, Dancing in the Street, Pinball Wizard, Lily the Pink, they were on every day, every night with Je T'aime Moi non Plus by Serge Gainsbourg and Jane Birkin always available as a slow dance mood enhancer for the bar staff who had 'pulled.'

Melting Pot by Blue Mink and Two Little Boys by Rolf Harris were on that jukebox too. Neither would get played on the BBC these days.

As avid travellers we've occasionally been asked, 'what's the point?' The enquiry is invariably genuine. A woman said to me recently in response to a remark I made to someone else about the joy I find in the solitude of a desert landscape, 'why do you have to actually go there and put up with the heat, the discomfort, all of that when you could just watch someone else show a video of a desert on YouTube?'

Would there be any common ground if I bothered to take issue with remarks like that? No, so I didn't bother. Marigold thinks I'm mellowing. 'About time too,' she added.

Still Banged Up.

Marigold Says...

Here we go, here we go, here we go. A football chant. Not relevant at all, well loosely. Words that we could do with not hearing again As it means everything is ok and we can talk about nice things again.

Charts

Pandemic

Virus

Diet

Deliveries

Germs

Cuddling

Masks

Elastic

Sourdough

Flour

Social distancing

Johnny Depp

Amber Heard

Exercise

Steps

May come back to that as there are probably quite a few more. In fact a simple Good morning, nice day today will suffice in the future. Even though we live in a genteel area we're more likely to hear 'Is it bin day?'

I have in the past been told "you must get one of these". It is still going on. Yes it's lovely for people to think we need all of life's non-essentials. Sometimes I buy them and they can languish in a drawer till I am making up a charity shop box or pass them on to people who can work out what to do with them.

The one I never fell for was the boiling hot tap, Quoocher I think it's called. Our friend in Spain bought one of the very first ones on the market. That friend who had it could have got a job as a demonstrator. Quite marvellous I was told and at £1,000 plus you save lots of money, eventually.

Wow, lots of dosh to lay out.

The spiel is brill going on about waste of water and boiling up a kettle perhaps 3 times. Blah, blah, blah.

The second visit to see them it wasn't working as it was gunged up with something or other and needed attention. We had also been told the kettle had become obsolete and now had a plant in it, so we were making drinks by boiling water in a saucepan, tinged with bits of vegetables.

Like being back in rural France.

We were there for three days and the part to repair it arrived on the last day and we left them with their heads under the sink shouting instructions to each other.

We carried on to a café for a much needed coffee. I am very happy with my Tesco £6 white kettle, which boils water, all I ask from it, and no amount of "you must get one of these" will change my mind.

Must admit I am easily swayed by comments about products but try and stop the usual "must have it" as half the time it is on a whim. I went to a saucepan party in the 1970's, now don't be jealous, it was either that or a party throwing your car keys into a circle. As we didn't have a car, no point really. Bought a few saucepans instead.

They were called Miracle Maid, the sales patter being they were made from the same metal as a spaceship or something outlandish. The trick was to use very little water and it acted as a sort of pressure cooker. Still have two so a good buy and I can leave them to the Space Museum. Our worst bargain was a Lada car for £85. It died after two days. Buyer beware comes to mind or predosterezheniye diya pokupatelya. Isn't Google great?

What is very strange with Covid stuff is when people say things like, "Aunty Flo came round with her poodle called Dolly, tottering in with her stroller containing her sandwiches and a flask of tea for a visit and we socially distanced in the garden, although it was raining and cold. I couldn't do her a hot water bottle as she can't eat or drink with her glasses steamed up."

Why does everything have to be prefixed with a Safety Notice, "social distancing," which actually means "We are following the rules". Why bother with all this when sometimes the people they're on about are in another country and you will never see them, or actually care. By the way I haven't got an Aunty Flo, but she sounds a very safe visitor, and am sure the dog ate the crusts.

I am wondering if in the future we will only meet up a tree or a mountain yodelling to each other. Just been reading that the Swiss Amish in America still do it, yodelling that is.

Do you ever have a neighbour who you never talk to, not for any particular reason, but because they are up the road and round the corner? Maybe the odd "hello". We've got one and became intrigued as he is not particularly friendly.

When you have crossed paths as he is setting off early for presumably work he wears a grey suit. We tried guessing his profession.

Me. A funeral director

G. A spy, as G has seen the light on in the night.

Me. Jehovah's Witness

G. Betterwear salesman

Me. Civil servant.

G. Estate agent. I said estate agents only wear trendy clothes now with pointy toes, both male and female. The list will go on till we find out.

G is now insisting he is an exotic dancer and I suspect he plays the triangle in an orchestra.

We have an adopted dog which when the mood takes us we "borrow" as it makes our walk more enjoyable and spurs us on. I suppose if we categorised him he would be called a "walk me wherever I decide I want to sniff" dog."

We walk, stop, have a wee, him not us, wait and carry on.

I can't give you a correct description of our charge as walls have ears. Needless to say, he wouldn't win Crufts. Or a beauty contest.

Yesterday on our borrowed dog walk, we went down a lane, were admiring a big pond, when a huge goose decided to see us off. We could hear the spitting bird before he arrived. We have come across this kamikaze pilot before when we have driven past and he tried to attack our tyres and were told he is only angry in the mating season early in the year. We have avoided this spot till yesterday. He really means business. The dog barked which didn't help, and we ran off in a scared screaming way, and felt lucky to be alive. He saw us off good and proper, and we will never go near his patch again. I am ordering goose for xmas with extra stuffing.

The other thing that gets on my nerves now you mention it, or even if you didn't, is why do arty types especially, have to say my father was a street gas lighter and my mother cleaned peoples' steps for a slice of bread to feed twelve of us and a donkey was tied up in our back yard, which we collected coal on, next to the tin bath and outside toilet.

So what! They now live in London, I know, I know, I am a Londonphobe, just made that word up. They go around mixing with all the luvvies and all that that entails.

Why are people embarrassed to say "I had a great childhood, 3 square meals a day and we went on holiday every year to Bournemouth", without garnering sympathy for a childhood like many others. Move on it is boring.

Anyway, if any luvvies are reading this G put me up to it and I will willingly accept any invitation to The Ivy or The Savoy at a moments notice, and I can regale you with details of my early childhood in a drain. I can even speak hoitie toitie after a couple of gins.

G was talking about him and his cousin going down the canal, sailing a tin bath he found on the tip, (G isn't at all arty), and they were racing other urchins. They raced the tin baths, with shovels as paddles, as far as the place where there was a dead cow in the water. They used to swim around the cow.

He said there was a horrible bloke called Dirty Reg, a sinister character who had been in prison for molesting wolf cubs, the children version, not the animals – and G and his cousin chucked him in the canal. Now that is a play date not to tell your mother about.

Have just been reading an article about jokes, which I adore. We saw Ken Dodd about 4 times, the maestro of jokes. His favourite joke: The man who invented cats eyes got the idea when he saw the eyes of a cat in his headlights. If he had been going the other way, he would have invented the pencil sharpener.

A Barry Cryer joke. Back in the day you would cough to cover up a fart. Now with Covid you fart to cover up a cough.

Last one: I told my wife she was drawing her eyebrows too high. She looked surprised.

G Says...

The French have a phrase, *L'esprit de l'escalier*, describing that moment on the stairs, as you're leaving the scene of a confrontation when you think of exactly the right witty riposte, just 10 minutes too late.

These delayed reaction 'wish I'd thought to say that at the time' moments, a mixture of self annoyance and regret, are familiar friends. I file them away as a subheading marked 'what I wish I'd said' in the vast mental filing cabinet bearing the title 'bitter regrets and missed opportunities.'

Wise after the event' may be the closest English version. Missing the moment, thinking of a witty or cutting retort when the moment has passed, is invariably accompanied by regrets, self recriminations and a desire to turn back time.

In Germany they say 'treppenwitz' to describe this belated repartee.* The moment has gone. Opportunity well and truly lost. Every writer suffers from this affliction. I try not to read my older published books as I want to rip out or add whole passages in a futile desire to improve them.

Too late, much too late. What's done is done.

*German is one of the very many languages in which I am resolutely illiterate, I've never previously written this word and am reliant on a faltering memory for context so if it actually means 'testicles' or something equally inappropriate, please forgive me.

A while ago now we were 'escaping' from an unspeakably dull social event. The hostess called it a Dinner Party even though it took place in the afternoon with 'finger food' on offer (her definition, not mine as sausage rolls, vol-au-vents and various stuff impaled on sticks aren't what I call 'food.) it wasn't dinner, it wasn't even a party, just a group of expats gathered together by reason of speaking a common language and with little else in common.

We barely knew this 'merry band' as more than one person had (inaccurately) described the group and there were many other expats whose company we cherished, but none of them were present on that day.

Okay, it wasn't all dull, but as Big Steve disrobed and threw himself into the pool after his twentieth beer at every single gathering not even that could raise the enjoyment level. Big Steve was larger than life in every sense. Morbidly Obese Steve would have been more accurate and Excessively Flatulent Steve even more so.

One of the guests came staggering after us. 'That was a right good do,' he called out. 'Plenty to drink anyway.' This may give some idea of the expectations of some of our fellow Brits on social occasions.

'I thought you would have picked up on Norman spouting his rubbish,' he added. 'What with you knowing about all that.' I nodded sagely and glanced at Marigold. No, it appeared she hadn't any idea who Norman was or what rubbish he'd allegedly been spouting either.

As he left us to drive home - not much attention was paid to the drink driving laws in Spanish mountain villages - we both tried to recall which of our fellow celebrants was called Norman. We finally narrowed it down to a very thin, tattooed chain smoker who'd not stopped talking for several hours, but we'd kept well away. He announced at one point he 'did a great Elvis' and justified this claim by singing a few lines of 'In the Ghetto. Marigold said he'd sounded more like Basil Brush than Elvis.

The only part of his racist, sexist, homophobic and resoundingly solipsistic diatribe I could recall was him referring to Germans – he wasn't a fan – as a hypo-aggressive nation.

It would have been pointless to interrupt him in full flow, but I could and, at the time thought I perhaps should have disputed his usage of the word hypo-aggressive by interjecting, 'I'm not familiar with that word. Surely you mean hyper-aggressive?'

As we toddled off home I thought, 'I could have added, 'surely the best word for aggression, relating to nations as a whole would be belligerent.' I said this to Marigold as an example of *L'esprit de l'escalier* which we had been chatting about to another drunken group who suspected anything said in a foreign language to have sexual connotations.

She gave me one of her well practised looks. 'Yes, you could have said that if you'd thought of it at the time, if you wanted to look as if you were as big a prat as him.'

She's absolutely right. The poor man's Elvis never stopped spouting offensive nonsense all afternoon yet the only thing I regretted not picking him up on was a single example of clumsy sentence construction and an unfamiliar word. Who'd be the prat then if I'd challenged him over something nobody else would have even given a moment's consideration?

What would I do without her?

I've been contacted rather a lot lately by well meaning people wondering why I stopped writing novels a decade ago and settled for writing something as trivial as a blog. I like contributing to the blog, even if only writing nonsense and the amount of actual work involved is infinitesimal in comparison to the gestation period of a novel. It's the difference between pleasure and duty.

I almost feel guilty about being happy. Even in lockdown. Possibly, especially in lockdown. 'Hell is other people,' according to Jean-Paul Sartre and only the other day someone I've known since my childhood asked me if I was still 'obsessed' with the great man of letters.

Obsessed? No, but it's true I went through a 'Sartre' period in my late teens. As a philosopher, novelist and playwright that was understandable for a 6th former with English Literature as one element of my A level studies. I don't remember having any problem in blithely disregarding his rather inconveniently obvious Marxism. He was French though and reading his works in his own language was way beyond my capabilities. I think the reasons for my fascination with Sartre had only a little to do with his novels. A leading existentialist, he explored the nature of 'humanity' and the underlying structures of human consciousness.

As the leading light of French café society where the Intellectual Movement was, and remains, an essential part of that nations' psyche, Jean-Paul Sartre was a colossus. He refused the Nobel Prize for Literature in 1964, at a stroke cementing his legacy as a free spirit even though I found his rejection of such an honour more than a little baffling.

My own ego, dampened down significantly over the years, was at its peak at that time of my life. Awards, prizes, recognition, isn't that what everyone wanted out of life? Strutting past the assembled ranks of my fellow students to accept a mere book token from some distinguished former pupil who none of us had ever heard of on School Prize Day may not have been a Nobel Prize but I don't imagine I ever considered declining to accept them.

Jean-Paul Sartre would have been an inspiration in the midst of a pandemic. Some of his sayings resonate very strongly in these difficult times.

'If you're lonely when you're alone, you're in bad company.'

'Better to die on one's feet than to live on one's knees.'

'Freedom is what we do with what is done to us.'

'We are our choices.'

Maybe my friend was right, I was obsessed.

'You can have your DNA tested,' another well meaning friend said. 'Would you be interested?' I'm not sure whether she meant we could share her own kit or whether they're on 3 for 2 special offer in Boots, but I just can't get worked up about the subject.

Leonard Rossitter once asked, 'if ignorance is bliss, why aren't more people happy?' It's a very good question, but on some subjects I am happy just to remain ignorant.

Where I came from, how I got here, all that was set in motion before my birth. Nothing to do with me at all, so why bother about it? I used to come across DNA testing in one of my former jobs, although it was very much in its infancy then and was both prohibitively expensive and long winded. Nowadays anyone can send off for a test.

I might see if Poundland stock them, not willing to risk any more than a quid. I will probably learn my origins are 98% Aborigine and the various ethnic percentages will add up to 312.

That's as useful as the proper test, ie not at all.

Oh well, I suppose it gives people with too much free time on their hands and not much idea of doing anything else to fill the hours of daylight something to get excited about.

A few months spent in quiet contemplation, sans distractions, it's like winning the lottery, isn't it? Well, no, not really. We miss 'stuff,' but most activities can survive a few months abstinence. No more dressing up to go out, no obligation to conform to the expectations of others, it's okay to be selfish as a byproduct of lockdown.

We never got the stage of thinking, 'what's all the fuss about, our lives are exactly the same' like we imagine many of the people we know have experienced. We're both sociable, gregarious people who love talking, meeting other people and exploring our world, but it's a few months deprivation, not being banished to a Gulag.

We can cope, we are coping and we will continue to cope with this temporary restraint. Like cockroaches, we're in it for the long haul. They haven't changed much in several million years – why strive to improve on what works? Nothing about that analogy is appropriate, apart from the essential truth therein.

It certainly didn't find much favour with Marigold.

There are men working on a roof over the road. Three of them. One is prising up roof tiles, another is stacking them into neat piles and the third member of the triumvirate is throwing something small, (peanuts? M and Ms?) into the air and catching them, or far more often not, in his gaping mouth. I'm unsure of his actual role in the roof renovation process, but I certainly can't fault his diligence.

There's no evidence of health and safety equipment or practice. Quite the reverse. I've had occasion to do roof repairs from time to time on our various renovation projects. I didn't go in for much in the way of safety equipment either, but relied on a knowledge of the practicalities and dire results of falling off.

We once employed a roofer, unlikely to forget him as his van had Fiddler on the Roof blazoned on the side. No, Fiddler wasn't his real name, but he told us it brought him a great deal of business.

Mister Fiddler, or whatever his real name was, clambered across our slippery slate roof, in pouring rain, to examine the lead chimney flashing.

This was a three storey house, so a very long way down, but he wandered up and down for several hours, finished the job and only slipped twice.

Fortunately not off the edge.

'Aren't you worried about falling off?' Marigold asked.

'Nah,' he scoffed. 'Been falling off roofs all my working life. Here, feel that.'

He offered his bald head in evidence which bore an enormous scar and a significant bulge.

'That's a metal plate, that is. Sets off the detectors at airports every time. Can't even remember getting it. My wife says I should be more careful, but I tell her it's just part of the job.'

We decided he was in the wrong job.

The tile remover over the road, quite a hefty frame for a roofer, is bending over, displaying that essential attribute of the building trade, a 'builders' bottom.' The medical term for this is intergluteal cleft, should you ever wish to offer it as a conversational titbit at a dinner party or similar tedious function.

Read all about it.

Marigold Says...

I have a very old friend in every sense of the word. She doesn't embrace technology from choice, so we only make contact fairly infrequently. She does write the most marvellous letters which is very refreshing in this day and age and I must say I quite enjoy writing back. She also does little illustrations as I read along. She writes a lot and loves painting, has been on her own for about 12 years and by her own explanation " I have seen off 2 husbands, one partner, 4 dogs, 3 cats and a whole tank of tropical fish." We met each other when we lived in France.

When we knew her she was with her partner, a great bloke, who used to fish and collect "stuff" and make marvellous things, or just paint them. We have a fair few dotted about. She is now on her own and happy to be so, not at all a recluse, as she is one of those sort of people who gathers friends. G adores her and so do I.

Anyway, the point of this is, I wrote a letter to her and we set off to post it. First box was sealed up, so the next day early we set off again and found one that was okay. Hope it gets there as unlike computers you can't just 'save' what you write.

Have been reading about the last remaining BlockBuster Video Store in Oregon which has been turned into an AirBnb. You can choose a movie from the racks, sit in your new BlockBuster Bed and watch it on the big screen. No breakfast is offered just popcorn and chocolate raisins. The thought of having chocolate raisins on tap while watching a film in bed with G doesn't fill me with glee. Just imagine if you spilled them in the bed, what would the cleaners think?

We have spent many a happy hour renting films from video shops and excitedly rushing home to view with a plate of sandwiches and our feet up. I remember when you could post them back to the shop. That added a new dimension of excitability. Also combined with taking your library book back and choosing another - happy days.

G Says...

Marigold is missing out on one of life's greatest pleasures during the perfidious restrictions imposed by a pandemic. I refer to what I call accidental conversations. Not missing out on actual conversations, with friends or even with complete strangers, that's bad enough, but those conversations which take place in one's presence, and of which one is merely a silent spectator. Privy to the words yet lacking the context. How exciting is that? Harold Pinter, who needs you?

I'm still savouring a snatched fragment of conversation between two dog walkers we overheard the other day.

'Never bothered me, the arthritis, but what with irritable bowel, a frozen shoulder, gout and now this wretched ear infection, I've had it up to here with trying to sound sympathetic when he goes on about his bad back.'

Now that's true comorbidity. Respect!

Marigold isn't alone. To the many men and women who cultivate a taste for accidental conversation a journey by train or bus, a walk through a supermarket aisle or just strolling along a busy street, is as good as a visit to the theatre. Not that the option of live theatre is available now either.

It's true that, as with much 'experimental' theatre such as we've had offered up at Edinburgh Festivals the scenes are apt to end abruptly, and the plots are often not sufficiently expressed; but against this must be set the variety and immediacy of dialogue and the immense variety of the stories. As with life being like a box of chocolates as expounded by Forrest Gump, you don't always get what you want. You certainly don't get what you expect.

A chance remark, when overheard in passing, lacking context or prior knowledge of both speaker and recipient, can be sufficiently engaging to occupy our own conversation for an hour or more. The more bizarre and inexplicable the better. A throwaway remark, devoid of any understanding of its antecedent history, can surpass anything produced by a television studio. All we need is imagination and there's never been a shortage of that in our house.

Imagination is a precious quality. Life would be very dull without it. My own imagination was nurtured from a very early age by an innate ability to 'play' by myself. (I almost wrote 'play *with* myself, which would have had unfortunate albeit unintentional connotations). For an imaginative child an empty room can be a castle or an entire solar system and my own imagination took wings when I discovered the escapist world of books.

I think it may be necessary to point out I read anything and everything put in front of me. I always have since I realised the written word was packed with possibilities at age five. Newspapers, magazines, books of all kinds, some very low brow indeed. Judging by the reaction of some of this blog's readers I have apparently been promoting myself as some learned scholar plodding through a series of dusty yet distinctly worthy tomes. Putting aside the current edition of Viz for the moment, I can assure you all this impression is very wide of the mark.

After certain uncharitable folk poured scorn on me reading the works of Plato and Pliny the Elder, (yes, there are some unkind people out there with distinctly plebeian tastes in literature) it took a moment or two's consideration before 'confessing' to reading The Decameron. After all, by Ancient Greek standards the 14th century is practically cutting edge.

The Decameron is a collection of short stories by the splendidly named 14th-century Italian author Giovanni Boccaccio – in translation, obviously. I struggle with the linguistic style of Chaucer, who would have been almost an exact contemporary, so medieval Italian would be impossible.

The Decameron is structured as a collection of short stories – think of Chaucer's Canterbury Tales - 100 stories told by a group of seven young women and three young men sheltering in a secluded villa on the outskirts of Florence while trying to escape the Black Death which was afflicting the city and indeed all of Europe. Very topical. Hence my interest.

In modern times we have the television set as our focal point, but for thousands of years humans huddled together around a fire and told stories. Boccaccio's group trying to avoid a pandemic are 14th century Italy's answer to Facebook and Netflix. As we now know only too well, pandemics are no fun at all, but the pressure of coming up with an entertaining tale when called upon appears to have promoted an aura of eustress and positivity within the group. Maybe we should all take a turn as story tellers.

Long ago reading became a lifelong affliction but also a pleasure not without its drawbacks. My weakness, one of many but this is a biggie, is books. I own a lot of books.

The Japanese have a word for this condition: tsundoku – the pleasure of owning more books than you'll ever have time to read. The word, thought to have been coined in the Meiji era is a meeting of two ideas: tsunde-oku – to pile things up and then forget about them, and dokusho – reading books.

You may have to accept that as an etymological fact. I did.

I read voraciously, happily reread old favourites and even isolation won't put a dent in my book a day addiction as I have untold numbers of books on Kindle as well.

Having moved house many times, books in large quantities are a big problem. They weigh a lot for a start. I try to do a bit of 'weeding' on the occasion of every move. The vast numbers of books I've held on to in the hope I'd appreciate them at some later date, the books given by friends insisting 'This one will be right up your street' – no, no, no - plus all those, mostly proof copies of still technically unpublished novels, sent to me in my 'writer' period to 'take a look at and let me know what stops it being a best seller,' (no pressure then), they're all packed off to good homes or that mythical 'farm in Wales' where excess and/or unwanted pets were reputedly sent.

Every time we move we vow to embrace minimalism. Each time we fail and books, in vast profusion, aren't very helpful. I'm not totally abrogating responsibility here, I'm looking on the bright side. Shelves of books aren't 'clutter.' They're furniture, ornaments, old friends. I'm fully embracing the concept of tsundoku.

All these books just waiting to be read and plenty of opportunity to do just that. It's one of the few bright spots of the Covid-19 era. A novel takes up a relatively small space on a shelf yet it's much bigger on the inside than on the outside. There's a vast world of imagination inside a book. That's true minimalism and reading a book has to be one of the least disruptive actions a confined person can indulge in. I suppose Marigold and I could learn to play the trombone in our freshly minted free time, but that's not showing much consideration for others, is it? Good manners still matter.

I've suffered from a surfeit of good manners all my life. Manners, behaving myself, not speaking unless spoken to in the company of adults, all this was drilled into me in childhood, and rigorously enforced. It's not made life easy.

I used to let people ramble on, never interrupting no matter how tiresome their conversation. I made a conscious decision not to suffer fools gladly a few years back and it's made certain aspects of life a lot less irksome, but as for the rest, I'm stuck with the legacy of my upbringing.

I still seem unable to pay for something with the exact change without saying 'I think that's right' as I hand it over, having already checked it three times beforehand, then hanging around while the cash is counted and some, usually unspoken, version of 'permission to leave now' has been granted.

On using a pedestrian crossing I do a strange little jog while offering an apologetic mini wave to any waiting motorists. They rarely acknowledge me, just sit in their cars wishing the weirdo doing the half skip half walk would stop waving his arms about and get off the road.

I apologise when someone barges into me, I apologise for not being able to provide the exact money in a shop, I say please and thank you about fifty times a day. Good manners are a chore.

Marigold is similarly afflicted. A neighbour misheard her name on first meeting her and has called her 'Marlene' ever since. Marigold says it's too late now to correct her, meaning she must live with her new name forever.

Names don't really matter, not really, as long as we all know who we're talking to.

I used to know a couple named Barnes who lived in Barnes which I thought to be the height of sophistication. We were living in Richmond at the time and it crossed my mind to change my surname by deed poll to Richmond, but nothing came of it. Mr and Mrs Barnes of Barnes had a daughter named Juliana and it's one of those names that sticks in my memory so when I read the other day about a book written by Juliana Barnes I took notice.

It was soon evident they only had their name in common. Ms Barnes from Barnes married a Kiwi and went off to run a sheep station last I heard while the one in the magazine was a nun. The book she wrote was The Book of Saint Albans. As it was printed in 1486 I don't imagine the two were even related.

The Book of Saint Albans is basically a list of collective terms for animals but also covered the topics of hunting, fishing, and coats of arms and provides the earliest list of collective nouns for every type of animal one could possibly imagine. It's been regularly updated as new species were discovered.

Originally, these nouns were used primarily as hunting terms, although it's hard to envisage a mediaeval hunting party setting out in pursuit of an ostentation of peacocks. A flock of ravens is called an 'unkindness' or a 'conspiracy,' both of which appear rather more weird than a simple 'flock.' A pride of lions, a prowl of jaguars, yes, I can see the logic there, but what about a wisdom of wombats? A murder of crows, a charm of finches, these I know, but a gulp of cormorants? Oh, come on, Sister Juliana, surely you can do much, much better than that. And what about a pandemonium of parrots or an intrusion of cockroaches...

Cognitive bias, what I usually call having blind spots, invariably manifests itself at the most inopportune moments. Certain areas of expertise are a closed book to me, yet I frequently offer up opinions on subjects about which my knowledge is minimal, at best, rather than my ignorance be exposed. Most of the time the habit is so ingrained I don't even know I'm doing it. It's very little consolation to find it's a common trait in humanity.

Confucius said, 'real knowledge is to know the extent of one's ignorance.' Okay, he said a lot of things, old Confucius, but that's one of his better ones.

Speaking to an Italian 'arteeest' in a Liverpool art gallery a couple of years ago I was reminded of how I've learnt over time to disguise this specific example of my numerous failings, but it's never been entirely successful. We were talking about art. Reasonable, given the surroundings, and my Italian new best friend, whom I'd never previously met, had decided I was obviously an erudite and cultured individual and the perfect person to engage in art appreciation discussion.

'Is this you?' He said. 'Does it reach out and grab you?'

I was tempted to say, 'Well, I know what I like,' but didn't. It's the usual get out of jail retort of those wretches like me who know naff all about the actual manner of producing art fit to hang on a wall, but can make a purely personal distinction between what works and what doesn't, but I'm still hoping to blag my way through this ordeal.

Sadly, events soon spiralled far beyond my bluffing capacity. 'Isn't it remarkable, the way the chiaroscuro practically leaps from the canvas? One could almost imagine Caravaggio nodding his approval.'

'Remarkable,' I agree, not having a clue what he was on about. When the conversation (lecture) moved on to ombreggiamento effects, I was torn between faking a seizure or dashing outside shouting 'fire!'*

*As most of this 'conversation' was way over my head I had to attempt to remedy my ignorance and look up much of what he was talking about at a later date. Having done so, I'm still none the wiser. Far from it. Okay, I now know 'ombreggiamento' is a fancy Italian way of describing 'shading,' but that's about it.

Marigold came over eventually and rescued me. She always seems to gravitate towards the source of lively and interesting conversation and leaves me at the mercy of the weirdos. Not that we don't like weirdos, we do; many of our best friends are very odd indeed.

'He's interesting,' she said, looking back at the Italian man. She'd not actually spoken to him, but had obviously concluded from twenty yards away he was far better dressed, far more handsome and, apparently, far more interesting than anyone else in the room. I resolved to cultivate an air of appearing 'interesting' in future. The well dressed/handsome aspects may be beyond my scope.

We'd been dragged along to this event to provide moral support for one of our very odd arty-farty friends who was exhibiting her beachcomber collage collection. We like her work, we even have one on our wall, but it's not to everyone's taste. In fairness, it's been battered about in transit during several house moves and quite a lot of 'bits' have dropped off. Not that anyone ever notices.

Arty-Farty had been busily eavesdropping on peoples' comments and would howl with joyous laughter when anyone 'dissed' her offerings.

'I get far more pleasure from the bewildered and the loathers than I do from mere praise,' she told us. See, I told you we had odd friends.

We got a lift back with our arty-farty friend's 'bit of rough' who turned out to be the gallery owner's dissolute son. He told us he was a great disappointment to his father which was evidently a source of immense pride. 'It's not exactly easy being the difficult one,' he confided, 'when one's perfect siblings set such high standards. It was the same at Harrow when I was the first pupil in the family for three generations not to be Head Boy.'

I suppose a 'bit of rough' is a relative term.

His car was a rusty relic of a bygone age, a Humber Super Snipe, way past its prime, but the fabulously battered leather seats made up for the scruffy exterior. Even the name, Super Snipe, has style.

I sat up front with the badly behaved one. 'Look at that walnut dashboard,' he said. 'I keep getting told I need a new motor, but where can you find quality like this nowadays?'

It's a fair point. He leant over and removed a pair of gloves. Yes, the glove box in this car contained gloves. Nothing else, just a pair of battered gloves. Okay, not string-backed gloves, that would have surely been a step too far, but even so. Where does he put all his 'stuff,' I wondered, thinking of my own car 'glove box' which had never seen a glove, I'd scarcely ever imagined it could be used in this fashion. There'd be no room for even a tightly rolled surgical glove anyway.

The last time I cleared out my car interior, the glove box yielded up a host of treasures. Documents, some of them even related to the actual vehicle, keys – mostly unidentifiable – a rusty pair of pliers and an electrical screwdriver, some wrapped throat sweets, a few tattered scraps of paper bearing the telephone numbers of people we hadn't seen for twenty years, a long lost 'favourite' pen, several items of 'jewellery ' worth about a fiver in total but highly prized by Marigold, and an asthma inhaler (expiry date 2012) which seemed to be in working order and about fifteen assorted nuts and bolts.

Covid Ramblings.

Marigold Says...

What I have noticed now we are venturing out a bit is the number of designer dogs. Never noticed that many before. Have they all been bought because of Covid? Most of them are a something or other mixture with the word poo at the end and a very exotic looking one we saw the other day had a diamond collar. Didn't ask what it was as the owner looked a bit shifty. The dog looked quite ridiculous.

We do see a regular walker who has a very fat bulldog. It waddles along and we can hear its laboured breathing from over the road. We talked to the owner once and she said it doesn't like other dogs, but looking at it, it couldn't do much harm as its jaws overlap. Was reading the other day that all these lockdown dogs are going to suffer once the owners go back to work, and will be wrecking the house out of frustration, and let's be honest they will end up dumped.

We had a rescue labrador for many years who was famous for escaping and eating anything. We had a bbq once and he pinched and ate loads of uncooked sausages, which he had dragged upstairs and was eating under the bed. You really can't have a bbq without sausages. Banana skins were a favourite and empty yoghurt containers, plastic and packaging he found delicious. He lived till he was 17 and we still talk very fondly of him. Another weird thing he liked doing was getting dirty washing out of the laundry basket and burying it. If anything was missing, we had to go and find freshly dug mounds in the garden.

We had our first coffee 'out' today since March. The usual latte tasted awful, as we have now got used to our dishwater strength instant brand. Maybe another time, we might try ordering food. It seems if you have food you have to give a code, didn't understand it all. It is so they can trace you in case of Covid or maybe salmonella poisoning. Who knows? Maybe they are marking you on table manners or your attractiveness.

We were meandering around the local YMCA charity shop. I went in for a treat for me for the sum of £3. Big spender. Told G not to touch the books 'cos of virus but he couldn't resist and was turning the pages with five pairs of plastic gloves on. Not really. What did I buy? Oh, just a bit of unwanted rubbish for an up- cycling project. Or for sticking in a corner for six months and then taking it back to a charity shop. I do this quite often.

When I went to pay, behind the plastic screen was a bloke with a name tag on saying Tommy. To try to describe him wouldn't do him justice. He had, I would think, probably once have been a skinhead but what do I know? Age - anything up to 60-80 with the usual tats but no face metal. Oh he had got one of those plastic things in his ear that stretch the lobe. If ever needed this description can be forwarded to the police I thought. He didn't have a pit bull as dogs weren't allowed in the shop.

While I was waiting for some change to arrive I said to Tommy 'you are very brown,' which was safe conversation – or used to be - and I thought wouldn't antagonise him. He replied with "well, I do gardening 3 days a week, can't do anymore as my back is knackered, and work in here two days as I get to sit down a lot. I have always been a sun lover and now they say it gives you cancer, but I am very stoic.' This next conversation then floored me. He said, 'have you ever read Marcus Aurelius?' I think he said he was in Gladiator. 'It was written two thousand years ago and is very prophetic today,' he went on. 'Also another good read which am reading for the umpteenth time is T.E. Lawrence, Seven Pillars of Wisdom.'

Never judge a book by its cover came to mind. I left feeling very ill educated, clutching my bargain.

Of course I have seen Gladiator but the character in it that I remember was Russell Crowe looking very fit, fighting a tiger, and thinking he was fab. I don't remember a philosopher.

I can remember when we lived in a country area where they were counting the numbers of badgers in view of the TB in cattle and the threat of a possible cull of said badgers. We used to nightly feed the badgers. It was something we got very excited about and of course developed a fondness for them. We had a couple of mothers as well bringing along their young. They seemed very organised and had very good table manners, a certain hierarchy and snuffled around for the scraps we left them. We stopped short of buying special food for them.

Along the way we met a former tree surgeon who had hurt his back and had been drafted in along with a couple of others to count the badgers in an area marked out. We asked how on earth do you do that? He said it is impossible, I look at last years figures and add a bit. Obviously with animals lives at risk, not the answer we wanted to hear. He had been chosen as it was thought he was a bit of an expert in country matters.

It was a lovely time in our lives and we remember the friendly fat badgers with affection.

At the same time we had a visiting cat that used to walk amongst them while they were eating and occasionally have some crumbs himself.

Badgers eyesight is bad, so maybe they thought he was one of them.

Don't know whether it is an age thing or just stupidity but I keep losing my glasses. Just recently they have been down the chair, under the bed and more than likely on top of my head. I am wondering whether to invest in a contraption that finds them, but what is to stop you losing that? It does my head in when you spend half your life looking for something again and again, going into the same space and checking again where you had been two minutes before. G sometimes helps and ends up following on where I have just looked. It is a eureka moment when whatever it is is found, only to be lost again later. NOT going to mention keys and pens. Wonder if they still have Lost and Found at railway stations. Always thought that was a great job. Bet some treasures were handed in. I often wondered what happens to all the stuff not claimed.

On a venture out donning masks, a water pistol and wearing surgical wraps, we tried Costa for a much needed cup of coffee. Told G to meet me at an outside table. I found negotiating the floor 2 metre ruling difficult when you get to corners.

First thing ordered two lattes, then they wanted me to provide phone number. I hadn't got my phone with me and anyway didn't know the number. Then they wanted my home phone number. I haven't got one. By now they were getting fed up with me. I was asked for my e- mail, but bossy-boots girl working the milk frother said that won't do, but eventually agreed on this occasion to take it. I felt very, very stressed, a rash appearing on my neck, sweat on my brow and if they had taken my temperature as a precautionary measure it would have been 104. Think everybody hated me.

The coffee didn't soothe me, as it took an hour of stress re-living the experience. Can't imagine what you have to go through if you want a full English, as I don't know my grandparents' names or where they went to school.

And another thing, since G saw Trump and his security men walking down the corridor with black masks on he has sent off for one which doesn't have the same status when he is wearing shorts a tee shirt and flip flops. I am persisting with paper ones, which I moan about as they keep slipping down.

G actually got personal and so did I. He said 'it's because your nose is a bit podgy.' I said "well your honker isn't exactly small". G said his nose was Romanesque. Is that even a word?

Anyway it isn't exactly Caesaresque, I said.

Touché.

G Says…

I got 'lumbered' with the man in the YMCA charity shop who told Marigold he was a Stoic. Marigold displayed typical low cunning by engaging the man in conversation, encouraging him to ramble on ad nauseum and then abandoning me to his diatribe while she went to study the junk table, 'everything here £1.'*

*If the sign referred to the entire contents of the table, not each individual item, it would still be too much!

The man behind the counter told me he read Meditations by Marcus Aurelius and Seven Pillars of Wisdom, alternately, every day and has done so for years. He used to be in the Army, is normally a gardener but works at the YMCA three days a week as he has a bad back. 'Never without pain'… oh, I know that feeling, Tommy. Maybe I should pay more attention to stoicism.

We did happen across the Stoa Poikile, literally meaning 'painted porch,' while meandering around Athens on a very hot and tiring day. It's not exactly 'fancy,' not even remotely comparable to the Parthenon on top of the hill, but that painted porch is where Zeno, the founder of Stoicism and his followers used to meet up for a chat.

It's still there, 2,500 years later. Every philosophical movement I can think of bears the name of its founder, but it's perhaps unsurprising that the humility so prized by Zeno led to the Stoic Movement adopting the name of the place where they happened to gather together, becoming Stoics, not Zenonians.

Marcus Aurelius didn't last long in Gladiator. He appointed Maximus, Russell Crowe, as his successor, but was murdered by his son, Commodus, shortly after so Richard Harris, playing the part of Marcus Aurelius, could get that heavy armour off and go on his holidays. Or down the pub. Richard Harris was a famous hell-raiser, the tabloids are fond of saying, but we were both bowled over by his son Jared in the recent drama, Chernobyl.

I was slightly distracted while 'chatting,' – by which I mean 'listening' – to the charity shop sage as he told me he'd been an army officer and his name tag said, 'D. Burgess.' I spent much of my 'education' years with a D. Burgess, who was about to leave school to start a career as an army officer when we last spoke. The age group was about right; he looked no more like an 18 year old than I did after so many years and as for the 'D'-

nobody at my school was ever referred to by anything other than surnames so D. Burgess could have been anything from a David to a Dante.

The D. Burgess I first met when we were both aged 12 claimed to be a direct descendant of a famous Japanese poet. The poet in question died in the 12th Century so he wasn't claiming kinship with anyone any of us had ever heard of. Considering he had the distinctly un-Asian name of Burgess I was initially quite sceptical, but when his tiny, enigmatic and very evidently Japanese mother turned up to watch us play rugby I revised my opinion. Why would anyone invent a 12th century Japanese ancestor anyway? Even twelve year old boys have limits on their imagination.

The ancestor in question was Kamo no Chomei and I distinctly remember wondering whether our English Masters (always 'Masters,' wearing full gowns, never just 'teachers') were actually up to the task of instruction as the name meant nothing to them, despite the avid protestations of Burgess. It was only after a pilgrimage to the school Library that we were finally convinced of the existence of Kamo no Chomei.

I hadn't given Burgess or his ancestors much thought in the interim – better make that none whatsoever - but as we walked home I mentioned him to Marigold.

'That man in the shop? He told me he'd been sent to Borstal when he was fifteen and only joined the army at 18 to avoid being sent to prison.'

Oh. I thought it was too much of a coincidence. I changed the subject but when we got home I looked up Kamo no Chomei. He apparently suffered some kind of midlife crisis and became a monk. Even the strict monastic life proved too racy for him and Chomei went to live alone in a tiny hut in the woods. Now that's more like it if you're talking about the solitary life, not this modern day watered down version with Netflix, the Internet and numerous other distractions.

I found an article: a critique of Chomei's memoir of his years living as a hermit. He described the hut in great detail. Not exactly palatial, ten feet square and seven feet high, he took it with him into the woods in sections and erected it himself. Ikea obviously had an offer on flat pack sheds in 12th Century Japan. Finding inner peace in utter simplicity is nothing new and surviving on roots, berries and water from a steam sounds like Bear Gryll's idea of Heaven.

It's a short book full of impressions of nature, pious thoughts on humanity and belief in gentle fellowship amongst all men and he ends it by chiding himself for ever imagining anyone will ever read it and cursing the vanity of writers. That's below the belt, Chomei.

If you're wondering whether my schoolmate Burgess was a chip off the old block and destined to become a rallying point for peaceful coexistence, I very much doubt it. On leaving school he went off to Sandhurst where his bloodthirsty nature would find its spiritual home in combat training.

Due mainly to the wider effects of this pandemic the U.K. National Debt - what we owe as a country - now exceeds Two Trillion Pounds. In the US the debt is over 26 trillion dollars.

Trillions? I can't cope with trillions. One trillion is a thousand billions, or equivalently a million millions.

It is a 1 with 12 zeros after it, that's 1,000,000,000,000.

One trillion seconds adds up to 32,000 years. Gulp! That's a lot of seconds. I need to go and lie down.

Numbers too vast to contemplate have always baffled me. As a young child the number overwhelming my brain was a billion. A trillion was a word that probably didn't even exist at that time. Just as well as the sheer vastness of a billion was far beyond my comprehension.

What makes up a billion of anything anyway? In real terms.

That's the question I desperately wanted to have answered as a young boy.

If a million is a thousand 'thousandths' (as I was always told) applying the logic of an eight year old to the concept I was certain a billion would be incrementally formed by multiplying a million by a million. Not at all. One billion is apparently 'only' a thousand millions. I was therefore convinced as a young lad that it was very hard to become a millionaire, but anyone having reached that stage and wishing to progress to becoming a billionaire had a much easier route to riches. With logic like that it's no wonder I was easily confused by high finance and the mysteries of space and time. I'm not much better even now.

Dermot, our next door neighbour at the time, was a very clever man. He told me so quite often, offering as proof the fact he had been off work from his job on the Liverpool docks 'on the sick with a bad back' for two years and was living the life of Riley. I never discovered who Riley was, but Dermot knew all there was to know about millionaires. It became clear at an early stage he wasn't keen on them.

There weren't many people Dermot was fond of in fairness. The 'can't stand 'em' list was very long and included every member of his family he'd ever met and quite a few other relatives he was unlikely ever to come across plus every other person in the street. He muttered imprecations at every person rash enough to walk past his door and had never even spoken to my (admittedly pretty scary) grandmother despite having lived next door to her almost all his life. I liked Dermot.

He explained the idea of scale to me one day using a woodlouse as a teaching aid.

'See this feller here,' he said, pointing to a woodlouse, one of several that had appeared from the gaps under the skirting board and prodding it with his finger. 'Here, hold it in your hand.' He picked up the woodlouse, risking his bad back in the interests of imparting wisdom and handed it over.

'That weighs next to nothing, right?'

I nodded.

'Just imagine a million of them. They'd weigh loads. A billion of them would weigh heavier than this house. That's how big a billion is.'

I told you Dermot was clever. I tried to explain the concept to my mother later, but she hadn't Dermot's brain power and was far more concerned about me removing the woodlouse from her kitchen and going to wash my hands. Even though I'd already washed them before breakfast and twice the previous day.

I haven't bothered to check the accuracy of Dermot's calculations until now and I found absolutely no reference point for the humble woodlouse as a unit of measurement. Best I could find was an ant. I know, I know, it's illogical, but an ant will have to suffice.

Apparently, eminent scientists and mathematicians all agree a million ants would weigh a little over 6 pounds. Dermot said a million woodlice* would weigh 'loads.'

(* how tempting to write 'woodlouses' as I undoubtedly would have said at age eight.)

Dermot said 'loads' and those modern scientists had said six pounds, but they'd used ants. About the same then. One billion ants, however, would weigh well over 3 tons. Has anyone ever checked this? Are we being hoodwinked? Are any ants harmed in the course of these experiments? Who collects them? Who counts them? I shan't sleep until I have a definitive answer to these questions.

Dopamine, can you get it from Amazon? I keep hearing about this mysterious chemical reaction spontaneously occurring in our brain whenever we do or experience something we find pleasurable. This enticing reaction is apparently not responsible for pleasure as such, but occurs as reaction to our cravings, basic urges and desires. This reward system goes back a long way. I wasn't surprised to find the two most basic triggers for 'reward' are food and sex. Two essentials for life itself ever since the cave man era. Sex addicts would have thrived in prehistoric times, doing their bit to keep the population up in dangerous times, while another addiction that's frowned upon now, addiction to food, would have been pretty useful a few thousand years ago when a gargantuan appetite would help make you the biggest, strongest person in the tribe.

Yes, I do appreciate I'm stretching a point in referencing atavistic behaviour in relation to our modern lives. So, dopamine is a good thing.

Oh, hang on, what's this now? The latest craze out of California – where else – is for dopamine detox. It seems these killjoys want to identify everything in our lives that give us pleasure and remove them. No more television, social media, cell phones, music, shopping for anything other than essentials, no more coffee, alcohol, fast food and, obviously, don't even think of having a sex life.

If we're to eschew pleasure, what's the alternative? Yoga is recommended. Meditation, thinking pure thoughts, okay that's five minutes accounted for. Can I read? Well, of course I can if I avoid any reading material that may be considered escapist so a maths text book will be fine.

I can at least eat food, but only if I derive no pleasure from the act of refuelling. The suggestion is to munch on a raw carrot, focussing on tastes and textures while being grateful for the availability of food in its natural form. Do all these things and you may discover a life free from mindless pleasure and addictive behaviour. People actually sign up for this putative depuration?

From choice? It's slightly reminiscent of the Transcendental Meditation movement espoused by the Beatles, but without the drugs. It won't catch on in our house.

Just as we're at the dipping a toe in the water stage of coming out of lockdown, there's widespread alarm at an impending second wave and localised restrictions are back in fashion. Marigold and I are refusing all offers to attend rave parties – no change there – but we have been out and about to a certain degree in recent weeks.

My former walking route, basically up and down the garden path, has now been extended to the wider world. We try to walk an early morning mile through a variety of virtually uninhabited streets, crossing the road whenever another pedestrian approaches within a hundred yards of us.

We're now expert 'distance greeters,' waving a cheery goodbye morning from the opposite pavements to the few people we meet. Occasionally we wander through the village shopping area, but usually at an hour when most people are still tucked up in bed. This is more likely to be populated, albeit not exactly thronged, but allows Marigold the opportunity to hear people other than myself speaking.

If we give any credence to the proposition that all life on Earth evolved billions of years ago from some mysterious primordial soup then whatever crawled, slithered or oozed onto land in Prehistoric times surely bears scant resemblance to the animals, fish, insects and reptiles we see about us in the 21st Century.

Distant ancestors of the group we saw exchanging unmasked air, fierce debate and occasional bonhomie outside the 'just about to open up' fishmongers had surely never slithered. Undoubtedly there would have been a Limo awaiting their arrival on that prehistoric shore.

Three couples, the men each wearing florid trousers, two bright red and the other an especially vivid shade of peach together with sweaters draped across the shoulders but not actually being worn. Their ladies, yes they must be classified as such, had identical shrieking laughs and appeared impervious to the inconvenience they were causing to the mere mortals patiently attempting to form a socially distanced queue outside the shop.

Parked alongside were two highly polished Bentley convertibles, one with the rear window festooned with stickers imploring us all to Save the Planet. A man with a more caustic nature than myself (!) may have pondered on whether a 'gas-guzzling' Bentley was an appropriate place to claim one's green credentials.

We walked past, tutting of course, but Marigold made an instant decision to adopt the walking speed of an arthritic tortoise when she realised the three men were not just ignoring their shrieking wives, but actually having what that class of person probably doesn't ever call a stand up row. All very mannered but there was venom enough simmering just beneath the surface.

'Correlation isn't necessarily causation,' one of the males bellowed.

'Aha,' I thought, 'just posh boys going on about pandemics. Same old stuff we hear all the time lately.'

As we lurked nearby one of the group looked about and decided I would make a good witness for the prosecution.

'Ask this chap what he thinks,' he called out.

'No, don't,' I thought, but in vain.

'What's your view on this mask wearing nonsense?' The irate Bentley owner asked, the tone of his question paying scant regard to the easily observed fact that Marigold and I were both masked. #

Marigold is convinced I prefer wearing a mask as it (normally) discourages unwanted conversation and allows greater leeway in acceptable facial grooming. Yes, my Covid era beard needs tidying up, but with a mask in place, who would know?

I muttered a reply of sorts, aiming for an unintelligible and completely unrelated mumble in order to be disregarded. All three men nodded sagely; either they're all pretty dim, I thought, or I was actually talking sense. I decided it was the former.

One of the men, the colour blind one in peach trousers, said, 'See, told you,' to his companions.

'Are you sure you've got speech recognition turned on?' retorted the one with an alarming comb-over. 'Cloth ears, that's your trouble.'

We walked on as they returned to their argument. That speech recognition comment was pretty much to the point, I thought. Adding 'cloth ears' was tautology though, plain and simple.*

*I can invariably be relied upon to think of the words and phrases I wish I'd employed at the time, but only five minutes too late. So often these days, sadly, they're buried amidst the other dross infesting what's left of my mind.

We carried on and found ourselves jinking and sidestepping our way through a group of dawdling window shoppers in the High Street. It was 07.30 so the shops weren't open and we'd expected to have the pavements to ourselves. The sunshine had obviously persuaded a few others to struggle out of bed.

How selfish. This is our early morning walking route, not yours.

Avoidance of unmasked and potentially infected humans is a skill we have developed over the past few months. We cross roads, repeatedly, duck into alleys, lurk in shop doorways until the danger has passed. We have gained the wariness and keen sense of impending threat of a meerkat.

One of the browsers was saying to another, 'I got shut of the lot of 'em. In one vile swoop.'

Well, that's an interesting variation, I thought. The subject matter remained unclear. What had been 'got shut of?' It could have been old shoes, unwanted presents or even annoying relatives, but the 'vile swoop' comment stuck in my mind.

I once uttered the original phrase 'at one fell swoop' in public when playing the role of MacDuff in a legendary* production of The Scottish Play.** Macbeth and Mrs Macbeth get all the best lines in the Scottish Play, but Macduff wasn't a bad part for someone whose only previous stage experience was in pantomimes I'd written.

My performances provided ample evidence of how becoming an actor was a most unlikely prospect as a career possibility.

'All my pretty ones? Did you say all? O hell-kite! All? What, all my pretty chickens and their dam at one fell swoop?'

*Legendary in the sense of being spectacularly bad.

**The Scottish Play. It's considered unlucky to use the actual name of Shakespeare's masterpiece after bad luck and a series of accidents accompanied the early performances and continued to do so. The Bard is said to have diligently researched ingredients of spells for his 'weird sisters' and did the job so well that 'real' witches placed a curse on the play in retribution.

Yes, the bizarre ingredients in the 'double, double, toil and trouble; fire burn and cauldron bubble' passage were supposedly taken from genuine spells. I can remember 'fillet of a denny snake, in the caldron boil and bake; eye of newt and toe of frog, wool of bat and tongue of dog,' but there were lots more. Imagine how difficult it must have been for the three witches – the black and midnight hags - to source their ingredients back in 1606 when the likes of Amazon, Ebay, Waitrose and Deliveroo were unknown concepts.

We Shall Overcome.

Marigold Says...
We desperately needed a spare key for the front door as I had lost mine, which I haven't owned up to. Went to the nearest local key cutter. Key man was standing outside having a fag and then assured me the one he got off the rack would fit.
Well it didn't, so back we go.
Key man said "I didn't think it would but worth a try! I will take a photo and order one. Ring me in a couple of days."
When I rang him he reckoned he didn't know what I was on about but to call in anyway.
Went AGAIN, he was sitting in the window in full motorbike gear reading VIZ and guffawing. I said 'are you working, or just going out?'
Key Man said "I was just off for a McDonalds".
It was 09.15.
He found the key which fortunately and miraculously looks like it will do the job. He is obviously such a workaholic he should get an award.
Not.
He also said "I am not very busy because of Covid, as nobody is going out". Think he is not very busy as he is totally incompetent. On the back of his leather jacket it said "Bikers do it really fast".
Yuk. In future I will go to Timpsons.
We got home, tried the key, it didn't work. Of course it didn't. I rang up and ordered yet another. It wasn't easy as he'd got Meatloaf blasting out in the background.
'Be ready Thursday,' he said. I think. We went back on Thursday and Mister Key Cutter was now wearing a motorbike helmet, with the visor down and a full set of motorbike leathers. I asked if the key I'd ordered was ready yet.
'Eh?' He pulled his visor up so he could hear me as I repeated the question.
'No idea, love, I've not looked at the post yet, just got back from the kebab shop.' Changed over from McDonalds then. He obviously supports all local businesses.
He took off his jacket but left the helmet on. 'Best idea ever, this. Can't be doing with wearing a mask, hurts my ears. I was supposed to have a plastic screen fitted to protect me from customers who aren't wearing masks, but already got this helmet and it's a lot cheaper.'

We got home and the key works now. I think I've lost it already, but am saying nothing. It will turn up.

For four days we have had scaffolders on the roof over the road in wet, windy and cold conditions. Two of them are wearing shorts and tee shirts, and the only thing to keep them warm is their tattoo ink and what is obviously a very vulgar sense of humour. Wish I could hear, but judging by the hand gestures probably better I can't.

G Says...

I was reading a Sherlock Holmes story, seeking comfort in familiar surroundings, and as I read a passage where Watson, in his usual pompous manner, declares, 'London is that great cesspool into which all the loungers and idlers of the Empire are irresistibly drained,' I glanced up at the television news – yes, I can multi task – and saw His Worship the Lord Mayor Sadiq Khan's face filling the screen. He was having a right old moan.

No change there then. It seems doom and gloom are the buzz words dominating everyone's life just lately.

'Will Christmas be cancelled? What do you think?' Our neighbour, one of those resolutely 'glass nearly empty or as near as damn it' characters, bellowed the enquiry as I was braving a trip out to the rubbish bin. Why ask me, I wondered. What difference will my thoughts have on events?

We all want to know, from a specific vantage point in the present, that things will be okay later on. Be better, in fact. But we can never know for sure. This is why it's erroneous to say we live now in especially uncertain times. The future is always uncertain; it always has been, it's just that we're currently very aware of it. As the ancient Greek and Roman Stoics used to emphasise, much of our suffering arises from attempting to control what is not in our control anyway and never can be. No amount of worrying or fretting can alter that.

We have a rather famous neighbour. Well, that's not strictly true, but one of the local residents looks exactly like Brian Blessed, he even has the booming voice which is pretty handy in the social distancing era. Everyone calls him Brian, although his name is actually Ken, so it's not just us who see the uncanny resemblance. Charlie Chaplin once secretly entered a 'Chaplin look-alike' contest – what Marigold calls a lookie-likie- and only came third, so if Brian Blessed moves to this area he can expect a few problems.

Brian was out, sweeping up leaves, when I went outside and from thirty yards away decided we should have a chat. I deflected his enquiry as to whether Christmas will be cancelled with one of my very best Gallic shrugs – the gestures have outlasted much of the vocabulary from our decade in France – and fell back on traditional fare, the weather.

'Bit nippy this morning.' He pondered a reply for quite some time. I was almost anticipating a reference to a period spent under canvas in Murmansk with polar bears rooting in the bins or the risk of frostbitten genitals on Everest ascents, but he was merely gathering his thoughts for something impressive.

'After Covid, we'll get another ice age,' he called out. 'Mark my words, it'll be like the Plasticine Age before long.' I moved on, trying to keep a straight face. The Pleistocene Epoch ended thousands of years ago and did indeed mark the last great Ice Age, but I've seen no obvious signs predicting an imminent reoccurrence. I have to say though, I do like the idea of a Plasticine Age.

We were going shopping, a rare occurrence, fraught with dangers. I'm getting close to regarding other people as The Walking Dead: infected, dangerous and hugely threatening so to actually be out in their midst is terrifying. Okay, I may be slightly exaggerating.

Marigold needs supplies and I'm sure she would only announce this if the situation was not at a critical point. Waitrose has wide aisles and shoppers in there are guaranteed to wear stylish face coverings, but Marigold announced, to my horror, 'Lidl will probably do and it's closer.'

Lidl, or indeed Aldi as my prejudices are evenly balanced, is not my favourite shopping experience. The last time I was in LIDL I wondered if I had somehow entered some form of alternative universe in which there had been different victors of the Second World War as most of the chocolate, jams, breakfast cereals and sundry other items bore Germanic names.

Everywhere we went in Germany the locals pronounced it Lee-Dell, while most of us ignorant Brits call it Lidd-Uhl or something very similar. Around 90 per cent of the products at Lidl are own-label brands specifically made for the company.That means Lidl can control manufacturing costs and cut out supply costs, so it can charge less and still make more profit than it does on big-name brands. Interestingly, the biggest surge in sales came from a gradual increase of the 'ten per cent,' those recognisable brands that customers actually recognise and trust. Aldi and Lidl have as few as 1,500 – at most 2,000 different products, while the 'big' chains such as Tesco and Sainsbury's have as much as 30,000, even 40,000 different 'things' on the shelves.

We walked in and stopped within ten paces. Social distancing? No sign of it in here. We did a swift about turn and went elsewhere.

Our trip out was an (apparent) urgent need for new saucepans. We were in town at just past 08.00 to play it safe. Wilkinson's were just opening up, we were the only people in the place apart from a single teenage girl on the only staffed checkout who appeared to be still asleep.

Saucepans mission accomplished we went to pay, waving our sliver of magic plastic at the credit card terminal and hoping it was recognised. I've no idea why the seeing the word 'approved' flash up on the screen brings me pleasure verging on joy, but it does. The girl on the till, now awake although certainly not 'wide awake' pushed our clanking pans back towards us and said, 'bet you're glad you didn't pick the set on offer, they're rubbish.' We hadn't actually noticed them or they would have gone straight into the trolley.

On the way out we saw a customer furiously banging the top of the hand sanitiser dispenser with his clenched fist. A sign next to it said quite clearly, 'foot pedal operated sanitiser.'

A barbers shop was just opening up next door. The (hand written) sign in the window said, 'One at a time, please, I'm clipping as fast as I can.' I like the sound of him. Not enough to tempt me inside though.

I've given up on looking smart. I don't even attempt 'tidy' lately. Marigold said recently I'm looking like a dilapidated building, just before demolition. 'Shabby chic,' it's my new look. From a quick glance at other (male) shoppers out and about, it's catching on.

The masculine 'look du jour' of 2020 is that of stressed out, weary ragamuffins. The serried ranks of newly minted Tatterdemalions of Britain are everywhere, a growing force in the land.

My hair has never responded well to instruction. It's no better now I have far less of it. I am reduced to two styles: the convict or the hostage. The convict, my usual 'look' in lockdown, is easy – clippers set to number one, basic sheep sheering. Alternatively, I let it grow unchecked and seemingly untouched for a few months. The result is more Charles Manson than Beau Brummel.

We were treated to a magnificent display of nacreous (or iridescent, as they are also called) clouds as we toddled back from our early morning excursion. Makes a change from the dark stuff containing yet more rain. I pointed them out to Marigold who seemed less than impressed. Maybe nature's wonders are best appreciated a little later in the day.

One of our friends lives in an area where Covid-19 is steeply rising and has voluntarily entered a recent drastic version of mostly self imposed lockdown. He's okay about being restricted as it allows a bit of breathing space from a massive row with a neighbour that's been ongoing for months. His hope now is that nobody tells the neighbour when the lockdown is eventually lifted as he's enjoying a rest from endless weeks' relentless strife conducted over the garden fence.

He attended the same school as me, he's a year older, but lived nearby and we both had three 'bus journeys each way every day so we got to know each other pretty well.

I remember the Headmaster singling him out on one occasion, in front of the entire school, saying 'you are without doubt the cleverest boy of your age in all England.' We were pretty astonished at the stratospheric nature of this rare praise, but after allowing an interval of at least ten seconds the Headmaster added, 'it's unfortunate that this is only your opinion and bears no relation whatsoever to the facts. On the contrary, you set yourself lamentably low standards of achievement and yet consistently fail to achieve them.'

Public humiliation of that ilk sticks in the mind. I certainly remember it, the gist of it anyway if not word for word.

As he reads this blog, I won't embarrass my friend by naming him - let's call him Ringo, it's actually his dog's name - but if I asked ten thousand random people in the North West of England who was the most awkward, cantankerous and argumentative person they'd ever met several hundred of them would utter his name.

Of course we get on very well with just the occasional difficult incident - only on every single occasion we meet and we rarely come to blows!

He knows when he's outmatched.

I've learnt over the years not to take any of his absolute statements of fact at face value as there's often very little empirical evidence to support them. He seems to subsist entirely on Guinness. It's only on very rare occasions he's seen eating anything that could be regarded, even loosely, as food. It's Guinness all the way.

'Food and drink in harmony,' he'd announce, knocking the top off a bottle of porter on the edge of the table. 'There's all the nourishment the body needs in every swallow. Plus, no need to wash up after a meal, just chuck the empties in the bin.' I've known him for many years and have yet to notice any deleterious effects on his health. Memo to self, order a crate of Guinness for the weekend.

Chocolate Digestives, fairly prosaic items, were the latest cause for diversion of views. 'Of course, the chocolate forms the base, not the topping,' Ringo pronounced as he handed out his customary ration, two for him, one for me.

I've devoured a great many chocolate digestive biscuits, a digestive biscuit with a chocolate topping, so was only too ready to take issue with his spurious claim that the chocolate formed the base of the biscuit.

To my horror, I read recently a press release by McVities stating with unassailable veracity that the chocolate on a McVities digestive is administered by a reservoir of chocolate, meaning that the chocolate side is the bottom of the biscuit, rather than the top. The same applies to Jaffa Cakes, also made by McVities, which is even more bizarre.

I fully intended to ring up Ringo and apologise and beg his forgiveness for ever doubting him, but for some reason it slipped my mind. Will this do, mate?

Digestive biscuits, the bog standard variety not the chocolate ones, have been around for a long time and were once heavily promoted as a health product. The idea was that the bicarbonate of soda used in the biscuit acted as an antacid and aided the digestive process, hence the name.

In 1836, Buss's Digestive Biscuits declared that they contained 'the greatest amount of farinaceous nutriment that can possibly be concentrated into a biscuit.' *'Farinaceous' simply means they contain a lot of starch, as do bread, potatoes and many other elements of our diet that we rarely hear being singled out as being beneficial to a healthy lifestyle.

Advertising has never paid much attention to actual facts when extolling the virtues of products and digestive biscuits have a dubious track record in this industry. J. Hutchinson, 'the original introducer and sole proprietor of Abernethy's celebrated Digestive Biscuits' proudly informed the biscuit buying public, 'these biscuits, when taken regularly by families, have the good property of keeping the body in a regular state, and in a great measure supersedes the necessity of having recourse to medicine.' My underperforming heart notwithstanding, no wonder I feel so fit.

Not that good health is always a blessing. Edvard Munch would never have painted his masterpiece, The Scream, if he'd been a well man. 'Without anxiety and illness I should have been like a ship without a rudder,' he said. I can only assume Edvard didn't care for the taste of Guinness.

'Others have seen what is and asked why. I have seen what could be and asked why not.' — Pablo Picasso

I'm usually reprimanded on arrival for failing to give due respect to Ringo's title. He's a baron, yes I have friends in the higher echelons of society, yet I invariably fail to refer to his ennoblement in a sufficiently impressive fashion. His title of Baron gets mentioned a lot, but not by me. It's the sine qua non of just about every conversation.

That highfaluting title, bestowed by a Monarch no less, is rather less impressive than it sounds. One of the many oddball acquaintances who have crossed paths with Ringo was a magnificently eccentric man named Roy Bates who discovered a rusting World War Two fort off the coast of Harwich, Essex in 1967 and unilaterally decided to take possession of it. Together with his wife Joan, Roy Bates declared his new home independent from the UK and became Prince Roy and Princess Joan, rulers of Sealand. They produced coins, stamps and passports, and the sovereign nation of Sealand was represented in the World Egg-Throwing Championships.

Sealand was in fact a former Maunsell naval fort, put in place in 1942 at a cost of £40,000 (which would be in excess of £2 million today), one of a series stretching from Clacton in Essex to Margate in Kent. I've come across a few of these forts, but only one had claimed independent nation status. Originally manned by 120 soldiers and fitted with Vickers anti-aircraft guns, the Maunsell forts protected the Thames Estuary from German bombers and were abandoned by the military in 1958.

Sealand, formerly known as Roughs Tower, was, crucially, outside British territorial waters. In those far off days when Radio 1 was unheard of it was fashionable to set up 'pirate' radio stations outside the reach of British laws beaming pop music to a deprived 'Yoof' audience. The best known was Radio Caroline, but there were several others and Roy Bates was not one to miss out. It wasn't luxurious; the 'facilities' consisted of a hole in the deck with a toilet seat on top of it and if a kettle was switched on, the record turntables slowed down.

Roy Bates died in 2012, aged 91, Sealand is now ruled by Roy's son, Prince Michael, who awarded the Sealand Peace Prize to Nelson Mandela and Sealand 'noble titles' to various people such as Terry Wogan, Ed Sheeran, Jeremy Clarkson and Ben Fogle, who are barons.

These notables would suggest Ringo, better make that Baron Ringo, is in good company, but alas for £199.99 anyone can become a Count or Countess and a mere Knighthood costs only £99.99.

If there's still no sign of a gong heading my way in the next New Year's Honours List I may yet have to lash out £199.99, if only to compete with Baron Ringo. Marigold has as yet expressed no interest at all in becoming a Lady.

A Covid Christmas.

Marigold Says... Happy Christmas.

G said, "whatever next, ginger is in short supply, so that will affect ginger biscuits. Put an extra six packets down on the order, we must stockpile". We have been rating them from our various sources, now sit down whilst you read this, M and S cheapo ones were the worst, sugary, little and not cheap. We actually now like Asda's own brand. They passed the dunk test. Asda are still the only supermarket who will deliver to us, interspersed with Waitrose when they can be bothered. It is like having a delivery from Harrods. I must say I have detected looks of "more money than sense" when the Waitrose van sedately drives up. Asda screech round the corner and are very rushed and gone within seconds of throwing the food on the mat but have been brilliant.

G is squirrelling the ginger biscuits away in his socks drawer along with mixed nuts and raisins. He thinks I don't know but the drawer is starting to sag, and there are crumbs on the carpet.

We bought our Xmas turkey crown ages ago as it would be one less thing to worry about. It is a frozen lump with a sell by date well into 2021. When I read about all of these glorious fancy breeds of this and that for sale, I was left wondering where my boxed one has come from. I covered it in herbs and bacon and gave it a nice send off in the oven as it might have had a chequered and unhappy life.

Had a huge Xmas card. Opened it and it had a Round Robin thing inside from Frank and Ann. Never heard of Frank and Ann. Had a look at the envelope and it wasn't for us, but was sent to our address. It had come from America. Anyway, read the Round Robin. Frank has had two teeth implants, a knee operation and some new glasses. He then went on and on in great detail about his new car, then the children and grandchildren, 6 of them, we were up to page 3 by now and I was losing the will to live. Finally on the last page he mentioned Ann who has got a lump on her nose and is having it removed. The lump, not her nose. I think. I have saved the real recipients a lot of boring reading matter. Gave it back to the postie who has never heard of them either. They will never know what they have missed.

We haven't sent any cards, mainly as I couldn't be bothered. We knew somebody years ago who used to get over 300. How stressful is that, as they will always get late ones and not be able to send them one back? The worry of it all.

Positives and negatives from this year. Mostly positives. Savings on clothes. I have probably worn a change of three clothes, because of not going anywhere choice went out the window. Same with G. I could tell him at a great distance because of colour combinations.

Every time we had messages they were always interspersed with "we were socially distanced of course". As they are not in my vicinity why do they need to tell me? I feel like writing, "we met, hugged and snogged, then sat on each other's knees whilst blowing in each other's ears."

We have become very good at avoiding corners on roads in case people are coming at us, and walking in the gutter avoiding traffic when head on collision with people is ensuing. We have been tooted by cars a few times but ignore the miserable gits. We will keep clear of the virus but end up being run over by a bus.

Have not taken up jigsaws, chess, Mar Jong, or anything at all fitness related. Was going to study a language but the library is closed and online learning just looks too complicated. Another blessing.

Oh and my cooking remains a choice of 5 recipes, using the excuse of not being able to get ingredients for anything more industrious. Funny when you can't get something, you crave it. Like chestnuts. Never bought them before but am sure our Xmas failed because of lack of them. We didn't get any wrapping paper so G used kitchen roll for my presents. Some of it looked second hand. I said I didn't want anything for Christmas and my lip started to quiver when nothing was produced, but G knows me very well and produced some great presents.

G Says...

***C'est Noël. Laissez les bon temps rouler* – It's Christmas. Let the good times roll.**

We aren't going out much, apart from a swift scamper around the block, avoiding all human life forms, when the sun comes out. Not that it's a problem as we can and do manage very well on our own. Occasional supermarket deliveries produce unbridled excitement and even checking to see if there's been any post can be a highlight. I got a card through the door from a courier service saying they were sorry they had missed me – I had been indoors and available, non stop, for at least a week at that time – but assuring me my parcel had been left in my 'safe place.' What a good system. Apart from my not expecting a parcel and, crucially, having not the faintest idea where my 'safe place' could be found.

I never did discover it, or the parcel. One day there will be a televised documentary on 'great mysteries of the Covid – 19 era' and I can expect to be asked to add my contribution.

Christmas. We have no tree, no decorations and made minimal preparations this year. Not unlike last year, actually, but for many people the restrictions on Christmas festivities have been hard. Those turkeys bought to feed a multitude on one day. will now last until Easter. I'd be okay with that, I like turkey, hot or cold, in any form.

As a complete contrast to the traditional gluttony of Christmas Day, I recently read a published rebuttal by a Soviet Labour camp doctor in the Stalin era to claims the wretched miscreants in his charge were undergoing unnecessary suffering. Here's what the doctor printed out as a flyer to be handed to each new arrival.

'You are not brought here to live but to suffer and die... If you live, it means that you are guilty of one of two things: either you worked less than was assigned you or you ate more than was your proper due.'

That's a pretty robust response.

Christmas is for kids; people keep saying this. In every other year it's also about eating too much, drinking (far) too much and spending all the money you can lay your hands on in an orgy of present buying and bonhomie. Well, there was a sea change this year. My parents would have approved.

In my childhood Christmas was first and foremost a religious festival. Exchanging presents was conducted at a (very) minor level, church attendance and listening to the Queen dominated Christmas Day, but even in such a joyless setting as my Grandmother's house in Liverpool my sister and I still managed to scour a modicum of enjoyment out of Christmas.

In the earliest years I can remember food rationing was still in force, which put enormous limitations on any (non-existent) plans for feasting and jollification. As the situation eased, I recall actually looking forward to the day itself. Not only would there be food of a nature and content available on no other day, but there would be guests for dinner. Not friends as I can't ever recall anyone my parents regarded as friends, but relatives. Two sets of uncles, aunts and cousins. All crammed into a two up, two down terraced house.

There were drawbacks of course. Nothing in life comes without cost and Christmas Day was no exception. On our return from church my sister and myself were often dragooned into performing the more menial chores such a gathering required. I had to chop wood for the fire, bring in coal for the kitchen range and see to the removal of spiders' webs, dust and anything else that had attached itself to the spare seating, a motley assortment of creaking chairs, stools and anything else I could find in the Anderson Shelter suitable for use as seating. One year myself and two cousins sat on upturned tea chests thrown out by a neighbour.

The round dining table was too small so it was augmented by the (oblong) table dragged in from the kitchen to be set alongside its more refined companion. The notable difference in height between the two was less of an inconvenience than the far more obvious threat of the ancient, wobbly, uneven dining table being at permanent risk of collapse.

Things got worse as the years passed. From the age of eleven and for at least the next three years I was required to sing two Christmas carols, standing on a chair in front of my ill assorted relatives to demonstrate the value of the superior education offered by the 'posh' school which I had the audacity to attend. Intelligence was regarded by my grandmother as an excuse for avoiding hard work and mixing with my 'betters' would only bring shame on the family.

Surprisingly, Silent Night always went down well. Sung in the original German version, *Stille Nacht*. I looked up the actual words, in the interests of accuracy. They were considerably easier to sing than if I had been asked to read them out loud.

Stille Nacht, heilige Nacht,
Alles schläft; einsam wacht
Nur das traute hochheilige Paar.
Holder Knabe im lockigen Haar,
Schlaf in himmlischer Ruh!
Schlaf in himmlischer Ruh!

Being the only person present who knew the words of the German version was a huge advantage. Phonetic recitals are not always entirely accurate, but nobody ever raised this issue.

The only other Christmas carol in my repertoire was O Come all ye Faithful, this time rendered in Latin.

Adeste fideles laeti triumphantes,

Venite, venite in Bethlehem.
Natum videte Regem angelorum.
Venite adoremus Dominum.
And so on...

I should stress there was absolutely no intention on my part to 'show off.' The urge to impress others had yet to join the rest of my lamentably bad qualities. These performances weren't voluntary, they were as much a requirement as part of the Christmas entertainment as the annual squabbles over board games.

These games made an appearance every Christmas, without fail, but I never recall seeing them at any other time. The Beetle game, Ludo and Mister Potato Head appeared from the depths of a drawer and caused friction almost immediately. One year Uncle Joe brought along a pair of rickety nets and we took it in turns to play Blow Football with a ping pong ball and a drinking straw on the sloping and uneven table. It was a fiasco, but that made it all the more enjoyable in my opinion.

Christmas Day was very different from any other, but some aspects never changed. Alcohol, of course, was banned, the horror of my Aunty Sally once inadvertently consuming a trifle laced with sherry at a Womens' Institute meeting was recounted every year. Uncle Joe liked 'the odd pint of ale' as he often remarked, but the house rules on temperance were set in stone.

Was the vast effort involved in preparing and serving a Christmas meal ever praised? Never. Did 'my' multilingual contribution to the post lunch 'festivities' ever receive a single handclap or nod of appreciation? Absolutely not. My resolutely dyspeptic grandmother usually said something along the lines of, 'that boy can't sing no matter what fancy language he uses' and the adults returned to discussing the unsuitability of hats worn by various women in the church congregation, the long obligatory walk to church, usually in the rain, having been the first and most irreplaceable part of Christmas Day.

Two Little Pricks. Covid Vaccination Day.

Marigold Says...

G got an appointment for his Covid jab as he is so old and withered. He only needs to keep breathing for another 33 years to become Britain's oldest man. He told me he's doing his best. When he got the news about the vaccine I told him they give it you in your backside as you drive through the car park with the car window open. Noticed he had a shower and put new pants on.

Arrived at the centre at allotted time. There was a woman who had collapsed outside and was sitting on a chair, being fanned with a clipboard by a worried looking volunteer. She was nothing to do with the jabbing experience, she was just waiting for her sister.

We joined a queue of five, one of which was a bloke of about 35, not decrepit like everybody else. He was wearing shorts, tee shirt, and doc martens. Of course it was all to do with showing off his tattoos, but did we really need to know the names of what were presumably his kids. Or a pack of beagles for all I know as there were some odd names included. As it was one degree out in the car park couldn't quite understand it. G said the bloke might come under the vulnerable category by now as he must be suffering from hypothermia. It turned out he had come to the wrong entrance as he wanted to collect his mother's prescription.

Said to G as it is only you getting the jab, don't speak and I will act as if I am your carer. As we got in I said to the desk volunteer, Amy, can I have mine as well, as we have had to come by taxi and obviously it is very expensive and we don't want to have to book another taxi when it's my turn. No problem she said. I was a bit miffed as she didn't say, 'it's only for the over 70s,' even though I do qualify I don't feel like it and G always says there must have been a mix up somewhere as I act like a five year old much of the time.

That's a bit much. He said I was immature last week. I said, 'if that's your attitude you can get out of my den and take your Dinky Toys with you.' Anyway, Amy asked a very jolly woman named Marjorie, rather bossily I thought, to go and get her a spousal form. Marjorie said to her, 'In a minute, Amy, better let me take your coffee order first.'

Obviously that was far more important. After much thought, Amy ordered a milky coffee with two sugars and a mint club. I could feel the virus taking hold with all those disease carrying people standing around while I waited for Amy to sort out her refreshments. Nobody asked if I would like a milky coffee and a Club biscuit.

Joined G at the sitting point opposite the toilets which had a sign saying "Toilets regularly cleaned". After seeing who came out I felt very grateful. I told G he could look normal now as he had been practising a vacant look. We had our jabs and then you have to wait 15 minutes to see if you collapse or start speaking in Swahili.

Drove off after we were released and unfortunately Amy who we'd told about arriving in a taxi was having a fag outside. She waved. Well for all she knew G could have been a taxi driver or suddenly recovered his faculties.

I read the list of possible side effects on the way back and felt quite ill. Apparently some people keep smelling burnt toast. G said "we have obviously had it already as that's all the house smells of until noon." If you are suffering from burnt toast syndrome, does that mean if you burn the toast it smells of something else, maybe polo mints? I find it all very confusing.

The leaflet didn't mention ravenous hunger. Cooked and ate bacon butties on return, followed by too many hobnobs. Then had a kip, after what in these times can only be classed as an exhausting experience. That's it for outings now until the next jab.

G Says…

Exciting times. I am awash with letters from the NHS just lately. Today's missive contained a 'poo kit.' My cup run over. Following the instructions, took ages to locate the version written in English, I obtained a very fine sample of my poo by scraping a plastic stick across a carefully collected section of the 'product' – the three cardboard strips system is no more – and posted it off to the offices of the Nasty Medical Conditions Affecting the Bowel Pie Company in Rugby for examination. What rewarding jobs some people have. The attached leaflet explained they only required a 'scrape' and specifically asked the donor to refrain from adding 'extra.' The envelope is quite large so I assume some people have been filling it to capacity in a misguided desire to please. Less is more when it comes to the examination of poo. Understandably.

Another missive in the post recently from my newest best friend Matt Hancock. We are mates by now so he just signs his many letters 'Matt,' and he is going to send me some Vitamin D tablets. He intimated he would send me a life time supply, but when they arrived in our post box there were only 120, enough for four months. I think I need to request a look at my medical records. Four months? Rather worrying. What does Matt know that I don't?

We went for a Covid vaccination, supposedly just for me but Marigold, whose invitation hasn't yet arrived and who hates missing out, managed to wangle a jab for herself as well. Awkward start to the day as the car windscreen was a sheet of ice, but we're used to minor setbacks and had added fifteen minutes to our trip to cover unexpected snags. Isn't driving a car strange? It seems so unnatural after all this time. I'm not sure the car appreciated being so rudely awakened early on a bitterly cold morning after a lie in of so many weeks.

We found the health centre, not one we'd been to previously and the car park was full, even at 08.30 am. I managed to squeeze in at the end and we made short work of the trip across the car park to the vaccinations entrance. Bare arms and short sleeved shirts make vaccinations easy, but don't do much to repel arctic temperatures.

The woman sitting behind the reception desk was wearing what I took to be one of those 'designer' fashion masks until I noticed the fancy script on it it said Mecca Bingo.

We were called into a room for the jab, we went in together, and there was a skeleton in the corner dressed as Elvis. Pretty good, actually. The doctor looked as if he had got out of bed about five minutes ago, was wearing clothes even I would think twice about wearing in public and had a photo of himself and his family on the desk. Five kids, no wonder he looked a bit rough first thing on Sunday morning.

Marigold drew my attention to the photo as the doctor went to find a relatively new needle for his syringe. The wife looked harassed and had a remarkably retroussé nose. That's a French word meaning tucked up used to describe a nose that turns up at the end. We usually call it a 'pig's nose', if we don't like the 'owner', which isn't quite as polite. Maybe some people look better when wearing masks. I'm sure I do.

Is it just me or do television news programmes only focus on misery these days? Evening news is where they begin with 'Good evening' and then proceed to tell you why it isn't anything of the sort and we're all doomed. Nobody on Sky or the BBC has blamed me or Marigold for any of the nation's woes so far, but I haven't checked Channel 4.

I usually lose interest in the tv news these days after a quick glance at the headlines. I still read (online) most newspapers every day. Yes, many articles still annoy me, but at least I don't shout out loud at a newspaper.

I have been busy lately rearranging our pandemic larder. There's a fair few tins. I am trying to organise them in sections - the contents we either consume regularly, quite rarely, scarcely, and never and also quite a lot of stuff we've somehow bought at some point for reasons that now escape us. These latter items make up the majority of our stocks. Things we don't eat, may never eat, have no idea what to do with, there's a fair few of them knocking about. After much denial and bafflement we remember the dark days of last March and April when confined to the house and unable to get anyone to deliver food to vulnerable old wretches like us. Yes, I know, when I say 'us' I mean 'me' as Marigold is younger, significantly more attractive and has a fully functioning heart.

The Council, ie the Local Authority, possibly after being told by our MP of a vulnerable VIP in the area – sorry about the acronyms, but they're everywhere just lately - delivered a food parcel to our door on three occasions. What joy as we unpacked the large cardboard box of goodies. We're well travelled, adventurous folk with wide experience of world cuisines, but some of the items in those boxes were obviously chosen by a computer with a rather serious wiring malfunction.

Of course we kept them. They're still here. Unloved and yet carefully hoarded away in case apocalyptic rumours prove to have been true all along. Fancy tinned artichoke hearts? We've got three of them. Tinned Brussel sprouts too. There's a product labelled simply 'lard with meat,' the writings in Polish and we've enjoyed many foods while travelling around Poland, yet somehow we've still not got around to trying this. Maybe tonight. Yum yum.

*actually, I love Brussel sprouts, just not from out of a tin.

I have now got everything in date order – come on, I'm in lockdown – and that's no easy task. Finding an expiry date is either dead simple or a task rivalling the Times crossword for difficulty. There's no middle ground. If you're interested, the tinned sprouts are deemed okay until May 2026. I shall place them on the storage area labelled 'vintage items' next to my last remaining 1990 bottle of Chateauneuf du Pape.

We lived within a few miles of that actual village at one time. You don't have to be rich to live in Vaucluse, or almost anywhere else on the Cote d'Azur, but it certainly helps! They soon found us out! Not every English resident of that era was named Peter Mayle.

That bottle of wine from 1990 is our last link with the region. It's one of the most recent vintages termed 'great' by the wine growing fraternity. Not merely a Grand Cru, but the far more rarified Grand Millesime and I may regret not having drunk it before my enforced abstinence became necessary.

Our lovely friend Gill rang us and said she was sending us an email of a word that describes me perfectly. Marigold emailed back and said, 'was it dickhead?'

Gill said I had 'Hyperthymesia' which is a condition that leads people to be able to remember an abnormally large number of their life experiences in vivid detail. It is extraordinarily rare, with only about 60 people in the world having been diagnosed with the condition. I wonder who the other 59 are.

*Just adding a dose of reality; if any of the few remaining attributes I possess was discovered to be so rare as to be thought remarkable I'd prefer it to be something other than the ability to retain endless recollections of trivial events.

One of my oldest friends still lives in Chateauneuf du Pape. He's a rather erudite friend and can usually be relied upon for a good laugh. He rang me the other day in far from jolly mode. He says he's 'marooned' in France, unable to return to England due to Covid restrictions and complaining bitterly about being denied the vaccine jab he would surely have been offered in England. He suspects he will be waiting a very long time before France has enough stocks to get around to vaccinating an elderly expatriate Englishman, resident in France for over 30 years but still regarded locally as the token Englishman, or Rosbif. In fairness, he's also widely regarded by his neighbours as a bien pensant. Roughly speaking that's French for a good bloke.

My friend insisted he was suffering from acedia, in an advanced and possibly terminal stage. Acedia, it's an interesting word, describing what so many are feeling in recent times. Acedia symptoms include – according to my venerable 'school' dictionary: - (don't trust online definitions), 'moroseness, weariness, fatigue, melancholy, gloominess, feeling overworked, discouragement, dejection, instability, activism, boredom, disenchantment, depression, languor, torpor, mediocrity, laziness, loss of interest and a compelling absence of joy and hope.'

Sounds about right in the Covid-19 era. I told him to stop being a miserable git, to buck up and start drinking the good stuff tucked away at the back of his wine cellar which he always assured me was reserved for my next visit. As I no longer imbibe - damn this useless heart - I cannot bear to think of my friend feeling forced to subsist on the thousand or so bottles of wine he regards as barely drinkable for a moment longer.

Visiting Karl Marx.

Marigold Says…
Not much from me today, again, been far too busy. Isn't lockdown marvellous?

I personally have saved lots of dosh by not wearing makeup, going to the hairdressers, not caring what we eat, not window shopping and lusting after stuff, not going out for coffee and treats or wandering around a supermarket.

Has all this doing without changed us? No, not at all. G's claims of his body being his temple are years out of date and now the temple just looks a bit more ruinous but with a newly thatched roof due to the absence of barbers. He would never have gone outside with long hair looking like Giant Haystacks but he does now. Its only long at the back and sides by the way as the top part is mostly baby hair.

Not having to hug and kiss people is great. I remember once somebody kissing me on the cheek and leaving a blob of tomato sauce stain from his own face.

Yuk. Keep your food stains to yourself.

If we ever shake hands with people again, we will immediately want to wash them. Will we ever want to use cutlery we haven't boiled or bleached? I would imagine the fad of sharing platters will be no more, but as I have never liked them it won't matter. My plate of food is mine and keep your paws off. People won't want to share crisps in a bowl. Thing to do is get in first and dive in filling your pockets before saying "now you help yourselves". They would all think "greedy". Would I care?

We have become obsessed with hearing "how many deaths today". Never thought we would be discussing that one. I still don't understand the R number. G comments on it, and I switch off. The other weird thing is not making plans, not because we think death is imminent but there doesn't seem any point. If we go over the channel all sorts of unsavoury people could be waiting in the mist coughing and spluttering in a Gallic manner.

We have been watching a lot of stuff on Netflix which may have been influencing our thoughts.

All the things I decided to do in first lockdown were to teach ourselves to become chess Grand Masters, make bread, do exotic cooking, lose loads of weight, read improving books, learn what the birds are in our garden, learn another language and have more patience.

The only one I have achieved so far are the names of several birds, but I knew those before, Magpie, crows, sparrows and starlings. Speaking of which we did see a hawk circling around. G said it was a drone and probably belonged to the council or police, looking for illegal swimming pools, naked sun worshippers or rave parties.

I am still waiting for inspiration to take up the other pursuits.

G Says...

I can only vaguely remember being able to get up out of an armchair without making sound effects. It's a gradual thing, age. It creeps up on you. The recognition I can't do some things any more, or certainly not as well, dawned on me long ago, but I heard from an old friend* recently who is finding late middle age, as I prefer to call it, a tad more difficult than most.

*When I refer to my old friend, I am of course referencing the breadth of years we've known each other not his chronological age. After all, he's the same age as me; no more than late middle aged then. A mere slip of a lad.

The most famous offering of Scottish poet, Andrew Marvell, turned up in a podcast I listened to the other day. Regarding podcasts, I mostly listen to learned people commenting on either news events or football. Mostly football, but somehow this one containing references to poetry sneaked in.

To His Coy Mistress is, basically, a plea to the poet's uncertain lady friend to hurry up, get a move on and become a little more free with her 'favours'. The opening couplet sets the tone:

'Had we but world enough, and time,
This coyness, Lady, were no crime...'

But, the segment of verse that's stood the test of time best is buried in the second verse:

'But at my back I always hear
Time's wingèd chariot hurrying near;
And yonder all before us lie
Deserts of vast eternity.'

That's the bit that can invoke despondency in later life. Not as much time left as we imagined in our youth and now we're in a pandemic, we're potentially wasting what bit of time we've got left. That's the stark reality facing many people now and my old friend isn't dealing with it very well. He's a born and bred Londoner, (not being judgemental, he can't help where he comes from) and in the far off days when I worked alongside him in the Kings Road, at that time the epicentre of 'Swinging London', we had spectacularly intense arguments about every subject under the sun. Bizarrely, we've been mates for almost fifty years now.

He was telling me of his daily exercise routine, wandering around Highgate cemetery. We've loved our visits there. One of Marigold's choices for a perfect excursion, forget about Alton Towers or Disneyland, is a trip around an old graveyard and Highgate is a belter. 170,000 'residents' in 53,000 graves – Ooh, budge up missus, room for one more – there can be few more fascinating places for a daily walk, but maybe a tad morbid in view of my friend's present and seemingly immovable melancholia.

When Highgate Cemetery opened, cemetery tourism was a big thing, not just in London. If you went to Paris in the 1830s, one of the top places to go was Père Lachaise – it was a must-see.

It still is in my view, if only to discover such unlikely residents as Chopin, Oscar Wilde, Edith Piaf and Jim Morrison all grouped together in one place. It's unlike any other cemetery we've visited and we've trailed around a lot of them. It took us ages to find the grave of Edith Piaf, even though the scenes of public mourning following her death had been mind blowing. She's buried in the family grave as Madame Lamboukas dite Edith Piaf, with the acknowledgment of her stage name only seen at the side of the monument, almost as if added as an afterthought. With hindsight, we should have just looked out for a grave heaped with masses of floral tributes. Even many years after her death, the 'little sparrow' still draws vast numbers of her fans to Père Lachaise.

Highgate cemetery opened in 1839, before London had public parks so it was a virtual day out in the countryside for city dwellers. More recently visiting cemeteries fell out of fashion with more and more people opting for cremation and Highgate, its costs helped out by being used as a 'horror setting' by Hammer films, became increasingly dilapidated and neglected until a group of likeminded people came to the rescue forming the Friends of Highgate Association. The success of their 'business model' means Highgate Cemetery draws 100,000 paying visitors a year, up from 63,000 seven years ago,

There are various guided tours available. I looked on their website and most tours omit the final resting places of Karl Marx and George Michael. I assume this is an attempt to restrict numbers at 'popular landmarks'. Marx observed in the Communist Manifesto: 'In bourgeois society... the past dominates the present.' I can't recall the context when I first read this but I'm fairly sure it was nothing to do with where and how he would end his days.

When Marx died in 1883, he was buried under a plain, flat slab on a small side path at Highgate, with only a dozen people attending his funeral. The grave was neglected for decades, hidden under overgrown weeds, until Marx's remains were moved in 1954 to a more visible location in the cemetery, and the monument was added, possibly for tourists, the original headstone being cracked and broken. He is buried there along with his wife, a daughter, two grandchildren and, a nice touch, the family's housekeeper.

There's CCTV around the Karl Marx statue now following two recent incidents of vandalism. The desecration or removal of monuments is in vogue, an unfortunate reflection of our era.

Karl Marx, Michael Faraday, Douglas Adams, Ralph Richardson, George Elliot, just a few of the notable grave sights I've seen in person at Highgate, including the most memorable of all in my view, those of the brilliant artist Patrick Caulfield and the not remotely famous 'resident,' Jim Stanford Horn who was only 34, but I've missed out many more. Since my last visit there's evidence that it's not necessary to be a Marx or a Faraday to be interred there. I offer up Jeremy Beadle and Malcolm McLaren in evidence. Ralph Miliband, father of Ed and David, is there too. As a prominent British Marxist in his day I assume he's happy enough to be close to his chief inspiration. I told my gloomy friend to buck up and get a grip. After all, things could be worse. He could be entombed in a Travel Lodge for ten days, the fate that now awaits anyone unwise enough to want to travel to the U.K. to savour the delights of our February climate.

The television news interviewed some of those poor wretches confined to one room in a hotel near Heathrow airport. Until I heard these harrowing tales I hadn't realised the quarantine process was apparently akin to recreating the Black Hole of Calcutta in deepest Middlesex. Restricted to one centrally heated room, containing a bed, a chair, a desk, table, refrigerator, access to both Internet and television and an attached en-suite bathroom, the inmates are being forced to collect all their meals from the doorstep. Where do the BBC find these people? Some of them appeared fairly 'normal' until asked for their opinion. More evidence of light travelling faster than sound - many people appear bright until they start to speak.

I can't imagine mentioning cemeteries without recalling our many visits to Tarifa on the far southern tip of Spain. The old cemetery perched above the town has appeared in this blog in the past and it's quite simply one of the best settings for a graveyard we can imagine. It's always beautifully kept and an increasing number of the, mostly above ground, graves are occupied by victims of unsuccessful immigrants trying and failing to cross the mere 8 miles of sea that form the Straits of Gibraltar, dividing Europe from North Africa.

Many graves bear just the simple, stark inscription, 'unknown African.' Those poor souls washed ashore receive a burial in the same graveyard as Spanish aristocracy and the locals ensure the graves of these unknown victims of the ocean are regularly provided with flowers and treated with equal reverence.

At Algeciras, in the shadow of Gibraltar, a few miles from Tarifa we saw a much more basic cemetery with at least 100 graves of people who drowned in the straits. Almost all are nameless. Only the date of burial and case number have been roughly scratched into the cement grave markers.

On our first ever trip to Morocco and North Africa, the first of many, we made the ferry crossing from Algeciras. We prefer the swifter ferry from Tarifa now, but visiting Algeciras for the first time was a real eye opener. The period celebrating Ramadan was imminent and the area was swamped with Moroccans and Algerians trying to get home to be with their families. Ramadan, one of the Five Pillars of Islam is observed by Muslims throughout the world as a month of fasting, prayer and community so the roads across Europe are packed with expatriate Muslims in heavily laden cars heading towards the ferries to get home. At night the hillsides around Algeciras are dotted with hundreds of tiny bonfires as the early arrivals await their turn to board a ferry.

Algeciras is far from attractive, it's a scruffy working port, but while wandering around the port area we came across a tiny 'monastery' run by a man I had heard about but never expected to meet. For more than 40 years, Padre Patera has been the first point of contact in Europe for thousands of Africans crossing the Mediterranean illegally by boat. He runs his charity out of a tiny monastery right next to the port. Illegal immigrants set off clutching only a scrap of paper bearing the name Padre Patera in the certainty that if they survive the perilous crossing they will receive a welcome meal and advice as to the next steps to take to achieve their dreams of living in Europe.

Many other memorable cemeteries come to mind: just outside a tiny hamlet in New Zealand we came across a hill side dotted with graves and stopped to look at the view across the mouth of a river to the sea. A great number of the headstones bore very similar names, all of them Scandinavian in origin, but the most striking aspect was that so many of the dates of death were the same. A tragedy involving the sinking of a vessel at the height of a storm as they reached landfall saw a score or more people, all ages, men, women and children, bearing the same name. We saw so many Andersons, Petersons and Eriksons, buried side by side, entire families laid to rest in one place.

I can't recall the name of that village, it was a tiny settlement far from any tourist route, but neither Marigold or I will ever forget it.

Other memorable graveyards are rooted in memory. Lacking the poignancy of that in New Zealand, but still utterly remarkable were the Old Jewish Cemetery in Prague with its ancient gravestones leaning against each other for support, the vast expanse of the City of the Dead in Cairo and the oddly named Cemeterio dos Prazeres (which translates Cemetery of Pleasures) in Lisbon which contains an absolutely gigantic mausoleum, the largest in Europe, constructed for the Duke of Palmela and his family in the shape of a pyramid and modelled on Solomon's temple.

Prague is one of our favourite cities. On our first visit we ate at a workers' café just off Wenceslas Square where diners took a ticket on arrival and waited for their numbers to be called to collect their meals. We sat, crammed together, on long wooden benches either side of long narrow tables, there was no choice, you ate what was offered, on that day it was a thick, meaty stew, and in a separate bowl everyone received a vast dumpling the size of a water melon. Neither of the two feeble British tourists could eat all of it, it was huge, but our fellow diners made sure our abandoned dumplings didn't go to waste.

As we waddled out, alongside well fed locals dashing back to work, a walk across the iconic bridge with its jazz bands, jugglers and other street entertainers and a climb up to the castle was just what we needed. The castle is impressive, but we loved the lively atmosphere of the Charles Bridge and its iconic statues just as much.

We found the statue of Prague's favoured son, Franz Kafka – it's hard to avoid references to Kafka there – but they've added a giant rotating Kafka head as well since we last visited which sounds interesting. We'd passed the Sex Machines Museum on the way but gave it a miss, (eaten too many dumplings for all that malarkey?) and the Jewish cemetery in the former ghetto proved an inspired choice.

It's neglected to the point of dereliction, with 12,000 tombstones – I didn't actually count them – most of them unable to remain standing without the support of its neighbour. The cemetery dates back to 1439 and as Jewish people were only allowed to be buried within the Ghetto it was soon filled beyond capacity. Jewish faith does not permit a body to be removed after internment so the dead are buried twelves layers deep in this relatively small space. An incredibly moving experience.

From the very small to the very, very large, the City of the Dead in Cairo has to be one of the world's most unusual cemeteries. If asked what aspect of Egypt left the most lasting impression Marigold and I would place this above the pyramids, the Sphinx and even the Valley of the Kings.

Cairo's population exceeds 20 million, the noise and bustle of its chaotic, crowded streets remain a shock for quite a while. It's one of the few places Marigold wasn't entirely comfortable on our first visit. On one occasion she momentarily released her grip on my jacket and took exception to being pushed aside by a group of pedestrians. They ignored her and directed their annoyance at me. 'Control your woman,' barked an irritated local. 'Oh, come on, mate', I muttered, 'I realised many years ago that was never going to happen.'

With such a vast population, housing is scarce and abject poverty forced many recent arrivals to get creative in the search for accommodation. Cairo's sprawling cemetery with its ornate tombs and mausoleums became home to several million people who still live there full time. I didn't take photographs for obvious reasons but the memories will be there forever.

I had another letter signed 'Matt' – he's the Health Secretary when he's not being my best friend and most regular correspondent. This one was to reiterate his ongoing concern for my well being and to advise I stay well away from the rest of humanity, Marigold excepted, until at least March 31st. That's no hardship whatsoever.

I read this piece in this morning's newspaper: 'English authorities have identified an extra 1.7 million people vulnerable to becoming seriously ill or dying from COVID-19 by combining factors such as age, underlying clinical condition, ethnicity, body mass index and local levels of deprivation.'

Does this now mean my 'special' status is to be diminished? Very disconcerting. The inclusion of body mass index is even more worrying. Suppose I am mistakenly grouped with the morbidly obese at risk in future? How very unfair after all my hard work in body mass reduction. Is there any sign yet of a badge detailing the incredibly specific medical conditions that have allowed me the 'privileged status' of being in a carefully selected group of clinically vulnerable citizens? It's rather awkward having one's status diluted. Marigold tells me not to worry as I'm much more decrepit than these nouveau vulnerables but I suspect she's just trying to cheer me up.

60s Swinging London.

Marigold Says…
Was outside minding my own business when one of the neighbours shouted to me, 'would you like to join an alternative spirituality class when all this is over?' I quickly climbed the ladder to the roof and sat on my perch so that I was safely socially distanced and threw the loud speaker down. She carried on, 'you do know what alternative spirituality is?'

I said of 'course, and I will let you know.' Rushed in and looked it up as I hadn't the foggiest. Oh dear, I don't possess any crystals or Birkenstock sandals. I will have to think of a good excuse.

I once went to yoga with a friend. They were all doing the dog, cat, budgie and snake poses or something like that.

I couldn't do any of that lot and invented a really bad knee. I have never known so many flatulent people in one room. At one stage I thought it must be compulsory. Apparently it is all the stretching. Nobody laughed except us and the best part was eating a bag of chips sitting on a bench on the way home. The teacher was a pony-tailed bloke wearing those funny trousers where the crutch comes down to way below your knees. He talked very quietly and used the word meditate a lot.

G Says…
Just had some students on the tv news bemoaning their restricted 'freedoms.' Just imagine not being able to concentrate on achieving a high score on their video game as their school keeps sending them online course work and insisting it takes precedence.

Kids these days, they don't know they're born. When I were a lad the snow were 10 foot deep from the middle of July. I had to walk 15 miles uphill to school wearing me dad's old pants, different sized pumps from Woolies, short sleeved shirt and tie and get fifty strokes of the cane off the teacher for being five minutes late. We ate raw potato peelings, soggy sawdust and gravel for us lunch and walked 15 miles, uphill all the way again, back home in 20 feet of snow, then had to work 8 hours down the pit. Went for a lie down on the kitchen floor for 20 minutes and then back up again for a thrashing from me dad for forgetting to dubbin his clogs then off to school in 30 feet of snow. Thems were the days.

I've had a complaint. Not the sort that can be eased by applying ointment; this was from a reader of our blog who grumbled about the absence of any actual 'travel' accounts recently in what started life as a travellers' blog. Well, travel isn't easy in a pandemic, but I take the point. I can't keep banging on about lockdowns and deprivation ad nauseam, but what else is there to talk about just now?

The answer came the next day when an old friend emailed me to bring me up to date with a house sale which has been ongoing now for well over a year. Three previous putative buyers had reached the final stages before the chain collapsed and stress levels have been stratospheric. Their most recent potential buyer had paid for a survey, all the legal work had been done, all going ahead. Result, only for the buyers to decide at the 11th hour that moving to an area where they didn't know anybody was out of the question.

'I should have told them to ring you,' my friend said, 'You pair move house all the time and you always end up in a place where you don't know a soul. You should write about that.'

It's true. We do exactly what she described. We've moved house and home twenty plus times, spread over a fair few countries plus a few years of having no fixed abode status while travelling around in a succession of camper vans. It's part of the attraction.

I decided I'd write about some of our earliest examples of 'upping sticks and venturing into the unknown.' They say if you remember the 60s you weren't there. Well, I was there and I remember it vividly. Obviously when it came to Sex, Drugs and Rock 'n Roll I skipped the drugs and concentrated my efforts elsewhere.

We started our life together as a couple in Newquay, Cornwall, in that glorious, golden decade the 1960s. We didn't know anybody there, we were jobless, skint and with all our possessions crammed into an ancient, temperamental Austin A35 van with holes in the bodywork necessitating the placement of a couple of newspapers underfoot to prevent my feet slipping off the pedals into a puddle of water if it rained. Accommodation was easily sorted. We bought a cheap tent from Millets, didn't bother with a groundsheet or sleeping bags, and just 'managed.'

I got a job as a bouncer at The Sailors Arms, the ultimate party pub in Newquay at that time, and Marigold worked at the Bilbo Surf Shop over the road. I also delivered custom made surf boards to customers all over Cornwall and Devon, the boards strapped to the roof but overhanging my tiny van both at the front and rear.

I'll leave Cornwall for now and move on as at the end of the summer season we were intending to go with our fellow beach bum mates to seek out the surfing scene in Morocco. We were all set and then decided at the last minute to go and live in London, then ranking alongside San Francisco as the epicentre of all that was 'cool' in that era.

We'd never been to London, knew nobody there, were jobless again, but we went anyway. I asked advice from one of the pub bar staff, a Londoner. He told me I'd hate it there and nobody would understand my Northern accent, but if my mind was made up I should head for Notting Hill Gate* as it was 'full of dossers and cheap housing.' It's become a haven for trendy celebs nowadays but back then Notting Hill was rough to the point of being seedy. Lots of scruffy hippies knocking about, run down houses divided up as cheap flats and not a wine bar in sight. Perfect, we thought.

*Nobody said Notting Hill back in 1969, always Notting Hill Gate, even though the original toll booths on the main route in and out of London had long since disappeared.

The Peter Pan Flat Agency, right next to the Tube entrance, gave us a list of available flats. We looked at five of them. Even after spending several months living in a tent they were grim. It's never a good sign on entering a room when the cockroaches look at you with disdain. The worst was in Rillington Place, but it wasn't at Number 10 where John Christie buried several of his victims. He worked as a projectionist at the Electric Cinema during World War II, but on the many occasions we went there to watch a film we never once glimpsed any likely serial killers amongst the workforce.

We watched films then, not 'movies,' and a night out was called 'going to the pictures' not the cinema. As for hot dogs, popcorn and the like, forget it. There was just the ice cream lady with her tray, but at the Electric Cinema you could buy a cup of coffee and a slice of carrot cake from a serving hatch at the back.

We went back to the agency for a new list. 'We just got this one in,' they said, handing us a scribbled address on the back of an envelope. 'It's top floor though and a bit pricey, £9 a week, and shared facilities but it's furnished.' Gulp! The flea pits we'd looked at so far were half that price. We left the van parked up and decided to walk to view the flat. Walking downhill towards Shepherds Bush took us into a very different area to Notting Hill. We were looking for a house in Holland Park Avenue and this turned out to be packed with gleaming white mansions.

The flat we'd come to view was in one of the biggest and smartest houses on a very smart road. Flat 12 was a one room bed sitter on the top floor, in the attic actually. The stone interior staircase went on and on and we were exhausted when we got to the top floor. There were three 'flats,' all one room bedsits. The other two bore the names Miss Foote and Dr Patel. Flat 12 had a Baby Belling cooker, a tiny sink and draining board, two old bentwood chairs, a chipped Formica table and, along one wall a double bed covered by a really revolting bedspread. It was tiny, the only light came from an attic window with a sit on ledge and we'd passed the only bathroom and WC on the floor below.

Marigold looked around and said, 'perfect.' This flat was to be the first in a succession of grim and dingy rented bedsits. We didn't care, this was the Swinging London era after all and after living in a tent for six months before moving to London anywhere with a roof was luxury by comparison and in our youth we weren't remotely concerned with creature comforts, but with hindsight our standards were lamentably low at that time.

Next door to the Peter Pan Agency was a large branch of Manpower, the agency of choice for casual/temporary workers. Marigold found work opportunities easy as typing and secretarial skills are always in demand, but I was rather more problematic. Being vastly overqualified is just as restrictive as the alternative option and I reluctantly agreed to take up a temporary job in Chelsea for six weeks while they found me a more suitable long term 'career.' A canny manager ensured I was promoted twice in the first month and so ended up staying in my temporary job for a year. I didn't even have to cut my hair, but flared loon trousers and tie dye tee shirts were frowned upon. I even had to wear socks at work, but at least I remained free of academia.

We didn't have a television so our entertainment options up in the attic were restricted. Occasionally my attention focused on a naked woman combing her hair while sitting in the window ledge of the bay window on the house across the road, directly opposite our apartment. For reasons I can't quite recall I used to spend rather a lot time perched on our window ledge.*

*Just for clarification I should perhaps point out I was fully clothed and the hair being combed was on her head.

Our house caretaker offered the information that the house opposite was a notorious 'knocking shop' where call girls in training, as he put it, worked to gain experience before heading to the private clubs of Mayfair.

We also witnessed more nudity, this time dancers in a circle, swaying and undulating in the ground floor of the same house. Our caretaker, Mr Anderson, a garrulous hippie known as Kiwi John who lived rent free in the basement in return for collecting everyone's rubbish and 'unblocking the khazis' if required, told us they were a 'bunch of weirdos' who met up twice a week to strip off and and 'prance around' the ground floor ballroom, chanting and burning incense. He also claimed the house in question had been raided numerous times by the police and had been a notorious address for about fifty years. He referenced 'camp boys' which meant nothing to us at the time, but the name stuck in my memory and the arrival of the Internet confirmed Kiwi John was on the right track.

In 1933, in what became known as 'The Lady Austin's Camp Boys Scandal,' 60 men were detained in a private ball room at that house in Holland Park Avenue. A squad of police officers had been watching them dancing, wearing makeup, dressed as women, and having sex. Twenty-seven men were arrested, charged with 'diverse lewd, scandalous, bawdy and obscene performances and practices' and sentenced to between 3 and 20 months imprisonment. The Club President, who organised these dances for his friends amongst hotel staff in the area, using the name Lady Austin, said in mitigation, 'There is nothing wrong in who we are. You call us Nancies and much worse but before long our cult will be allowed in this country.'

Simon Cowell, Robbie Williams, Elton John, Jimmy Page and David Beckham all now own houses within a stone's throw of our former apartment They're all more likely than us to get a blue plaque on the outside wall. Not fair – bunch of nobodies. In 1969 the only famous person in the road, to our knowledge, was a Chelsea footballer and as he wasn't Peter Osgood or Alan Hudson, 'only' football stars but well known 'faces' in the Kings Road scene, nobody cared very much.

Neighbours – although not remotely famous – who also became friends lived in a dingy flat in the vast property known as Woodland House, then owned by the parents of Michael Winner, but later by Michel Winner himself. We visited the house on a few occasions when a frequent talking point was the Led Zeppelin guitarist, Jimmy Page, living in the house next door. Michael Winner ran up huge debts restoring the 46 roomed Woodland House and after he died it was bought by Robbie Williams for £17.5 million.

We loved our time in Holland Park. As long haired hippies we'd thrived in Newquay and Swinging London afforded so many more opportunities. Holland Park tube station was only just across the road, past the gloriously named Fags and Mags paper-shop, and it didn't take long to realise fare payments on the tube could be purely voluntary as ticket inspectors back then were unknown as long as we were happy to take the back stairs avoiding the barriers. We travelled all over London, but in fairness it may have been wiser to just buy a ticket as some of the staircases were very demanding. 320 steps at Hampstead tube station, we didn't go there very often. We liked Covent Garden, but with 195 steps to climb it was easier to get there by jumping off at Charing Cross and walking down there via The Strand.

A few days after we arrived in London we went to view an event everyone was talking about: 200 or so squatters, described as 'hippies,' in the press, but who people in the crowd who knew many of them personally called the Dilly Dossers, had recently occupied 144 Piccadilly on Hyde Park Corner. The building was an 18th century five-storey mansion, once the home of former Prime Minister Lord Palmerston. Next door (number 145, and built at the same time) was the childhood home of the Princesses Elizabeth and Margaret before the Second World War. The house was surrounded by a dry moat over which the intruders built a makeshift drawbridge.

Squatting was a comparatively recent phenomenon, but finding free accommodation, usually in derelict houses, was common enough and we knew a fair number of people who did that. Moving on to occupy empty houses was a comparatively short step and when I eventually returned to an established career pattern my new job brought me into contact with a great many of them.

Arriving at Hyde Park Corner we joined the hundreds looking on from the opposite pavement and were enjoying the (mostly friendly) banter between squatters and spectators when suddenly matters escalated. As the drawbridge was briefly lowered to allow a (as it turned out later, fictional medical emergency) a couple of hundred police charged in. A hail of missiles rained down on the police, but the resistance was very short lived. As they were taken away we commented on how they were mostly our age or even younger. Just kids mucking about as one person in the crowd said.

Most of the squatters were arrested, but released later as the police action did not have the correct paperwork in order.

The building stood empty for three years and then was demolished despite its listed status. It is now the site of the Intercontinental London, Park Lane which is very smart indeed. Not that we have ever stayed there, not even as squatters!

When arranging to see friends for a night out, we usually met up at the well known statue of Eros in Piccadilly Circus. Buskers, dancers, rent boys, prostitutes and pickpockets all congregated there every evening. It was never dull. I remember being told, in haughty tones, by a very drunken man wearing a Brigade of Guards tie as a bandana that although the statue is generally known as Eros, it was created as an image of his brother, Anteros. It turned out he was right.

We loved the vibrancy of Speakers Corner where the racist, sexist and homophobic outpourings of those brave enough to stand on a soap box would have horrified the present 'woke' generation. We made friends with a man tattooed from head to foot, including his face, who told us he had taken these drastic changes in his appearance after once being wrongly identified as a murder suspect and decided to become uniquely distinctive.

Portobello Road was within easy walking distance, and there we discovered Seed, the UK's first macrobiotic restaurant and shop, and later Ceres where the bread was baked on the premises and 'something from Ceres' became our Saturday morning treat. The owners were Craig Sams and his brother Gregory.

Nebraska-born, Craig Sams imported Afghan coats that he had spotted on his travels in Asia to sell on Chelsea's King's Road. Among his first customers were the Beatles and a fashion trend was born. Craig Sams was a pioneer of the 'organic' movement and without his influence the supermarkets and high street shops of today would be very different. There were sacks of flour, lentils and rice inside the doorway and freshly baked bread on offer.

On September 18, 1970, his girlfriend found the great guitarist Jimi Hendrix unresponsive in her apartment at the Samarkand Hotel in Lansdowne Crescent, Notting Hill. One of the first instances of what would become the classic rock star death from drug overdose. We walked past the hotel that evening; it was thronged with people standing several rows deep in silent mourning.

Three weeks later, October 4, 1970, the legendary rock star Janis Joplin was found dead of a suspected heroin overdose in her Hollywood hotel room. We had just done a 'big shop' at MacFisheries on the corner of Kensington Church Street and the Evening Standard seller outside was bellowing, 'First Jimi, now Janis, is it the end?'

Enigmatic, but perhaps because of this I remember it vividly. Barefooted, long haired, kaftan clad locals milled about, clutching at each other for support on hearing the news and when I went to my usual kiosk to buy the current Rolling Stone magazine the girl behind the counter was in tears. Seven years later Elvis Presley would die in similar circumstances at age 42, promoting a worldwide surge of grief, but for our age group, in this era, these two untimely deaths were pretty devastating.

After surviving a few temporary jobs Marigold worked in the West End as secretary to an eccentric, but high powered, solicitor with many VIP clients. In those early days of 'temping' we used to set out on a 'recce' every Sunday evening, plotting her route for the following day. Three stops on the Central Line, change at Earls Court for the Eastbound Circle Line, then again at Trafalgar Square for the Northern Line, then it's the third stop.' That sort of thing, all carefully written down in readiness for the Monday rush hour dash to a new job. On one of these trips I said something like, 'not long to wait now, our train is next, due in three minutes.'

Marigold: 'how do you know that?'

Me: 'it says so on the notice board.'

Okay, Marigold didn't actually say 'what notice board,' but she couldn't read a word on it. An urgent trip to the opticians for some distance glasses was called for!

As for Swinging London fashions we eschewed the tackiness of Carnaby Street but adored the Kings Road where we spent many weekends browsing and exclaiming at the shop fronts, the cars and, best of all the peacock styles of our fellow pedestrians strutting their stuff. Garishly painted psychedelic Minis, pink Cadillacs, Rolls Royces painted decidedly non standard colours ruled the roads while the pavements were even more colourful. Celebrities received far less attention than they do now. Pop stars, footballers, actors, we saw so many it scarcely warranted a mention.

The Granny Takes a Trip shop was never dull and Bazaar, the store owned by Mary Quant, was always busy. She claimed to have invented the miniskirt, whether she did or not she certainly did more than anyone else to make it a ubiquitous item of clothing. We loved the Mary Quant philosophy when applied to clothing, 'rules were invented for lazy people who don't want to think for themselves.'

It's not a bad slogan, is it?

Perhaps our favourite store front belonged to a shop at the far end of the Kings Road. Let it Rock appeared in 1971, selling uniquely wacky clothes, bits of fetish wear and with a (very loud) jukebox playing non stop, it attracted an 'off the wall' clientele. It was not so much a shop as a meeting point and an opportunity to explore the outer regions of fashion and music. Set up by two acknowledged geniuses of the day, Malcolm McLaren and Vivienne Westwood, this was where the Sex Pistols and the punk era began. We weren't great fans of punk, but we thrived on the excitement surrounding it. Let it Rock has long gone, but was succeeded, in the same place, by Too Fast To Live Too Young To Die, then SEX which was almost entirely devoted to fetish clothing and objects – we never went in there – and is still there, now called Worlds End.

Away from the Kings Road, that infamous fashionista Marigold loved Biba for its fashions and unique style and we were frequent visitors, firstly to the chaotic shop inKensington Church Street where Marigold bought a favourite classic minidress* and later after Biba moved to what used to be Derry and Toms department store with its brilliant roof garden in Kensington High Street.

Polish born Barbara Hulanicki began her career in fashion in the early 1960s. Her husband, Stephen Fitz-Simon, (whom we knew slightly as the friend of a friend,) was an advertising executive. They opened a mail order clothes shop and her designs were so successful the innovative Biba boutique shop phenomenon took off. Biba dresses, often accompanied by the signature black lipstick, swept London and then all of Europe in the late sixties and early seventies.

*We saw the exact same zig zag patterned mini dress a few years ago at the Victoria and Albert Museum.

We often walked through Holland Park, where there were 'real' peacocks, past the copper roofed Commonwealth Institute building to Kensington High Street. There was quite a small marble slabbed fish counter shopfront on the right hand side, one of the early branches of Sainsburys. Our supermarket shopping choices were few and far between in 1969 and MacFisheries accepted luncheon vouchers as cash so we went there in the main. I'm aware the concept of luncheon vouchers, a perk of Marigold's job at the time, may be alien to many readers, but like Green Shield Stamps and ubiquitous electricity meters they were part and parcel of life in that era.

Barely scratched the surface of our time in London. Our next move would be to Bayswater and a flat once owned by Peter Rachman, the infamous slum landlord who included both Christine Keeler and Mandy Rice-Davis amongst his 'mistresses' as the newspapers of the day always termed these arrangements. That will have to wait for another time.

My First Murderer.

Marigold Says...

The things I remember from our flat-living time in London starting at Holland Park are the many flights of stairs to our top flat and the shared telephone at the bottom. If somebody rang and it was for us, your name was shouted once by whoever answered. You had to be quick. It was obviously a source of entertainment for one of the old ladies on the third floor as you always heard her door creak open and she listened to your end of the conversation over the balcony, sometimes tutting. She was very much a Miss and used to leave handwritten notices on the door of the shared toilets, always pinpointing the many vagaries of men.

One I will always remember said "Can the gentlemen please close the lavatory seat after use". Somebody soon added underneath, "Can the ladies please not sh*t on the floor". It was hastily removed, but to this day I still find it highly amusing. No it wasn't G who wrote it.

Miss Dowler who lived underneath us in her bedsit used to have a loaf of bread delivered every day from Harrods. She would use any excuse when I returned from work to invite me in and give me a sherry and tonic. Those old ladies were of a bygone age with a very old fashioned nostalgic view of the world. Her nephew worked at Buckingham Palace of which she was very proud. She was leaving all her money to him as he was the only one who visited her "regularly" which was about twice a year. I had to eventually knock the sherry trips on the head as sometimes I couldn't safely make it up the two flights of stairs home.

I was temping when we first arrived in London. The travelling on the tube frightened me to death. Every single Sunday night G used to map out and do a practice run with me to my new assignment. The words Country Bumpkin come to mind but I was still a teenager and London was just so BIG.

Temp jobs were sporadic and I eventually got a permanent job in Bentinck Street, next to Harley Street, working for a prestigious firm of solicitors. I was Legal Secretary to the senior Partner, Mr Muscat. He was tiny, inclined to go into furious rages and very eccentric. He had numerous celebrity clients and refused to allow them to have a coffee or a biscuit if they called at the office in case they imagined he was impressed by success. Everybody else, the plebs as he called them, got tea, coffee and biscuits. He always worked with the office windows open and when anyone on the telephone annoyed him he used to throw the phone out of the window. I had to pull it back up on its dangling flex.

One day G was waiting in reception to collect me and I had been delayed by one of my bosses tantrums. As I walked down the stairs to meet G a tiny, dishevelled figure ran down after me shouting, 'I love you, don't leave me.' He used to say that quite often after one of his rants at the world and it was a good job that G was very understanding.

If you worked on Saturday mornings they provided a Jewish buffet, rolls with different weird fillings, all of which I loved, dishes of pretzels and home-made pickles. I adored my time there and it opened up a new world.

I worked some evenings when G was out working as a sports coach at a hotel just at the end of Holland Park Avenue, near to some very big mansions that were all foreign Embassies. One night Nana Mouskouri was staying there and we were all told we had to pretend we didn't know who she was as she hated a fuss. It was easy for me as I didn't care. Her backing band, the Athenians, had to sleep in a much lower standard hotel in Shepherds Bush because she was the 'star'.

The woman who owned the hotel was always very smart with bouffant hair like a film star and one night she asked me to make a cup of coffee and take it to her room. When I went in she was sitting on the bed and combing her wig. She was completely bald. I screamed and when she said, 'go away, stupid girl' I ran out and couldn't stop laughing. My friend on reception said the owner hated her own hair and had shaved her head as she preferred to wear wigs,

I also managed to get a Saturday job later on in Selfridges on the button counter. I lasted 3 weeks and was asked to leave. I was supposed to measure 20 yards of ribbon, which I did, forgot how much half way and was told off. The final straw was when a woman customer had the handles of her crocodile bag cut and the thief ran off with the bottom part. She shouted "somebody has pinched my crocodile" which I thought very funny and was told off again for laughing. What a supercilious place it was. I had a dismissal letter that day in with my wages. I was delighted.

My next Saturday job was at Wallis in Bond Street. That was great. We shop girls earned 1p in the pound commission. The old shop floor ladies fought for every customer who looked rich, and cries of "mine dear" rang out. It certainly hardened me up. I can still get to the front of any queue before anybody else.

G Says…

'Portobello Road', from the musical Bedknobs and Broomsticks, 1971.

Portobello road, Portobello road.
Street where the riches of ages are stowed.
Anything and everything a chap can unload,
Is sold off the barrow in Portobello road.
You'll find what you want in the Portobello road.

Portobello Road by Cat Stephens, later known as Yusuf Islam, from the album *Matthew and Son*.

'Nothing is weird, not even a beard
Getting hung up all day on smiles,
Walking down portobello road for miles,
Greeting strangers in Indian boots,
Yellow ties and old brown suits,
Growing old is my only danger.'

Our arrival in London in 1969 was at a time of huge change throughout all society, about previously unconsidered freedoms, particularly among the young and rampant experimentation in art, fashion and music. Despite this breadth of options virtually everybody we knew had the same albums, still largely referred to as LPs, by the Beatles, most probably Sergeant Pepper, and Simon and Garfunkel playing constantly and listened to the surreal and faintly anarchic Kennie Everett on the radio, 10.00 to 12.00 every Saturday morning. He got the boot from the BBC in 1970 for making a fairly innocuous quip wondering if the wife of the Minister of Transport had offered the examiner a bribe to pass her driving test.

When we decided to move from genteel and distinctly upmarket Holland Park it was in search of a more affordable flat - we were finding the weekly rent of a top floor small bed sitter, accounting for about three quarters of our income, a bit of a financial struggle and also wanted a tad more floor space. Our (normal size) bed took up half the room, so it was a bit of a squeeze.

A turning point came one Sunday morning after a dispute with a neighbour, Doctor Patel. We never actually discovered where Doctor Patel worked as we never saw him go out, but our other top floor neighbour, Miss Foote, was convinced he was an eminent surgeon and had operated on several members of the Royal Family. We thought this unlikely as his bed sitter was only the same size as ours, hardly befitting the lifestyle of a top surgeon.

We'd soon realised Miss Foote wasn't the most reliable source of information. She was friendly enough, always said, 'good morning, Clive' when we met on the stairs. My name isn't Clive and on many occasions it wasn't in the morning either, but the greeting never varied. Marigold did not rate a name at all, just a curt 'good morning.'

Our ablutions took place in the bathroom on the floor below, a dingy little room with a rusty bath, toilet and basin where hot water was obtained by lighting a wall mounted gas boiler that bellowed loudly when it was eventually lit. Our resident wise man was the caretaker. Kiwi John wasn't even a New Zealander – he was Irish - but had lived there for ten years so became known as Kiwi John when he returned to differentiate him from the many Irish Johns in the area. Yes, it was a bit confusing. Kiwi John told us about the temperamental boiler, how it was difficult to light first time and responded best to a system of switch the gas on, wait for up to a minute and then strike a match near the gas jet.

'That sounds dangerous,' I said.

'Oh, Jaysus, it's that all right. Best stand right across the room and throw matches at it.'

Right. That explained the vast numbers of matchsticks on the floor and the permanent smell of gas. Marigold refused to even enter the bathroom until I had dealt with the boiler and survived the blast of flame that burst forth. It wasn't a very large bath, but we were young, fit and nimble then so usually shared a bath as the metered gas supply didn't last for long. One day we were going out in the evening so Marigold nipped out of the bath first and went back upstairs as she invariably needed more time than I did to get ready.

Of course this meant the door was now unlocked. I stayed in the bath, using the hot water to have a shave. I had no sooner applied shaving cream to my face when the door opened and Miss Foote rushed in. She didn't say 'good morning, Clive,' so I just kept very still and tried to be invisible. Miss Foote wasn't a large woman, she was very thin and always well turned out, but until you have experienced someone using a lavatory about two feet away from your face you can't really say you know them. I can only compare the sound effects and general ambience of the occasion to being what I imagine it's like sitting immediately adjacent to a difficult and protracted birth in a maternity ward. She finally arose, understandably looking a little weary I thought, and wandered off out again.

Doctor Patel, like many of the residents, left his rubbish outside the door for Kiwi John to collect as part of his caretaker duties. His only job as far as we could see. On one occasion Marigold noticed a pair of desert boots on the landing and came in very excited to say they were just my size. I had a look, tried them on and they fitted perfectly. Superb recycling we thought and I wore them to work the next day.

Several days later a notice went up in the entrance hall referencing the theft of some new shoes left outside flat 10 by Mrs Patel for unspecified reasons. I went back up, removed the shoes, reluctantly, and placed them outside the door opposite. Miss Foote told us later that Mrs Patel had thrown missiles from her window at Kiwi John as he sat in the garden and told him she had contacted Scotland Yard to report his theft of the valuable shoes.

Maybe it was time to move out.

We looked at Earls Court, lots of flats, lots of Antipodean accents, lively area, but had no luck as Aussies and Kiwis had already snapped up the good flats, happy to share an apartment with a few like minded mates. We met a girl we'd known from our surf bum days in Cornwall, seated outside the Sun in Splendour pub in Notting Hill. This pub introduced us to the recently arrived concept of 'pub grub' and their specialty, 'sausage hotpot' was to become Marigold's most appreciated dish when we had dinner guests in the future.

Our rediscovered surfing friend worked at I Was Lord Kitchener's Valet, a clothing boutique which sold antique military uniforms as fashion items. Regular customers included Eric Clapton, Mick Jagger John Lennon and Jimi Hendrix. Peter Blake, the artist who designed The Beatles' Sgt. Pepper's Lonely Hearts Club Band album cover, said that he and Paul McCartney got the idea for the record sleeve while they were walking together past the shop. She also told us about a two roomed flat in Paddington that had just become vacant. Even more interesting.

St. Stephen's Gardens couldn't make up its mind whether it was in Paddington, Bayswater or Westbourne Grove – locals used all three definitions with impunity. Whatever it was called, the area wasn't remotely comparable to Holland Park. The houses had been smart enough in their day, but their peak had long since been passed.

The landlord, a Polish man with heavily accented English, was Mister Fenkul. The flat was on the ground floor, at the rear, with a (communal) lavatory outside the door and the bathroom on the next floor up. As for the anticipated two rooms, well technically it was one room with a dividing wall separating living space from the bedroom extending halfway across the width of the room. There was the familiar sight of a small sink next to a Baby Belling cooker to form a 'kitchen' but our initial attention wandered to the colour scheme. Two walls painted vivid purple and the other two a bilious shade of orange.

Plus points? It was half the cost of our Holland Park flat, Portobello Road was just around the corner and Paddington/Bayswater/Westbourne Grove had plenty of shops that stayed open all night. It wasn't much, but it was enough. We agreed to move in and Mister Fenkful said he would call to collect the rent every Saturday morning at 08.30. 'On the dot.'

The big talking point in the Bayswater area at the time of our arrival was a vast concrete monstrosity scything through the area, bisecting Portobello Road. The Westway was Europe's longest elevated concrete roadway carrying the A40 trunk road, which was formerly a motorway, linking the western outposts of London to the centre. Hundreds of houses had been demolished to facilitate the building of the flyover, intended to ease the notorious traffic bottleneck around Shepherds Bush, yet it had remained empty of traffic for many months. It wasn't a complete waste as a thriving shanty town grew up beneath it and the local drug dealers and alkies, of which there were many, appreciated it as a place to shelter from the elements.

The scent of cannabis was all pervading under the flyover and marked a major point of difference. Beyond the antique stalls and the fruit and veg sellers, the traditional market that had been in existence for ever and a day, was a very different world. We could walk there from our flat in five minutes and were so captivated we made the short trip almost every Saturday. It didn't take long to realise Portobello Green, a leafy little area of trees, lawns and benches right next to the Westway which had somehow evaded demolition wasn't the restful oasis it promised to be. Winos, drug dealers and wiped out 'users' filled the benches and fights were common.

When we first discovered the seedier end (the best bit of Portobello Road in our view) from under the Westway onwards usually called Portobello Village, or just 'the village,' it was just a scruffy area where the Market Inspectors didn't seem keen to show their faces. Second hand clothes and the sort of 'junk' you saw in skips were on offer, very cheaply, along with a thriving stall selling cannabis paraphernalia: bongs, large size rolling papers and Rastafarian knick knacks. A couple of years later the stall morphed into a shop called Alchemy, Britain's first 'head shop.' It became a Village institution and only closed its doors very recently. This area of Portobello was where we first encountered organic, vegetarian and vegan food, these concepts being virtually unknown in 1969.

If we took an alternative walking route through Golborne Road, which we often did, there was another street market selling battered furniture and stalls specialising in ethnic food. Yams, spices, goat meat, horse meat, jerk chicken, these weren't readily available in any of the shops and supermarkets we'd ever been in; it was literally a glimpse of another world. We loved the different accents, the friendly banter and the realisation that bartering a price downwards wasn't considered an insult here. We bought food – what we thought were huge unripe green bananas that turned out to be plantains and virtually inedible until cooked on one occasion, never repeated – clothes and many items of furniture, all at knock down prices. The leather sheepskin lined flying jacket, in dreadful condition, I bought there in 1969 for 'ten bob,' (pre decimal so 50p), has only recently given up the ghost despite it being banned from numerous successive wardrobes on the not unreasonable grounds of being throughly unsanitary.

The Westway flyover opened in July 1970 – we were there – and it was a raucous occasion. Michael Heseltine, Parliamentary Secretary to the Minister of Transport, officially opened the road and as he was trying to cut a thick strip of white ribbon, with apparently very dull shears, the noise from the crowd/mob was deafening. All along the tops of a row of terraced houses opposite was a huge banner that read 'Get Us Out Of This Hell, Re-house Us Now'.

After the crowd dispersed we drove along the new road, both ways. Amazingly, it proved less of a life enhancing experience than we'd expected.

Life in the new flat was similarly underwhelming. Our nearest neighbour, a wild haired Greek man who told us he was 'in hiding' from unspecified threats played Greek folk music, very loudly, all day and for most of the night. Like living under an aircraft fly path, we didn't notice it after a while. He'd been a tenant for many years and complained bitterly, in his almost incomprehensible Greek accented English, about the number of 'foreigners' who were living in the house. There were 14 flats in the house, some no bigger than the proverbial shoe box, bringing in a fair income yet the landlord dressed like a tramp and collected the rents from all the tenants in a plastic carrier bag. He collected cash from five other house in the road, but was said to be 'well protected' ensuring he would never be robbed.

In the week we took possession of the flat a film crew turned up in the road outside. In an episode of *Steptoe and Son*, Harold left the family home after the unannounced arrival of Albert's supposedly long lost Australian son and moved to a particularly run-down bed-sit in a particularly run-down terrace of houses.

The location chosen was St Stephen's Gardens and our front entrance was the one chosen for filming. A member of the film crew confided to Marigold on one of her numerous attempts to appear 'in shot' during filming that they wanted to film in a decaying and run-down area and chose St. Stephen's Gardens as it had once been an early part of Peter Rachman's property empire and the first house he purchased and used for his infamous multi-occupation was this very house.

After extensive demolition in the mid 1970s this area is now very smart indeed and a similar tiny bed-sit (now of course it would be called a 'studio apartment') to the one we lived in in what's left of the very fashionable St Stephen's Gardens, will cost an obscene amount of money. A current Notting Hill resident, Damon Albarn had once lived in St Stephen's Gardens, but presumably under significantly more salubrious circumstances than we once did.

Peter Rachman – his name invariably prefaced by the description 'infamous slum landlord' – worked as a 'fixer' (his actual title being 'investment consultant'), for the 'Maltese' family, the Messina Brothers who dominated much of London's organised crime 'rackets' for over 20 years. The five brothers, Salvatore, Carmelo, Alfredo, Attilio and Eugene whose father was Sicilian but had married a Maltese woman built a prostitution empire in Malta before exporting the trade to London where the term 'white slavery' first came into use. The family name was DeBono, but they adopted the surname Messina to confuse the U.K. authorities.

'Houses of ill repute' as brothels were termed back then were highly sought after and Peter Rachman proved adept at finding new properties. The Messina brothers were long gone from the scene when we reached London, but I worked with a man, a former police officer, who had attended dozens of raids on brothels in Bond Street and Mayfair and gave me a tour of dubiously acquired properties once owned by Peter Rachman. Of course, the tour started at our front door.

Rachman bought up hundreds of almost derelict houses in Bayswater and Notting Hill and converted them into small flats. He neglected to improve the fabric of the buildings and charged exorbitant rents, mainly to immigrants who were unable to show references or bank details required by more reputable agencies. He has the dubious honour of having his name added to the Oxford English Dictionary. Rachmanism is defined as the exploitation and intimidation of tenants by unscrupulous landlords. In other circumstances, a penniless Polish refugee who died a multimillionaire would have been applauded for his business acumen.

Christine Keeler and 16 year old Mandy Rice-Davis who lived with him for two years were heavily involved. After he died after a sudden heart attack, Miss Rice-Davis was so upset the only words she could bear to utter were, 'did he leave a will?'

The Rachman Empire crumbled on his death as details of his vast wealth were only ever stored 'in his head' and thereby untraceable after his demise. Those Swiss bank accounts remain unclaimed. Naturally we peered into every crevice in our flat hoping for hidden loot, to no avail.

We were still managing to cope without a television as there was so much to do and see. Highlights were the free concerts in Hyde Park. We'd missed out on seeing The Rolling Stones in July 1969 and the next offering just after we arrived in September didn't appeal. From memory the headline acts were Soft Machine and Al Stewart, but we did join half a million others for the summer concerts of 1970.

I can remember seeing Pink Floyd, Edgar Broughton and that most unlikely offering at a 'rock concert', the soft voiced Roy Harper who despite having the appearance of a middle aged geography teacher reduced the vast audience to a rapt and appreciative silence.

On another occasion King Crimson topped the bill, but I remember being blown away by Jack Bruce, beginning a solo career after the break up of Cream and his successful collaboration with Eric Clapton and Ginger Baker.

It was one of those occasions, three years after the 'summer of love,' when the twin slogans of the age, peace and love, were at risk. Security for the half million spectators was provided by a motley group of Hells Angels and one particular faction were being particularly aggressive in our vicinity. It was getting out of hand, numerous fights were breaking out and the arrival of a dozen or so skinheads spoiling for a fight didn't help at all.

Having (fairly) long hair and a sizeable moustache had already caused me a few problems in London I'd not previously experienced elsewhere. Skinheads tended to go around in groups and thousands of 'long–haired hippies' all in one place were fair game. Faced with the choice between extirpation of my facial adornments or the potential for strife I chose strife and there had been a fair few 'hairy' moments if you'll forgive the expression. A mass brawl on a sunny day in the park wasn't in the plan for almost all of us.

A familiar face stepped up to rescue the day: Roy Harper again who must have been permanently available as this was his third Hyde Park appearance. The tranquility of a lone folk singer accompanied only by his acoustic guitar calmed the mood and prevented the threatened riot. Even the skinheads went off to mug old ladies somewhere else.

We still had our A35 van, but it was only rarely used as public transport was much easier than the frustrating search for a parking space. On one occasion I parked it up in an unmetered zone near to our flat and on returning a few days later found it festooned in stickers advertising a fairly recent innovation, designer clothing.

Zandra Rhodes had opened a boutique just around the corner from my place of work called Fulham Road Clothes Shop. In the weeks after we moved to the new flat we'd noticed these flyers advertising 'Paddington's Latest Design Studio' and we'd seen what Marigold described as an apparition, a woman with bright green hair, exotic clothing, wearing theatrical makeup and with dangling ornaments clanking at every step. Even in bohemian Westbourne Grove she was noteworthy.

We'd first seen her walking through Whiteley's Department Store, all commerce ceasing as everyone turned to stare, but now saw her almost every time we went out as her Solo Design Studio was at the end of the road. By the time we left the area we were on nodding terms and the green hair was now pink. She obviously liked pink best as the last time I saw her on tv she still had the exact same shade I remembered from fifty years ago.

I'm not able to talk about certain aspects of my working life. I was not a Police Officer but my job brought me into frequent contact with many 'undesirables,' including a few murderers. In our early years in London I was occasionally asked to take charge at the London Emergency Centre at a dingy office at Alexander Fleming House, Elephant and Castle, long since turned into a block of flats. This was a weekend centre for the indigent flotsam and jetsam of London society, open from ten am to ten pm on Saturdays and Sundays. Runaways, victims of crime, people delivered by police officers, they came seeking help, advice or just a government funded 'handout.'

I had a fund of cash available, delivered to me with great ceremony by a man in a grey uniform, always the same man, from the Treasury who never spoke, not even good morning and insisted on me using only the pen he brought with him for the signature on his clipboard. My interviewing staff of about a dozen were keen to impress on me at my first day on the job that the vast majority of the hundred or so people an hour who called seeking help were scroungers 'trying it on' and I should not be swayed by sob stories.

It took only a single morning to change me from a gullible person to a fully formed cynic. Excellent training for life. I mostly made decisions based on the evidence provided to me by my staff. On the rare occasions I interviewed a 'customer' in person I soon realised my very experienced staff knew what they were talking about. I doled out small cash sums to people whose wallet containing their wages had been lost or stolen and tried to find safe lodging or a place of safety for life's unfortunates. I would estimate we believed only ten per cent of these tales of woe and yet my staff still shook their heads at my rampant generosity.

They weren't being unkind, the vast majority of callers were indeed trying it on and many of them said 'oh well, worth a try' after being refused. It was never dull. I remember a drunken woman coming in asking for a new winter coat as she was cold. I'd just had a call from a Salvation Army hostel to say they had room for one of my customers and they'd mentioned a large quantity of clothing being available. I told the woman I was arranging for a coat to be provided shortly, but she became abusive insisting she wanted money to go and buy one from Selfridges.

I moved on to deal with another matter and within five minutes we had to evacuate the waiting room to put out a fire. The woman had collected a pile of newspapers, set fire to them and was 'getting warm in front of the fire.'

Over a thirty year period a statistically high number of people fell to their deaths in front of tube trains on the Northern Line. Sadly, it's a fairly common experience and both Marigold and I heard the station announcer informing waiting passengers of a delay in service 'owing to a body on the line' on several occasions. My route to work at the Elephant and Castle involved a trip on the relentlessly grim Northern Line of London Underground. After cashing up and locking up on Saturday and

Sunday evenings I didn't ever relish a late night trip on the tube with assorted drunks and druggies for company and the Northern Line was pretty grim back then even in daylight.

One of the 'regulars' was a local rough sleeper who came in fairly often to ask for money to buy 'just a bit of comfort.' He was a hardened drinker, well into the stage of imbibing methylated spirit, and inclined to become violent even though he was very short and slight of build, as befitting the jockey he claimed to have been in his native Ireland.

Alcoholics, rough sleepers, down and outs, I have come across a great many of them over the years. They're prone to exaggeration, wild flights of fancy and unsubstantiated boasting so I didn't take the claims of Kieran Kelly to have pushed his best friend under a tube train and repeated the act with strangers on several occasions at all seriously.

I did on one occasion mention his name to a police officer who came to collect a teenage runaway who wanted to go back home to Leeds. It had been a frustrating episode requiring confirmation from the police in Leeds that a 14 year old runaway would be cared for back home as I was about to issue a rail travel warrant. The boy's parents sent a message back along the lines of, 'keep him, we don't want him back' and it was while I was still trying to resolve the problem that I drew the attention of the police officers to the claims of mass murder on the Northern Line only to be told, 'oh, he tells everyone that. Ignore him.'

Between 1953 and 1983 when he was finally sent to prison for life, Kieran Patrick Kelly committed at least 18 murders and possibly as many as 24. Kelly, a vagrant alcoholic was well known to the police and had a long history of drunkenness, violence and thefts to support his alcoholism. These murders were all recorded as suicides, often as a result of a helpful member of the public providing a statement saying he had been standing close to the person and seen them leap in front of the approaching train. Nobody ever bothered to note the same helpful person on each occasion was Kieran Kelly.

Over that thirty year period Kelly would be arrested for robbery or drunkenness, serve a few months, come out of prison, be arrested again and be back in prison within days. Finally, In 1983 he was arrested for stealing a ring and a watch from a 65-year-old man on Clapham Common in south London and while in the cells of Clapham police station he killed a fellow vagrant William Boyd because the other man was snoring. He readily admitted killing Boyd but claimed he had killed many others by pushing them under tube trains.

Computers as an aid to linking events were unknown then and it had never been noticed before that soon after Kelly came out of prison, someone committed suicide on the Northern Line. Even more remarkable was the evidence finally gained from British Transport Police files revealing Mr Kieran Patrick Kelly had been a witness at each of the reported suicides.

Murder trials are costly so the Director of Public Prosecutions only tried Kelly on five murder charges. When he was found guilty of murdering William Boyd and Hector Fisher, another vagrant who was found stabbed in a graveyard in 1975, and given a life sentence the DPP decided not to proceed further. Despite his confessions, later rescinded on legal advice, he was never convicted of any of the 16 Northern Line murders.

My lead receptionist, Harry, a middle aged man who wore half a dozen wristwatches on each arm, part of his 'stock,' all available for sale, and ran three market stalls on Petticoat Lane as his day job was the most cynical man I ever met. He would have said he was a realist and any con artists who tried to get a free handout soon realised they'd met their match.

His market trader expertise in the garment industry had been the inspiration behind his friends Ronald Wolfe and Ronald Chesney writing The Rag Trade, a hugely popular tv sitcom starring Peter Jones, Miriam Karlin and a very young Barbara Windsor. He was also the man behind my introduction to a world I never knew existed, the otherworldly and distinctly seedy area of Whitechapel. It may be trendy now, but like many areas of London* now considered desirable it was a real eyesore.

*Islington? Not a celebrity, fancy restaurant or wine bar in sight in 1969. It was one of the many places best avoided after dark, like Brixton or Notting Hill.

One day Harry and traipsed through Petticoat Lane to go and queue at Blooms, the Jewish delicatessen for a lunch meal I will never forget. I had salt beef sandwiches with pickles. I can taste that sandwich even now. Most customers were Hasidic, ultra-orthodox, with long side curls known as payos below their hats, dressed in black and speaking Yiddish. I couldn't believe we were still in London. Being with someone who knew everybody else meant listening to a dozen conversations at once. The waiters and serving staff were conspicuously rude, surly and unhelpful. This was said to be their trademark, the USP (unique selling point) of Blooms.

As we left to rush back to work I was still trying to compose myself in readiness for real life again so paid little attention to the fiftieth person who had stopped to   say hello to Harry. Very small, very perky with a rather vulgar laugh, that's all I remember. After she'd gone I realised it was Barbara Windsor.

Printed in Great Britain
by Amazon

34978785R10242